Crying All The Way To The Bank

By Revel Barker

Foreword by Vera Baird QC

In the High Court of Justice, Queen's Bench Division

Monday June 8, 1959

L1901

Before Mr Justice Salmon, sitting with a jury

Between:

Wladziu Valentino Liberace (Plaintiff)

And

Daily Mirror Newspapers Ltd and William Connor (Defendants)

Revel Barker
Publishing

First published by Revel Barker Publishing 2009
Copyright © Revel Barker 2009
Court reports reprinted with permission
Official court transcript excerpts from Royal Courts of Justice:
Crown Copyright © reproduced under licence.

ISBN: 978-0-9558238-7-9
Revel Barker Publishing 66 Florence Road Brighton BN2 6DJ
United Kingdom
revelbarker@gmail.com

In the High Court of Justice, Queen's Bench Division
Monday June 8, 1959 L1901
Before Mr Justice Salmon, sitting with a jury

Between:
Wladziu Valentino Liberace (Plaintiff)
And
Daily Mirror Newspapers Ltd and William Connor (Defendants)

Mr Gilbert Beyfus QC, Mr Helenus Milmo and Mr David Morris
(instructed by Messrs M A Jacobs & Sons) appeared as counsel on behalf
of the plaintiff.
Mr Gerald Gardiner QC, Mr Neville Faulks QC and Mr G Ellenbogen
(instructed by Messrs Nicholson, Graham & Jones) appeared as counsel on
behalf of both defendants.

INDEX

Revel Barker started writing for newspapers at a penny a line while still at school in Leeds and worked for two weekly papers in the West Riding before joining the *Yorkshire Evening Post* at 17 and the *Daily Mirror* at 20 – in each case the youngest reporter either newspaper had ever employed.

He spent 27 years with Mirror Newspapers, during which he covered investigations and major trials and was later a columnist, foreign editor and finally managing editor.

He now publishes books about newspapers and journalism. His current titles include *Cassandra At His Finest And Funniest* – a collection of *Daily Mirror* columns by the co-defendant in the trial reported in this book, and *A Crooked Sixpence* by Murray Sayle, who was one of the witnesses.

Vera Baird QC was born and educated in Oldham then at university in Newcastle upon Tyne where she first practised as a barrister. She moved to London and specialised in mainly criminal work as deputy head of Michael Mansfield's chambers. She is a visiting fellow of St Hilda's College Oxford, visiting professor of London South Bank University and visiting fellow of Teesside University.

Elected as MP for Redcar in 2001, she was a member of the parliamentary committee on human rights (2001), parliamentary private secretary to the Home Secretary (2005), was under secretary of state for justice (2006) and was appointed Solicitor General in 2007. She has published books and numerous articles on the law of evidence, rape law, and criminal procedure and has been a regular commentator on legal and political affairs.

For Paula
With love... and to explain
what makes us all like this

Foreword

By Vera Baird QC

This is the story of a fabulous historic court battle, from a different age. Liberace sued the *Daily Mirror* for defaming him in a deeply critical column which he complained, among other things, alleged that he was a homosexual (a 'homosexualist' as it was called in the trial). Being gay, as we call it now, was illegal in 1959, so that allegation was a serious slur both about 'sexual perversion' and about breaking the criminal law.

William Connor, writing as 'Cassandra', was an eclectic wordsmith whose range of vituperatives will probably never be surpassed; he wrote the offending newspaper column. These days he would not stand out so much as the Mr Nasty he occasionally set himself up to be in the fifties, because the press has taken a nosedive overall. But he might still be special, with phrases like 'the biggest sentimental vomit of all time' as his stock in trade. He told the court he was astonished that he was thought to have alleged homosexuality, but he and the *Daily Mirror* admitted that the rest of his piece defamed Mr Liberace. Their defence was that it was all fair comment.

At the time Liberace was a fey, handsome, popular pianist, who avowed in every stage appearance that he loved his 'Momma' and his brother George. He played abbreviated classics on a grand piano with candelabra on top and wore sequinned suits, sometimes in pink, with piano-shaped cufflinks, piano-shaped signet rings and candelabra embroidered on his white silk handkerchiefs. *Ave Maria*, accompanied by a soaring chorus of ersatz nuns, was one of his more popular tunes, and therefore a fairly regular feature of his act. He was certainly sickly for some tastes, but he made a fortune. He was utterly individual, a show-business star who appealed in particular to middle aged American women, but who played to packed audiences on both sides of the Atlantic. There was something about the combination of being rich and wearing glaringly expensive and flamboyant clothes, while talking from his piano stool in a naive, boyish and personal way, that brought the otherwise out-of-reach glamour-world into the TV watcher's life.

His case, at court, was easy. His work was sincerity epitomised. He was a family entertainer. People either liked him or disliked him and most people liked him: women and children as well as men. He gave middle aged women the love they didn't get from their sons. He loved his mother and feared God and all were upset by this immoral allegation, which must surely have been made to sell newspapers, at his expense.

He must have felt extra confident when, counsel and the judge having held lengthy legal submissions on whether films of the Liberace television show could properly be admitted in evidence, the jury foreman told the court 'only two (of us) have not seen them'.

For Cassandra, it was harder. It was difficult to sustain the assertion that calling somebody 'fruit-flavoured' in a piece that was bound to be read in America, where it was often syndicated, did not refer to 'fruit', then slang for gay in the US. Although it was not a term used in England, and may have meant nothing to its primary readership, it had no other logical sense and seemed, in itself, to demonstrate what the article really intended to say.

It was tough, too, to insist that the phrase 'a sugary mountain of jingling claptrap wrapped up in such a preposterous clown' was not intended to ridicule.

And even more difficult to assert that:

> this deadly, winking, sniggering, snuggling, chromium plated, scent-impregnated, luminous, quivering, giggling, fruit-flavoured ice covered heap of mother-love

was not intended to 'depreciate Mr Liberace in the public eye', as the pianist's counsel, Gilbert Beyfus QC, put it.

It was a nasty article, which nobody was going to like, whereas Liberace, even if sickly and actually insincere, gave pleasure to lots of people. My mother said he irritated her, but she always watched him when he appeared on television.

The *Mirror* didn't seem to have a plan for the trial; Gerald Gardiner, later a Labour Lord Chancellor, can't have felt comfortable in cross examining Liberace; he fully realised that he was facing one of the most experienced interviewees on the planet, a man who was a well-practised expert in handling the most pertinent (and often impertinent) questions about his personal life. Browbeating a popular family entertainer, whose trademark was outright niceness, could only engender sympathy for the witness.

Nor can he have found any comfort within Cassandra's mostly sullen evidence. Neville Faulks who was Gardiner's junior (and was the uncle of the author Sebastian Faulks) showed an amiably self-deprecating wit, but got nowhere in cross-examination.

Beyfus, for Liberace, was highly regarded in his day but seems stagey now. His elaborate gesture of cupping his ear when asking for repetition of an answer a witness had not wanted to give, would probably also have irritated my mother. When a witness said something that he didn't like he would ask in a rhetorical challenge: 'You realise you are on oath?' This is comment pretending to be question and it was never fair. He had to show that the whole defence was cooked-up and these gestures of surprise towards contentious replies were fairly commonplace at the time, although judges would probably not allow them now.

Elaborate, lawyerly and remote styles of advocacy are long gone. Nowadays jurors are often as well-educated as barristers, and as well-travelled and well-informed. They are sceptical about posers, see themselves as equals and need to be befriended rather than impressed. Perhaps, in a case like this, they felt entitled to be entertained too. For many jurors, in everyday cases, their experience in court can provide after-dinner conversation for years. This celebrity battle had potential for the rest of their lives.

And Beyfus was certainly up to providing entertainment. He drew Cassandra easily into a totally stupid, pointless, time-wasting argument about whether the *Daily Mirror* could rightly be described as sensational. Beyfus knew what he was doing; Cassandra missed the plot. Hugh Cudlipp, the editorial director, and a stream of editors actually boasted that the newspaper was sensational. Cassandra would not tolerate that from Beyfus. He could easily have conceded that 'sensational' was acceptable to him, so long as the understanding was that it meant 'vivid', and that 'violent' was fine to describe his own work, insofar as it implied only total bluntness. Beyfus knew that he could not compete with the witness's exceptional vocabulary, but he rightly calculated that he, a bewigged and begowned Edwardian old Harrovian, could make the cantankerous columnist from a workingman's newspaper appear as the most pompous person in the courtroom.

In many ways, then, the parties had the lawyers one would expect. Plainer and down to earth, though inevitably in those days, top-drawer, for the anti-Tory working-class *Mirror* and an elderly, somewhat remote and old-fashioned QC brought in for his traditional style, for the over-rich American.

The trial generally ambled in often pointless directions, with nobody seemingly hurrying. The newspaper called people to the witness box to give credibility and sources for the bulk of Cassandra's text (although none of his damning adjectives was substantiated) and Liberace said that somebody had shouted 'Fairy' at him during a theatre performance, which he thought sounded 'queer' – perhaps an odd choice of word – shortly after the offending column appeared, although no evidence was produced to support this claim, while the *Mirror* produced witnesses who said that if anybody had used that word none of them had heard it.

Beyfus's argument, that Cassandra's words could only bear the meaning that Liberace was gay, without uttering it in so many words, was persuasive: there was no other explanation for some of the phrases. However, damages for this part of the column were only part of the claim. The remainder would be for the rest of the invective, likely without doubt to bring the plaintiff into 'hatred ridicule or contempt' in the eyes of right thinking members of society, represented by the jury.

It might have been smarter to accept what Cassandra meant to hint at and still plead fair comment in the public interest. Liberace always posed as a supporter of orthodox family life and had affected to be looking, while in the UK, for a girl to marry. Cassandra's evidence would have been less laboured on that tack, so perhaps more attractive and even believable on the rest. He would have been helped by a song in a nightclub review, skitting Liberace:

'But my fan mail is really tremendous
It's growing so fast my head whirls
I get more and more; they propose by the score
And at least one or two are from girls.....
I'm so coy with Tchaikovsky
I mince through Moskovsky
With Albinez, I'm so light and airy
But my fans all agree that I'm really most me
When I play the sugar plum fairy'

The jury heard about the skit. If, rightly or wrongly, it was common currency that he was gay, the damage from this column might well have been less, and perhaps even incontestable. Indeed, on reading some of the background commentary to the trial, one is tempted to believe that this is the course that Hugh Cudlipp, Cassandra's boss, suspected that the trial was most likely to follow. But the stubbornly dishonest defence on that issue led to dishonesty on the rest of the case and probably infuriated the jury.

Just before the trial, in 1957, the Wolfenden Committee, set up following the arrests of a number of prominent gay men, had recommended decriminalising adult homosexual acts in private, while introducing harsher penalties for 'public acts'. Oddly enough, homosexuality was not specifically identified in law. Its criminality was called 'unnatural offences', gross indecency or importuning. It has been said therefore that Wolfenden had to define homosexuality in order to recommend it be decriminalised.

It would be ten further years before the recommendations became law and undoubtedly being gay brought social opprobrium, even prosecution, in everyday life before then. I have an abiding memory from my childhood of our window cleaner, a beefy and amiable man who certainly did not irritate my mother. She and I both liked him and we all chatted on the doorstep when he called for his pay. One Sunday morning, there was a police car outside his house, blood on the pavement and a front downstairs window was smashed. 'What happened to Clifford?' I asked. 'They broke in to arrest him,' said my mother. 'He turned out to be one of those homosexuals.'

10

After the legislation, a significant number of performers – and politicians and newspaper columnists – gradually came to feel comfortable in 'coming out' or being 'outed' as gay – idioms not heard of in Beyfus's day. Ordinary people presumably took longer to gain the confidence. But Liberace's contemporaries, many of them famous people who took tough-guy or romantic leads on stage and screen, strove to take their sexual secrets to the grave, as he himself contrived to do (in spite of being sued for palimony by his alleged live-in boyfriend, Scott Thorson) right up to his death, from AIDS, in 1987. The next generation would learn of the agonies endured by film stars like Rock Hudson and Anthony Perkins, while caring little about the sexual inclinations of entertainers such as Boy George, Freddie Mercury, Elton John, or George Michael. But in the 1950s public opinion had hardly changed since 1895, when Gilbert Beyfus was ten years old and Oscar Wilde had lost a libel case he brought after being accused of homosexuality, and had been arrested immediately afterwards and jailed for offences of 'gross indecency'.

This trial is, in another sense, from a lost time. In the fifties, lawyers and journalists belonged to the same village in the city of London. At the end of the day they relaxed shoulder to shoulder in the appropriately named Wig & Pen Club, El Vino or the Cheshire Cheese. Fleet Street ran alongside the Temple, from The Strand to Ludgate Circus, and although it was the generic name for the entire area from Holborn to the Thames, now it refers only to the one thoroughfare named after the sewer beneath it; another sign of a lost age. Most reporters' offices were in the old courts and alleyways off it, as were the barristers' chambers. While lawyers, years ago, formed themselves into 'Inns', journalists had 'chapels' (run by a 'father of the chapel'). There, too, dispersed about the Fleet Street village, was 'the print'.

Now most newspaper connections are long gone and many lawyers work elsewhere. I spent many months, as a young barrister from chambers outside the Temple, defending protest cases when the first newspaper workers had to relocate to Wapping on what they saw as unfavourable terms, and sometimes on no terms whatsoever, for their jobs disappeared with the move. Lawyers started to need more space as the profession expanded in the sixties and seventies. The courts have stayed put, and a core of the profession remains close by, but it is numerically larger, more diverse and many come to court from much further away.

At the end of the Liberace trial it was difficult to identify the winners and the losers. In the following years the *Daily Mirror* increased its sales by a million copies a day. Cassandra continued with his daily diatribe. Liberace continued to play to packed theatres. And QCs continued to play to sometimes packed courts.

'Who is Liberace?'

Right at the start of his opening speech on June 8 1959 Mr Gilbert Beyfus QC, representing Liberace in his libel case against the *Daily Mirror* and its columnist William Connor, who wrote as Cassandra, referred to the tradition in British courts of explaining to the jury who famous people actually were.

'I think it would be most convenient if I tell you something about the plaintiff. You probably have all heard of him, and some of you know something about him, but in these courts there is a presumption that neither the judge nor the members of the jury know anything at all about the persons who come before them; and, indeed, if Mr Harold Macmillan were the plaintiff in this case it would be necessary for me to tell you that he was the Prime Minister and to call evidence to that effect.'

There is also a historical presumption; fifty years on it would almost certainly be necessary to inform – or at least to remind – people who Mr Macmillan was, had he been a plaintiff, and to introduce him if he were a witness. Perhaps more importantly, it served as the tear-jerking rags-to-riches vehicle for the counsel's opening, for there would have been little likelihood that anybody in the court room on that first day of the trial could have been unaware of the identity of Wladziu Valentino Liberace.

Put simply, he was a superstar in an era when stardom implied international recognition and esteem, rather than the mere 'celebrity' status that would become a benchmark in the following half century. A number of film actors, from Charlie Chaplin and Charles Laughton to Elizabeth Taylor and Laurence Olivier were genuine British 'stars', recognised worldwide, but for general entertainment the public in the United Kingdom was turning increasingly towards Hollywood and the United States for its idol worship. And Liberace was a million-dollar-a-year idol. To put this in a show-business context in terms of mass public appeal, 1956 (the year in which the alleged libel was published, coinciding with Liberace's first visit to London) was the year in which Elvis Presley effectively started his career; The Beatles were a creation of the 1960s.

The British population, now emerging at last fairly rapidly from the experience of grey wartime austerity, had been enthralled by photographs of the performer's extravagant lifestyle – his gold-lamé or diamond studded suits and his many accoutrements, from swimming pool to signet ring, bed headboard, coffee table and even ashtrays, all shaped like a grand piano, that illustrated the millionaire status of a pianist who could perform Chopin's *Minute Waltz* in 37 seconds because, he said, 'I leave out all the dull bits'.

Television, introduced widely just in time for the 1953 Coronation, was still a comparatively new phenomenon. At the start of 1959 – the year of this trial – vast areas of the UK were able to receive only one (BBC) channel on TV and regions like the north-east (Northumberland, Durham, North Yorkshire), Anglia (central-east England) and Ulster (Northern Ireland) still had no commercial TV franchise; the Independent Television Authority had been launched only in 1955. In 1959 commercial TV was advertising cigarettes (You're never alone with a Strand) and toothpaste (You'll wonder where the yellow went, when you brush your teeth with Pepsodent) while introducing British viewers to what they presumed to be typical American urban life (*I Love Lucy*) and cop shows (*Highway Patrol*), whereas the BBC was largely maintaining its charter to educate the masses, with such titles as *A Year in Kathmandu*, or a programme about a psychiatrist talking to a Christian Scientist.

While commercial television had America's *Liberace* every Sunday, the BBC offered Vera Lynn – although interestingly Beyfus saw no need to explain her to the jury, despite the fact that she figured obliquely in the evidence (she had retained popularity as a singer after being widely known as the Forces' Sweetheart during the Second World War and was a household name, as was Gracie Fields, another English entertainer named but not explained).

Although within a few short years it would become commonplace to see pictures of thousands of adoring fans throng to international airports to welcome visiting performers, in the 1950s transatlantic travel depended mainly on luxury liners. It wasn't until 1961 that air passengers outnumbered those crossing by ship. National newspapers kept staff reporters and photographers based permanently in Southampton solely to cover such arrivals and departures. Beyfus had heard that instructions had been given to clear masses of flowers from the quayside, thrown by supporters to mark Liberace's arrival at Southampton, so as not to impede his fellow passengers. If anybody had given that instruction, said the entertainer, it hadn't been him.

In the 1960s, every national newspaper would base photographers (some of them also stationed staff reporters) as 'resident press' at London Airport, as Heathrow was then still known. Tradition was always slow to fade in the newspaper business. Thirty years after the Liberace trial, when asked why the *Daily Mirror* still maintained a staff presence at Southampton, the only forthcoming excuse was 'in case Bing Crosby [who had died in 1977] arrives on the Queen Mary [which had been decommissioned in 1967].'

The QC apparently deemed it unnecessary to greatly enlighten the judge and jury about other popular American performers, including rock and roll singer Bill Haley (*Rock Around The Clock, See You Later Alligator*) and

Elvis Presley – whose first name the court's official shorthand writer recorded as Alvis – who were also referred to during the trial.

But he felt the need to explain that a tuxedo was what they called a dinner jacket 'in the States', and to define the term 'patter'. And he said he thought that 'fans' was 'the modern expression' to describe people who gathered to see entertainers.

Yet the expression 'bobby-soxer' was not clarified when it was used in court. This was a term that had originated in America in the 1940s to describe teenage girls who were forbidden to wear shoes and danced in ankle socks at functions in school gymnasiums, to avoid damaging the wooden floors. It became most widely used to depict fans of singer Frank Sinatra, and was then applied commonly to female audiences who tended to scream, squeal and occasionally swoon as mass hysteria became associated with popular singing stars (still many years before the advent of 'Beatlemania' in the UK). Shirley Temple, a child star, had featured in a 1947 film, *The Bachelor and the Bobby-Soxer*.

For the defence, Mr Gerald Gardiner QC (who would achieve fame later defending the publishers of *Lady Chatterley's Lover* against charges of obscenity and later still as Lord Chancellor) did however need to explain, at least in part, who Semprini was. English-born Alberto (Albert) Semprini was, like Liberace, a pianist of Italian ancestry. He had his own popular light music show on BBC radio, introducing each performance with the words 'Old ones, new ones, loved ones, neglected ones'. It would run for about 25 years, but at the time of the trial had been on air for less than two years. He was a successful entertainer, said Gardiner. Apparently not all that successful, replied Liberace, because he had never heard of him.

Nobody thought it necessary to explain Charlie Kunz, another American-born pianist who had lived in England since 1922 and, until Liberace appeared on the scene, was (perhaps equally with Winifred Atwell another pianist mentioned but not explained) the most popular musician in the UK. He played solo piano in music halls and on BBC radio, and led an orchestra that backed Vera Lynn, among others.

Perhaps most remarkably, no reference was made to the implied social stigma of the period that would automatically follow the imputation of homosexuality – other than the obvious one, at the very core of the trial, that it would inevitably lower a person in the esteem of members of the public.

Part of the defence would be that neither Cassandra nor the *Daily Mirror* had ever intended to suggest to their readers that Liberace was what would be described in court as a 'homosexualist' (or, in other instances, a 'homosexual pervert'). Sexual jargon has come a long way since 1959, and the defendants might surely be forgiven for their ignorance of the fact that, in an American dictionary of slang expressions, the term 'fruit' –

14

Cassandra had described Liberace as, among other things, 'fruit-flavoured' – implied homosexual.

Perhaps it should also be explained to younger readers (younger in this instance meaning those under pensionable age) that the 1950s was the era of mass readership of newspapers. Television news was in its infancy and the population relied for the bulk of its information – and almost wholly for its news pictures – on the print media. At the time of the trial the population of the British Isles was slightly more than 50million and the circulation of the *Daily Mirror* around 4.5million, from which the total actual readership was calculated at something more than 14million. In other words it was a reasonable assumption, mentioned during the trial, that approximately one person in three saw the newspaper six days a week.

Cassandra appeared in the *Mirror* on five of those days. Even if, as its own circulation survey suggested, only about half the paper's readers read Connor's column on a daily basis, he didn't need any more help in being identified and explained than Liberace did.

In addition to being a columnist, he was also a reporter at large. His (unwritten) contract stipulated that no major world event should occur except in his presence. He had reported Nazi storm-troopers stomping their jackboots past the remains of the Reichstag in Berlin, attended Nazi rallies in Nuremburg and produced a wanted poster describing Hitler. He covered wars and accompanied the Pope to Bethlehem and the Queen to Australia, he had a one-to-one interview with Kennedy in the White House, stared blinkingly back at Adolph Eichmann behind his bullet proof dock in a war crimes trial, and witnessed the testing of the H-bomb off Christmas Island – 'a dress rehearsal for the end of the world... like an oil painting from hell.'

Nevertheless, he would probably have found amusement in becoming part of that legal tradition in which things needed to be explained. In 1937 he had picked a quote out of a newspaper:

> He found that he was suffering from what he (counsel) said was vulgarly and commonly known as a 'hangover'.
> 'A what?' asked Mr Justice Hawke.
> 'I am just as ignorant as your Lordship,' replied counsel.
> Mr Justice Hawke then severely rebuked people who laughed at this.

And with the words, 'May I hasten to assist his Lordship?'... Cassandra fashioned an amusing column on a helpful series of definitions.

Similarly, he would have known as much about the background story of the entertainer called Liberace as the plaintiff's own counsel. More. For one of the supreme ironies of this case was that, when offered the brief Beyfus, whose musical appreciation was restricted to listening to palm

15

court orchestras on the radio, had to ask his clerk, Donald Woods, who Liberace was.

But the presentation was not for his benefit so much as for the jury – only two of whom admitted to not having seen him on television – and for the court, for the readers of the next day's newspapers and for history.

Amusement – for themselves, their in-house legal team and even possibly for their readers – was as much as Cassandra and his ultimate boss Hugh Cudlipp, the newspaper group's editorial director (editor-in-chief), expected to result from the article.

The office protocol was that each day Bill Connor would send a copy of his Cassandra column to Cudlipp, a close friend; it was a matter of courtesy, not a requirement. Cudlipp would not necessarily read it immediately; it was rarely dangerous stuff, dealing more frequently with cooking, cats, gardening, travel and atrocious puns than with abuse of people in the public eye, but in the event of a challenge from the editor or the lawyers Cudlipp would exercise a casting vote. Another carbon copy went to the editor, one to the features editor, another to the chief features sub-editor (who was instructed not to alter it in any way), one to the lawyer and yet another was transmitted by wire to Manchester where the *Mirror* ran a parallel but separate printing operation.

It was in Manchester in the afternoon of Tuesday September 25, 1956, that an eyebrow was first raised, by a young part-time lawyer, Mark Carlisle (later the Rt Hon Lord Carlisle QC). He telephoned his misgivings to Mark Goodman, a barrister who headed the team of staff lawyers in the paper's London headquarters, and Goodman took the half-size folio of feint copy upstairs to discuss it with Cudlipp.

It was, both men agreed, a classic Cassandra piece. But, in describing the world's most popular pianist, wasn't

> this deadly, winking, sniggering, snuggling, chromium plated, scent-impregnated, luminous, quivering, giggling, fruit-flavoured, mincing, ice-covered heap of mother-love... this superb piece of calculating candy floss... the biggest sentimental vomit of all time... a preposterous clown...

going a bit over the top, even for him?

Didn't it, asked the lawyer, hold up Liberace to ridicule and contempt? Certainly, said the editorial director who claimed to keep *Gatley On Libel* as bedside reading: but not, he thought, to hatred – nor, in his opinion, to any greater extent than Liberace himself consistently held himself up by his own ridiculous and contemptible buffoonery.

Maybe the column exposed him as a clown, but what jury would ever find against that? Here was a man who, between bouts of hammering the ivories, larked about on stage and joshed with his audience in theatres and

16

at press conferences. A performer who would say: 'I've had so much fun tonight that honestly I'm ashamed to take the money – but I will!' Or ask his adoring fans: 'Do you like my outfit? You should – you paid for it!' Not only a buffoon, then, but a fairly cynical buffoon.

Typically, the yardstick that newspapers apply to contentious copy is: Is it true? Could they sue? Will they sue? If they sue, will they win? If they win, what would it cost us? If we have to pay out, is it worth the money? There are plenty of opportunities within that discussion process to kill copy.

Cudlipp's view was that it would be a greater sin to suppress an excellent column than to embarrass Liberace. If the piano-player chose to sue over it, he would most likely be laughed out of court; if he sued and won – What the hell, said Cudlipp, it would be money well spent.

When Cassandra phoned him to report that 'the legal eagles are having kittens', Cudlipp's response to the cat-loving columnist was: 'You look after the kittens, Bill; I'll look after the writ. We're publishing the column untouched.'

The writ landed on October 22, by which time a second reference to Liberace had appeared in Cassandra's column.

Lew (later Lord) Grade, who was boss of Associated Television which also owned the London Palladium Theatre (and in which the *Mirror* newspapers were the principal shareholder) offered to intercede. He knew Liberace well, and was concerned about his friends falling out. Such mediation would have required an apology, however slight, from both newspaper and columnist. Cudlipp's reply had been: 'Thanks but no thanks. Much appreciated, but I can't let Cassandra down, or the newspaper, or the public – who will enjoy the hearing.'

Largely because of his hectic pre-booked schedule of performances, it would be nearly three years before the pianist had his days in court.

It would be difficult to claim that the publications had had any damaging effect on his career – in the interim he topped the bill at the London Palladium and when he arrived in the capital for the trial he also had bookings in London – including a Royal Command Performance in front of the Queen Mother, another television appearance at the Palladium on the Sunday night and shows at the Empire theatres in Chiswick and Finsbury Park on two evenings after appearing in the High Court during the day.

Liberace's publicity machine had spent the intervening years trying to plant stories about his heterosexuality claiming, for example, that he had lost his virginity to a night club singer called Bea Haven, and linking his name – as they say – with characters as diverse as ice-skater Sonja Henie and aging American icon Mae West. It didn't wash, however, with the gossip writers. *Hush-Hush* magazine asked on its front page: Is Liberace a

17

man? And under the headline, 'Why Liberace's theme song should be *Mad About The Boy*', the Hollywood *Confidential* said that one of its photographers was left 'fighting for his honor' as the 'hefty piano player made goo-goo eyes at him'.

Ironically, it had never occurred to the worldly wise professionals in the *Mirror* – in those days they were based at Geraldine House, Breams Buildings, between Fleet Street and High Holborn and within a short walk of the Royal Courts of Justice – that any suggestion of homosexuality had been implied in the offending articles.

The pivotal paragraph of the first column was apparently the one that Cassandra himself had chosen as the 'pull quote' – the extract that would be highlighted in a box at the top of his column. It read:

> He is the summit of sex – the pinnacle of Masculine, Feminine and Neuter. Everything that He, She and It can ever want.

It was not until the case started that the defendants accepted they had been formally made aware of the argument that this wording implied that Liberace was a homosexual. They might have thought, or suspected or even been fairly certain that he was. But describing him as the pinnacle of all sexes didn't amount to saying that... did it?

Gerald Gardiner, the *Mirror*'s QC, had objected to the issue of homosexuality being introduced. 'There is no suggestion and never has been anything of the kind,' he interrupted when the subject was first mentioned in the trial. Liberace clearly had a bee in his bonnet about homosexuality, the QC would say later, many times, trying to dismiss the accusation as a red herring. But the plaintiff's counsel insisted that this was the clear and intentional innuendo of Cassandra's carefully, professionally, chosen words. Beyfus put it straight to his client:

'Are you a homosexual?'

Liberace said: 'No, sir.'

'Have you ever indulged in homosexual practices?' – 'No, sir, never in my life... I am against the practice because it offends convention and it offends society.'

Liberace was prepared to lie to win his libel as flagrantly as Oscar Wilde had. But Oscar Wilde had lost. And the *Mirror*, apparently naively unaware that this was the essence of the case they were committed to defend, had not accumulated a single shred of evidence to combat it. Nor could they, because to admit they were implying it would have required their proving it was right; and not even the keenest investigative journalists on Liberace's home ground had been successful in doing that.

While protesting that they had not even obliquely referred to it, the *Mirror* must have been fully cognisant that the entertainer's sexuality had been discussed fairly openly in the American media – certainly in the more

18

colourful Hollywood scandal sheets but also, only slightly less forcefully in some of the mainstream press – and Cassandra would tell the court that before writing his column on that fateful day he had read virtually everything that had been published about him, in both the UK and the USA. Between the issuing of the writ and the appearance in court, it is impossible that Cassandra and the *Daily Mirror* – or their legal advisers – could have been uninformed that in 1958 the pianist had taken a similar court action against Hollywood *Confidential*. He had won that one through a technicality: on the basis that on one of three otherwise well-documented assignations with a handsome young press agent he had not been exactly where the magazine had described him as being.

Now Liberace would claim that the *Mirror*'s evil accusation had so shocked his mother (who had read it on the day it appeared) that it nearly killed her. Now he would say: 'On my word of God, on my mother's health, which is so dear to me, this article only means one thing, that I am a homosexual, and that is why I am in this court.' But while that – for a God-fearing mother-loving plaintiff – may have adequately described why he had issued a writ, it was not quite the same as declaring on the word of God or on his mother's health that he was not a homosexual, even though he had sworn to tell the truth in court.

If the pianist could claim that his reputation had been besmirched, it might be fair to consider, even briefly, what was said about the columnist. Liberace's QC called Connor 'a literary assassin who dips his pen in vitriol, hired by this sensational newspaper to murder reputations and hand out sensational articles on which its circulation is built.'

And the *Daily Mirror* itself, 'when not devoted purely to sensationalism, is devoted to dealing with sex...'

In addition to its biggest-selling newspaper and (probably) its most highly-paid columnist, Fleet Street itself did not escape serious criticism.

Liberace had denied talking about his tax affairs during a press conference he had given on board the Queen Mary, en route from Cherbourg. He surely had discussed them, because so many journalists had a note of it. The problem was that the notes varied considerably.

Stanley Bonnett, for the *Daily Mail*, had him talking of the trials of earning $1,000,000 a year: 'You see,' he said, parting his lips around his milk white almost-too-perfect teeth, 'I get only nine cents out of every dollar I make.' But Bonnett had also said that the grand piano ring on his finger was made of ivory, whereas pictures showed it was composed of diamonds.

Jack Frost of the *Daily Telegraph* said Liberace had been talking about his suit: 'It cost me $400, but to be able to pay that I have to earn $4,000. I earn about a million a year and could earn more if I tried harder; but I only manage to keep nine cents out of each dollar I earn.'

Charles Stuart Reid of the *News Chronicle* quoted Liberace as saying that he grossed from $10,000 to $60,000 a concert, adding: 'Sounds a lot, I know, but how much do you think I keep from every dollar I earn? Not more than nine cents.'

Whether he said it in respect of his annual earnings, the cost of his clothing, or his fee for a concert was hardly important, either to the journalists or to their readers. What mattered to the defendants was that it was pretty certain that he had said it before Cassandra had lifted the quote from one of them. But for the plaintiff's lawyers it was another example of the sheer recklessness and unreliability of the newspaper world, where both the columnist and the newspaper sat comfortably at the top. This had a fairly salutary effect on Fleet Street and for years afterwards, following any form of joint interview, reporters would gather with their notebooks and agree precisely what they were going to say had been said to them.

One journalistic distinction that was unknown to, or had been overlooked by, the lawyers was the relatively important difference between news reporting and feature writing. By definition a reporter was expected to report facts and get quotes 'straight' – not necessarily strictly in the order that they were made, because very few interviewees ever talked in logical sequence – but certainly to get them accurately and essentially in context. On the other hand by some unwritten law, and certainly by Fleet Street tradition, a 'writer' was assumed to be entitled to shift quotes about a bit, because his role was to describe the overall mood of an interview or of an occasion, to add what in those monochromatic days was known as 'colour'; he would position the quotes where they best fitted the narrative.

Most of the journalists who followed the Liberace trail would have described themselves as writers. It could never have occurred to them that one day their compositions would be compared and contrasted, one against the other, under a forensic light, with their carefully thought-out paragraphs being dissected line by line and even on occasion word by word.

The court case was a massive learning curve for Fleet Street's finest.

Cassandra, as the defendant, fared worst of all. Some unfortunate researcher had clearly been despatched to the archives to pore over every word – Cassandra's own estimate was a million words and 6,000 columns – that he had written for the paper since 1935. The careful gleanings did not produce much that was worthy of criticism, but there had been noteworthy attacks on royal commentator Richard Dimbleby, on popular radio personality Wilfred Pickles, and on family doctors in general; and there was even an apology printed in the paper for a caption (written, it

20

would transpire, on the basis of a totally concocted and false memo submitted with a picture from a staff photographer). There had also been official criticism of a one-line caption that Cassandra had written for a cartoon during the war that had incurred the wrath of the government. It would all come out in court, calculated to cause the defendant discomfort and to prove him 'reckless'.

Among several journalists who gave evidence, two stood out as remarkable, for quite different reasons.

Dail Betty Ambler, a freelance journalist and pulp-fiction novelist, had been commissioned by *The People* to write an in-depth series on Liberace during his 1956 English concert tour, and somehow also – within a few days of the issuing of the writ – been asked to contribute an interview with Cassandra for the *Picture Post* about 'famous people and their cats'. Even the judge thought that was a remarkable coincidence... especially after she told the court she had discussed the case at the Connor home and been told by him that they had no defence and would lose the case; and when another witness (a *Daily Mirror* reporter) said that he had actually heard Miss Ambler suggest to Liberace that he should sue. It did not help her credibility much when she said she could not remember whether her publisher had been sued for obscenity on the basis of one of her novels.

By contrast, reporter Murray Sayle told the court how he had helped an unfortunate colleague and unexpectedly interviewed Liberace in Paris. The colleague – from a competing newspaper – had been on his way to the interview but was turned back at the airport because his passport had recently expired. Sayle volunteered to do the job for him, and telephoned a report back to the rival paper for him, and three years later found himself being criticised in court because the article appeared under a name other than his own, and because he had not protested about material being added to it in the rival office.

There was as much in this trial to entertain and educate lawyers as there was for journalists. The cross-examination of Connor by Beyfus would be read by barristers to relish its technical brilliance much as Oscar Wilde's, by Edward Carson, had been read by previous generations. And despite the occasional frustration of examination and cross-examination there was a fair amount of good humour and even of inter-professional respect (and sometimes of lack of respect). There were times when witnesses could not hide the fact that the court system – judge and barristers – was tiresome and apparently pointlessly repetitive, and equally when the lawyers clearly thought that the witnesses from down the street were being devious or even perverse in their answers.

Towards the end of his closing speech Gerald Gardiner told the jury: 'You can compare that vitriolic language of Cassandra, of which you have heard several examples, with the language of Mr Beyfus in his final speech to you. I trust I shall offend no-one if I prophesy a dead-heat.'

Beyfus, an outstanding advocate and a frustrated writer, was game for the challenge. 'Might I suggest that this newspaper is vicious and violent, venomous and vindictive, salacious and sensational, ruthless and remorseless... I don't think that is up to Cassandra's standard, but it is the best I can do.'

Cassandra joined in the general laughter. He thought it was no contest.

But he didn't yet know what the jury was going to decide.

Vicious and violent

Liberace had been disappointed to learn that John Jacobs, his American attorney and business manager who had persuaded him to issue the libel writ, would not be allowed to represent him in the English high court. He was even more disappointed when the man Jacobs had chosen for him arrived for a preliminary meeting at the Savoy Hotel.

The pianist had been expecting a thrusting young photogenic lawyer like the brilliant advocates he had seen in American films and on TV. Instead he was introduced to a man who looked as if he had stepped out of a particularly dusty volume of Dickens. A crumpled Old Harrovian in a crumpled suit, grey in countenance, deaf in one ear and with a disconcerting twitch in one eye, Gilbert Hugh Beyfus QC was 73 years old when he first met his latest client, and anticipating the last case of an illustrious career.

'We wanted the best lawyer in London, not the oldest,' said one member of the Liberace entourage. Then it was explained to them. Not for nothing was Beyfus known, from the pubs of Fleet Street to the Inns of Court, as 'the Old Fox'. Partial deafness could be an advantage in a trial if only because, cupping his bad ear with one hand, he could excusably ask for damaging evidence to be repeated; the twitch – the result of an injury caused by a kick after having been thrown by a horse during a barristers' point-to-point meeting – could become a devastating tool for distracting and disconcerting jurors and even witnesses.

Consulting the London Law List from Hollywood, John Jacobs may have been naturally attracted to the firm of M A Jacobs and Sons. He may not have known that David Jacobs, now the senior partner, who had a two-tone pink Bentley, three chauffeurs and a table permanently booked at the Caprice, was gay, but he could not have made a better choice; happily for him they were well practised in high-level libel cases and had a large number of show-business clients. David Jacobs recommended Beyfus, the top libel man of his day, who years earlier had often been his father's first choice for High Court advocacy. However, as a close associate of the QC he knew a secret: Beyfus was suffering from a terminal illness. Diagnosed the previous October with cancer, he had then been told that he was suffering not from cancer but from tuberculosis and had spent ten weeks in a sanatorium. Then in April he learnt that the original diagnosis had been correct and he underwent an operation for cancer of the bowel. Within three weeks of his discharge from hospital his clerk offered him the brief from Jacobs. He reminded the solicitor about his state of health and said he would not be offended if his friend offered the case to someone fitter. But

Jacobs didn't know a better man for the job. And Beyfus, if he was going to be forced to hang up his wig, wanted to end his career on a high note.

More to the point, he convinced Liberace when he met him that he could and would win the case for him. He was a performer, too; he even had a fan club – a handful of legal aficionados who followed him from trial to trial to enjoy his wit and erudition. He would often affect an air of total distraction, apparently misplacing important pieces of paper for which he needed to search on the table in front of him and occasionally confusing inconsequential dates in evidence. He sometimes gave the impression of being unsure whether he had stumbled into the correct courtroom and perhaps of being involved in a trial for which he was unprepared. Like many in his profession he was, in fact, a consummate actor.

But the crowds, mainly women, who lined the pavement outside the black railings of the Royal Courts of Justice in The Strand and who packed the public gallery on Monday, June 8, had not gathered to see the theatrics of Gilbert Beyfus QC. Mounted police were on hand, if needed, to control the enthusiasm of Liberace fans, many of whom had been waiting for three hours – since 7am – for a chance to see him in the flesh. Opening day of the trial was like an opening night in the West End.

As the court date had loomed ever closer Liberace had become less confident than his counsel and started believing that it had been a mistake to have issued the writ. He entered Court Number Four convinced that he would leave it a loser with his reputation in tatters and his career finished. When Gerald Gardiner – younger by 15 years than his own QC – was pointed out to him in the courtroom, he said: 'That's the lawyer we should have got.'

The jury – ten men and two women – was sworn in. Mr Helenus Milmo made a formal announcement of the case before them and Beyfus rose slowly to his feet, clearing his throat for his swan song.

The action, he told Mr Justice Salmon and the jury, was in respect of two libels published by the first defendants (Daily Mirror Newspapers Ltd) and written by the second defendant (William Neil Connor).

'The first is an article published in the *Daily Mirror* on September 26 1956, which is as vicious and violent an attack on the plaintiff as could be imagined – and written, as you will probably think before this case is over, by as vicious and violent a writer as has ever been in the profession of journalism in this city of London. The second article was a very short one. That which is complained of consists in effect of one sentence. That was published in the issue of October 18 1956.

'The writer's name, as you will have gathered, is Mr Connor, who writes habitually for the *Daily Mirror* and who writes not under his own name but disguises his identity, as many writers do, under the nom-de-plume of

24

Cassandra, a somewhat curious one for a man to adopt, as Cassandra, according to legend, was a Trojan princess who constantly prophesied evil – a somewhat sombre nom-de-plume to choose but one which Mr Connor no doubt thought suitable to his style of writing.'

Liberace, the QC continued, was born in Milwaukee in 1919 with music in his blood. His Italian immigrant father struggled, largely unsuccessfully, to earn a living by playing the French horn; his mother, Frances, an American citizen of Polish descent, was an accomplished amateur pianist, and came of a family with a long musical history.

Although a competent musician, Mr Salvatori Liberace did not earn enough to support a wife and four children, but he opened a grocery business for his wife to run and she developed it into a vegetable market and finally an ice cream parlour, but even with those resources they had to rely on state welfare for subsistence.

'That early period and his mother's struggle on behalf of him and his family made a deep impression on the youthful Liberace and he has two other special and grateful memories of his mother – how when he was nine years old she nursed him through a serious attack of pneumonia from which he nearly died and which probably caused the spinal weakness which prevented him from joining the armed forces of the United States in 1941. Secondly, and perhaps a good deal more important, when he had a poisoned finger at the age of about sixteen, and a doctor was called in and insisted on an amputation of his hand, which of course would have stopped the career which he was then expecting as a pianist, she sent the doctor away, and tried her own efforts, poulticing and so forth, and saved his hand.

'That came just at a time when, young as he was, he had been offered employment as a soloist with the Chicago Symphony Orchestra. From his very earliest age my client had shown considerable disposition to play the piano, and his mother had started to teach him at the age of four. At the age of seven and for many years thereafter he had outside lessons. There was no need, as is so often necessary in the case of children, to insist on his practising because, as I said, music was in his blood and he adored playing the piano. At one stage Paderewksi, the famous pianist who was later prime minister of Poland, visited the home and complimented the child on his playing. Even so his father, with his somewhat unhappy experiences of the lot of a musician, tried to dissuade him from becoming a professional pianist and wanted him to become, of all things, an undertaker.

'But he was quite decided that he was going to become a professional pianist, and he had his way.'

The youngster's 'one, purely classic, period' had been that tour as a piano soloist with the Chicago Symphony. When it ended he played with dance bands – 'not so classical but much more remunerative' – and the bands for which he played, the places where they performed, and the money that he earned all improved. By 1951, when he was 31 and playing in first class hotels and night clubs he was probably earning as much as $50,000 [about £18,000 at 1959 conversion rates] a year.

At that time he played in 'ordinary, normal clothes', a dinner jacket and a black tie, or tails and a white tie, said Beyfus. 'He had no sort of gimmicks, except that he adopted the idea of having candelabra with candles on his piano. That idea was taken from a film of Chopin in which he had been engaged. It became popular and served as a sort of trade mark for him, something like Mr Maurice Chevalier's straw hat.'

While playing in the comparatively intimate atmosphere of hotels and night clubs, he was developing his personal style – 'which he has since perfected, of, if I may so put it, so projecting his personality as to get on intimate terms with his audience. He achieved this largely by talking to his audience, by developing a line of what is professionally known as "patter". It was impromptu, simple stuff, in which he talked about his mother and his brother George who was to be the distinguished violinist associated with the plaintiff in many of his musical ventures, about his home and his 'early days of poverty and struggles, and his views on life and music; everything indeed that came into his head which he thought would create the intimacy with the audience which he was trying to achieve. And it was successful. He succeeded in getting that sort of close intimate relationship between himself and his audience, and in imbuing them with the idea that it was his general wish to share with them the delights and joy of the music he was playing to them.'

But when he did four television performances in New York in 1951 he had to comply strictly with the orders of those who were directing them. The candelabra on the piano were disallowed; he was told not to look straight at the camera. To what extent this was successful Beyfus did not know, nor did he think his client knew, but those shows made no great impact, he said.

Everything was to change at the beginning of 1952. He was playing at the Coronado Hotel in San Diego where his act impressed the vice president and general manager of a television station in Los Angeles who invited him to perform. He 'took precisely the opposite view to that which had been taken in New York the previous year. He wanted Mr Liberace to try to put over on television the intimacy of his night club performances – not perhaps a very easy thing when the performer, instead of facing a close gathering in a night club or hotel, is merely facing a camera. But my client attempted it, having been given a 13-week contract at, I think, $1,000 a week.'

Liberace was a tremendous success from the start, and at every subsequent performance the audience figures increased. 'His fame spread like a prairie fire, and within a few months he became a national figure.' Within about six weeks a big bank started to sponsor his show, and from that time he never looked back.

Beyfus said: 'Music critics in the United States, and I think the music critics in England, who are perhaps inclined to be somewhat highbrow, have never liked his performances, but the masses have. They have responded to his intimate style, and my client has always recognised that. One of his jocular observations of it has been: Nobody loves me but the people.'

One hostile critic compared him with a literary digest which sought in a short space to provide the gist of a great book, saying that similarly, in a short time, Liberace tried to give the essence of great music. 'He recognises, of course, that there is a great deal of truth in that criticism because it is impossible, when performances are given on television where time is limited, to do more than give extracts from or to give the kernel of some long piece which takes twenty to thirty minutes to play. Of course it takes much ability to be able to give in a short time the kernel of some great piece of music, but in that sort of way he has been able to introduce first class classical music to the masses who probably otherwise would never have heard it at all.'

Those performances on television in Los Angeles created such a demand for Liberace that he was soon giving live concerts. Then in July 1952 he was booked to appear at the Hollywood Bowl (which the QC explained was 'a vast natural amphitheatre just outside Hollywood').

And this performance was a turning point in the pianist's career.

'July in Hollywood is a pretty hot period, and he conceived the idea of appearing in completely white evening dress. Of course, in hot countries many men wear a white tuxedo jacket, but he conceived the idea of appearing dressed in white from top to toe.

'The Bowl was crowded. There were 22,000 people present. When he appeared clad entirely in white he received a terrific ovation, and it was such a success that, with the approval of and, indeed, at the instigation of some of his sponsors he developed the idea.

'He gradually acquired an elaborate wardrobe of what could be called fancy dress, and he started to appear in these glamorous garments, such as a gold lamé jacket, a diamond studded tail coat, and a bugle-beaded tail coat which had been created for his role in a film called *The Great Waltz* in which he played the part of the young Johann Strauss. His sponsors approved because it became quite obvious that the American public liked to see him in these glamorous clothes, and he catered for their taste.'

Lest the English consider disparaging the American public for enjoying this show-business glamour, suggested Beyfus, 'or before we jeer at Mr Liberace for acceding to it', they should remember that less than 150 years ago, in the Regency period, 'people dressed like peacocks'. And what about the guards at the palace and in Whitehall, or the Beefeaters at the Tower, the robes of Knights of the Garter, or even a hunt ball 'where tough hunting men prance around in pink coats with silk lapels of various colours'? Look at the judge and the barristers in court, he said, shifting his hand from his wig to his gown: 'Because we dress like this in the performance of our duty it does not mean that we dress like this in our ordinary daily life. Nor does Mr Liberace.'

The jury and members of the public in the gallery were clearly obliged, at that point, to note how the plaintiff was dressed. And there, sitting immediately in front of him, was his offended client, in a dark blue suit, white shirt and blue tie (the gold wrist watch, gold cuff links and gold ring, each in the shape of a grand piano, were not visible to the onlookers).

There were other occasions, the QC continued, that were public appearances, although not on a stage or in front of studio TV cameras. 'For example, in Hollywood, at a first night, crowds assemble to see the stars arrive, and on occasions Mr Liberace, who acquired a white beaver overcoat, appeared at first nights so clad.' Press conferences were also public occasions at which he would dress more showily than he would in his ordinary private life. 'At any rate, however that may be, dressing up became a feature of Mr Liberace's performances. The audience liked it and, liking it, expected it.'

His success appeared unstoppable and in 1954 he performed at the Madison Square Garden in New York to an audience of about 15,000. After the performance his dressing room was besieged and he spent until two o'clock in the morning signing autographs.

He was at the height of his fame in the United States. He sold more than a million records in three years. He also made a film called *Sincerely Yours*, which was the story of a modern Beethoven, a composer who was afflicted with deafness. The film was only moderately successful in the USA, but extended his fame internationally. His own television show was by now being broadcast on 197 stations all over the United States. 'Most of his television shows were films. They lasted about twenty-seven minutes, and he performed some six different numbers, giving him an average of four minutes each, with about three minutes for patter. That at least was the general pattern and, of course, playing each number for four minutes did not enable him to play anything like a piece of classical music in full, and he was obliged to abbreviate them.'

Liberace built himself a home in the San Fernando Valley, near Hollywood. The house itself was normal enough, said Beyfus, 'but the

28

piano motif and the black and white colours of the keyboard were very much in evidence in the decor. Behind that there was a swimming pool in the shape of a grand piano, of which you have probably seen photographs, with a terrace painted in black and white to represent the keyboard.'

Having enlightened any non-readers or non-viewers about the biographical, theatrical, wardrobe and domestic details of his client, Beyfus eventually reached September 1956, the month in which the libel was published.

'When he came to England he was known to many thousands, I think probably millions, because of his film performances which had been presented by Independent Television on Sunday afternoons for a considerable period. He came to England to give concerts, and one television show, *Sunday Night at the Palladium*.

'One would have thought that it would at least have been decorous to have abstained from criticism until he had given his first performance, but that was not the idea of the defendants.'

Liberace had arrived on board the Queen Mary, via a short stop at Cherbourg. Inevitably there had been 'the sort of tremendous hullabaloo which greets the arrival of famous entertainers in this country nowadays, firstly at Southampton and afterwards at Waterloo Station when he arrived.' Beyfus conceded that this might have been contributed, at least in part, to the performer's own publicity team who had hired a special train, dubbed the Liberace Special... 'to bring him and his party, and some of his fans – I think that is the modern expression – who had travelled to greet him, to Waterloo.'

The QC said he thought he could not be fairer to the defendants than to read their own account of this arrival, both at Southampton and at Waterloo in their issue of September 26, the day after it had happened. He handed copies and photostats to the judge and jury; it was the same edition that contained the libel.

There were four articles in the paper dealing with Liberace. On the front page was 'Wunnerful!' says Liberace, with a photograph of him:

Liberace mops his brow and fixes his famous smile as he arrives at Southampton yesterday.

WHAT a welcome! But an even greater one awaited him in London.

Last night he called it: 'A fantastic, wunnerful welcome.'

He added; 'It was not just a curious crowd - they were very happy people with a look of devotion on their faces. I have seen crowds who just looked at me as if I were a freak.'

More Liberace quotes last night: 'I shall have to go out late at night when there aren't too many crowds. I like to walk about at night. It makes me rest well...

29

'The secret of my success? It is a very simple thing - everyone in this world wants to be loved and I express that love to my viewers and listeners and they seem to respond to it...

'The majority of the people who welcomed me at Southampton seemed to be men. I began to wonder if the ladies had given me up!'

The story and pictures of the 'wunnerful' welcome are on page 5. On page 6 Cassandra describes Liberace as 'a superb piece of calculating candyfloss'. And on the back page Liberace relaxes in his London hotel.

On page 5 the caption for the main photograph was:

He's here! And a group of Liberace fans, a man, young women - and one not so young - smile and wave a welcome at Waterloo Station.

By the look of them, said Beyfus, they seemed to be women of all ages: 'At the bottom left hand corner a girl apparently plants a kiss for Liberace on the train window at Southampton as his Mom looks on and he presumably does the same thing on the other side – all good publicity, I imagine.'

Another caption read: 'The welcome is over. Brother George, Mom and Liberace relax in their London hotel', the photographers having followed them to the Savoy.

SQUEALING women... weeping women... screaming women... fainting women... Liberace got the lot when he arrived in London yesterday.

Three thousand fans swarmed and jostled around the platform at Waterloo Station as the special Pullman train bringing The Casanova of the Keyboard from Southampton steamed in.

Most of the fans were women - young and middle aged. They cheered him as the train arrived. They waved their 'Welcome Liberace' banners.

But when they saw the dimpling, dumpy pianist smiling at the train window, cheering was not enough. They squealed. And they never stopped.

As he stepped from the train the women showered him with paper rose petals, with messages of love printed on them. And all the time Liberace smiled.

He even smiled at an opposition group of students carrying a banner which said: 'We hate Liberace... Charlie Kunz for ever'.

Liberace posed for the TV cameramen - still smiling. Then, with his Mom and brother George, he stepped into a waiting car to drive to his hotel.

That was too much for the girls and the middle aged Moms.

They surged through the crush barriers, sweeping aside the police cordon and descended on the car in a squealing, screaming mass.

They showered it with rose petals. They threw paper roses in its path. They hammered on the windows and several shouted: 'He's lovely.'

Some women fainted. Others wept as they saw the car slowly drive away.

It took five minutes to travel the 100 yards from the platform to the exit. And through it all Liberace smiled his dimpling, roguish smile. And that squealing never stopped.

Sixty members of the Liberace 'Sincerely Yours' fan club travelled from Southampton with their hero on the special train.

One of them, attractive Barbara Bacon, 24, of Upton Park, London, founder of the fan club, said; 'This is the most exciting moment in our lives. We have tickets for every one of his concerts throughout the country and will get there even if we have to hike.'

Another fan, a fifteen year old girl, had 'I Love Liberace' embroidered across her black sweater. She had stayed away from school - all for Liberace.

'They can expel me for all I care,' she cried. 'I've met him. I touched his hand. That's all that matters.'

Some girls, with their hair in curlers to look their best for Liberace, camped out overnight at Waterloo Station. Then they travelled to Southampton by the early morning milk train to pick up the Liberace special train.

'Of course,' Beyfus told the jury, 'you probably know that this is not the first time that, when some distinguished musician or otherwise has arrived in this country, there has been a somewhat hysterical welcome.'

The back page showed the pianist reclining on a sofa in his hotel.

Tonic sofa! Mmm - that's swell!... Liberace relaxes on a sofa in his London hotel suite after a squealing, screaming reception from thousands of women fans yesterday. He doesn't seem to worry about crumpling that elegant £125 suit of silky tweed with golden thread through it. Why should he? He has brought another fifty suits, including his famous gold lamé creation.

So much, said Beyfus, for the news.

'We now turn to the libel, which is on page six. The *Daily Mirror* have been very kind, very kind to me at any rate, because the very worst part of the libel they have repeated and put in a little box at the top, as showing what the editor of the *Daily Mirror* considers to be the vital part of the article. Let us see what Mr Cassandra says. He starts with a little reminiscence of the drink which he seems to have had in Berlin':

On August 20, 1939, when war was absolutely inevitable between Great Britain and Nazi Germany, I went and had a drink - I needed it more than anything in my life any time before or since - at Berlin's most violent, most vulgar and most picturesque bar, the Haus Vaterland in the Potsdamer Platz.

This vast establishment had about twenty bars representing the drinking habits of all nations ranging from ersatz English pubs to ersatz Cuban bars. It was a round up of the drinking customs of the world staged in suitable theatrical scenery.

In the Yachting Bar (Why can't the Royal Navy and the Kriegsmarine love each other like brothers?) they had the drink to end all drinks. It was called *Windstarke Funf* - or Windstrength Five. It was the most deadly concoction of alcohol that the Haus Vaterland could produce in those most desperate days.

On behalf of Mr Chamberlain and Mr Hitler I had five.

'That has very little to do with what follows,' said Beyfus '– although one perhaps might think that the article was written immediately after he had had those five deadly drinks and not many years afterwards...'

I have to report that Mr Liberace, like *Windstarke Funf*, is about the most that man can take. But he is not a drink. He is Yearning-Windstrength Five. He is the summit of sex - the pinnacle of Masculine, Feminine and Neuter. Everything that He, She and It can ever want.

And if the jury looked to the top right hand corner, they would see that 'enclosed in a little box there, in considerably larger print, the editor thinks it right to repeat it –'

Cassandra says - 'He is the summit of sex - the pinnacle of Masculine, Feminine and Neuter. Everything that He, She and It can ever want.

The column continued:

I spoke to sad but kindly men on this newspaper who have met every celebrity arriving from the United States for the past thirty years.

They all say that this deadly, winking, sniggering, snuggling, chromium plated, scent-impregnated, luminous, quivering, giggling, fruit-flavoured, mincing, ice-covered heap of mother-love has had the biggest reception and impact on London since Charlie Chaplin arrived at the same station, Waterloo, on September 12, 1921.

This appalling man - and I use the word appalling in no other than its true sense of 'terrifying' - has hit this country in a way that is as violent as Churchill receiving the cheers on VE Day.

He reeks with emetic language that can only make grown men long for a quiet corner, an aspidistra, a handkerchief and the old heave-ho.

Without doubt he is the biggest sentimental vomit of all time. Slobbering over his mother, winking at his brother, and counting the cash at every second, this superb piece of calculating candy-floss has an answer for every situation.

On Religion. 'I feel I can bring people closer to God through my appearances. I happen to be a religious man, and I want my marriage to be blessed with my faith.'

On Mother Love. 'I think it is my mother love which so many of them (middle aged women) do not get from their children.'

On World Love. 'I want to spread the world of Love, Love of Family, Love of God and Love of Peace.'

On Money. 'I think people love lovely things - and they are deductible from income tax. I earn about a million dollars a year and could earn more if I tried harder; but I only manage to keep nine cents out of each dollar I earn.'

On the occasion in New York at a concert in Madison Square Garden when he had the greatest reception of his life and the critics slayed him mercilessly, Liberace said; 'The take was terrific but the critics killed me. My brother George cried all the way to the bank.'

Nobody since Aimee Semple McPherson has purveyed a bigger, richer and more varied slag-heap of lilac-coloured hokum.

Nobody anywhere ever made so much money out of high-speed piano-playing with the ghost of Chopin gibbering at every note.

There must be something wrong with us that our teenagers longing for sex and our middle aged matrons fed up with sex, alike, should fall for such a sugary mountain of jingling claptrap wrapped up in such a preposterous clown.

'All that,' said Beyfus, 'before my client had given a single performance in this country…'

He said the jury 'may think it is about as savage a diatribe as could be given. It is, as you can see, an attack on him not just as a performer and entertainer but as a man, and a grave, serious attack upon his morals. Nothing, I venture to submit, could be clearer than that the words, which the editor has thought fit to repeat in larger print in the little box at the top, meant, and were intended to mean, that my client was a homosexual. That is about as clear as clear can be. Otherwise I venture to suggest that they can have no meaning at all. You may imagine that article caused my client the most intense distress. He tried to keep it from his mother, but he could not. She saw it, and was most upset, and that increased his distress. As the time passed, and he could see the effect which it had, his distress increased.'

The defendants were not denying that the article was defamatory, he said. The ordinary, standard definition of 'defamation' in English law was writing something that held a man up to hatred, ridicule or contempt. 'Quite obviously this article holds my client up to hatred, ridicule and contempt, all three of them. That is not denied.'

What then was the defence? The fairest way to deal with the defence would be to read it – 'then I certainly cannot be accused of misrepresenting it.'

In so far as the words complained of… consist of statements of fact they are true in substance and in fact; in so far as they consist of expressions of opinion they are fair comment made in good faith and without malice upon a matter of public interest namely the television and other performances of the plaintiff and his mannerisms and tricks therein and the propaganda put out on his behalf and with his authority.

Although the judge would direct the jury about the law later Beyfus said he thought it right to explain what was meant by 'fair comment'.

'First of all, where a defence of fair comment is made upon certain facts, it has to be established by the defendants that the facts are true. You

33

cannot have fair comment on facts which do not exist. That is why the defence starts by [claiming] that, in so far as the article consists of statements of fact, they are true. The second thing about fair comment, and indeed the defence recognise it, is that it must be honest. It must be the honest opinion of the man who writes it, but it need not be fair in the sense that you think it is reasonable and fair. It need only be such that in your opinion a reasonable man could have written it.'

Therefore, while listening to the evidence in the case, the jury should be aware what it was that the defendants had set out to prove – (i) all the facts were true, (ii) the article was written honestly and represented the honest opinion of William Connor, and (iii) that in the jury's opinion it was such a comment as a reasonable man could have written.

'In substance all the abuse is said to be comment, with this exception, that with regard to the expression scent-impregnated the defence say that, if that be a statement of fact, then it is true. Let me give you an example. Under the words "Not since 1921", it says "They all say that this deadly, winking..." etc. The words from "deadly" to "mother-love" are comment and not fact. One of the questions which you will have to decide is whether they are right in saying that sort of description of a man is in fact comment or whether it is fact.'

Perhaps the highlight of the defence, Beyfus thought, was that his client was 'alleged to have made a disparaging remark with regard to Princess Margaret' during a TV interview with American broadcaster Ed Murrow. The interview had taken place in Liberace's home and the QC read the transcript to the jury verbatim, from 'Good evening, I'm Ed Murrow', to 'Goodnight,' explaining where the commercial breaks came during the programme.

> MURROW: Not since the silent movies, and the idols they produced, has Hollywood witnessed the sort of pilgrimage that is now going on. Each day, oblivious of time, weather, and the state of the world, sightseers head in the direction of California's San Fernando Valley, for there, at the end of the tourist line, is Sherman Oaks and the home that Liberace has built for himself and his mother. This is the front... and no one knows how many people have seen that view. And this is the back of the house, and that's Liberace's bedroom. Good evening, Lee...'

(His client was generally known by the name of 'Lee' among his friends, Beyfus explained.)

Some time later, the interviewer asked: 'Well now, Lee, that you're so successful, do you find that on occasion you have to be just a little bit tough skinned?' – Liberace: 'Well, I don't exactly ignore criticism. A lot of criticism that is fair and just, I do pay attention to. In fact, it's been very helpful to me in my life. But then there's the other kind of criticism that's on the destructive side, and I'm glad that God has made me tough-skinned, as you say, so that I can ignore it.'

MURROW: Well, then the apparent lack of enthusiasm so far for that picture *Sincerely Yours,* it doesn't particularly bother you?

LIBERACE: Well, actually, Ed, I'm very, very thrilled about the encouragement this picture has brought to me. It's my first venture in making motion pictures, and we found that it was the first picture since *Going My Way* to win the highest honours from the Legion of Decency, and I'm very, very proud of that fact, as well as the fact that it was made for family entertainment. And I find now that where the picture is playing at neighbourhood houses at popular prices where entire families can afford, to go, the picture is doing very well. I'm going to make some more, too.

MURROW: Tell me, is your brother in that picture, or can't we put any of the blame on him...?

That question provided the opportunity for Liberace to introduce his brother George, his sister Angie, and then his mother who, he suggested, was possibly interrupted by the TV crew while she was trying to watch the wrestling (rather, apparently, than watching her son, reportedly being interviewed live on the screen.)

He hoped he would not embarrass his mother by referring to the hard times when 'I used to wear George's hand-me-down clothes and George and I used to go to the county relief to get rations from the relief department.'

And he revealed 'a little bright side to all of this, too... Ed. I can recall being in Milwaukee just recently and the relief department said that now apparently I was doing well and they wanted me to pay them back for all the groceries, so I gave them a check for $132. That doesn't sound like a lot, but in those days that bought a lot of beans, rice and barley; didn't it Mom?'

Angie, the viewers learnt, was married, which prompted the question: 'Lee, what about you? Have you given much thought to getting married and eventually settling down?'

LIBERACE: Well, actually, I have, Ed. I have given a lot of thought to marriage, but I don't believe in getting married just for the sake of getting married. I want to some day find the perfect mate and settle down to what I hope will be a marriage that will be blessed by faith and will be a lasting union. In fact, I was reading about lovely young Princess Margaret, and she's looking for her dream man, too. I hope she finds him some day.

MURROW: Have you ever met the princess?

LIBERACE: Not as yet but I have great hopes of meeting her when I go to England next season. I'm going to give a concert in London and I'd like to meet her very much because I think we have a lot in common. We have the same tastes in the theatre and music, and besides, she's pretty and she's single!

35

That last sentence, said Mr Beyfus, was part of the defence justification that their comment was fair.

'I venture to submit there is nothing in it at all but a rather dull part of this interview. It was introduced as a little jocular observation: I should like to meet her. She's pretty and she's single. You must remember that the royal family in this country cannot really expect, and do not expect I am sure, to be treated in the United States with the same sort of feelings and respect and unwillingness to make any sort of jocular observation as we do here.'

In fact Liberace had been 'tackled' about it after the programme –'critics are always after him' – and he immediately expressed his regret if he had said anything in bad taste or that he ought not to have said.

After the interviewee had talked gushingly about his happy life, Murrow asked: 'Well, surely something must get under your skin once in a while, doesn't it?'

And the jury, Beyfus suggested, would be astonished to hear that the reply was something on which the defendants rely in the case: 'Well, about the only thing that bothers me is when people accuse me of having a following only of nice old ladies. I have nothing against the nice old ladies, but I like nice young ladies, too.'

About as harmless a sentence, said the QC, as you could possibly imagine.

He then turned to what he said was proof of 'how little those responsible for the newspaper really believed that the plaintiff was the revolting person which he would appear to be if there were any sort of truth or substance in the libel.'

In October Patrick Doncaster, a *Daily Mirror* feature writer, had written to Liberace's manager about arranging a picture feature in a London pub:

> …Some other newspapers, I fear, have a similar idea and I am therefore anxious to try to keep this exclusively to the Mirror – with your kind co-operation – because we have been planning this with some eagerness.
>
> I know that requests and calls on Mr Liberace must be overwhelming, but at the same time I would be grateful if we can discuss this feature as soon as possible.
>
> I can assure you that, if it is exclusive to us, it will be given the utmost prominence and display in the Daily Mirror - the paper with the greatest daily sale on earth.
>
> Miss Heppner [an agent] assured me on the phone today that 'everything would be all right'. She asked me to ring her again 'in a day or two'. Meantime, I would be pleased if you can give the matter your consideration and possibly suggest a tentative date.
>
> Best Wishes, Yours sincerely,
> Patrick Doncaster.

'As it was the invariable practice of Mr Liberace (and those who advised him on publicity matters backed him up in it) to co-operate with the press in every possible way, and thinking that possibly this libel was an individual effort of Mr Cassandra, they determined to carry out what they had half promised in Hollywood,' explained Beyfus. 'So Mr Liberace, accompanied by Mr Doncaster and another reporter, went out with them on what the paper calls a pub crawl.'

He handed a book of newspaper cuttings to the jury – the judge already had his own copy – and read them the text. The heading was:

> This is wunnerful, just wunnerful being with you grand folks.
> Liberace on a pub crawl, by Pat Doncaster and Tony Miles.

It was all fairly inconsequential stuff. Trivial at worst; knockabout at best. The jury smiled, occasionally even laughed, especially at the quotes attributed to the apparently typical cockney sparrows that the reporters had stumbled across during their evening foray. Perhaps they even thought it was all a bit silly; certainly out of place in the dignified surroundings of the Royal Courts of Justice, with a scarlet clad judge and bewigged barristers trying to take it all seriously. But Mr Beyfus was having none of that amusement or bemusement. He intoned the text as though he were reciting the Magna Carta:

> He daren't go shopping because he might be mobbed. When he does go out he has to have police protection. Night and day he's almost a prisoner in a plushy hotel suite... But at the weekend he escaped for an hour...
>
> We took Liberace on a pub crawl. And for the first time since he arrived in Britain he became just one of the crowd.
>
> He slid out of a rarely-used side door at the Savoy Hotel, huddled in a corner of a car that swept him across the river to London's Cockney Borough area. We pulled up outside The Bell in Webber Street, SE1.
>
> The public bar was bursting at its seams. A friendly crowd rushed the car. 'Come and give us a tune on the old Joanna, mate,' cried a Cockney voice.
>
> But Liberace's manager, who had come along, got scared that his million-dollar charge might get damaged in the crush. So we rolled on to the seventeenth-century coaching pub, The George, in Borough High Street.
>
> Liberace looked up at the inn sign, put on that marshmallow smile and wisecracked: 'Gee... named after my brother!'
>
> Then in he walked, straight to the counter and said; 'I'll have a shandy, please.'
>
> Hardly any of the customers looked up at the chubby figure in the mustard-yellow sweater, chocolate slacks and crocodile-leather shoes.
>
> Fascinated by the beer pumps, Liberace drawled: 'Can I work those?' At the landlord's invitation he went behind the counter and drew himself a pint of bitter.

'Pull me a pint, too, mate, while you're there,' said Bermondsey docker William Welsh, 46. And Liberace did.

Office cleaner Bert Anderson, 53, sitting by the window, remarked: 'I reckon he's a decent sort - the kind of bloke you don't mind having a pint with.'

Next we bowled into The Tiger close by the Tower of London - just as they had finished playing a Liberace record on the gramophone. You could have knocked barmaid Violet Blandford down with a bung-plugger.

'Oor, if it ain't Liberace - 'ere, in our pub!'

But three regulars standing next to the famous dimpled face at the bar kept right on sipping their beer.

Dick Regan, lorry driver, murmured to Stan Peasley, a caretaker: ''Ere, that's Liberace!'

Stan nodded casually and said; 'Yer, so it is.'

Then, to be matey, Stan turned round and said to Liberace: 'Have one with me.'

That started it. Others wanted to buy him a pint. Dark-haired Mary Dorsett, who has a fruit stall outside the Tower, put her arm round Liberace's waist and said: 'Every mother would want a son like 'im. 'E's a wonderful fellow to his mum, bless 'im.'

Dick Regan asked for an autograph. 'It's for the wife,' he said. 'She'll be thrilled and won't mind me being late for dinner.'

Then a fruit stall-holder from Aldgate adjusted his choker and cap, fished out a £1 note from his leather jerkin and went up to Liberace and asked 'Could you sign this, mate?'

His 'mate' did. What will the fruit man do with the note? 'I reckon I can flog this for more than a quid,' he said.

Liberace started playing the beer pumps again. Everyone rushed to buy a Liberace-pulled pint. And the million-dollar fingers with the grand-piano ring took the money and worked the cash register, too.

'This is wunnerful, just wunnerful being with all you grand folks,' he said with a grin as wide as a keyboard.

Then the bell rang for time. He signed an empty cigarette packet for a man in a cap. Then we went off. It was back once more to the plushy hotel suite, the spotlights - and the candelabra!

That article had appeared on October 8. Meanwhile, Liberace had been performing on stage, in a Palladium Sunday-night television show, and at the Royal Festival Hall, said Beyfus.

'When he arrived there were some hostile groups outside with hostile placards, and at the opening he found an unpleasant attitude in the audience. From all his experience he can sum-up the feelings of an audience, and he found some hostility at the beginning. He had to win them over; and that happened throughout his stay in England. The same thing applied at Leicester and at the Davis Theatre, Croydon, and on October 8 at Manchester.

'On October 11 at Sheffield it was quite worse, because he was greeted by the audience with cries of Fairy and Queer, which, as you know, are the slang expressions to denote a homosexual. That was really the last straw for him, because when he arrived at Dublin two days later he rang his lawyer in California for advice about bringing an action. Never before had he brought any sort of action in respect of any of the criticisms which had been directed against him.'

From Dublin he returned to London and on two nights packed the Royal Albert Hall – justifying, his QC said, his slogan that 'Nobody loves me but the people.'

The writ was issued on October 22 by which time a second libel had appeared in Cassandra's *Mirror* column. Under the heading Calling All Cussers, the columnist had quoted biblical extracts from Isaiah, and continued:

> I think we should return to these greater and more sonorous maledictions. For those were the days when a cuss-word was a cuss-word and, when well and truly laid, the recipient knew that what had been said was no term of endearment but a prayer that his liver should be devoured by maggots and that his children should be fatherless before nightfall.

The libels against his client, said Beyfus, were 'not that his liver should be devoured by maggots, but that he should be avoided and shunned by all decent men and women.'

Then that day's column continued, under a smaller heading, What's on.

> In their daily programme of events called 'Today's Arrangements', *The Times* was yesterday at its impassive, unsmiling best.
>
> St Vedast's, Foster Lane: Canon C B Mortlock, 12.30. St Paul's, Covent Garden; The Rev Vincent Howson, 1.15. St Botolph's, Bishopsgate: Preb H H Treacher, 1.15. All Souls', Langham Place: Mr H M Collins, 12.30. Albert Hall: Liberace, 7.30.
>
> Rarely has the sacred been so well marshalled alongside the profane.

Clearly, that was 'an accusation of profanity on the part of my client.'

The QC said he planned to call a number of witnesses who would tell them that whatever criticisms may be made of his client's performances the one thing which was quite and absolutely clear was that they were not sexy, that there is nothing in them which could possibly justify the expression 'The summit of sex'. He said: 'They are, you will be told by a witness, wholesome, homely, indeed homey, and in parts sentimental. There is nothing in them which could possibly be described as sexy and nothing which could be said to be calculated to stimulate sexual feelings. Indeed, they will tell you that they are in fact the very reverse. Parts of the article by Mr Cassandra indicate the same sort of thing, that in his opinion (although he had never seen my client, at any rate certainly in a live show) they are over-sentimental; indeed, he says, The biggest sentimental vomit of all time.'

He also intended to prove that Mr Connor did not believe his own side's defence. He would produce a witness who had interviewed him for the magazine *Picture Post* and had asked the columnist how he thought the case against him would go.

The answer had been: 'He will take a lot of money off us. It was libel,' and he'd said the libel was contained in the phrase 'He, she or it'.

But he had told the reporter: 'The *Mirror* thinks it will be worth it for a week's publicity, and I do not know who will look the bigger buffoon in the witness box, him or me.'

On the subject of fighting the case, he said Connor had continued: 'We could object to the jury, and we will make sure there are no women on it. They will be very distorted, so we will make sure we have all men. Men don't like him.'

As for who would appear the bigger buffoon, Beyfus said: 'It is no part of my case that Mr Connor is a buffoon. A buffoon may well be a kindly person, which is the very last epithet which could be applied to Mr Connor. It is part of my case that, far from being a buffoon, Mr Connor is just a literary assassin who dips his pen in vitriol instead of in ink and is hired by this sensational newspaper to murder reputations and hand out to the public day by day those sensational articles on which its circulation is dependent.'

He explained to the jury that he was asking for damages on two bases. 'First, the ordinary and normal basis is damages to compensate my client for the damage to his reputation which this savage article must have caused and for the distress which it has caused him;

'Secondly, if you come to the conclusion – and, of course, only if you come to the conclusion – that the publication of such an article was deplorable, indecent conduct on the part of this newspaper, conduct which ought to be punished, then you are entitled to grant Mr Liberace what are known as punitive damages – damages which are deliberately designed to punish the defendants for their misconduct. They are sometimes known as exemplary damages, damages which are awarded so that they may afford an example and a warning to other newspapers not to follow the same deplorable path.'

That, he told members of the jury, was all he had to say in opening.

'I will call Mr Liberace.'

Wladziu Valentino Liberace having been sworn in, Mr Beyfus affected to have difficulty pronouncing his first name. It was all part of the act, because there was no need for him to mention it at all; but in case anybody was interested he got the plaintiff to agree that the name could be rendered in English as Walter.

–Were you born – in so far as you know it, at any rate – in May 1919? – A: Yes, in a suburb of Milwaukee known as West Dallas.

Mr Beyfus then led him through the biographical details he had outlined earlier.

Yes; his parents were both accomplished musicians. Yes; when he was 15 or 16 he had a poisoned finger and doctors had suggested amputating his hand to prevent the spread of infection, but his mother had refused to allow it and had applied poultices for several weeks which drew out the infection. Yes; his family was so poor it had needed to resort to what was known as county relief. Yes; he had found work as solo pianist for two performances with the Chicago Symphony Orchestra and then played with dance bands and at supper clubs and hotels. In 1947 he had started putting candelabra on his piano as a trade mark. He got the idea from a motion picture about the life of Chopin.

–During these performances did you develop a certain technique? – A: Yes... I studied my performance very thoroughly and took into particular notice the reaction of my audiences to certain types of entertainment that I was giving them, and I noted that they particularly enjoyed the kind of entertainment that was of a personal and intimate approach. This is the approach that I used in my performances, the conversational approach with the audiences... I discussed various episodes in my early life and training, and discussed the members of my family who had played a very important part in my early life and training. I also discussed my musical views as well as some of my philosophies of life... Yes, it was very successful.

When he was invited to appear on a Los Angeles TV station he asked the general manager about the type of performance he wanted, and was told to play as he performed in the supper clubs where he had been spotted.

'I remember his words very distinctly, and I have had many occasions to remember them since; he said: Do not think of the television camera as being the means of putting you over to thousands, and perhaps eventually millions, of people, but think of it as one separate individual to whom you are speaking and trying to entertain with your music. I believed this so strongly that many times, when I would bump into this camera I would say Excuse me.'

He was given a contract for 13 weeks at $1,000 a week, and from the start the series had been a success, with viewers telephoning the station 'congratulating the station on this new programme and on my efforts as a television performer.'

–Did that success increase as the weeks and the months passed? – A: It did, as you said, spread like a prairie fire.

41

The Citizens National Bank of Los Angeles offered him sponsorship and it was followed by 'products and services aimed at family consumption' including 'food products, automobiles, services such as electric and gas, and products that are used by families in homes.'

He was also booked to give live performances in southern California. And for his concert at the Hollywood Bowl he decided to appear in a full dress suit of tails, all white. All 20,000 seats were sold out for the show, and an estimated 2,000 were sitting on the hillside. He was greeted by an ovation when he walked out on the stage, and later was referred to in the newspapers as 'Mr Showmanship'.

This convinced him that the audiences to which he played enjoyed seeing him dress in clothes that might be termed as glamorous clothes… Other performers in his profession, he said, began to copy his way of dress. 'This was flattering to me, but at the same time it created a situation in which, being considered a top name in my profession, I had to dress above the other performers who were copying me, and set an example. I found difficulty at times in topping my previous self.'

This involved higher and higher flights of fancy, he agreed with Beyfus: 'I recall one particular instance in Las Vegas when the man who had hired me asked what I was going to wear. I told him that I thought I would wear a gold lamé jacket, and he said: That is old stuff by now; you wore it last time you were here; you have got to give us something new because people expect it of you. Then he cited a few examples of performers who had copied my gold jacket, giving the name of one young man who was just coming up at the time – Elvis Presley.'

Liberace topped the gold jacket with a suit of tails threaded with lamé silver. 'It sparkled in the lights and looked extremely glamorous, I also thought of a suit of black mohair, the tails of which had diamond studded buttons on them. It was given much publicity and valued as being worth $10,000.'

So accoutred, Liberace made a number of guest appearances on TV shows and performed 117 of his own. They were usually 30-minute slots on film of which, to allow for commercial breaks, his performance would usually last about 24 minutes, and consist of six 'units' of music.

Four minutes a piece, he agreed, was insufficient time to play any classical music in its entirety. He said he was 'not ashamed' of that… 'I had on some occasions in my television programme tried to do numbers which were more than four minutes, but the balance of time, the difference between the four minutes and the time I took to perform a particular number usually wound up on the cutting room floor…'

During the lunch adjournment Beyfus realised that he had forgotten to ask about the fur coat his client wore for movie premiers and opening nights of theatre productions. Possibly superfluously, he asked: 'Did you acquire a somewhat glamorous coat?' Yes he did... It was white beaver ... He wore it on special occasions, for example on the first nights of films and on his own opening nights.

He'd made a jocular observation about Mr [President] Truman having a similar coat in tan, and said 'We pianists must stick together'. So, did the president have a similar coat, except that it was tan? – Yes, he did.

–You made a joke about 'We pianists must stick together'; I suppose he plays the piano too? – A: Yes, it is a known fact that he does.

–Not for his living? – A: No, not for his living.

The questioning then swung to the number of press conferences Liberace gave. A great number? – Yes. He confirmed that, at press conferences, he was asked questions by reporters; on every conceivable subject, which he endeavoured to answer; but he was in no way responsible for the subjects covered.

Liberace spoke about his appearance in 1954 at Madison Square Garden, then agreed that he had sold more than a million records, appeared in a stage play and as a comedian on the Red Skelton show and as a beachcomber in a film called *South Sea Scene* in the US, but *East of Java*, elsewhere.

BEYFUS: 'I do not want to lead, but I suppose as a beachcomber your clothing was not extremely glamorous?' – A: No, it was that of a beachcomber.

By the time he reached London in September 1956, he had reached what some people presumed was the summit of his career and was, he agreed, 'earning a very large income'.

He confirmed that he had arrived with 'quite a retinue', for the purpose of giving concerts, and that the press had been there when the Queen Mary put in at Cherbourg and when it docked at Southampton where he was also greeted by 'a certain number of what we must call fans'.

Then on the next day there appeared in the *Daily Mirror* the three accounts of the preceding day which had been read, and the pictures... 'and in addition the article which is written by Cassandra, of which you are complaining here?' – Yes.

–How did that article affect you? – A: After reading that article I was deeply shocked, and my only thought at the time was that it would certainly have to be kept from my mother. The reason I felt this so strongly is because my mother has a hypertensive heart condition; and I further know that she is extremely proud of all her children, perhaps a bit more proud of me... but it was brought to her attention by someone... She became immediately very ill, and was attended by a physician. It was decided by everyone concerned for her welfare and myself that she leave the country.

–I ought to ask you this at once: are you a homosexual? – A: I am not.
–Have you ever indulged in homosexual practices? –

Mr Gardiner, representing both the *Daily Mirror* and Cassandra, had presumably overlooked the earlier reference. Now he was on his feet before the question could be answered: 'There is no suggestion, and never has been, of anything of the kind!'

BEYFUS: I do not know. The defence is that the comment is fair. I do not agree there is no suggestion. At any rate, I am going to ask him... Mr Liberace, have you ever indulged in homosexual practices? – A: No, never in my life.

–What are your feelings towards homosexuals? – A: My feelings are the same as anyone else; I am against this practice, because it offends convention and offends society.

Beyfus moved quickly on through the concert itinerary, *Sunday Night At The Palladium*, then the Royal Festival Hall the following evening.

When he arrived at the Royal Festival Hall were there any hostile groups outside? –Yes, there were some 'hostile' groups and he had to stay in the car until policemen arrived to protect him and take him inside. There were also 'unfriendly' placards.

On that day Patrick Doncaster of the *Mirror* had written about arranging 'what the papers called a pub crawl'. It had first been suggested in Hollywood and Liberace and his manager thought it would result in good publicity. The paper's account of the night outing was quite accurate, he said.

After the Festival Hall he sensed a 'mood of hostility' in audiences at Croydon and at Belle Vue Manchester at the beginning of his performances, but during the course of the performance he was able to win them over, he said.

–When you appeared on the platform at the City Hall at Sheffield did you hear any cries from the audience? – A: Yes, I did....The cries seemed to come from the gallery, and they were queer and varied, and such things as 'Go home, Queer'.

–Did that upset you? – A: Very much and it upset the audience too, because I would say that a good many people in the audience were at variance with those comments.

–So far as you could judge, did you win that audience over before the end of your show? – A: Yes, I worked very hard to win them over.

He was so upset that two days later, while appearing in Dublin, he rang John Jacobs, his lawyer and business manager, in California. Then he returned to London for two engagements at the Royal Albert Hall where on each occasion he played to a full house.

'The very dignity of the Albert Hall seemed to spread over the audience, and they were a better behaved audience than I had enjoyed in some of the other theatres... There were some hostiles outside, but they did not continue into the Hall itself.'

He left England for Rome on October 18 and the writ was issued four days later. He had returned to London to give a Command Performance at the Palladium for the Queen, but the event was cancelled at short notice because of the Suez crisis, and he had returned to the United States very disappointed.

In 1958 – the year before the trial – he fulfilled a two-week engagement, again at the Palladium, taking over the second half of each night's performance and playing for about 65 minutes each time.

Oh, Mr Beyfus had forgotten to ask...

–During your first visit in 1956, apart from the concerts which we have gone through, you also played at the Café de Paris, a restaurant in Coventry Street, London? – A: Yes, I gave six performances at the Café de Paris.

–I think there the artist makes his first performance by walking down some rather steep stairs... As you walked down those stairs did you have any reaction from the audience yourself? – A: There seemed to be a feeling in the audience that might be termed resentful, and it thereby made it necessary for me to prove myself to these people. I am happy to say that after opening night this feeling did not prevail.

–I want to ask you about the nature of your performance. You have told us how you developed this patter. That, I gather, you continued on television, and have continued ever since... Was there anything at all sexy about any of your performances? – A: No. I have never been termed that by the American public.

–Do not let us bother for the moment about the American public. Let us take your own view. Is there anything at all sexy about your performances? – A: I am not aware of it if it exists. I am almost positive that I could hardly ever refer to myself as a sexy performer. I have tried in all my performances to inject a note of sincerity and wholesomeness because I am fully aware of the fact that my appeal on television and in personal appearances is aimed directly at the family audience.

–What sort of subjects have you discussed in your patter? You told us what they were in the origin. Do those subjects remain today the same, the principal subjects that you discuss? – A: Yes. I learnt in time in discussing these subjects which I have referred to beforehand to develop them in such a way as to make them pleasing to the audience and sometimes amusing to the audience, and I have always tried to use my so-called patter in such a way as to make it an entertainment portion of my programme.

–The subjects of your mother, your brother, your early struggles, your poverty, your love for music, your philosophy, all remain subjects which you discuss? –A: Yes. My experiences sometimes were the motivation in talking about various subjects.

–Did you ever tell what we know as a dirty or smutty story in the course of any of your performances? – A: I have never been known to tell any so-called dirty stories. I have told experiences that happened to me that might have been termed double meaning, things in referring to some of my sponsors who have at times given us various samples of their products. Among them was a very famous paper company who amongst their products made toilet tissue, and when I mentioned my various sponsors to my audience I included them because they were one of my biggest sponsors, and the audience found it amusing; but it was in no way offensive.

–In the articles there is one thing which is, I think, quite accurate. It is said: 'On the occasion in New York at a concert in Madison Square Garden when he had the greatest reception of his life and the critics slayed him mercilessly, Liberace said: 'The take was terrific but the critics killed me. My brother George cried all the way to the bank!'... You did say something like that, did you not? – A: Yes, something like that. I perhaps put it in slightly different words, but the meaning was that, yes.

–That was a jocular retort to your critics... Is that rather typical of parts, at any rate the more amusing parts, of your patter? – A: Yes.

Beyfus resumed his seat with the air of a man unsure whether there might yet be something he had forgotten to ask, or a point that he ought to have made. He handed his client over for cross-examination by Gerald Gardiner, who made a brisk, but unexpected start, as though inviting the witness back home for an evening in front of the wireless.

–Mr Liberace, are you doing anything on Thursday evening? – A: Yes.

–You are? – A: I am, yes.

–You are engaged? – A: Yes.

–Will you be engaged in a public restaurant or in a home? – A: Neither; I will be in a theatre.

–Do you know a pianist, well-known here, called Semprini? – A: Would you repeat that?

–Do you know a pianist, very popular over here, called Semprini? – A: No, I do not.

–You have not heard him play? – A: No.

–I asked you about Thursday because in the event of this case lasting so long I was going to ask you whether you would listen to his regular programme *Semprini Serenade*; but you will be in the theatre. – A: Yes, I will.

Gardiner was not deterred by rejection: You, of course, have a large and very enthusiastic following, have you not... From what may properly be described as an adoring public... Of men, women and children... Of all ages... And in all walks of life... As you have told us, you fill the largest halls in the United States? – A: Yes.

He took the jury through what was becoming fairly familiar ground, revisiting information much of which they were hearing for the third time in the same day.

He had filled the Madison Square Gardens; he had more than 200 fan clubs in the United States; he received between 6,000 and 10,000 letters a week, and 27,000 valentine cards; about 12 proposals of marriage a month, including one from a lady 'who offered to put $200,000 down'; he earned about $1,000,000 a year from TV and concerts alone, in addition to record sales, real estate investments and a company that gave piano tuition. He gave mainly single-word answers: Yes... yes... yes...

–When you came to England in September 1956 I think you came on the Queen Mary... Had interest in you here been such that a number of English newspapers had got reporters to go and interview you while you were in Hollywood... And did most of the English newspapers when you came over here on the Queen Mary fly reporters to Cherbourg in France in order that the British public might have the advantage of the first words which you might think fit to utter on the Queen Mary... And on the Queen Mary on the way from Cherbourg did you have a press conference? – A: ...Yes.

Mr Gardiner asked the witness to look at two pictures that were handed to him.

–One is a photograph of you, is it not, greeting the press... That is the silk tweed suit with the gold, thread, is it... Which I think you described as 'my English suit'... And the other is a picture of you giving the very well-known Liberace wink... Which is an integral part of your performances, is it not? – A: Yes.

At Waterloo station somebody had a placard saying 'We hate Liberace – Charlie Kunz for ever' but no; Liberace was not suggesting that the *Daily Mirror* had put them up to it.

–This article of which you complain says you had the biggest reception and impact on London since Charlie Chaplin arrived at Waterloo. I suppose you do not suggest that that is in any way defamatory of you? – A: Obviously not.

–As far as your concerts at the Festival Hall and the Albert Hall were concerned, were they full? – A: Yes.

–But were there again some people outside the Albert Hall with placards supporting rival pianists? – A: They were not all 'We hate Liberace –

47

Charlie Kunz for ever' placards. They were placards saying 'Go home', 'Don't chop up Chopin', or something.

–It is the fact, is it not, that while you have this very large adoring screaming public there always have been a number of vociferous critics... A strong opposition... So that you have always been a figure of considerable controversy? – A: Yes.

–Broadly speaking, your critics have been of two kinds, have they not; first of all the musical critics. They have been pretty well unanimous, rightly or wrongly...? – A: Rightly or wrongly, they in recent years have attacked my musicianship, yes; but I have on record reports of my musicianship prior to my advent on television which were praiseworthy.

–But not since? – A: No.

–The other main criticism has been of the extent to which you exploit the emotions and of your sugary ingratiating approach? – A: I have never referred to my performance as such.

–As perhaps a fair specimen of what is said on both sides, I wonder if you would mind looking at an article in a rival paper called the *Daily Sketch*, which I suggest puts pretty fairly what is said on both sides of the controversy. This is February 1, 1955. I chose it as being fairly old and as showing how old the controversy has been:

> A shockingly handsome young fellow is planning to visit London in the spring, to give some concerts. He is pianist and singer Wladziu Valentino Liberace, who has hit a note in the American heart harder than any pianist ever struck a key before. The result is called 'the Liberace frenzy'. There has never been anything else like it. His playing sends women of all ages into ecstasies; they swoon and love it. Even bankers behave like bobby-soxers when they hear him.

...You would not, I hope, suggest that the *Daily Sketch*, in saying that not only do women swoon but that bankers behave like bobby-soxers when they hear him, mean by that that you are homosexual? – A: No. I have never seen bankers behave like bobby-soxers.

–Perhaps you would not recognise the bankers when you saw them. – A: I am sure I would. They were my sponsors.

> –He has put the piano back into the American parlour; makers bless him as sales hit new highs. So do music teachers; they have hordes of new pupils. And Liberace - pronounced Libber-arch-ay - is earning £350,000 a year! Yet two years ago he was almost unknown. Thick wavy hair, dimples and a toothpaste-advertisement smile have helped create the 'Liberace frenzy'.

...Then there is a heading 'Critics are caustic':

> For many critics are frankly caustic about this most-successful-pianist-that-ever-was. They accuse him of exaggerated crescendos and 'prodigious skill at faking brilliant runs up and down the keyboard'. But

his friends say he plays the piano just the way the average woman would like to hear her son play it.

Critics writhe when he produces his mother at concerts and he introduces her as 'My Mom'. But audiences wriggle with delight. If the mood takes him he waves his arms, tosses his head, sings, sits on the edge of the stage and lets grandmothers kiss him.

He has taken piano playing out of the rarefied atmosphere of the classical virtuosos, and brought it to millions who unabashedly revel in his style and don't care a hoot what the highbrows say.

Albums of his records sell by the hundreds of thousands. At New York's Carnegie Hall, which the greatest keyboard masters seldom fill, women were turned away weeping from the box office. Twenty thousand people crowded the Hollywood Bowl to hear him. In New Orleans he was kept signing autographs for 2½ hours after his performance.

...That is because you always put a note in the programme, is it not, saying 'Do come round and see me afterwards'? – A: That is not true.

–You have had such a note in your programme, have you not? – A: Not to my knowledge, unless it is put there by someone without authority. I have never personally authorised its display.

–His fan mail rose to (and stays at) 10,000 letters a week. He is swamped with gifts. One was a gold fly-swatter with his picture on it.

The attacks help him on. Critics still don't like him.

One, a woman, wrote: 'Such dimpling and winking! Such tossing of curls and fluttering of eyelashes and flashing of teeth! Such nausea!'

...Is that a fair summary of the sort of thing which for years, since 1954, has been said in this controversy on one side or the other? – A: It is typical, yes.

–The words 'nausea' or 'nauseating' and the word 'emetic' have been common, have they not, in criticisms of you? – A: I would not say so; not common, no.

–You do not read them? – A: I would say that the article in essence in regard to my performance and the type of people who attend my performance is accurate; but the part about the nausea and the tossing of eyelashes and that sort of comment was few and far between.

–I suggest that there have been in fact a number of articles in which the words 'nausea' or 'nauseating' or references to an emetic have appeared. – A: If you say so, I do not doubt your word.

–There is one paragraph in the article of which you complain: 'Nobody anywhere ever made so much money out of high-speed piano-playing with the ghost of Chopin gibbering at every note'. Is Beethoven's *Moonlight Sonata* a work which takes a concert pianist many minutes to play? – A: Yes; approximately 17 minutes.

–On the television do you do it in four minutes flat? – A: I play an excerpt of the *Moonlight Sonata* and it does last approximately four minutes, yes.

49

–Is it the first movement? – A: It is the first movement, the adagio movement of the *Moonlight Sonata.*

–That first movement takes a concert pianist eight minutes, does it not? – A: Approximately that long.

–You have been known to do the first movement in three minutes flat, have you not? – A: I have been known to do it in approximately that time because I only play an excerpt of the first movement depending on the time that is available.

–You do not even play the first movement, on television? – A: In its entirety? No.

–This is one part of your work on which music critics have commented most strongly and usually unanimously? – A: Yes.

–Is Tchaikovsky's *Piano Concerto No.1* a piece in 153 pages of music? – A: Yes, it is.

–When you play it do you usually play the first 13 pages and the last 11 and four bars in the middle which are not there at all? – A: That is true.

Liberace told Gardiner he did not remember meeting a reporter called Mr Sayle in 1955 at the airport in Paris and had not said: 'Professionally I just use my surname, like Chopin'. He met a great many journalists. But, he said, he had been described a number of times as 'The Chopin of TV'. And he admitted that the use of candelabra on his piano had been inspired by a film about Chopin.

–At the Madison Square Garden concert to which Mr Beyfus referred was there a Chopin medley which you played immediately following a song about a cement mixer? – A: It is very possible, yes. I play in one programme music of all types and nature, and it is very possible that Chopin's music might be followed by a number such as the cement mixer. This is the individuality of my programme that makes me different from anyone else.

–I was going to suggest that is not strictly correct, because there are other pianists – indeed, Semprini the concert pianist is one – who make a mixture of popular modern music and classical music. – A: Evidently he does not do it quite as successfully, because I have never heard of him.

–That is, if I may say so, a very pertinent answer, because one of the questions to be considered here is whether the reason why you have not heard of Semprini is because of the quality of his playing or because he has not got a fan club and does not produce his mother on the stage or have a high-powered publicity organisation. – A: I would not know what the reasons for it are, but it does remain a fact that I do not know this gentleman you speak of and I cannot make any comparison since I do not know his performance or what he does.

–As far as you know, are you the only pianist in the world who performs the *Minute Waltz* in 20 seconds flat? – A: I have never claimed that.

–Is it true? –A: It is not true.

–Do you know anybody else who does? – A: I do not know of anyone else who makes that claim, no.

Gardiner then wanted to test the accuracy of what the plaintiff's own publicity machine had said about him. He handed him a copy of a book called *The Liberace Story* by Anton Burney, published specially in advance of his British tour.

The opening paragraph said: 'The following story of my life, written by my friend Anton Burney, is accurate in every detail, and I am indeed grateful for this opportunity to further acquaint myself with the wonderful people of Great Britain.'

It continued: 'No artist of our time has met with such savage criticism' and gave, said Gardiner, 'much the same reason as the music critics'.

He read the text:

> Perhaps this unquestioning faith lies behind Lee's generous response to the malice of his critics – this faith, and a bubbling sense of humour. No artist of our time has met with such savage criticism, and it is easy to see why. His technique is revolutionary, and the critics are reactionary. They boil with rage if he plays in five minutes some great composition which another artist cannot perform in less than eight…

Yet in the article he complained about, the wording had been:

> On the occasion in New York at a concert in Madison Square Garden when he had the greatest reception of his life and the critics slayed him mercilessly, Liberace said: 'The take was terrific but the critics killed me. My brother George cried all the way to the bank.'

That had been a standard gag of his, Liberace admitted. And if a critic wrote an unkind notice he would sometimes reply: Thank you very much for your criticism. I cried all the way to the bank –'or words to that effect'.

–Would it be right to say that you spend a good deal of time jingling your money in your pocket and talking about how much you earn? – A: No, that is not true.

Gardiner then returned to the performer's wardrobe, which included about 60 suits and 80 pairs of shoes… a white jacket with a million bugle beads on it, which sparkled in the limelight… six pairs of tails in white, black and blue… a diamond studded silk mohair coat that cost $10,000… a white beaver overcoat… a gold lamé dinner jacket lined with real gold… a bow tie studded with silver beads…

Then counsel produced a cutting with a photograph of him wearing the beaver coat in the company of his mother.

'The article states that you said to the press conference on the Queen Mary, when asked to what you attributed your very large following among

American matrons: I think it is my mother-love, or my love for my mother, which so many of them do not get from their children.'

Liberace replied that he did not use the expression mother-love, but agreed with the QC that it was 'difficult' to attend one of his piano recitals without hearing more than one reference to his mother, who he usually referred to as Mom, and who used to attend all his concerts. The spotlight would focus on her and he might say: 'I give my applause to my mother,' and the audience would clap her.

He agreed that a standard reply, when asked about marriage, might be: 'I am looking for a girl like Mom and of whom Mom would approve.' But he had never heard it said that he appealed to 'the Mom complex'. He was unaware that, five years ago, *Time* magazine had referred to him as 'The musical momist'. And he denied telling reporters: 'So far, my girl is still my mother.'

Back to accuracy...

Liberace had said he was born on May 16, 1919.

But, said Gardiner, 'All your officially passed booklets, like the one I put to you in which you said that every word was true, say you were born on June 16, 1920. How is that? Perhaps I have got a misprint or something, but I suggest they all do, do they not?' – A: It is very possible that this date is given as a convenience to people who try to rapidly determine the age of persons such as myself. It is easier to figure out one's age if a round figure is used rather than an odd number such as 1919... 1920 is much easier to figure out.

The material for the book came from Warner Brothers studio, he said. 'The only acquaintance I have with the actual writing is the foreword. I did not write it myself; it was submitted to me. I signed the book; and I hasten to add that the signature that appears at the end of that foreword was written not by me but by my secretary Susan Roberts.

And yet, said Gardiner, he claimed the book was 'accurate in every detail'... He continued reading:

> Liberace has a great sense of family relationships, and that old album is often in his lap, calling up old memories. By its aid he can tell chapter after chapter of family history. 'Here's George!' he'll say, quizzically, looking across at his violinist brother.

...And so on. Was all this an invention?

Liberace said: 'These are not quotations from me, because I have never met Anton Burney and I have never been interviewed by this man; therefore the quotations he uses are pure invention, yes.' As far as he knew there was no such family album.

–Did you read this before you signed or authorised your secretary to sign a statement that it was accurate in every detail? – A: No, I did not, speaking of the book itself.

–It is all good for publicity, is it, whether it is true or not? – A: I did not read the book, no.

–But you authorised somebody to sign your name. Any of your fans would think that, would they not, knowing your signature? This is a deliberate imitation of your signature, Liberace? – A: Yes. She does it very well.

–And you authorised her to do it? – A: Yes, I often do.

–You authorised her to sign this… knowing quite well that there was an introduction which purported to have been signed by you saying that every detail was accurate? – A: Yes, I knew that.

–Did you think it was right, knowing this was going to be sold for money, to authorise your secretary to imitate your signature to a preface which said that it was accurate in every detail? – A: I did think it was right at the time because the importance of having advance publicity reach England before my arrival was stressed. They stressed the importance of this book, and they also stressed the accuracy of the book and impressed on me that no liberties would be taken with my life or my life story, and it would be based on material that had been submitted to them by Warner Brothers, and it was intended to be accurate in every detail. I trusted their intentions and therefore I authorised my secretary to sign the foreword.

Part of the book was also published in *TV Mirror*, described as 'his only authenticated biography'. It began:

> To you, Liberace writes: It is difficult for a man to express his feelings when he sees his own short life made into a story which is spread out before him. Now, reading it, I find that I have been moved by every sentence, at times so much so that tears have sprung into my eyes. I have had to remember so many things that might otherwise have stayed forgotten, and for this, if for no other reason, I am deeply grateful to *TV Mirror* for wanting to tell this story.

This was the same story word for word, as was in the book, he said.

–Did you get money for that article? – A: I do not know.

–Did you write it? – A: I did not write it, no. I have never written those words you have just spoken.

It ran for six issues in the magazine, but was all fake then, said Gardiner. – Yes.

He referred him back to the book by Anton Burney, with the signature written by the secretary, *Sincerely yours, Liberace*.

–Is it just an accident that if one looks in the middle page one sees 'Birthday: May 16th, Place of birth: Milwaukee, USA (1920)'? – A: It is not an accident. Like other performers in my country, I find it advisable to make the birth date a round figure; I have never been seriously accused of being a liar for one year. Therefore, I took the liberty for my publicity and not for any other purposes legal or otherwise of using the birth date of

1920 rather than 1919. I followed the idea, if I had been inspired to do so, from Jack Benny.

–You do, I suppose, ordinarily look at the newspaper cuttings about yourself, do you not? – A: Sometimes I do.

–And you have held a very large number of press conferences, have you not? – A: Yes.

–Have you noticed many press people interviewing you have said that of all the celebrated people that they have ever interviewed they consider you the quickest and most adroit in answering awkward questions? – A: Yes, I have been attributed to have fast answers.

–And if your real birth date had been 1916, 1920 would still have been the nearest round number, I suppose? – A: My birthday was 1919... I would say four years is rather more difficult to hide than one.

–You agree, I understand, that when asked about marriage, it is a standard reply of yours: 'I am looking for a girl like Mom'? – A: That is not the standard reply, no. I have many views about marriage and I have expressed them from time to time. That may be one of them, yes.

–You say you do not say to them 'So far as I am concerned my girl is still my mother'? – A: That is not a quotation of mine, no.

–Has she appeared in your television performances? – A: Yes, she has.

–Sitting on the stage? A: Yes, she has.

–While you sing to her: 'I shall always call you sweetheart; that will always be your name'? – A: Yes.

–Then you kiss her? – A: Yes.

–Then George kisses her on the other side? – A: Yes.

–The result of that is simply this, is it not, that with the majority it goes down splendidly but it makes a few people feel rather sick? – A: If that is the reaction, it is not my intention to derive that reaction.

–These things are very much a matter of opinion, are they not? – A: That is true.

–And, as with sugar, though it is very nice up to a point, there comes a point where too much sugar makes people feel sick? – A: That may be true, yes.

–And individuals differ as to what the point is? – A: That is right.

The next thing in the article complained of was about the world of love, said Gardiner: 'I want to spread the world of love, the world of family love, love of God and love of peace.'

Liberace said he had used words to that effect... 'Because I am frequently asked by reporters to discuss my philosophies, and this philosophy is based on a book about positive thinking. I have found this book to be most helpful to me in my life and in my career, so much so that I have been asked to write a foreword to it because I do strongly believe in its philosophies and statements... this is the only publication that I have ever honestly written myself, for the book *The Magic of Believing*. It states, and I mention in my foreword, that in order to be loved one must give love; in order to be a success one must think successfully; in order to be wealthy one must think wealthy, and words to that effect. In order to be loved, one must give love. I believe this very strongly, and these are my philosophies.'

–As far as the thinking wealthy side leading to being wealthy is concerned, that appears to be right? – A: It is a policy in this book that I referred to that the overall purpose behind this book is positive thinking. I think in positive lines and in so doing I make other people believe in me, and I build up a following. This philosophy is probably responsible for my success on television.

–Are the things one says at a press conference about oneself things one wants to get into the papers? – A: Yes; I would say so.

–'I want to spread the world of Love, Love of Family, Love of God and Love of Peace.' In practice, that all helps the box office? – A: If it does, it is not said with that intention in mind, I am sincere in stating my philosophies in the hope that they will be helpful to people in all walks of life.

–In the next paragraph, on money: 'I think people love lovely things – and they are deductible from income tax. I earn about a million dollars a year and could earn more if I tried harder, but I only manage to keep nine cents out of each dollar I earn'... It reads as if, when you were asked by the *Daily Mirror* representative about your clothes, you said first of all that you thought people liked looking at lovely things, and that as far as your stage dresses were concerned they were deductible for tax purposes? – A: I did say that my clothes I wore on the stage were deductible, and that people liked them, but the article, as you quote it, says that lovely things are tax deductible. This is not so; I am well acquainted with the tax laws of my country, and for me to say that all lovely things are tax deductible would be an inaccuracy for which I would be held in ridicule.

–Nobody thought you meant that. Did you then say, 'I earn about a million dollars a year and could earn more if I tried harder; but I only manage to keep nine cents out of each dollar I earn'? – A: I did not say words to that effect. I probably stated my annual income as being one million dollars a year, but as to keeping nine cents out of each dollar I would have no exact knowledge of that figure. My business manager and lawyer and my tax people in Hollywood handle that aspect of my income.

–You must know pretty well. Did you not in fact say it? I suggest it is rather unlikely that two or three different reporters on different English papers would hear you say, or understand you to say, you only managed to keep nine cents out of each dollar, because if you did not say it how would they know that? – A: I would not have any recollection of saying I keep nine cents out of every dollar, no.

–You do receive reporters, do you not? I gather you interview them in considerable numbers at your Hollywood house? – A: Yes, I have.

Did that cost something like £40,000 to build? Liberace said he didn't know how much it cost in pounds.

–I am only asking you because in the material for which you ask your fans to pay one shilling and sixpence as no doubt they do, it says: 'Nearly £40,000 English would be needed to build this house.' That is also untrue, is it? – A: Well, actually it is, because they use the expression 'to build this house', and in there were appointments, furnishings, which totalled more than $100,000, but actually to build this house cost somewhere in the neighbourhood of $60,000.

–Is it right that one piano alone is worth $50,000? – A: It is valued at $56,000.

–Have you got tables shaped like pianos? – A: Yes...

–And ashtrays shaped like pianos? – A: Yes.

–Do you remember March 1956 when you saw in Hollywood Mr Donald Zec, a reporter of the *Daily Mirror*... Did you see him on the Queen Mary and did you put your arm round him and say. 'Thank you, Donald, for the article you wrote about me'? – A: I may have.

Back to the cuttings book and an article:

> With apologies to Liberace for not making this page piano-shaped, here is Donald Zec's story of a dizzy day. At home with the golden boy of syrup.

–Syrup, honey, treacle, sugar have been very frequent among the articles written by your critics? – A: Well, we have two so far. That first one you mentioned, and this one.

–So far... which have been called to your attention in this case, but I am asking is it not the fact that for many years the words treacle, honey, syrup and sugar have been frequent in public criticisms of you? – A: No.

Gardiner continued reading:

> I sat down at a glass-topped piano yesterday and played *The Rustle of Spring* to Liberace, with a winning but slightly nauseating smile on my face. It was my final tilt at this dimpled cavalier of the keyboard. But it went way over his glossy head like all the things I said to him in that lush, musical oddity he calls his home.
>
> He had phoned me. 'Dahnald, this is Liberace', he had said, his voice a cloying extract of goo and golden syrup, 'Why don't you come over this afternoon?'
>
> Well, I wanted to say a few things to Mr Liberace. So I drove over the mountains to his home and rang the bell which played a tune.

'Come in', he said at the door with a smile (and the dimple).

You have read in the *Mirror* before about this outrageous home with pianos thrown at you wherever you stand, sit or lean. Now it's even worse. The cushions are shaped like pianos. The ashtrays are shaped like pianos. The coffee tables are shaped like pianos. Oddly, the goldfish are shaped like goldfish. Liberace was dressed in a black monogrammed sweater with ivory trousers (like the pianos). It was a relief to see all his teeth were white - and not blacked alternately (like the pianos).

'Liberace', I said, stubbing my cigarette out on F sharp, 'I'd like to have a straight talk with you. Are you sensitive?'

'Only to beauty', he said pianissimo. 'The sight of a lovely ballet dancer brings me out in a cold sweat.'

'You have the same effect on me,' I said candidly, 'but for different reasons.'

'Can't please everybody,' he said with a smile (and the dimple).

'You discovered that, with your film *Sincerely Yours*.' I said, leaning against a treble clef. 'Wasn't that a big flop?'

The smile (and the dimple) on his chubby face faded. 'The trouble was the film came two years too late. I have had tremendous exposure on TV. The excitement of seeing me on the cinema screen just wasn't there. The people didn't think I needed them. It's doing very well in the Philippines though.'

'Could it, be,' I suggested, 'that the public are getting a little restive over that Liberace smile and that intimate Meet-me-in-the-boudoir routine of yours?'

He got up and did a springy little walk round the piano. 'I dedicate myself to the common people,' he said with emotion. 'I make them forget the drab reality of their lives.'

'But you irritate thousands,' I said.

'I please millions,' said Liberace, with a smile (and the dimple).

...That is very promptly and very naturally your answer always: 'Nobody likes me but the people'. – A: Yes, that is true.

–'However strongly the minority may feel about it, the majority are on my side'? – A: That is the illusion I labour under, yes.

–It is no part of my case that it is an illusion, but it is part of my case that this is a point on which there are very strong views both ways.

He introduced me to his famous mother, a quiet homely lady, wearing a blue apron and pendant diamond earrings. Then he showed me round the house, which was like a nightmare in the Royal Albert Hall,

And when we weren't trapped by pianos, we were confronted by grinning portraits of Liberace, which beamed down from every wall.

'How can you stand meeting yourself in every room?' I asked.

'Fans paint them,' he shrugged. 'The least I can do is to exhibit them.'

Bedroom: The bedspread is monogrammed with a gigantic embroidered 'L' (guess who). The huge bed back is a satin piano, complete with keyboard.

57

'This is the end,' I said thumping the black notes. 'How can you sleep nights with eight octaves hanging over you?'

'It was given to me,' Liberace explained with a smile (and the dimple), 'like most of the things in the house.'

Bathroom: It is all mirrors so that Liberace can always see Liberace, even when Liberace's back is turned. There was 'Liberace' on the mats; there were pianos on the towels...

Mr Gardiner interrupted his flow: Is that right? – A: Yes.

–...I must say that one major item in the bathroom was not shaped like a piano. There is a limit even for Liberace.

'Why don't you get married?' I asked him as we went out to view his wardrobe.

'I suppose I will one day - when the right girl comes along', he said. 'I'm singing a song about that in the show I'm going to put on in Las Vegas. It's called *The Girls in My Life*.'

He sat down at the piano (shaped like a piano) and sang it to me with a smile (and the dimple). It was all about fancy dames - including 'Gloria of the Waldorf Astoria who was thrilling - and willing...'

...Is that right? –A: That was part of the lyric... The song about the girls in my life was written for me as a special material song. With my audiences this was amusing. It was actually based on fancy and fiction rather than fact.

Gardiner asked what did 'willing' mean. Liberace told him: 'The song took five minutes to perform. I doubt if I can remember the words because it was several years ago that I did it, but the *Gloria of the Waldorf Astoria* is referring to a fictional girl in the song, whom I fictionally, supposedly, met at the Waldorf Astoria, who was given to drinking champagne, and that is all I can remember about that.'

–Was she thrilling and willing? – A: Well, she is a fictional character. How can I say what a fictional character was?

–What did 'willing' mean... What did you mean when you sang it... Willing to do what? – A: I do not know: I never know.

–At the end of it all he's single - 'but I've still got my mother.'

Then he did a soft shoe shuffle for me. After which he imitated one of the show girls who has to lift her skirt coyly to show a wicked garter; Liberace lifted one trouser leg coyly to show a wicked sock.

'Let's see the wardrobe,' I said swiftly - and I felt queasy at the first glance. He draped a black hand-beaded suit over his arm. Next a Christian Dior shot-satin job followed by a Spanish style suit with ruffles. 'I wear a lot of silks', he said. 'Wool bites.'

...You have got a Spanish style suit with frills on the shirt? – A: On the shirt, yes.

–Then he held a pink linen suit against himself and I shuddered. 'It's ghastly', I said. 'Do you really like this sort of thing?'

58

'Believe me', he said earnestly, 'the public are starved of glamour. This is what they want'.

He played some records for me - of Liberace. He introduced me to his white parakeet - learning to screech 'Liberace'. Then he sat down at the piano again and played like Liberace - with a smile (and the dimple).

So, as I said, I tried it on him. I sat down at the opposite piano and played *The Rustle of Spring* to Liberace, with a big, coy smile (but no dimple).

'How do you like it?' I challenged.

'Very nice', said Liberace, and played *The Rustle of Spring* right back at me with a smile (and the dimple).

The fact is, nothing can hurt Liberace, because he is wrapped around with an impenetrable cocoon of self-adoration. He is unquestionably a competent pianist, pleasant vocalist and friendly host. He is a vain, unblushing, sugary piano player who has insinuated himself deep into a million maternal hearts.

In spite of his enormous ego, his piano crazy home, and his frilly, foppish wardrobe – I like him. With his smile (and the dimple).

Gardiner asked: 'Is that the article for which you thanked Mr Zec?'

Beyfus rumbled to his feet: 'I think…'

Mr Justice Salmon said he thought Mr Beyfus was objecting. He was:

'I would point out to my friend that above the last two paragraphs, in large print, there are the words *I Like Him*, which he has omitted.'

Gardiner was obliged: 'I am afraid I omitted the headings. The first cross-heading is *Now It's Worse* the second is *The Smile Faded*; the third is *The End*; the fourth is *It's Ghastly…* and the fifth is *I Like Him.*'

And Liberace had thanked Zec for writing it, even though he didn't recall having read it. But 'it has always been a policy of mine to thank the press for writing about me… I can assure you further, if I may, that there are many discrepancies in this article. He is wrong saying he put his cigarette out on my piano keys. I would have thrown him out.'

GARDINER: He does not suggest that. He says that the ashtrays are piano shaped… All he is suggesting is that he stubbed out his cigar [sic] on one of these ashtrays which were piano shaped. He puts it graphically. He stubbed it out on F sharp, or whatever it was.

Perhaps it was all getting a bit trivial for the judge, who asked: 'Are there any other discrepancies in the article, Mr Liberace?' – 'Yes, my Lord. One starts at the top. Mr Donald Zec did not sit down at my glass topped piano and play *The Rustle of Spring…*'

Never mind the facts. Gardiner got him to confirm that he had thanked Zec for writing about him, and asked whether he took the view that any publicity was better than none. No: Liberace did not.

59

–Would it be right to say that you jingle your money in your pocket so that your large income makes more publicity and more publicity makes more money? – A: Well, it is a very necessary requirement that people in my profession must be publicised in order to be brought to the attention of the public. And we have on many occasions employed publicity people to carry out a publicity campaign and further acquaint the public with my performances and myself as an artiste, and I am grateful to the publicity which I have received up to the point of the article which is the reason I am in this court.

Beyfus was back on his feet: 'I am sure my learned friend did not mean this, but he prevented the witness from answering your Lordship's question of what other discrepancies there were. He had related one on this very first item.'

Mr Justice Salmon: 'I do not mind, Mr Beyfus, when he tells me – but at some stage I would like to know what the discrepancies are.'

BEYFUS: I thought the right time was the time your lordship asked the question.

MR JUSTICE SALMON: I do not want to interrupt. Mr Gardiner has probably got his cross-examination planned.

BEYFUS: Very well, I am sorry; I thought we might overlook it otherwise.

GARDINER: I will come back to that tomorrow, but may I make it quite plain that Mr Zec, who is sitting behind me here, says that what you have just said is quite untrue, that he did sit down at your piano and he did play *The Rustle of Spring*? – A: I do not remember that. I am somewhat fussy about who plays on my piano.

The QC pressed on. –Is it right that you use your sex appeal... When I say 'sex appeal', Mr Liberace, do not think I am suggesting anything improper... and the fact that you are not married, to increase the publicity for your piano recitals? – A: No.

–When you came to Britain and when you went to France, when reporters asked about your marriage prospects, did you say, 'Well, I hear you have got some pretty girls in your country. One never knows'... I am not suggesting there is anything wrong in that? – A: That is right.

–Do you say that is divorced from sex appeal? – A: I am always looking. I stated that when I went to France, yes.

–The Ed Murrow *Person to Person* programme is about the largest viewing programme in the United States, is it not? – A: It is one of them, yes.

–When you were asked by Mr Murrow about your marriage prospects, why was it necessary to refer to Princess Margaret? – A: Mr Murrow's interview referred to members of the royal family, and Mr Beyfus related the entire transcript of that programme.

–He did, and up to the time when you were asked about your marriage prospects there had not been a single word about the royal family, had there... You say: '...I have given a lot of thought to marriage, but I don't believe in getting married just for the sake of getting married. I want to some day find the perfect mate and settle down to what I hope will be a marriage that will be blessed by faith and will be a lasting union. In fact, I was reading about lovely young Princess Margaret, and she's looking for her dream man, too...' Then Mr Murrow asks have you ever met the princess? And you say: 'Not as yet but I have great hopes of meeting her when I go to England next season. I'm going to give a concert in London and I'd like to meet her very much because I think we have a lot in common. We have the same tastes in the theatre and music, and besides, she's pretty and she's single!'... Why, when asked about getting married, did you think it necessary to refer to Princess Margaret? – A: I did make the statement, as you read it, to her, but I was referring to Princess Margaret not as a marriage prospect I can assure you, and if any interpretation was given on that I have apologised for it since. However, I was referring to Princess Margaret solely on the premise that she is known and widely publicised as having accepted American performers who have come over to England to appear, such as Danny Kaye, John Ray and many others, and since it seems to be a foregone conclusion that I only appeal to matronly women it would be very lovely and very wonderful to be accepted in my performance by a lovely, young princess and, furthermore, to have her single would make it even more lovely; and therefore I stated that I had hopes of meeting her, but that was not with the intention of asking her to marry me. I can assure you that was not my intention at all.

–What had she got to do with your marrying? – A: Nothing.

–That Liberace-Murrow interview was sheer good publicity in the United States? – A: I think that the association of my views on marriage and the fact that Princess Margaret was mentioned in the same paragraph was probably brought about by the fact that at that particular time considerable publicity regarding Princess Margaret and Peter Townsend had reached our shores, and it was evident at the time that she was considering the young man. It also was later publicised that she had given up the thought of marrying a commoner, which he was, so that it was not to be assumed by me that being a commoner I would have been suitable as a mate for Princess Margaret. I merely stated that I wanted to meet Princess Margaret because it is a great feather to have in one's cap that someone such as me would be accepted by a lovely young princess, and to have her single would make it even more acceptable.

–Isn't one of the things which you have said that you did not look on yourself as a commoner? – A: No.

–Could you not possibly exist on your abilities as a pianist without all this dragging in of your money, your mother, sex appeal, the British royal family or anything that may come in handy? – A: Well, the answer to that is yes, I could exist.

–But not at the rate of £367,000 a year? – A: I would say it has nothing to do with my earning capacity, the fact that I have expressed my devotion to my mother, and on many numerous occasions it was borne out by my early training in life where I was taught to observe the commandment of God which states that one must love and so honour one's parents.

–Your own organisation puts out the story, does it not, that shortly after your television films started, the wireless shops got a great increase in broken television glasses from infuriated husbands, and that lipstick was found on the glass? – A: That may be true, yes.

Gardiner told him: 'In the morning I am afraid I shall have to ask you about one or two other matters, including religion, which I suggest you drag in to all your performances and publicity matters, as well as the things to which I have referred, for the purpose of making money and to increase publicity.'

And that, he suggested to the judge, might be a good point to adjourn for the day.

He, She and It

The prospect of a trial always presents a serious dilemma for people who genuinely believe they have been libelled. While they are obviously eager to have the defamatory statement contradicted and withdrawn, going to public trial inevitably risks drawing the original article to the attention of a far wider public. Millions may have read the references by Cassandra that Liberace complained about, but millions of others would have missed or overlooked them. The entertainer and his professional advisers must surely have been fully aware that the fusion of an outrageously dressed mega-star who could pack the Albert Hall on consecutive nights and the pomp of a trial in the Royal Courts of Justice would extend the awareness of the public to what had been said against him, about which he strongly objected, and which he believed exposed him unjustly to hatred and contempt. The plaintiff must also have been warned that anything known or suspected about his past was likely to be dredged up to cause his further embarrassment.

Sure enough, the following day's papers were full of it. There were photographs of the main players arriving and departing at the law courts, and no detail was spared. The *Daily Telegraph* devoted six broadsheet columns to the trial, even mentioning what the plaintiff's team had for lunch during the adjournment (it was ham and chicken, brought from the Savoy hotel at the other side of The Strand). Rival publishers may have seen the trial as an opportunity to score points against the newspaper with the highest circulation, but for most, it was simply show-biz – no more and not much less than that.

The headlines did not vary much. Although a few dwelt on the alleged 'vitriol and viciousness' of the original article, the Fleet Street favourite by far was 'Summit of Sex'. 'Liberace called The Summit Of Sex'... 'Newspaper Sued Over Summit Of Sex'... 'Liberace: I Am Not A Sex-Appeal Artist'... and 'The Pianist And The Princess', while, across the Atlantic, the *New York Times* reported, flatly: 'Liberace Denies He Is Homosexual'. Superstardom and sex is always an incendiary combination for headline writers and coining phrases like that was Cassandra's forte. He was, after all, the former advertising copy-writer credited with promoting a lavatory cleaner with the immortal words: 'Clean round the bend'.

Beyfus had made an early start, combing the various reports, presumably to confirm that all of them – especially, no doubt, the *Daily Mirror*'s own three-page reportage – were both fair and accurate. He actually thought he had been misquoted by some of them, and made a note, intending to refer

63

to it immediately the trial resumed, but he forgot about it until the lunch adjournment.

Instead, Gardiner re-started and handed the cuttings book back to Liberace. 'You were going to tell us in what ways you suggest that Mr Zec's article was incorrect...'

'First of all I would like to state that yesterday was the first time I had ever read Mr Donald Zec's article.' He had been told that he liked him and considered him a fine pianist. 'So I went over and I thanked him. So much for that...'

He brought up the subject of the stubbed-out cigarette again, and Gardiner again brushed it aside. Then: – Referring to my motion picture flop, he said that I said 'It's doing very well in the Philippines though.' I told Mr Zec that it had not been a success in the United States, but it was doing very well in the foreign market. I never mentioned the Philippines. A little further down it said: 'He got up and did a springy little walk round the piano.' This would be an impossibility. I would have had to go through the wall in order to walk around my pianos, because they are against a wall... 'He introduced me to his famous mother, a quiet homely lady wearing a blue apron and pendant diamond earrings.' This again is his opinion. My mother does not wear diamond earrings. She was wearing rhinestone earrings...

–With an apron? – A: Yes, She has pierced ears and she wears them all the time.

–I am not suggesting she should not, but it was a thing which struck Mr Zec. – A: I think most women that have pierced ears wear earrings all the time. I did not perform for Mr Zec in my home. I did not sing a song about fancy dames, including 'Gloria of the Waldorf Astoria'. It says: 'He sat down at the piano (shaped like a piano) and sang it to me with a smile (and the dimple).' It also said that I did an imitation of one show girl who has to lift her skirt coyly. I gave no imitation of such show girl lifting her skirt coyly.

–I suggest you in fact did. – A: I suggest in fact that I did not.

–What else? – A: I never said 'wool bites.' I never owned a pink linen suit, so consequently I could not have referred to it, saying 'This is what they want.' I have never owned a parakeet that screeched the word 'Liberace'.

–Did you have a parakeet? – A: I had a parakeet. It does not speak a word.

–Did you tell him that it was learning to say 'Liberace'? – A: I did not. I have no recollection of Mr Zec playing my piano, *The Rustle of Spring* or any other composition.

–There were two pianos in the room, were there not... I suggest he sat down and played *The Rustle of Spring*; he gave his best imitation of you. – A: I suggest he did not.

–And then you took over and performed the real thing. – A: I did not. The only thing I am grateful to Mr Zec for is the fact that at no time during this article did he use the expressions 'he, she or it', 'masculine, feminine or neuter' or 'fruit-flavoured', all expressions which in America are termed homosexual. Therefore, I have no reason to take any offence to Mr Donald Zec's article, and that is why no action was necessary in the way of libel against this reporter. In fact, I would thank him again, if I had the opportunity, for saying 'He is unquestionably a competent pianist, pleasant vocalist and friendly host', and 'I like him'.

–Did you say that the gold lamé suit had been made by Christian Dior? – A: I did not.

–That is another thing that is inaccurate, is it? – A: That is right.

–An invention of Mr Zec? – A: Perhaps it is.

–I think you said you had not noticed, in reading your press cuttings, that there were many in which the words 'nausea' or 'emetic' appeared? – A: No, I have not noticed that.

–Would you look at the *Daily Herald*. These had all, of course, been published before Cassandra wrote his article. You see at the bottom of the first column:

> The screams of his adoring fans drown the small, quiet voices of the critics - who say he is not an outstanding pianist - and the moans of nauseated husbands.

–Do you observe that? – A: Yes, I do.

–The *Evening News* was a paper for which you wrote a series of articles when you were over here, did you not, or at least they appeared under your name? You see the one with your signature on it: 'Liberace says Au Revoir: You've taught me good manners', and ending 'My sincerest thanks to my new English friends, Liberace'. That appeared in the *Evening News*? – A: That is right.

Another cutting from the *Daily Herald*:

> I can understand women swooning for Johnnie Ray. I can understand men drooling over Marilyn Monroe. What I can't understand are the people who devote their time and energies to organising fan clubs for them. But now another one has been started. This time for the man I vote the most unlikeable on our television screens. The man whose leers and dimples make me heave. None other than Laughing Boy Liberace.

Back to the *Evening News*:

> America's romance-starved matrons become limp when his image appears on their television screens. They go dreamy-eyed when he pounds his grand piano and they swoon when he smiles... Liberace - half Italian, half Polish - has few fans among the bobbysoxers. He is derided

by serious critics. He is the butt of most TV comedians, but millions of middle aged women here think he is the greatest heart throb since Rudolph Valentino...

A second asset is a smile of rare brilliance which is all wonder and romance for the deadlier half of the species. Honesty compels me to reveal that upon me it has a mildly emetic effect.

LIBERACE: They sure have a lot of people who want to throw up here; [Laughter] that is all I can say; and I further state, if I may, that this emetic language, as you so aptly put it, is new to me and is certainly not evident in all my press cuttings. I have had, in all modesty, I would say, over a period of 25 years, millions of press cuttings, and this emetic language does not appear in all my press cuttings.

–I am not suggesting, of course, that the word appears in every press cutting about you. – A: Thank you.

Then, in Liberace's official book:

It was not after all until the advent of commercial television in September 1955 that the British public were able to judge for themselves the merits of this phenomenal performer about whom they had read so much. Reaction in Britain was typical, to say the least. The press critics - the national press, that is - sailed into Liberace with almost as much vitriol as had their American counterparts not so long previously.

–Is it right to say that your critics in America had been even more vitriolic than the critics here? – A: No, it is not right to say that, because no critic in America has ever referred to me in any words similar to these for which I am alleging libel, and therefore I have no reason to complain of any American criticism that I have received to date. No American critic has ever said 'he, she or it', 'masculine, feminine or neuter' or 'fruit-flavoured', all expressions that denote homosexuality.

From the same book:

Sincerely Yours was the story of a pianist whose ambition was to play at Carnegie Hall, but who was suddenly stricken deaf. Of course, all came well in the end; true Liberace fans loved it, but once again the critics gave it a slating and box office returns were indifferent. Not that this sort of occurrence would be likely to worry Liberace. He had a wow of a time making the film, as the film company handouts clearly showed. 'His dressing room at the Warner Studios is tastefully decorated in silver, white and black', reported the publicity blurb. His monogram on the door is executed in stainless steel; couch and chairs are upholstered in silver grey. Liberace wears dressing gowns of the richest silk, and...

Gardiner paused for dramatic effect. The QC actually said: '*Wait for it!*'

...and sports gold lamé suits designed by Christian Dior.

–Do you see that? – A: Yes, I see it.

–Do you still say you had not told Mr Zec in Hollywood that your gold lamé suit was designed by Christian Dior? – A: I still say that my gold lamé suit, coat, jacket, or whatever they are referring to, was not designed by Christian Dior; I have never met Christian Dior, may his soul rest in peace. I do not have any recollection of meeting this man. The report that you have just read is only one man's opinion, He says that the critics gave my motion picture a slating, which is not true. This is the one experience in my entire career where I had unanimous praise from the press, and it was still a flop.

–Now will you answer the question? – A: What is the question?

(The court shorthand writer then read 'Do you still say you had not told Mr Zec in Hollywood that your gold lamé suit was designed by Christian Dior?')

LIBERACE: I still say that I told Mr Zec no such thing.

GARDINER: I am not suggesting it is true. I am only suggesting that you were saying the same untruth about it to Mr Zec in Hollywood... Do you tell the members of the jury that it is just an extraordinary coincidence that what Mr Zec thought he heard you say in Hollywood is to be found in a publication from the sale of which you were drawing money in England? – A: I do not know what you are driving at. You are making an issue over the fact that I have a gold lamé suit or jacket designed by Christian Dior, and I do not know what you are driving at.

–The article goes straight on; I ought to have pointed it out.

> This delightful flamboyance is all part of the Liberace character that has been deliberately built up by Lee and his publicity advisers since he rocketed to television fame in 1952.

–Look at the next page. Do you see a heading 'Mother complex'?

> If there is one thing on which the critics have seized, in concentrating their attacks on Lee, it is what is sometimes described as a mother complex, or 'Momism'.

–Did you tell us yesterday that you had never heard of anybody referring to a mother complex or momism in relation to you? – A: I do not think I did. I said that I personally never referred to my love for my mother or my devotion to my mother as a mother complex, mother love or Momism. Other people may have referred to it as such. I never have.

The QC read from the transcript:

> (Q) It has been said a good many times, has it not, that you appeal to the Mom complex? (A) I never heard it put in that way. (Q) Your well known American magazine *Time* five years ago coined the expression 'Momist'; they referred to you as 'the Musical Momist'? (A) I am unaware of that. I do not recall that, (Q) I suggest five years ago in 1954 they were calling you 'the Musical Momist', (A) I was unaware of that if they were. I have been called a lot of things but I do not remember that one.

Then Mr Gardiner directed him to the issue of *Time* magazine with the heading Musical Momist:

What is Liberace's magic? It could be merely the irresistible appeal of his shining mediocrity. But there is also his quality - which comes out in his bounciness, his sweet smile, his nasal voice, his my-oh-my prose style - of being just a big little boy. And a good boy, too, who would never swear or drink or leave his poor old mother while he ran off with some young hussy.

Liberace is fully aware of this appeal. Says he: 'Unfortunately, there are too many lonely mothers around today, deserted by their children when they need them most'.

–*Time* is one of the weekly magazines with the largest circulation in America? – A: Yes... What is your purpose in referring to the *Time* article? Is it to prove that I said: 'Unfortunately there are too many lonely mothers around to-day?' I do not understand why he is referring to this article.

JUDGE: Mr Liberace, in this country the witness just answers the questions asked of him. – A: I see. I am confused, because I do not know what the question is, if there is a question.

JUDGE: If you do not understand the question I am sure Mr Gardiner will repeat it.

GARDINER: Do you still say that in spite of the expression 'Momist' being used by *Time* and being found in connection with mother complex in *Liberace* which was sold in England and on which you drew money, you had never heard the expression 'mother complex' or 'Momist' used in relation to you? – A: I heard it. There is a difference. I have heard it, but I have never used it myself.

And this was *The Liberace Story*.

Magnificently illustrated souvenir album... Life story... Signed portrait... Revealing details of.... the women in his life... His ex-fiancées... Fabulous house... His adoring fans... Ambitions... TV, discs and films... His childhood and early struggles... Flamboyant personality... Brother George and the Liberace family... Views on marriage... His amazing swimming pool, clothes, pianos, secrets, hobbies...

He confesses that every month, on average, he receives about a dozen proposals of marriage - he has accepted none of them, as he says he is still looking for 'A girl like Mom'.

–Is that right? –A: I would say that was right, yes.

...But there is hope yet for all those girls whose one prayer is that Lee might some day settle down and decide to marry.

–Do you suggest that you and your publicity have nothing to do with sex appeal? – A: I would say so. I have never considered myself as being a sex appeal artist.

–Adoring fans... Those fans: You know, the ones fiancée No 3 disliked so much. They seem to follow the pattern that surrounds everything Liberace does, the pattern that creates new precedents of its own instead of copying other people's. What other artist ever had a letter from a fan, asking for tickets for a concert, and ending with: 'We want to be so close we will feel the breeze from your eye lashes when they flutter.'

–Had you received such a letter? – A: I suppose I had, yes.

–Nothing to do with sex appeal? – A: I do not think so, no.

–You mean that quite seriously? – A: I do not think eye lashes are very sexy. I am sorry.

Then how about this…

Last St Valentine's Day, Lee received no less than 27,000 (yes, twenty seven thousand!) valentines. And one fan, overwhelmed by the Liberace piano technique, sent him a gold fly swatter, while yet another frantic fan gave him her shoe to autograph…

Fans bake for him, fans knit for him. And in some American homes, if you see a dirty great smear of red lipstick on the glass of a TV screen, it's a pretty safe bet that *Sincerely Yours* was on not so long ago…

–Still nothing to do with sex appeal? – A: No. I have no control over the reactions of the viewers. They are aimed at a family audience, and if some viewer takes that interpretation of it, I have no control over it whatsoever. If they find me that attractive or something, I have no control over that.

–You still say, do you, that what is sold for money, you receiving some of the money for this story, about lipstick on the television glass, had nothing to do with sex appeal? – A: It has nothing to do with sex appeal, yes.

–Would you like the truth or otherwise of your other answers in this case judged by the jury by that one? – A: I would like the truth of all my answers to be judged by the jury. I am under oath.

–Is this the position, that you do not mind at all what they say as long as you get the money for it? – A: That is not the position. I in good faith gave the authority to this publication being written providing it was based only on these things that appeared on this cover. They have gone beyond that authority… I never read it.

There was another official volume of biography. *The Liberace Story* – Thrilling. Revealing. Authorised. The fabulous Liberace story. The loves of Liberace.

–And there was a picture of you kissing a girl on the outside. Inside was a paragraph about a performance at Miami:

A policeman who was there at the time said that it was like a tidal wave. 'Ten thousand women descended on Mr Liberace and nearly crushed him to death,' the officer said. 'The women acted like wild animals, we had to fight them off from nine in the morning until six at night.'

…Nothing to do with sex appeal? – A: The policeman made the statement, not I. I would say it had nothing to do with sex appeal, no.

–Compression is obviously one of Liberace's neatest tricks. Grieg, Chopin, Johann Strauss, they're all easy for him to reduce to manageable length. Liberace recreates. If a composition is too difficult, he simplifies it.

…Is that right? – A: That is not the reason I do it, no.

–Did you get some money from this book too, for giving your authority to the publication? – A: Yes.

> – 'I really do love the critics because they have increased my viewing audience every time they have written a particularly vehement piece of criticism about me,' Liberace told us when we asked him how he feels about the critics. 'Let the critics say anything they want, but don't let them stop talking or writing about me,' Lee went on, 'because when they do I will be through.'

LIBERACE: That is true, yes.

–'Nobody in years has been the butt of so much criticism'. Is that right? – A: Criticism, right. Criticism directed at my performance. There is a difference.

–There are pictures of you inside, kissing girls, and on the back two girls kissing you? 'No-one loves like Liberace! Heart-throb of forty million women... hottest personality to ever melt the TV airwaves...' Still no question of sex appeal? – A: No, I do not think they are referring to sex appeal there. I consider sex appeal something possessed by Marilyn Monroe and Brigitte Bardot. I certainly do not put myself in their class.

–Are those words nothing to do with sex appeal? – A: No.

–Is one of the quotations in this article you complain of this: 'I feel I can bring people closer to God through my appearances. I happen to be a religious man, and I want my marriage to be blessed with my faith'? I think in answer to an interrogatory you said; 'I may have said it to the reporters on the Queen Mary, but I have no recollection'... I think I have already asked you about an interview I suggest you had in July 1955 with a Mr Sayle at Orly airport. Do you remember saying to him: 'I try to give viewers some of my simple faith in God. I often go from the *Ave Maria*' – that is sacred music, is it not? – 'straight to the *Beer Barrel Polka*; but the contrast is never offensive, never. In fact, I have often been called the Billy Graham of music. Billy and I are tremendous admirers of each other'? –A: I never said that.

–There is another paragraph in the article complained of: 'Nobody since Aimee Semple McPherson has purveyed a bigger, richer and more varied slag heap of lilac-coloured hokum'. Was Miss Aimee McPherson a lady who in 1920 went to Los Angeles with $10 and a tambourine and combined religious fervour with marked financial ability? – A: I would have no recollection of that. In 1920 I was just a year old,

–Had you ever heard of her? – A: Yes.

70

–You know she built a million and a half dollar temple? – A: No, I did not know that.

–She came over here and took the Albert Hall. Did you know that? – A: No, I did not know that.

–She was the subject of acute controversy. – No, I did not know that either.

–Did you tell the reporters on the Queen Mary this – you yourself saying it, you understand – 'There is no one like Liberace. What the people want of me they want of no one else. I am a missionary'? – A: No, I did not say that, sir.

–Do you in fact go from the *Ave Maria* to the *Beer Barrel Polka*? – A: I do not. These numbers often appear on the same programme but I never go from the *Ave Maria* into the *Beer Barrel Polka*.

–It may be the next item on the programme? – A: No. I never would treat the *Ave Maria* with a sacrilegious attitude and follow it with the *Beer Barrel Polka*. The fact is in the same programme I play music of different types, religious music included, and this music is treated with the proper respect and when I play the *Beer Barrel Polka* in my programme at some later time it is done with the proper introduction and proper facial expression and a number such as the *Ave Maria* is given proper reverence and respect and it never is in the same composition with the *Beer Barrel Polka*.

–Have you played the *Ave Maria* in your television programme... With somebody singing it from the stage? – A: Yes, there was a choir singing it.

–And then the curtains go back and disclose a stained glass window... With a woman framed with the statue of the blessed Virgin Mary... And as the camera gradually pans up to the face of the actress who is playing the statue so her emotion considerably increases, does it not... And then does the choir boy, or a boy dressed as a choir boy, come up and put candelabra on your piano? – A: Yes... The number was done because it is one of the most highly requested numbers on the television programme.

–Do you think some people might think that to make your piano playing more attractive by having an actress praying in agony to a statue of the blessed Virgin Mary is profane? – A: I do not think so because the manner in which this number was presented on television met with the approval of every dignitary of the church I have ever met who had seen this particular performance, including Archbishop Cushing of Boston...

Mr Gardiner referred to another film in which the entertainer showed viewers his home.

–And having shown them round did you say: 'Well, I hope you like my home; Mom and I live here, so does my French poodle... And there is someone else who lives with us and to whom I speak...' and then are the

71

lights lowered and do you sing: *'Bless this house O Lord we pray, make it safe by night and day'?* – A: Yes.

–Who is the 'someone else'? – A: It is our belief that God is in every home and we hope he is in our home and it is to him I spoke when I sang the song *Bless This House.*

–I suggest that while you may be perfectly sincere an honest man could take the view that to introduce God living in your house for the sole purpose of making a cue for a song... – A: I would say, sir, no honest man has ever objected to that film. It has been repeated more than any other television programme I have ever done and it is one of the television shows that has been approved time and time again by members of the clergy of all religions as being a good, fine and wholesome tribute to family life of religion and faith in God.

–I am not suggesting many people might not honestly take that view. All I am suggesting to you is that there are honest people who might object to it. – A: If there are it never came to my attention. I have never received any objection to that particular television film.

–I think you have agreed, in answer to interrogatories, in September, 1956, just before you came over here you said to Mr René McColl: 'People who have never walked before start walking because I ask them to. At my request, people leave their iron lungs. In fact only the other day in the Hollywood Bowl two couples arose and walked at my command'? – A: That is true.

–So far in history there has been thought to be only one person with that ability, has there not? – A: I have never professed to be a faith healer. That incident related to a girl and it was witnessed by many people and it actually happened.

–People who have never walked before... How old do you suppose they were? – A: I believe they were in their twenties.

–You really suggest that two people who had never walked before started walking because you asked them to? – A: I suggest that they probably walked for me because they thought they could, yes... In fact it was such a startling thing that we did make enquiries about them and this was what we found out, that they had never walked before.

–And 'At my request, people leave their iron lungs'; is that right? – A: I am particularly referring in that statement to one particular girl named Mary Kittsmiller who left her iron lung to come and see my concert in Chicago at the Civic Opera House. That also actually happened. I talked to her doctor afterwards and he said it was her extreme will that made her want to get out of her iron lung and want to come and see the concert because I had invited her to see it a few months earlier and her will to do so made it possible.

72

–That is the incident you are referring to, is it, as your justification for the statement: 'At my request people leave their iron lungs'? – A: I never made that statement, sir, in exactly those words. So often when I relate an experience as I have just related about Miss Mary Kittsmiller, when it is retold by a member of the press it is told in a general way to infer that all people in iron lungs leave their iron lungs at my request. I never said this. I merely stated that a certain one did.

–Do you know the celebrated American critic, Art Buchwald of the *New York Herald Tribune*... Was he at a press conference you gave on September 29 1956, in Paris when you referred to your press criticisms? – A: Yes, I believe he was there.

–Did you say to the press conference, a few days after the Cassandra article: 'Everyone has to expect a certain number of non-believers, and even enemies; I suppose that's why they shot Abraham Lincoln and crucified Jesus'? – A: Those are supposed to be my actual words? I would say no, I did not say that, because they were not my actual words and I did not say them.

–Did you say: 'Everyone has to expect a certain number of non-believers, and even enemies'? – A: I may have said that, yes.

–Did you say: 'I suppose that's why they shot Abraham Lincoln'? – A: No.

–Did you refer to both Abraham Lincoln and Jesus? – A: In the course of the conference I did refer to both Abraham Lincoln and Jesus.

–Was not that putting yourself in a rather high class? – A: Not necessarily. I was quoting the advice which had been given me by a gentleman I mentioned earlier today who was a dignitary of the church, Archbishop Cushing. I had a private audience with Archbishop Cushing in Boston and he was aware of the fact that I had been receiving some caustic comments in the press and it was his comfort to me when he stated that when your head rises above the crowd one must expect to have stones thrown at it. And I was quoting Archbishop Cushing further when he said: 'Look, my boy, is not it true that even Jesus had enemies and therefore he was crucified, and take our own President, Abraham Lincoln, who was shot because he had an enemy.' And it was told to me and I repeated this to the press and when it came out in print it came out in the manner you stated in the interrogatories.

–When was this interview with the Archbishop? – A: I believe that was in 1954 or 1955.

–The object of a press conference is to create publicity, is it not... I suggest in your press conferences and publications and in other ways you use your love for your mother, your president, your money, the British royal family and God all in the cause of publicity. – A: I suggest I do not.

73

–May I take the adjectival paragraph of the article complained of: 'Deadly, winking, sniggering, snuggling, chromium-plated, scent-impregnated, luminous, quivering, giggling, fruit-flavoured, mincing, ice-covered heap of mother-love'... So far as winking is concerned, of course that is one of your standard items, is it not... Your trade mark... And you occasionally sing a song into the microphone, do you not... And occasionally you do a little dance... – A: Yes.

The QC handed him two photographs: –It is the one of you in your white tail coat at the microphone... And the other is you doing your little dance... Do you let women come up to the stage to feel your clothes and touch your knees? – A: Yes.

–And when you let women come up to touch you does that usually result in hysterical screams from the women section of the audience? – A: Yes, it usually does.

–So far as chromium-plated and luminous are concerned you wear these diamonds and sequins and things to reflect the lights, do not you? – A: They reflect the lights?

–The spotlights. – A: They are attractive on the stage, yes.

–And in the criticism of your performances in the press here and America would you regard 'Mincing, quivering, giggling' fair comment? – A: No.

–Are you suggesting an honest man could not think you minced and giggled and so on? – A: I suggest that an honest man would give it a different interpretation, and honest men have.

–Let me come to one example. Will you take it from me – say so if you don't – that the *Manchester Guardian* is not a paper which is likely to be influenced by the *Daily Mirror*? – A: That is right.

It was back to the cuttings book and Liberace's Festival Hall performance, headed: The clowning of Liberace.... Indifferent Technique.

–Outside the Festival Hall students paraded with banners reading 'Is this America's answer to the Suez crisis?'... 'All this for Mum'... 'Surely Mums deserves more'... and 'We loathe Liberace'. Two girls form a smaller diversionary procession with a banner inscribed 'Bring back Johnny Ray.' And they at least looked as if they meant it.

Inside the hall, a piano with a glass top and candelabra stood in front of the George Melachrino Orchestra. In front of the orchestra sat an audience - 90 per cent female - and suppressed its hysterics, though not very well, particularly when Liberace's Mum appeared.

George was received with loud, prolonged, and girlish cheeps; they died away, the half-lights dimmed, a spotlight pointed its trembling finger at the yellow curtains and Liberace was here.

An unnerving squeal, like 40,000 Persian cats having their tails trodden on simultaneously, went up. Eventually the squealing stopped; not so the

74

smile. He sat down, and after cracking a joke (of Mr Bob Hope's) about the height of the piano stool, he played *Chopsticks*, giggling like mad.

Another few minutes of howling (from the audience) and he played, with many a coy little joke and many a soulful look, *Clair de Lune*. Then he sang. Then he played some more. The smile stayed riveted where it was and the screaming between items grew louder.

The clowning, the giggling, the grinning, the winking, and a great deal of arm-waving covered an indifferent technique; with eyes shut I could imagine myself in the palm court of some seedy south coast hotel.

...You are quite used to all that from the critics? – A: I would not say I was; I am not used to it but I would not take exception to this article, although I have not read it before just now, because he does not say the offensive words that were used by the columnist in the *Mirror*. The reason I am in court is because of these offensive words.

–Do you use scent or scented lotions? – A: I use after-shaving lotions and under-arm deodorants.

–Which are scented... And it is common enough at a press conference when you come in to the press conference a noticeable odour comes in with you? – A: I would not say it was an odour, I would say it was a sign of good grooming to smell clean and fresh and I always smell clean and fresh.

–Have press correspondents mentioned that to you? – A: I do not believe so, no. I have noticed their scent many times. [Laughter.]

–Do you remember having met Peter Stephens at Le Bourget airport in Paris in September 1956? – A: I do not recall the gentleman, no,

–Do you remember talking to Mr Peter Stephens for some five minutes? – A: I do not recall Peter Stephens. I talked to many press people; I cannot remember them all by name.

–Do you remember his asking what scent you used because it was so strong? – A: No, I do not recall that.

–Did you say: 'That's American toilet water. But I hear the French make really wonderful perfume. I hope to buy some of it'? – A: I did not make that statement, but I probably did buy some perfume in Paris, everybody does, to take back to America for their mothers, their sisters, my sister-in-law, my girl-friend.

–Is it eau de cologne you use? – A: I sometimes use men's cologne and men's toilet water and always deodorants.

–Scented ones? – A: Made with scent. Well, it has to be that way, they are all...

–You authorised the publication of an article in London which purported to have been written by your mother which begins:

I know that today I am the envy of every Mum in Britain. For my son is the sort of boy every mother would like to be able to call her own.

75

Then there's other folk who criticise him because he likes flowers and colognes. Why shouldn't my boy like these things? I read him my history books. In them it said that some of the greatest men in history, especially in the days of your own Queen Elizabeth, liked flowers and scent.

...Do not think there is any reason why you should not use scented after-shaving lotion, but I understood you were complaining this had been said of you, and it is true, in fact, is it not? I am not suggesting it is any offence. – A: It is not a criticism against me, sir, but what I believe the paragraph implied is that it tends to support the accusation I am a homosexual, sir.

–'He is the summit of sex – the pinnacle of masculine, feminine and neuter. Everything that he, she and it can ever want.' Are you seriously suggesting that these ordinary English words mean you are a homosexualist? – A: That is the interpretation that was given and understood by everyone that I have come in contact with who has seen this article. I mean without exception, sir.

–I suggest that is quite fantastic, but it is a matter the jury will have to decide. Many artists have a lot of sex appeal, have they not... Which they very properly use in their stage performances... So far as bobby-soxers are concerned is it true that you publicised the number of proposals of marriage you have had and so on? – A: Yes; it has been publicised; I did not publicise it myself.

–Are you suggesting that the scenes which took place as they did at Southampton with girls screaming and fainting and trying to kiss you through the window happened without your ever having done anything to create it? – A: I would say that it was one of the biggest surprises of my life to be greeted by so many thousands of fans and it is a performer's right to create publicity and my coming on a special train was merely to lend publicity to my appearances in England.

–I am not suggesting that there is anything in the world wrong with your exploiting your sex appeal. – A: I beg to correct you there. I am exploiting Liberace as a performer; I have never exploited my sex appeal or advertised it in any way, shape or form.

–But you make money out of books which tell these things about lipstick on the television screen and 'No one loves like Liberace, heart-throb of 40 million women'? – A: I did not write that.

–You got money out of it. – A: I believe I did receive a royalty.

–Did you say to Mr Sayle: 'I appeal to women as Marilyn Monroe appeals to men'? – A: I did not say so.

–I am not suggesting there is anything wrong in it. – A: I did not say it in exactly those words. I do recall saying to this reporter it is not an unnatural kind of adulation for a man performer or a male performer to receive the adulation of female fans nor is it an unnatural kind of adulation for a female performer to receive the adulation of male fans.

76

–So far as the ladies are concerned you trade on sex appeal... I am not suggesting there is anything wrong in it. – A: Sir, I do not trade on it. I would rather believe, in fact the strong belief that I have had all my life as a performer, that my appeal is to people who want to be entertained with the type of entertainment I give them which is primarily wholesome entertainment not directed to sex whatsoever.

–Did you say to Mr Sayle: 'I appeal to women exactly as Marilyn Monroe appeals to men'? – A: I did not say that.

–Did you say to the press conference on the Queen Mary when you were asked about sex appeal: 'If people notice it, I am happy'? – A: I did not say that.

–Are you quite sure? – A: I am positive.

–And do you say that it is not true to say that in your close-ups on the television you flirt outrageously with the women? – A: If winking is flirting, yes, I guess I am guilty of that.

–But the way in which you perform is intended to affect your women listeners. – A: The way in which I perform has been very successful and I will continue to do it for the rest of my life.

–I am not suggesting there is anything wrong with it. – A: Thank you.

–All I am suggesting is you deliberately, and in no way improperly, use your sex appeal over women. – A: I use my musicianship and my ability as a performer to put myself across to the public which consists of people of both sexes of all ages and I do not use sex appeal to do this. I use my training as a performer. I have studied for a period of nearly 25 years and I have found this formula to be successful as early as the age of eleven and I can assure you that at the age of eleven I was not selling sex.

–Do you consider winking as part of musicianship? – A: I would not consider that as part of it; I would say the style of performance I am attributed with is a style that is intimate and the fact I wink and smile to create intimacy in my performances is the thing that has made me stand out from the rest.

–Has not the size of your public always been due to the fact that you exploit all the emotions simultaneously, ordinary love, mother-love and other emotions of what a mother would like her son to be, the love of God, mass assault of emotion; is not that largely what the size of your public has been due to? – A: I would not say so. I would say that they... Did you say it was an assault?

–An assault on the emotions with a view to rouse the emotional temperature. – A: It is the purpose of every performer particularly myself to create a series of emotions on an audience which consist of humour, sadness and a general feeling of being entertained in a happy way, and sometimes people find my performance such they can be entertained and in a serious vein as well. I have had my audiences howling with laughter and I have had them crying, and that is one of the great attributes which a performer such as myself can ever hope to possess. I was not always capable of doing this but I am happy that now I can mould the mood of an audience based on my experience as a performer and to be able to do this is not based on anything derogatory but is based on a sincere approach to my profession.

–Is it done to raise the emotional temperature? – A: Emotional temperature? I do not believe I have ever had that intention in mind, no.

–If you look at your official life again:

> In the same way, it must be emphasised that these mannerisms, his tricks before the cameras, are contrived and deliberate, and no greater television artist is now performing. Lee knows that the TV performer must be larger than life. His performance is a perpetual close-up, even when the cameras pan away, for the close-up is not measured by distance but by emotional temperature.

…Is that right? – A: That is right, sir, yes,

–Your second name is Valentino, is not it… And he was a man with enormous sex appeal, was he not… Rudolph Valentino? – A: Yes.

–I expect you have read his life? – A: I have read many books based on his life, yes.

–When he died 15 American women committed suicide? – A: Yes.

–Your brother is Rudolph… You are Valentino… And men used to see him in large numbers, didn't they, because of his sex appeal? – A: Men went to see him as well.

–In large numbers. – A: I do not know why they went to see him in large numbers.

–They went to see him because he had got sex appeal; I do not mean anything improper. – A: I could not say why men went to see Rudolph Valentino, whether it was because of his sex appeal or whether perhaps they thought he was a good actor or an interesting personality or perhaps their wives dragged them along.

–Perhaps they hoped to learn a thing or two. – A: Perhaps they hoped to learn the technique, yes.

–Would you look at *The Truth About Me by Liberace*. This is in the *American Weekly*.

> I'd also like to smash the idea that my fans are all women. Some newspapers have added to this impression. Friends mail me these comments in the press. This one was printed in St. Louis:
> 'His women fans quite literally went wild. He could do no wrong. Wearing a coat of many colours, he smiled upon his flock and they were stunned deliciously. A couple of women fainted. Dozens wanted to touch him. The bolder ones kissed him and went home starry-eyed.'
> Well, I've got news for a lot of people. At every concert, I play a number with a piano break where the audience shouts: 'Hey'.

On the first chorus I invite the whole audience to yell. On the second, I ask for women only. On the third I say: 'Come on, boys!' You should hear *their* shouts.

...You have said yourself, have you not, that you attracted large numbers of men as well as women? – A: That is right. I would like to add that this account of this particular number is distorted by the very fact the word 'their' is put in italics, adding some innuendo.

–What is the innuendo? – A: The way you read it, it sounded like an innuendo.

–It certainly was not meant to be. – A: I took it that way.

–Did you read everything as meaning you are a homosexual? I suggest there is nothing in it that refers to homosexualism.

Gardiner read the extract again, and asked: 'What on earth is there in that to suggest you or anybody else in the world is a homosexualist?' – A: It was in a leading paper, that I objected to, and there is something in this article to suggest I am a homosexual; there has never been anything in any other paper that suggested that sort of thing and that is why I have never been to court before in my life to bring a libel action against any columnist or newspaper or magazine because nobody has ever suggested prior to this article written by the *Mirror* columnist which in no uncertain terms states this untruth about my morals.

–I suggest it does not say anything of the kind, but that is for the jury to decide. There is nothing wrong in your attracting men, women and children, is there? – A: No.

–It is part of your sex? – A: Yes, it is.

–Have you seen the film *Gigi*? – A: Yes.

–There is an artiste of great sex appeal. – A: Who is that?

–Maurice Chevalier. – A: I would say 'charm' was the word.

–I would suggest both 'charm' and 'sex appeal'. – A: I do not know if he is capable at his age.

–You have seen the film? – A: He did possess charm. I loved it.

–Over seventy, is he? – A: I think Maurice Chevalier possessed the greatest charm of any man in his seventies I have ever seen.

–And the greatest sex appeal in his seventies? – A: No, I will not say that. You cannot put those words into my mouth.

–Did you say at a press conference 'When I do a show I exude love'? – A: I do not believe I ever used the word 'exude'. I express love, yes.

–I suggest it is quite fantastic. These are ordinary English words: 'He is the summit of sex – the pinnacle of Masculine, Feminine and Neuter. Everything that He, She and It can ever want.' It is quite clear, is it not, that what that means is that you have great sex appeal and you attract all sections of the community, not in any improper sense. – A: I would suggest this is the most improper article which has ever been written about

79

me, and it has been given that interpretation. It has been widely quoted in all parts of the world, especially in my own country. The article has been reproduced exactly as it appears in the paper, and it has been given this interpretation. I have in my possession a magazine which is recently in print, which reproduces this article and which states in headlines '*Is Liberace a man?*' This is the interpretation that this article has been given by peoples in every part of the world, including your country of England.

–I suggest to you that a lot of people must have singularly filthy minds if they think the ordinary words, 'He is the summit of sex – the pinnacle of Masculine, Feminine and Neuter. Everything that He, She and It can ever want', imply you are a homosexual. – A: Yes, it does imply that. I say the expression 'fruit-flavoured' implies that. It is an expression which is very common, which is directed at homosexuals.

–I suggest that also is nonsense, that 'fruit-flavoured' is merely a reference to your sugary manner. – A: I suggest it is a reference to homosexuality.

–Do you know that it is usual in this country – it may not be in America, I do not know – if you are threatening someone with litigation, to write a letter to them first, telling them about what it is you are complaining? Do you know that the writ in this action was issued without any letter having been written or, indeed, accompanying it? – A: I did not know that, no. This matter was handled by attorneys, my attorney in California and my barrister and defence representatives here in London, Mr Jacobs and now Mr Beyfus. I do not know of the letter writing procedure.

–Is not the normal and natural thing to do, if you have got a complaint against a newspaper, to write and tell them what your complaint is?

Beyfus interrupted: 'That is not a question which an American citizen can answer, as to what is usual in this country. I have my own views about it, having regard to the nature of the libel.'

Gardiner continued: –Do you know that in your statement of claim in this action, which sets out what your case is, there is not one word to suggest that the words complained of mean that you are a homosexualist? – A: I maintain that there are many words that can only mean this interpretation which has been taken by people in all parts of the world, unfortunately by people in a respected profession and theatres, and certainly by a great many members of my audiences, both on television and in personal appearances. This is the only interpretation that these words contained in this vicious article have meant to the people upon whom I am dependent in carrying out my life's work.

–Have you any knowledge what the question was? – A: The question was do these words mean...

Mr Gardiner asked the shorthand writer to repeat it. –Have you read your Statement of Claim? – A: Yes.

–Did you observe that there is not one word suggesting that any part of the article complained of means that you are a homosexualist? – A: I believe there is. In my claim the morals issue has been brought into it.

The QC asked the witness to look at his Statement of Claim. The judge intervened: 'Mr Gardiner, I do not suppose the witness is very familiar with the Rules of Pleading.'

GARDINER: If he read it he must have observed that it does not in fact contain any allegation of homosexuality. I am not suggesting it was necessary because Mr Beyfus might say it is not, because it is there by innuendo. I appreciate that, but I thought it proper to put to him that there was nothing in his Statement of Claim about it.

–Mr Liberace, do you know that when Mr Beyfus made this statement in court yesterday that was the first official occasion on which you or anyone on your behalf has ever suggested that the words complained of mean that you are a homosexual. I do not mean – I want to be clear about it – that news had not reached the *Daily Mirror* that that was one of the things you were going to allege, but you realise that from beginning to end there is no letter or document of any kind which was ever written to the defendants, either of them, saying 'What I am complaining about is that I say this means I am a homosexualist'? – A: The reason I am in court is because I thought this article attacked me below the belt on a moral issue, and therefore...

–Mr Liberace, I have not interrupted you before, however long your answers, but would you apply your mind to the question. Do you realise that until yesterday morning, when Mr Beyfus said it, there has never been one line in writing – in the pleadings, letter or any document – in which you or any one on your behalf has alleged to the defendants that what you are complaining of is that this means you are a homosexualist... – A: The actual word may not have been used.

–Or anything of the kind. – A: Yes.

–The question is quite a plain one: Did you know that, until Mr Beyfus said whatever he did say yesterday, there has never been a line in writing from you or anyone on your behalf to the defendants, or either of them, to say 'What I am complaining of is that this means I am a homosexualist', or words to that effect? – A: Everybody else said it for me. I did not have to say it. It has been said all over the world, that this is the interpretation of this article, and it has been given that interpretation. This is the interpretation that we give it, my counsel and I.

–I suggest to you that neither at Manchester nor at Sheffield were there shouts. I think it is only at Sheffield that you say someone in the audience said things, or was it at Manchester as well? – A: When I yesterday referred to hostilities I was referring precisely to some shouts and cries taking place outside the theatre. When I am asked for details, it was only in

Sheffield that the cries and shouts I mentioned yesterday were heard from the stage, from people who had entered the hall. Fortunately they did not occur in the other places inside the hall, but only on the outside. When I spoke of hostilities those were the hostilities to which I referred, not to the hostilities, so-called, about 'Charlie Kunz for ever'. I do not care if he lives for ever. I have no reason to resent those placards which paraded outside this place at which I played. The hostilities to which I objected were the hostilities of these various shouts which were made by men mostly and which actually came from inside the confines of the auditorium where I was giving a performance. In the other places, because they were sold out in advance, these people could not get in, even if they wanted to.

–I suggest to you that all that happened at Sheffield was that there were a certain number of university students in the gallery, who had come to make fun of you; that no one shouted 'Queer' or 'Fairy', and that the university students threw paper arrows down to you; and I am not sure that someone was not thrown out. – A: I can prove that they did. I have witnesses to prove that they did.

–Did you know that before you came over here there was a revue called *For Amusement Only* running in London? – A: Yes, my attention has been directed to it.

–In which an artiste was giving an impression of you? – A: That is right.

–Did you book two seats to go and see it? – A: I did not

–Were they booked for you? – A: They were not booked for me. I did not book them. I never saw the show. I have no idea of the actual performance to which you refer.

–Do you remember speaking to a *Sunday Express* correspondent... this was when you were at Miami, just before you came over here, early in September... You asked him this 'Is anyone impersonating me in London at the moment?'... And did he tell you that you were featured in a revue showing in London? Then did you say, 'Oh, goody, I must get tickets; I love to watch myself being impersonated'? – A: I may have said that, but I never did get tickets for it because I found out later that it was a vulgar impersonation of me.

–Did you say 'You have a wonderful line in hokum'? Although you did not see it, you did hear what it was about, did you not? – A: I heard that it was vulgar.

–Did you hear the nature of the song? – A: No, I did not. I made no further enquiries about it.

–I suggest in fact you did? – A: No, I did not.

–Was it performed by Mr Jimmy Thompson? – A: I believe that was the young man.

–I suggest that if – which I suggest was not the case – anybody had made any such remarks to you they are much more likely to have come from the song which Mr Jimmy Thompson was singing. – A: You suggest that? –Yes. – A: All right.

–Just let us see if I cannot refresh your memory about it. Was this, as I suggest, the song which Mr Thompson was singing?

> Thank you, ladies and gentlemen. Thank you very much indeed. The name's Liberace. Each Sunday quite archly you are exposed to my dentifrice grin. I'm a sort of a Winifred Atwell combined with all the nice aspects of Vera Lynn...

Mr Beyfus objected to that. 'With the greatest respect, my learned friend is not entitled to read a song which is supposed to have been sung by someone, which my client says he has never heard and knew nothing at all about it, unless he is going to call Mr Thompson as a witness. If he is, then I do not object to it, because it will come in sooner or later.

GARDINER: I am going to call Mr Thompson.

BEYFUS: Then I do not object.

Gardiner resumed his recitation:

> –The name's Liberace, each Sunday quite archly
> You're exposed to my dentifrice grin.
> I'm a sort of a Winifred Atwell, combined with all
> the nice aspects of Vera Lynn
> My sequin dress suit is a bit of a brute,
> But it does take your mind off disasters,
> That occur. It is true, when I'm leering at you,
> Instead of the piano, when I play the masters.
> But my fan mail is really tremendous,
> It's growing so fast my head whirls,
> I get more and more, they propose by the score,
> And at least one or two are from girls.
> I'm so coy with Tchaikovsky,
> I mince through Moscovsky,
> With Albinez I'm so light and airy,
> But my fans all agree that I'm really most me,
> When I play the sugar plum fairy.
> And my programme is very artistic,
> Oh the stage and the cheers and the noise
> In a frenzy of bliss I made two children kiss,
> In spite of the fact both were boys,
> As I sexily render the classics,
> I've caused many a happy divorce.
> I send thrills down their spine playing Beethoven Nine,
> Cut down to two minutes of course.
> I've a piano-shaped bar, and piano shaped car
> In the piano-shaped house where I dwell.

I've a piano-shaped hearth, a piano shaped bath,
And a piano-shaped piano as well
   I've a Chinchilla coat and a dress suit that's stoat
And a tail coat of new marmoset.
When Momma and I wear our mink coats, oh my!
To tell us apart takes the vet.

...That is the song. – A: After hearing it, I would say that it was very vulgar, yes.

–You know that was performed every night for a year and three-quarters in London. – A: No, I did not know it lasted that long.

–Did you know that it had been on television prior to your coming over here? – A: Really? I am shocked.

–And after you came over it was on again both in *Chelsea at Nine* and in *Sunday Night at the London Palladium*. – A: I am shocked to discover this. When you tell me you allow this on television in England, I cannot believe it.

–Are you telling my lord and the jury that while you were in England in 1956, with your publicity people, theatrical agents, and all your fans, you never knew the contents of this song? – A: So help me God, I never knew it, and until you spoke the words of this vulgar song at this very moment, on my word of God, I swear it, I never heard it.

–Has it not been your experience that your fans, when you are attacked, always rush to your defence? – A: Yes, it is true, they do.

–You saw in the *Daily Mirror*, because the *Daily Mirror* published them, some of the letters which Cassandra received from your fans, most of them saying 'May you drop dead'. – A: They may have said that, and meant it.

–Do you say that none of your fans, legal advisers or your London theatrical agents... Was one of the first things which you got, when you came to England and arrived at the Savoy, these flowers made up in the shape of a dove of peace, from Jimmy Thompson? [Photograph is shown to witness] – A: Yes, I received these flowers.

–Did you know they were from Jimmy Thompson who was doing this impersonation of you? – A: I believe the name Jimmy Thompson accompanied the flowers, in the form of a giant replica of a telegram, and a dove of peace.

–Did you know that it was from Jimmy Thompson who was doing this impersonation of you? – A: Yes, I did.

–Are you still telling us that you have no knowledge of what the impersonation was? – A: No, I did not. Individuals, of course, give impersonations of me, but they have never been vulgar ones, and I laugh the loudest. I think they are marvellous, but I have never seen one which was vulgar. I would have no idea that this particular one would be any different from the other impersonations which have been done by Jack

Benny, Red Skelton and all those different people who have done impersonations of me. But Jimmy Thompson's impersonation I never witnessed, and when I got this thing, this dove of peace and this replica of a telegram, which said 'Welcome, from Jimmy Thompson', I remember distinctly asking the people who were assembled in my suite at the Savoy 'What is the meaning of the dove of peace? Am I to assume from this that Mr Jimmy Thompson is doing a devastating impersonation of me?' It could be devastating in the term of being an unkind impersonation, where he is making fun of my clothes or the way I comb my hair, but I had no idea at the time I received this that Jimmy Thompson was inferring in his impersonation of me that I was a homosexual.

–Do you suggest that all the time you were in England, mixing with the press, the theatrical people, your fans and so on, you did not know the nature of Jimmy Thompson's song? – A: I did not. No one ever suggested that it was that. They merely said 'Do not go and see it. It is terribly embarrassing. It is extremely vulgar.' I did not go and see it.

–You did know that it was terribly embarrassing and extremely vulgar? – A: More reason why I should not go and see it.

–Did you not ask anybody in what way? – A: I think it sufficed and satisfied me to know that it was vulgar and embarrassing, and my presence at such a performance would condone this sort of thing, and I do not condone an impersonation of me which is below the belt and vulgar.

–Did you go up to Jimmy Thompson when you were performing at the Café de Paris? – A: Yes, I met this...

'Did you put your arm around him, and have you both photographed together? – A: That was true, yes. I did not at the time know that his impersonation of me was a vulgar one.

–Oh, come! – A: I did not.

–I thought you said a minute or so ago that you had been told by people that it was embarrassing and vulgar? – A: Yes, I did make enquiries about it.

–You were told by people? – A: Yes. A lot of people at the Café de Paris, when Jimmy Thompson was there that night, asked me 'Have you seen Jimmy Thompson's devastating impersonation of you?' and I answered, 'No, I have not'. They said, 'Please do not go and see it. He is here to-night.' And they just let it go at that. I made further enquiries after meeting this boy and allowing myself to be photographed, and I was shocked to learn that the impersonation that he did in fact was a vulgar one.

–Where were you on April 22, 1958? Did you come to England in April 1958? – A: Yes, I did.

–You were here until the end of April, were you? – A: Yes, I was a fortnight at the Palladium, and I did spend some time here.

85

–Did you see Jimmy Thompson again in April, at the Savoy? – A: No. I do not recall seeing Jimmy Thompson again.

–Did you again send for a press photographer and have Jimmy Thompson doing his act at the piano, and you looking admiringly on? [Photograph is handed to witness.] You can look at that. It says on the back: 'The following Tuesday he was doing it again on television in *Chelsea at Nine*'. – A: It says, 'Liberace watches sceptically while Jimmy Thompson...'

–Is that a photograph of you and Jimmy Thompson... That is taken at the Savoy a few days before April 22 1958? – A: I believe it was, yes,

–Did he tell you that he was re-doing his show on television in *Chelsea at Nine* on the following Tuesday? – A: I do recall Mr Thompson telling me that he was going to appear on television but what the nature of his performance was to be was certainly not known to me. I assumed that he would not do anything vulgar on television because I assumed that you have a decency code, as we have in our country, which prevents anything vulgar being shown on television. I thought I was safe in having this picture taken together because I assumed that this man was a performer who had not given a vulgar performance in a television show.

–When I asked you about the picture in the Café de Paris I understood you to say that of course was before you had been told that the performance was embarrassing and vulgar, and that, of course, if you had been told that, you would not have posed for a photograph with him? – A: That is right.

–This is afterwards, is it not? – A: This is after, yes.

–Did you realise that the show had been running in London for over a year and three quarters? – A: Yes, I understood that.

–Are you telling my lord that, after a performance on television before you arrived in this country and in spite of the fact that it was to be re-televised a few days afterwards, you still did not know in April 1958 the words of the song? – A: No. I did not until this very morning, a few moments ago, when you read the words of that song, so help me God.

–If anybody in this country did think that of you, they would be much more likely to do so from that, rather than a small paragraph in a newspaper. People soon forget what they read in a newspaper. – A: I doubt it, because I doubt if Mr Jimmy Thompson is as widely quoted and as widely read as the *Daily Mirror*.

–Night after night, day after day, in the West End of London for a year and three-quarters, and these three times on television? – A: I suggest that if I had known this to be true, that the contents of the song were so viciously aimed at my morals, I would have probably sued Mr Jimmy Thompson for libel.

Mr Beyfus intervened: 'It is not too late…'

GARDINER: So far as the *Daily Mirror* is concerned, had you told their Mr Doncaster, when he was in America, that when you were in England you would like to see some ordinary pubs? – A: Yes.

–On October 6 1956, ten days after the Cassandra article was published, did you accept the *Daily Mirror*'s hospitality to arrange for you to go to The Bell in the Borough and The Tiger on Tower Hill? – A: Yes.

–Was that written up by the *Daily Mirror*? – A: Yes, it was.

–In point of fact, although someone might think, reading that, that you stood everybody a drink, all the drinks given there were paid for by the *Daily Mirror*. – A: I have no idea who paid for them.

–You did not, did you? – A: I never recall paying for any; I do not handle English money.

–If you really thought that the *Daily Mirror* had said you were a homosexualist, are you telling my lord and the jury that you would have accepted their hospitality after that? – A: I have more or less proven the fact that I had promised him to do a pub crawl with the *Daily Mirror*, at my home in California, and when I arrived in England, in accordance with that promise, I kept it.

–I suggest it is exactly the other way round, that you had said to Mr Doncaster that when in England you would like to see some ordinary pubs and he said he would do his best to arrange it. That did not oblige you to go through with it at all. – A: The letter which we have states that extreme desire to take me on a pub crawl. Mr Doncaster wanted it, and he wanted to have that exclusively so that other newspapers could not do the same thing. I have in my file over there this letter, and I will submit as evidence, through counsel, if necessary.

–If you really thought that the *Daily Mirror* had said you were a homosexualist, do you say that you would, in order to get further publicity, have accepted their hospitality? – A: I would say that this is true, that I would go on a pub crawl, yes, with the *Daily Mirror* because I had promised to do so back in California before this vicious article had been printed.

–A few days later, on October 10, were you in Miss Winifred Atwell's dressing room at the London Palladium in the evening when Mr Doncaster and other reporters came in? – A: I believe I was.

–Were they taking photographs? – A: Yes, they were.

–And did you say, 'Let us have one for Cassandra'? – A: No, I did not say this.

–Was there a Miss Ambler there? – A: I believe she was.

–Was she in your employment? – A: No.

–Did she write the articles which were published in *The People*, which purported to have been written by you? – A: She did not. She edited those articles, and she was hired by the newspaper to edit these articles because I

87

have a habit when writing newspaper columns of saying in too many words what Miss Ambler could edit into a few and say just as well. That is why she, understanding the newspaper profession, said that rather than limit me to a certain number of words just say anything that I wanted to say about my visit to England, and she would get the essence of that article condensed in a sort of *Readers Digest* form; and after she had done it she would submit the finished article to me and I would approve of it. Usually I would commend her for putting it in so few words.

−Do you say that she was not paid by your organisation at all? − A: Yes, I do say she was not paid by my organisation at all.

−I suggest that when you said 'Let us have one for Cassandra' Miss Ambler said 'If Randolph Churchill can get £5,000 from *The People*, Liberace should be able to get something from the *Mirror*.' − A: I have no recollection of those words being spoken by Miss Ambler, no.

−Do you remember Mr Doncaster saying 'Are you going to sue us'? − A: I have no recollection of that, no. We may have been thinking about it, but I do not recall saying anything about it.

−Did you then say, 'No, I am not'? − A: No, I did not say that.

−Then did you go on to say that you read his article about the pub crawl and − I do not suggest you used these words − you thought it was just great? − A: Yes, I do remember commenting to someone, I do not know who, that the article on the pub crawl was a step in the right direction. In saying that I am meaning that most of the caustic comments which I receive in the English newspapers were based on hearsay that were written prior to my arrival in England. I noticed that while I stayed here the newspapers themselves seemed anxious to make amends for saying caustic comments, and there was a sort of turnabout face, as we put it back home, about the newspaper profession. In 1958 this prevailed even more so, and the newspapers, with which I have always tried to co-operate, both in England and in other countries, seemed to realise my sincerity in wanting to be co-operative; and this pub crawl was the first article written by any newspaper that seemed to want to give me a chance to prove myself a regular fellow.

−Mr Liberace, I am most anxious not to stop you from saying anything you want to say. The question whether you said this was a very short one, and your learned counsel Mr Beyfus will have an opportunity of re-examining you and asking you further questions in all these matters. Could you keep your answers a little shorter, because we have the time of the jury to consider? − A: I will.

−When you said 'I thought it was just great', did Miss Ambler say 'Why don't you ask Cassandra to lunch?' − A: No.

Mr Beyfus was on his feet again: My learned friend is putting into my client's mouth words which he did not say. He did not say 'I think this is great'.

GARDINER: I am so sorry. Let me go back. Mr Liberace, did you tell Mr Doncaster that you had read his article? – A: I may have, yes.

MR JUSTICE SALMON: I think you agreed that you approved the article? – A: Yes.

–And you probably said so? – A: Yes, I probably said it was a good article, yes.

Mr Gardiner continued: When you said that, did Miss Ambler say 'Why don't you ask Cassandra to lunch'? – A: I do not recall Miss Ambler saying that.

–Did you say 'Maybe I will'? – A: No, I did not say that.

–On October 18 were you in a cabaret at the Café de Paris? – A: Yes, I believe so.

–In the course of your performance did you say 'I will now dedicate my next number to the stinking press, and in particular to Mr Cassandra'? – A: No, I did not say it in those words. I said that I would like to dedicate my first number to some of my critics, and I played *Jealousy.*

–Perhaps I had better complete the whole thing. First, did you in fact say: 'I will now dedicate my next number to the stinking press, and in particular to Mr Cassandra. I am going to take him to lunch. If he does not come, I will know he is one of them. Does he not use a woman's name?' – A: No, I did not say that.

–Just think… – A: No, I remember what I said. Would you like to hear it?... I said: 'I am going to dedicate my first number to some of my critics, particularly to one whose name I shall not mention. I do not wish to make him more famous.' Then I played *Jealousy.* Those were my exact words. I have witnesses who were at that performance, who will testify to the integrity of that statement.

–I suggest that in fact you mentioned his name. – A: I did not mention his name because I did not wish to, but everyone knew to whom I was referring.

–How old are you now actually? – A: I lie about the year. I have to think for a moment. I am forty.

–Are you suggesting that women do not flock to see a woman who is reported to have outstanding sex appeal? – A: I am not suggesting that, no.

–You agree that is true, do you, that women do? – A: Women do, perhaps not as many as men, but women do, yes.

–There is nothing improper in that? – A: No, nothing whatsoever.

–Nothing homosexual – A: No.

–Are the opening words of your theme song, *I don't care as long as you care for me*? – A: Yes.

–That is addressed to the whole audience, whether men, women or children? – A: Yes.

–There is nothing improper in that? – A: No

–At page 45 of *The Liberace Story*, in the last three lines, your authors have suggested this:

> They listen not only to his music, but to his voice, his words. Such a man could do great harm, if his heart were not true. He could preach war and a nation would spring to arms.

...I suppose the part of the nation which would spring to arms would be mainly men, would it not? – A: I would say both men and women have fought for their countries; yes, mainly men.

–You have great appeal, as I suggested when I started, and that is what these words mean. You have great appeal to all sections of the community, all ages, whether men, women or children? – A: I would like to believe that, yes.

–Is this right, 'Liberace is a pretty unusual human being. He has millions of grandmothers, matrons and bobby-soxers agog, to say nothing of similar number of fans of his own sex.' There is nothing wrong in that? – A: No.

–Could you explain this to me: you talk a great deal about love in your performances I am not suggesting in any improper sense... – A: Well, it is an underlying theme of my performance, the underlying theme being the love you speak of. It is not always spoken in words. It can be the expression which forms on one's face. An expression of love can be understood by an audience, as they do in my case. I do not necessarily have to say 'I love you', but they know that I do by the way I treat them and by the way I perform before them. This is the expression of love which I use. I do not go round and say the words. You know what I mean.

–You do appreciate, do you not, that I am not suggesting there is anything wrong in the sex appeal? – A: No, I do realise that.

–I am suggesting that all sections of the community and sexes and ages are interested to see it? – A: That is right.

–Then when Cassandra says 'He is the summit of sex – the pinnacle of Masculine, Feminine and Neuter. Everything that He, She and It can ever want'... how on earth do you get out of that the meaning that you are homosexual? It is all your appeal. – A: It is not the same. There are millions of people in this world...

–Would you explain it then to my lord and the jury? – A: This is the interpretation that I give it because people in all parts of England and in all parts of the world, on whom I am dependent for making my livelihood, have given it this interpretation. I am intending to prove that in my testimony, and because of this interpretation – and regardless of how you interpret it, this is the interpretation by millions and millions of people on who I am dependent for my life's work – this article has given me untold agony and embarrassment; and it has made me the subject of ridicule; and it has cost me many professional years of my career I can assure you.

–I suggest to you that is not so at all, that what has hurt you and hit you is the fact that Cassandra has said rather more sharply and rather more bitingly what most other critics have said about you for a long time? – A: I do not say that at all. No one has ever intimated that I am a homosexual before this report.

–Where do you find it? – A: The article was so brilliantly and viciously written that the interpretation which was given this article was that I was a homosexual, in no uncertain terms.

–Where do you find it in terms? I am only asking you to explain your case to the jury. – A: You just ask me to explain it, and then you will not allow me to do it. Did you ask me to explain it to the jury?

–Yes – A: Members of the jury, I am a performer who travels in all parts of the world. On my word of God, on my mother's health who is so dear to me, the interpretation of this article has only meant one thing, that I am a homosexual, and that is why I am in this court to fight this libellous accusation.

–I am sorry to interrupt you, Mr Liberace, but I did not ask you to make a speech to the jury. I asked you to explain to them quite simply how the words 'Everything that He, She and It can ever want' can possibly be understood by anyone outside a lunatic asylum to mean that you are a homosexual. Would you explain to them? – A: I will try.

–Where do you find it in these words? – A: 'He, She and It'... 'It' refers to the sex, supposedly in between 'he' and 'she', right?

–That is what you are suggesting, is it? – A: That is what it means, yes.

–I thought you were going to suggest that 'It' was animal. It is not masculine. I apprehend you to say it is the word 'It'. – A: I object to this entire article because it is all slanted to mean that I am a homosexual. It means further that all the things said in this article – besides 'masculine, feminine and neuter' there is the episode about 'fruit-flavoured' – all these associations which I am supposed to be a fancy dresser, the fact that I love my mother, all the things which appear in this article all point to that thing, that horrible fact, which has damaged me in my career and in my profession. It has made me the subject of ridicule, has caused me great embarrassment, and has been responsible, ladies and gentlemen, for losing almost the life of someone who is most dear to me, and that is my mother, who to this day is a sick woman because of this vicious attack.

–If you do not mind confining yourself to the question... – A: Yes, I did.

The judge asked: 'When did your mother first have this article drawn to her attention?' – A: I believe it was on the very day when it appeared in the paper. It has been the practice at the Savoy to have the papers delivered each day to the room, which is a courtesy they extend to their guests.

–It made her very ill? – A: It did. It made her so ill that she was advised by her physician that she return home immediately.

Mr Gardiner resumed. –She attended all your concerts the same night? – A: She attended my concerts because she said in her opinion – I remember so well my mother saying this – 'If I go home now it will make all the people think that this is true about you'... 'this' meaning this horrible charge.

–She was in the theatre in her usual place the same night?

Something was puzzling the judge. 'You must have been in a very forgiving mood,' he said, 'when, after your mother had been taken ill in the way you have told us, you accepted the hospitality of the paper.'

Liberace said: In doing the pub crawl? Yes. I have known it to be a fact that by being co-operative, particularly with people who have never met you personally, to give them an opportunity of knowing me as an individual and to meet me at close quarters, I have found in many hundreds of instances that by being co-operative, in allowing people to change their opinion of me, including members of the press and journalists... they turn about face. Many times reporters have said: 'I used to hate him, but I like him. I would not write anything bad about him now because I have met him, and he turned out to be a nice guy'.

GARDINER: You are always stressing the fact that you exude love, and you want the people to love you... there is nothing homosexual in that? – A: No.

–Men, women and children? – A: That is right.

–I suggest you really summed it up yourself in a sentence which you said at Southampton, and which was published in the same issue as the offending article, when you talk about expressing your love to your viewers. It is in the issue of September 26 1956, on the front page, in which you sum up for yourself what you describe as the secret of your success. 'The secret of my success? It is a very simple thing. Everyone in this world wants to be loved and I express that love to my viewers and listeners and they seem to respond to it.' Your viewers and listeners include men, do they not? – A: Yes.

–When you said they respond to it, you did not mean that in any improper sense? – A: No, I did not. I was speaking of love, humanity, brotherly love, the love between peoples. That I feel is sadly lacking in this world.

–That I suggest is exactly what Cassandra was obviously referring to when he so described the universality of your appeal? – A: Yes, I believe he was referring to that.

Gardiner paused to let the answer sink in. Liberace had finally agreed that the 'He She and It' phrase described 'the universality of his appeal. There was just the question about his claim that it had damaged his career.

–Are you now appearing in *Sunday Night at the London Palladium*? – A: Yes, next Sunday I will be there.

–Is that the highest paid position in the British Television Authority? – A: I believe it is.

–And then at the *Royal Variety Performance* before the Queen Mother? – A: Yes.

The end of Mr Gardiner's cross-examination coincided conveniently with the lunch adjournment. When the court reassembled it was Mr Beyfus's opportunity to re-examine his client on points raised since his evidence-in-chief. But first he referred to something he had noticed over breakfast.

'My lord, before my client goes back into the witness box, may I say something which I intended to say at half past 10? I see that I have been reported in the press as saying that I was going to call witnesses to establish that my client's performance was "wholesome, homely and over-sentimental". I certainly did not intend to say "over-sentimental". I do not think I did say over-sentimental.

The judge said no; he did not think Mr Beyfus had said that either.

'If I did say over-sentimental, it was a slip of the tongue. What I intended to say, and what I think I did say, was in part sentimental.'

That matter having been cleared up, Liberace returned to the witness box to face his QC.

BEYFUS: I want to go back to the beginning of your cross-examination when your attention was directed to the big book, an article by Mr Bill Parsons of February 1 1955, when my learned friend directed your attention to what might be called the worst part of the article... There is a heading 'Critics are caustic'. The caustic part was read out. It ends:

> He has taken piano playing out of the rarefied atmosphere of the classical virtuosos, and brought it to millions who unabashedly revel in his style and don't care a hoot what the highbrows say.

...Then my learned friend read that one woman who did not like you wrote:

> Such dimpling and winking! Such tossing of curls and fluttering of eyelashes and flashing of teeth! Such nausea!

...He did not read what follows:

> But whenever anyone attacks Liberace his myriad admirers attack back with speed and venom. A week later, while wrathful letters still poured in on her, the critic admitted: 'I have kicked up a hornet's nest... They impugned my honour and had grave doubts about my patriotism.'

...You explained yesterday, and again today, that you expected *The Story of Liberace* to be quite accurate because you knew, or thought you knew, that all the material was being supplied by Warner Brothers... Did they have all the necessary material about the history of your life? – A: Yes.

–You were cross-examined yesterday and today with regard to press conferences. There was a press conference when the Queen Mary arrived at Cherbourg... Another when the Queen Mary arrived at Southampton... And am I right in saying there was another one when you arrived at the Savoy... I just want to ask you about these press conferences. Take Cherbourg, for example. Did you invite reporters on board the Queen Mary at Cherbourg, or did they come of their own accord? – A: They came of their own accord.

–Knowing, of course, that you were on board... When they came on board you received them in a conference... Would you dictate at all to any of the reporters the questions which they put to you? – A: In actual substance the questions put to me by these reporters were about my career, about my philosophies, about my family.

–Who chose the questions? – A: The reporters did.

–If one looks at the Statement of Claim in this case and at the libel in it, it refers to your answers on four questions on religion, on mother love, which you have changed to 'love for one's mother', on world love and on money. It was put to you in cross-examination that every one of those matters was dealt with at the press conference at Cherbourg. Who chose those questions on love for one's mother, on religion, on world love and on money? – A: The reporters.

–When reporters put questions to you on matters not connected with your performances, your entertainments, do you still do your best to answer them? – A: I do.

–You were asked about the various articles in your house which were shaped like pianos, I think ashtrays, cushions, tables for smoking materials and so forth. How did you acquire those different articles? – A: Those articles you refer to were given to me by friends and admirers as gifts.

–I think you dealt with the discrepancies in the article of Mr Donald Zec... When he came to your place and you gave him an interview and showed him your house, did he appear to be friendly or unfriendly? – A: He appeared to be friendly.

–Had you any idea when he left that he was going to write a mocking article about you? – A: No, I did not.

–Modified only by the last words which suggested that he liked you. – A: Yes.

–So far as your public entertainments are concerned, do you simplify music? – A: No, I do not.

–You said with regard to the film that you made with regard to your home which ends with a hymn that no man has ever objected to that film... We know that the defendants have sought to collect all the adverse criticisms they can find of you. Have you found any adverse criticism of that film in any of the documents disclosed by the defendants so far as you

94

know... I am not saying it may not exist, but have you found one? – A: I have not, no.

–Then you said that there was one girl who came by willpower out of her iron lung... Is there any doubt at all about that actual fact? – A: There is no doubt about it.

–With regard to the expression 'scent impregnated', you were asked about that and I think you said you used after-shave lotion... And deodorants? – A: Yes.

–You were asked about the article which was published under your mother's name. Did you notice that the word used by the writer, 'perfumes', was crossed out, and the word 'colognes' substituted... Do you in fact use eau de cologne... I suppose various types of eau de cologne? – A: That is right.

–Apart from using eau de cologne, do you use scent? – A: No, I do not.

–You were cross-examined with regard to your name Valentino. Did you have anything to do with the choice of your name when you were christened Valentino? – A: No, I did not.

–And in fact, so far from trading on it, you have already told me you are known throughout the United States as Liberace without the addition of either of your Christian names? – A: That is right.

–You were asked about accepting the hospitality of the *Daily Mirror* to go on what the *Daily Mirror* calls a pub crawl. You remember that... And asked who paid for the odd beer or two which was drunk. – A: Yes.

–You told my lord and the members of the jury that you, or somebody on your behalf, promised to do that in Hollywood. – A: That is right.

–The second paragraph of the letter which reminds you of that is: 'Some other newspapers, I fear, have a similar idea and I am therefore anxious to try to keep this exclusively to the *Mirror* – with your kind co-operation – because we have been planning this with some eagerness'... It was in order to fulfil your promise of which you were then reminded that you went. – A: That is right.

–Lastly, you were cross-examined very severely at great length on how on earth you could say that the words in the libel suggested you were a homosexual. You remember that? – A: Yes, I do.

–And you said that you could produce and would produce a magazine in the United States which reproduces that article and is headed 'Is Liberace a Man?' – A: Yes.

[A document was handed to the witness].

–Is this the magazine to which you refer? I think it is called *Hush, hush*, is it not? A: Yes, it is, and this is the magazine.

–And is it headed: 'Is Liberace a Man?' – A: Yes, it is.

Mr Gardiner objected: 'It is, I gather, a document published in some other country. There is, of course, no reliance for the purposes of damages on some alleged repetition anywhere because, of course, that would have to have been pleaded. The position, in my submission, is this: if it is convenient to do so, I would like to base it upon another submission which I can see I am going to have to make in view of what Mr Beyfus said in his opening, because the submission I am now making depends to a large extent, I think, on that one. Mr Beyfus did intimate that he was going to call witnesses to say what they understood the words to mean.'

BEYFUS: No, my Lord. I concede that in law I cannot call witnesses to say what the words mean, and my client could not have given evidence on that point if he had not been cross-examined on that point. I am not going to do it because I cannot. They are ordinary English words and I am not allowed by English law to call people to say what they mean. That is a matter for the jury, judging ordinary English words. Therefore, I am not making any such attempt.

GARDINER: I had, of course, to put to the plaintiff my case, which is that these words do not mean this and that no reasonable person could think that they did, and I thought it right to give him an opportunity to explain his case on that to the jury. But as my friend now concedes that, in a case where there is no innuendo, it is not open to the plaintiff to call some witness who can say 'I thought it meant so and so' or, of course, equally for the defendants to call witnesses to say 'Well, we did not'. Having put that to the plaintiff (as I had to do) that does not mean, in my submission, although one cannot in fact stop what one witness says in cross-examination, that he is entitled to get in by hearsay in re-examination the very evidence which he was not allowed to call. If he is not allowed to call Smith to say 'This is what I thought it meant', he cannot, in my submission, say 'This is what Smith told me'. The mere fact that I put my clients' case to him strongly, as was my duty, and saying that it was quite fantastic to suggest it and no-one would think so, does not entitle my friend to do this. The question whether anyone would think so is to be decided in law, not by on the one hand calling witnesses to say what they thought or on the other hand by giving secondary evidence of what somebody else has told you, or producing a document which shows what somebody else thought, but by submitting the words to the jury and the jury deciding, where there is no innuendo, from the words themselves what the ordinary reasonable person would understand them to mean. Therefore, although I had to put it to the plaintiff in that form, 'nobody would think it meant this', that does not, in my submission, let in re-examination at second hand the very evidence which would not be admissible.

BEYFUS: My answer to that is first of all that my learned friend was under no obligation at all to put to my client in cross-examination...

MR JUSTICE SALMON: I think that is right; but he did invite your client to explain, looking at the words, 'How do you say they mean what you say they mean?'

BEYFUS: Yes, and he put it to him that it was fantastic and that no person could possibly form that opinion. My learned friend repeated the word 'fantastic' two moments ago. As he put to my client 'It is fantastic and no person could possibly form that view', my client is entitled to answer, as he did: 'So far from its being fantastic, so far from it being the fact that nobody could form that view, I have in my hand a magazine published in the United States of America which shows what you are saying is absolutely wrong'. It could not come in except as a result of cross-examination which invited it.

MR JUSTICE SALMON: You have got the answer from the witness. I should leave it there.

BEYFUS: The only reason I thought it my duty to go a little further is that we like the best evidence in this country, and if a witness refers to the contents of a document, I thought it my duty to put the document to him. If your lordship thinks I should not, I am quite prepared to leave it. I was only trying to do my duty and not introduce evidence of what a document contained without producing the document.

MR JUSTICE SALMON: I think the way Mr Gardiner put it was that no-one outside a lunatic asylum, or no sane person, would think so and so. We do not know anything about the publishers of *Hush, hush* or anything.

BEYFUS: There it is, my Lord. I tendered it in order to confirm, amongst other things, the honesty and reliability of my client in saying that he had such a document here. If your lordship thinks it better not to put it in, I will not press the point, because the evidence is there. It is evidence which is unchallenged and as to which I have produced the document. If your lordship thinks I had better not put it in formally, I will not.

MR JUSTICE SALMON: I think strictly it is not admissible in evidence in this case.

BEYFUS: My learned friend produced this document. [He showed the judge a photograph.] What it is supposed to be, I do not know, or whether it has been put in evidence, and, if so, on what ground it has been put in evidence.

GARDINER: I asked the witness whether one of the first things he did not see when he arrived at the Savoy was those flowers made up in the shape of a dove of peace and whether he did not think that they had come from Jimmy Thompson.

BEYFUS: Are those flowers?

GARDINER: Those are flowers made up in the form of a dove of peace.

BEYFUS: They look like feathers. I think the answer was 'No'.

GARDINER: No. The answer was 'Yes'.

BEYFUS: He did see that?

LIBERACE: Yes, I did.

BEYFUS [to the witness]: You were asked with regard to the words in the Statement of Claim in the libel. Would you look at them? You said that in your view they certainly suggested that you were a homosexual? – A: Yes.

–Let us look at them. They are the words in the box at the top repeated in larger print: 'He is the summit of sex – the pinnacle of masculine, feminine and neuter'. Then: 'Everything that he' – meaning some other man – '...can ever want', under the words summit of sex. What do you think those words mean? – A: I have the opinion that these words mean that I am a homosexual.

–Can you conceive of any other meaning properly...

GARDINER: That is a slightly leading question.

BEYFUS: Do you object to it?

GARDINER: I thought the question 'Can you conceive' was a slightly leading question.

MR JUSTICE SALMON: That is a point of view, Mr Beyfus.

Beyfus started to ask his client: 'Can you think of any other meaning...?' Then he gave up: 'My lord, it is difficult to frame it otherwise than in the form of a leading question, so I will leave it.'

And on that point Liberace left the witness box, six hours of testimony completed.

The jury, if they were paying attention, may have been a little confused at this point. Liberace, who had brought the case, was complaining that in the phrase 'He She or It', it was the word *It* that he found offensive; it referred, he had told Gardiner, to 'the sex, supposedly in between He and She.' That was what denoted homosexuality, he was saying. But Beyfus, who was pleading his case, thought that the offensive element was the *He* word, 'meaning some other man'. The plaintiff's side may be singing off the same hymn sheet, but they were not singing the same hymn.

The second witness was Arthur Coppersmith, musical director and orchestra leader at the Café de Paris, who said he was a married man with two children, had worked in the entertainment world for the last 30 years, and had seen Liberace's performance at the restaurant during October 1956.

Helenus Milmo, Beyfus's junior, asked: 'What would you say was the appeal of that show?'

But before the question could be answered it provoked a legal argument – not about the nature of the performance but about the nature of evidence: could comment be considered fair and reasonable even if other people disagreed with it?

GARDINER: My lord… I am sorry, but of course obviously a great deal of evidence may depend on this. If my learned friend will allow me, what, as I understand it, is being contended is that on the questions which are questions of comment, because they are not alleged by the defendants to be fact, it is open to the plaintiff (and presumably the defendants) to call evidence to this effect:

'I do not agree with the opinion expressed in the *Daily Mirror*. It did not seem to me that it was a mincing sugary performance. It did not seem to me that he was using his sex appeal. It did not seem to me that he was talking about his mother more than he should, and I do not agree at all with the matters of opinion expressed in the article', and so on. I say 'opinion' because, as your lordship knows, defendants have to specify which are the allegations of fact and which are the allegations of comment, and they have said here that what they said about his arrival at Waterloo is fact. Whether or not the plaintiff made the statements to the press correspondents set out in the article is, of course, fact. Whether *The Times* published what it is alleged to have published was a question of fact, and everything else is a matter of opinion, that is to say, comment.

If that is so, of course, it is open to the plaintiff to say: 'We do not think that some of what you say is comment, is comment; it is fact'. If that is so, of course, the defence would fail; but, on the basis of the plea, it is not, in my submission, open to either party to call evidence of people who agree or do not agree with the article.

MR JUSTICE SALMON: That is right, Mr Gardiner; but on the issue of fair comment the plaintiff's case will be that no fair minded man could honestly believe what was written about the plaintiff's performance. It seems to me in those circumstances they are entitled to call evidence factually as to the nature of his performance.

GARDINER: Your Lordship says 'factually'; but the performance of an artist is really entirely a matter of opinion. This would, in my submission, apply to every case of fair comment. Somebody goes to see a play. One person thinks it is very good, and in particular that a particular actor was extremely good. Somebody else who sees the same play thinks it is very bad and that the particular actor was very bad and says 'For one thing, he gives a very dramatic ham sort of performance', but the other does not think so at all. If it is open to the plaintiff in this case to call evidence that they did not think that the performances were of the kind which the *Daily Mirror* did, and if they can call 50 witnesses of that kind, it must be open to the defendants to call 100 witnesses to say the opposite.

MR JUSTICE SALMON: You must not try and frighten me. [Laughter.]

GARDINER: I apprehend that the reason why the law is so is really that common sense reason, because if it were not so, granted that this is the field of opinion – and I am not making this submission as to any of the matters which are alleged by the defence to be questions of fact – and granted that this is restricted to questions of opinion, it is not, in my submission, open to the plaintiffs to call a number of people to say 'We do not see how any honest man could have formed that opinion', because that is the very thing the jury has got to decide, any more than it is open to me to call a number of witnesses to say 'We could not have agreed with Cassandra more. We thought that this performance was perfectly frightful'.

MR JUSTICE SALMON: You are knocking at an open door, if that is all you are submitting. I agree with that. I do not quite know what the witness is being called to prove. He may be going to say what the plaintiff did when he was at the Café de Paris.

GARDINER: I thought he was being asked about the nature of his performance. I hope I have not taken up time unnecessarily. I thought he was being asked what his opinion was of the nature of the performance. Might I just add this: I should have no objection at all, and I was happy to find the plaintiff in agreement, that if it would assist the jury to see some of his television performances – because, after all, that is what everybody has been commenting on – then they could judge that for themselves. I should have no objection to that, and I am told arrangements could be made to do that tomorrow or at any later time that was convenient; but on any view this is in a sense second-hand evidence.

BEYFUS: My Lord, I do not want to mention this in the presence of the witness, the object of calling this evidence, but I indicated to my learned friend in my opening I wanted to call evidence of this sort that the nature of the performance was such that no reasonable person could honestly have formed the extreme opinions expressed by the defendants.

MR JUSTICE SALMON: I think you can call evidence as to the nature of the performance and what the plaintiff did, but you cannot ask the witness: 'What did you think about it?'

Milmo took the hint and resumed his examination: –What was the nature of the performance? – A: The programme consisted of the *Blue Danube*, Gershwin's *Rhapsody in Blue*, I believe Mr Liberace sang *September Song*, I cannot remember, but it was that type of quite popular appeal.

–Was there anything dirty about the performance from start to finish? – A: There were no risqué lyrics of any sort.

–Was there anything suggestive about it? – A: Nothing whatsoever.

–Would you have said that it was or was not a sexy performance – A: Definitely not a sexy performance.

–I suppose that occasionally you do have performances with a sexy appeal at the Café de Paris? – A: Yes, we have had all sorts of artists of different types.

100

–During the time that Mr Liberace was performing there did you meet him personally behind the scenes so to speak? – A: Two or three times, yes.

–Did he do or say anything during the whole of that period that suggested to you that he was homosexual?

GARDINER: I object to that question, with respect, for this reason that it is put with a view to trying to get the jury to think that it is the defendants' case that he is a homosexual. I have made it clear at the earliest moment the suggestion was made that the words did mean that he was a homosexual, that so far as my clients are concerned there was no suggestion of that kind and their case is that they never intended that. Of course the plaintiff is entitled to say: 'well, what does it mean', but, my lord, once having made it perfectly plain so far as the defendants are concerned their case is that it does not mean that, that it never has been that, these repeated questions as to whether there was any truth in it can only be put not because they really go to any issue in the case but to try to persuade the jury in some way or another it is still part of my case he is.

MR JUSTICE SALMON: I am sure the jury understand what you have made so plain again just now but I shall allow this question none the less.

MILMO: Mr Coppersmith, can you remember my question? –A: Yes, I believe I can. I went into Mr Liberace's dressing room and we had photographs taken and we were together as musicians and artists are at prior rehearsals and we discussed various aspects of the music which was going to be played by my orchestra in accompanying him and I have spoken to him at odd times.

–You still have not answered the question which I put to you. Did you see him do anything or say anything which would suggest that he was a homosexual? – A: No.

–I want you to help us, if you can, about the first night. Can you tell his lordship and the jury what the reaction was of the audience on the first night? – A: Yes, there was a sort of tension...

GARDINER: My Lord, I again object...

MILMO (to the witness): Will you tell his lordship and the jury what was the initial reaction of the audience at the Café de Paris when Mr Liberace appeared on that first night? – A: All first nights at the Café de Paris have certain tenseness in the atmosphere but in the case of Mr Liberace I think there were an awful lot of people there who would have liked to have made fun out of the entrance, sort of thing, but in actual fact once he started to play he had the audience absolutely in the palm of his hand. A customer, a patron, did say to me... I do not know whether I should say this...

–No. Was the initial reaction in your experience a friendly one or an unfriendly one, the initial reaction? – A: It was not as friendly as the other first nights.

–Put it that way if you like... was it? – A: No; it is very hard to say... I did not speak to anybody, but the general atmosphere was... how can I put it in words...

MR JUSTICE SALMON: I think you have conveyed your meaning quite well to the jury.

MILMO: Have you read the article that is complained of in this case? – A: No.

It was the defence's turn. Mr Gardiner asked whether the witness had seen *For Amusement Only*. And whether he remembered Jimmy Thompson's skit of Liberace. Mr Coppersmith said he'd seen it and remembered it.

–And did Mr Thompson come to the Café de Paris while Mr Liberace was there? – A: I would not know. I do not know Mr Thompson personally.

–You read some of the papers, I suppose? – A: Yes.

–And, of course, before Mr Liberace gave the performance of which you have been speaking he appeared at the Festival Hall? – A: I believe so.

–I am not sure what you read, but do you know that there had been highly critical comments about Mr Liberace in the *Daily Express*, the *Daily Herald*, the *Daily Mail*, the *Daily Mirror*, the *Daily News*, the *Daily Sketch*, the *Daily Telegraph*, The *Evening News*, the *Standard, Everybody's, Illustrated, The Observer, The People, Reynolds, Reveille*, the *Star, the Sunday Dispatch*, the *Sunday Express*, the *Sunday Graphic*, the *Sunday Pictorial, TV Mirror, The Times, Time* and the *Manchester Guardian*?

BEYFUS: Do not answer for a moment. Even double questions are not allowed but in this case it is a multiple question. If my learned friend wants to put them I ask him to put them individually.

MR JUSTICE SALMON: Did you know that after the Festival Hall performance he had a bad press generally? – A: Yes.

Next witness was George Militiades Melachrino, musical director and composer, who said he specialised in popular classical music performing 'pretty well all over the world' and that his orchestra had appeared with Liberace on his tour. He presided over all the rehearsals and at every concert except the one in Sheffield, when he had a long-standing engagement elsewhere.

MILMO: Would you tell his lordship and the jury what the appeal was of the plaintiff's performance?

GARDINER: I make the same objection as before, my Lord.

102

MILMO: What was the *nature* and the appeal of his performance? – A: Light popular classical music and patter with a degree of amusement and light entertainment.

–Was it in any way a dirty performance? – A: Never at any time.

–Was there anything suggestive about it? – A: Nothing at all,

–Would you describe it as a sexy performance? –A: No, not at all,

–Have you read the article which is complained of in this case? –A: I have.

–You know it has been written of the plaintiff by the defendant, Connor, who calls himself Cassandra. 'He is the summit of sex – the pinnacle of Masculine, Feminine and Neuter. Everything that He, She and It can ever want.' From your observation and experience of the plaintiff both in his performances and privately, can you tell the court whether you have seen anything which would enable a fair minded person to come to that view?

MR JUSTICE SALMON: Mr Milmo, I do not think that will do.

MILMO: My lord, one of the questions which the jury will have to…

JUSTICE SALMON: It is the very question the jury has to decide.

MILMO: What this witness can speak to is this: that he is a person who has experience of theatrical performances and of musicians, that he has seen the plaintiff at such performances and, my lord, subject to the evidence supporting my learned leader's opening, it is going to emerge that the person who wrote this libel has never seen the plaintiff at all, and in those circumstances, my lord, I would submit that it is admissible for this witness to say not whether the words are true or whether they are false, but whether he has seen anything which would warrant a fair minded man writing those words.

MR JUSTICE SALMON: Very well.

MILMO: Mr Melachrino, perhaps you can tell us this. Have you had an opportunity of judging the plaintiff as a musician? – A: I have, yes; I did at all rehearsals and performances.

–Where would you place him in the category of musicians? Is he a good musician, a bad musician or what? – A: He is a very good musician; he is not the greatest in the world, but he is a very, very good one.

GARDINER: That is in your opinion? – A: My personal opinion and the opinion of my orchestra also.

–You know, I expect, most of the musical critics take a different view – it is a matter of opinion, is it not?

BEYFUS: My learned friend cannot really say that unless he is going to call them, with great respect. He is entitled to cross-examine my client on it but unless he is going to call these critics he is not entitled to put to the witness they think he is not a good musician, in my humble submission, at any rate.

MR JUSTICE SALMON: I shall not stop it.

GARDINER: Did you see *For Amusement Only*, a review which was on for a year and three-quarters at the Apollo? – A: No, I am afraid I did not.

–What newspapers do you read, Mr Melachrino? –A. Pretty well all of them. I do not read all of them every day, but I keep in touch with most of them because in my profession I have to.

–It is quite right to say, is it not, and I have never suggested anything to the contrary, that Mr Liberace is not a blue comedian, does not tell dirty jokes, that is right, is it not? – A: In my experience he does not do that.

–Are wriggling and winking and arm waving ordinarily regarded as musical accomplishments? – A: Not in the pure sense of the word, no.

–Did you see his television performances? – A: I did, yes.

–Would it be right to say that so far as he has sex appeal he used it quite properly in his television performance? – A: I would not say sex appeal; I would say charm.

Miss Dail Betty Ambler of Crowborough Sussex said she was an authoress, script writer and journalist who had written about 25 thrillers and the dialogue for an Errol Flynn film in 1949. In 1956 she did some freelance journalism for *Picture Post* and was commissioned by *The People* to do a series of articles on Liberace which necessitated seeing him on a number of occasions. *Picture Post* had commissioned an article on Cassandra for a series on famous people and their pets, and in October 1956, four days after the writ had been issued, she had gone to his home in Henley on Thames with a photographer to interview him about his cat. She had written up her notes of the conversation on her way back on the train.

BEYFUS: First of all, what was the subject matter of the conversation? – A: I had to do a story on the cat, and after that Mr Connor brought up the subject of the writ.

–Which had been issued against him by Mr Liberace? – A: Yes. He was laughing about it really, and seemed to take it very lightly. He said: 'This is going to be quite a bit of fun.' I said, 'I cannot think how it is going to be fun. I do not see how it can be anything but a libel.' He said: 'Of course it is libel, and he will take a lot of money out of us.' I said it certainly was a libel, all the words of it, and he said, No; it was really in the phrase 'He, She or It'. It was in that phrase.

The witness was allowed to consult her notes, then continued: …I said, 'If it was a libel, why did you write it and why did they print it?' and he said: 'They think it will be worth it for a week's publicity.'

BEYFUS: Did he go on to say anything else? – A: Yes. He said: 'I do not know who will look the bigger buffoon in the witness box, he or me.'

–How did it go on? – A: That being the case I think I asked him how on earth it could be defended, and he said 'It cannot be defended, but the lawyers are looking up everything which has been written about him to see

104

if this line has been taken many times before.' I think it was at that point that he made a telephone call to London, I think it was to his secretary, for some photostats of an article which had appeared, written by a man called Beeby. It was the article Mr Cassandra had written, and it had been reproduced by this man Beeby in a Nevada paper.

–At any rate, he telephoned to his secretary about that. Then how did it go on? – A: The other thing was about the jury.

–What did he say about the jury? – A: He said, 'We can alter the jury because men do not like him. So we will make sure there are only men on the jury.'

–Did you say anything in answer to that? – A: Yes, I said I thought that could cut both ways... If there was an objection on one side, there probably could be on the other, but he did not comment on that. I also asked him at this time if he'd ever met Mr Liberace, and he said 'No'.

–Was anything said about any ex-employee? – A: Oh, yes. That was at the time of the lawyer business. He was saying about the lawyers looking up what had been written about him before, and he said there was also a man who worked for Mr Liberace and had left with a flea in his ear, and they were trying to contact him to see if he would be of some assistance.

–Then did Mrs Connor come in? – A: Yes. She heard the comment on it, and she said 'Liberace will like it anyway as long as it is publicity. He is so vain.' I said 'Have you met him?', and she said 'No'.

Cross-examined by Mr Gardiner, Miss Ambler said on Wednesday, October 10 she had been in Winifred Atwell's dressing room at the Palladium with Liberace enjoying an after-show drink. She did not remember which other reporters were present and said she did not know Patrick Doncaster of the *Mirror*.

–Had you been to see the show with Mr Liberace? –A: Yes.

–Were you the only person who accompanied him in his car to Leicester? – A: No. I think there was always the dresser with us.

–Did you go with him to Leicester? – A: There were so many places, Sheffield, Manchester, Dublin. I cannot remember.

–You went to most places with him? – A: I cannot remember whether it was Leicester.

–When you said you were in contact with him a great deal, what period would that cover? – A: Pretty well from when I met him on the night of the first press reception and went back to his hotel with him, when the arrangements for the articles were fixed up, and we went to the Café de Paris after that, and I think I left him about four that morning. I saw him early the following morning, and from that time on it went rather like that.

–You were with him practically the whole of every day? – A: Pretty well every day.

–After the taking of one or two photographs, Mr Liberace said 'Let us have one for Cassandra'? – A: I cannot remember that, I doubt it.

–Did you then say 'If Randolph Churchill can get £5,000 from *The People*, Mr Liberace can get something from the *Mirror* – I know the *Mirror* has a million'? – A: I never said anything like that, and never would... It is an extraordinary thing to say, trying to get someone involved in a libel suit.

–Are you sure you did not say that? – A: I am absolutely certain I never said anything like that.

–Do you remember Mr Doncaster asking Mr Liberace 'Are you going to sue us?' and Mr Liberace saying he was not? – A: I do not remember this conversation at all.

–Did you say 'Why don't you ask Cassandra to lunch?' – A: No, I cannot remember that.

–You cannot remember that at all? – A: No.

–When you went – I am afraid there is a very serious conflict of evidence here – to see Mr Connor at his house, I suggest in the first place that it was not October; it was November. – A: [After a short pause] I thought it was October, but I cannot remember. It certainly was when Mr Liberace was away in Rome.

–Was it about eleven in the morning? – A: Yes.

–Had you rung him up, given your name as Miss Ambler, and asked whether you could go and interview him about his cats? – A: No. I never rang him at all. It was all arranged by *Picture Post*.

–You say it was arranged by *Picture Post*? – A: Certainly. I had to go into the office to collect my railway ticket, and meet the photographer.

–His recollection was that you rang him up? – A: I did not have to ring him; it was all arranged.

–Had you ever met him before? – A: No, never.

Miss Ambler said she had arrived about 11am with a photographer, Mr McGhee; Mrs Connor invited them into the sitting room and they sat down and talked about the family cat.

–Did Mr Connor suggest that he might write an article, What he thought of the cat, and another article, What the cat thought of him?... You said you thought it was rather a good idea. – A: Yes.

–Then, first of all, the cat had to be photographed... The cat objected to being photographed... Decided to go upstairs... Then Mr Connor and the photographer went upstairs. – A: Yes.

–And, I think, in fact photographs were taken and published in *Picture Post*, showing him trying to find the cat upstairs. – A: It went under the bed.

–Did you say to Mrs Connor that you had met Liberace at a party, and she thinks you said 'In Winifred Atwell's dressing room'? – A: No. I did

106

not discuss Liberace until the question came up from Mr Connor. We were talking about cats.

–What I suggest to you is that it was you who first mentioned Liberace. – A: No.

–Did you see him when he came back from Rome? A: Yes.

–You knew a writ had been issued against Mr Connor. – A: Yes.

–Was the article about the cats an excuse... An excuse to go and see Mr Connor? – A: I did not arrange to do this. *Picture Post* wanted me to go and see him.

–Did you say to Mrs Connor that you had met Liberace at a party? – A: No, I never mentioned Mr Liberace to anyone. It came from Mr Connor.

–At the party – I am not suggesting it was true – did you tell Mrs Connor that Liberace had asked 'Who is this guy Cassandra? Is he one of those?' and there being general laughter, and did Mrs Connor then say 'What a ridiculous thing to say'? – A: No. This conversation I do not think took place. I cannot remember any of it at all. We did not discuss Liberace until Mr Connor brought up the question.

–I suggest it was you who in fact brought it up. – A: No.

–After some general conversation about the action or saying it would be a sensation – I am suggesting Mr and Mrs Connor seem quite clear in this recollection – you said – they cannot remember your exact words – that you had met Liberace quite recently at a party, as though you were a mere acquaintance who had just met him once. – A: It was never discussed. Mr Connor brought up the question first, started talking about the action, and after that that was when it was discussed, and Liberace...

–You never mentioned Liberace? – A: No, I was there to see him about his cat.

–Did he say there would be two buffoons in the box, and the jury would have to decide which was the bigger buffoon? – A: What he said was, 'I do not know who will look the bigger buffoon, him or me.'

–And some reference to a Nevada article – A: Yes.

–That is why I suggest your date must be false. I do not know whether you realise it, but the date of publication in November is the date you have given as the date of the interview. – A: I could be wrong. It is a long time ago.

–It is quite untrue otherwise to say that Mr Connor said any of the things you say he said. – A: No. Mr Connor said exactly what I have said, exactly.

–To a complete stranger? – A: That is how it was.

–Did you say, Miss Ambler... is it Miss Ambler? – A: Yes.

–Your name is Ambler? – A: Yes.

–You described yourself as an authoress? – A: Yes.

107

–Are you the authoress of *The Elusive Husband*? – A: That may have been one of the paper-backed ones. It goes back a long time. I did a lot of paperbacks.

–Very few authors forget what their books are, do they not? – A: Well, I think you will find those people who have done a lot of paper-backed books in a sort of fiction factory style, which I did at the beginning, when one is turning out forty thousand words a week, very soon forget.

–You know that a bookseller in this country was fined for selling that as an obscene book. – A: No, I did not know that.

–Did you not make a statement to the press about it at the time?... Just think... – A: Oh, yes. It is a very long time ago, but I do remember.

MR JUSTICE SALMON: You had forgotten it a moment ago! – A: Completely forgotten it. It goes back to about 1949.

GARDINER: 1950, 1952? – A: Before that.

–1950? – A: Was it 1950? 1949 or 1950.

–I suggest that the date of the conviction was July 27 1950. – A: If you say so, it must be.

–May I assume, as of course I do, that is the only obscene book which you have written, or any book which has been alleged to be obscene? When I asked you whether you were the authoress of *The Elusive Husband* was your answer, that you did not remember, a genuine one? – A: Yes, completely, because one is doing an awful lot of these books. When I mentioned twenty-five thrillers, there were a great deal more coming under different categories, like romances etc. I used to turn out one a week.

–This is the one and only book, is it not, which you have written in which the unfortunate bookseller selling it has been convicted and fined for selling an obscene book – there is no other one? – A: Not as far as I know.

–Surely you would remember that one, would you not? – A: I was not involved in that, was I? Someone else was fined for it.

–You were just the authoress? – A: I was not fined for it.

–I suggest that, when you pretended that you could not remember whether *The Elusive Husband* was among your books, it was not an honest answer. – A: No, it was perfectly honest. I had forgotten.

–...And that your evidence with regard to this conversation with Mr Connor is equally not honest. – A: No.

–Were you trying to give the impression to Mr and Mrs Connor that you had just met Mr Liberace once at a party, when really you were quite inseparable from him throughout the whole of his English visit? – A: I did not bring up Mr Liberace's name. Mr Connor was the first to talk about him.

–Having been with him throughout the remainder of this tour, did you see him again when he came back from Rome? – A: Yes.

108

BEYFUS: You told my lord and the jury that your association with Mr Liberace originated from *The People*? – A: Yes.

–Who paid your expenses in connection with your journeys with Mr Liberace to his various concerts? – A: *The People*.

The witness was finished, no doubt certain in her mind that, whatever her success had been with commissions from the national press, none was ever likely to be forthcoming from the *Daily Mirror*.

Don Fedderson, examined by Beyfus, confirmed that he had been vice president and general manager for a television station in Los Angeles and had seen Liberace perform at the Coronado Hotel in San Diego and been impressed with his performance. He also saw him in Chicago, New York, Los Angeles and Las Vegas, and then approached him to go on television. 'I asked if he could do it as close to the same eminent performance that he did in the night club or the supper club.' He signed him a five year contract at $1,000 a week, increasing to $2,500 a week, which he agreed was very high salary for television.

BEYFUS: What was the result of his first performance? – A: The first night he appeared it was fantastic, and the following weeks it became unbelievable. He went up to a No. 1 show overnight in Los Angeles, which is the television capital of the world... Los Angeles in the United States.

–Apart from performing on your television he has told us that he gave three or four concerts before he appeared at the Hollywood Bowl? – A: Yes. I think the first one was San Diego, California. We were very interested, because we owned him, so to speak, with his contract.

MR JUSTICE SALMON: There was no cross-examination on this.

BEYFUS: That is why I was leading all through. At any rate he gave three concerts, and then he appeared at the Hollywood Bowl... As we heard, in this completely white suit. Did he discuss that with you at the time? – A: Yes, he did. I believe it was in July that he gave the concert. He had appeared within the region there in three concerts, and he asked me what I thought of him wearing completely white tails from head to toe instead of his normal custom at that time, which was the normal black jacket and a white tie. I thought it was an excellent idea.

–It was a complete success? – A: Yes. When he came out it was dazzling. Twenty thousand gave him an ovation. It was showmanship.

–In view of my lord's reminder that there was no cross-examination I want to take this as shortly as I can. Thereafter he wore all fancy dress on a number of performances, and the fancy dress became more and more elaborate as time passed? – A: Yes.

–Is that popular with American audiences? – A: Very popular.

–In the years which followed did you see a very considerable number of his performances... Both live and on television... Did you ever see

109

anything suggestive in any of his performances? Did he do anything suggestive, or say anything suggestive, or sing anything suggestive? – A: No. In America we have a code on television and all of our performers live up to that code. When Liberace began his concert they expected to see him as though he was appearing on television and I have never seen him do anything other than what was OK by the code.

–Did he ever tell any dirty stories, or sing any dirty songs…?

GARDINER: I never suggested that.

BEYFUS: …So far as when you were watching or listening to his performance? – A: Never to my knowledge.

–Did you ever see anything sexy about his performances? – A: No.

–By the way, in the course of the years – I do not think Mr Liberace gave any evidence about this – did he ever win any awards? – A: Yes, from the Academy of Television Arts and Science in 1953 for his performances in 1952. He was voted by the workers, the management and everybody who participates in television to be the most outstanding masculine programme and the most outstanding male personality… So-called Emmys which are comparable with Oscars in motion pictures.

–Did you ever see anything about him or hear anything said by him which could suggest to anybody that he was a homosexual? – A: Most assuredly not.

It was getting towards the close of the court's day. Neville Faulks, for the defendants, may have confused the Los Angeles witness by telling him: 'Mr Gardiner wants to change the bowler to see if we can get a quick wicket before the close of play.'

–Do you still own Mr Liberace? – A: No.

–When did you cease? – A: I left the station and went in business myself. I have a 10% interest in Liberace films, in 117 films.

–You have owned him, and now you only own a very small part of him? – A: By owning him I mean the control of his appearances, not the money.

–You made a lot of money out of him? –A. Yes, but nothing compared with my other income.

–Your original interests were in advertising, were they… It was just a stroke of luck that you happened very intelligently to spot this very brilliant young man… Since then you and he have done jolly well together? – A: Well, I have eight other shows on American television.

–The object, as far as you were concerned, of the alliance between you both was that each of you should fare well financially… And fare well financially you have… You have nothing to say against Liberace, and would not have if I asked you questions for two or three hours? –A: I am not influenced here by money.

110

–The fantastic and unbelievable success which he achieved was one which you perhaps were the only person to have the good sense to foresee, or someone else would have booked him up. – A: Perhaps.

–When he achieved this fantastic and unbelievable success, the first thing which was apparent was that he appealed tremendously to the opposite sex? – A: No; to the family. Our banks in America are perhaps as conservative as your banks. They are very careful whom they sponsor.

–Let me put it in another way. You first saw him in cabaret in a night club... What struck you about him was not his playing like Paderewski but the fact that he projected his personality so amazingly into his audience. – A: He had humour; he played well; he had honesty; he had charm.

–Shall we put it in one word, that he had personality? – A: I think it is a combination of a lot of things which makes any artiste.

–There were matters other than his being a mere virtuoso of the piano... I may have got this wrong, but I think we have heard that it was you who had the inspiration to tell him, when he went on television, to turn right into the instrument. Was it you who did that? – A: Yes, but I would like to explain it. In the early days of television many people were making the mistake of appearing as though they were appearing in front of thousands of people. We felt at our station – we had other stars besides Liberace – that this was an intimate moment, that the people at home were being appealed to as though they were in their home, and I suggested to him that he sang to one home, to one person rather than to millions of people.

–Excellent advice, which he took, and that advice being taken did it make a difference to the acceptability of his programme? – A: Well, many things were the culmination of his success.

–As a result you got fan mail from all over the country... It is right to say that in addition to women he had great numbers of men who came to his concerts at the Hollywood Bowl? – A: Yes, and children.

–We can say of him quite fairly that he was a person who attracted all kinds of human beings of whatever sort? – A: Yes. He had a very, very great honesty, a kindness which came...

–A sort of pied piper, I mean? – A: No.

–Is that offensive? I did not mean it like that. Someone who had such charm that anybody was going to be attracted to them, all sorts and kinds of all ages and genders? – A: He had, I think, a family appeal.

At the end of that evidence, with the wicket still standing, the judge asked counsel whether the jury were going to see any of the TV performances they were hearing so much about. Beyfus told him they were still working out the practicalities.

111

Gardiner suggested that, if a number of different films were available, each side could perhaps choose two half-hour films to show. The judge told them they should be able to agree on a procedure, and if not they should bring it up with him later. So saying, he adjourned for the day.

Bring me a grand piano

Word had got out as, somehow, it always does, that there would be another all-star line up at Court Number Four on the third day. Liberace, his evidence finished, would of course be present, even if not actually performing. Cicely Courtneidge – actress wife of light comedy film and theatre star Jack Hulbert – was on the list. Bob Monkhouse, popular comedian, actor and script-writer, would be making an appearance. Cabaret and film star Helene Cordet would be appearing. Mantovani, leader of the 'cascading string' orchestra consisting mainly of violins, who featured regularly on television, had been booked. So had a reputedly Perry Mason-style hot-shot lawyer from Hollywood. And there was a strong chance that Cassandra himself would be in the witness box and facing gruelling questioning from Beyfus before the day was out.

Mounted police were again on hand to control the pavement gawpers, and two cars collided in The Strand as their drivers craned their necks to watch the famous names arriving.

The hard wooden seats of the public gallery were packed again. Apart from the people actually employed in the proceedings, the only person guaranteed a seat was the judge's wife, Jeanie, who would be present, sitting in an upholstered chair beside her husband on the bench every day, and who said later that she 'would not have missed a moment of it, for anything.'

Purely as a matter of form, Mr Milmo said to the witness sworn in as Mrs Cicely Hulbert: 'The court takes judicial note of very little, but are you Cicely Courtneidge?' – I am.

– I do not think I will ask you anything more about your theatrical career, except this: Are you now appearing in the lead in *Fool's Paradise* at the Apollo Theatre? – A: Yes, I am.

She said she had seen performances given by the plaintiff, Liberace, and had seen nothing in them that could be described as 'dirty' and nothing that was 'suggestive'. Over the years she had seen his shows she had seen nothing that amounted to a 'sexy performance' nor anything 'making an appeal to sex'.

That was all Milmo had to ask.

Faulks asked whether she had seen the revue, *For Amusement Only*, including Jimmy Thompson's 'skit' on Liberace. He was relieved that she had. He was keen to get a witness to admit that, because it had run for 21 months, so many people must have seen it that somebody, surely, would

113

have mentioned it to Liberace; and yet the plaintiff had still appeared on chummy terms with a man who, far more blatantly than the defendants, had implied that his stage and TV shows had homosexual overtones.

–I suppose there were not many people in the theatrical world in London who did not see that skit? –A: I would not know that.

She could not remember a 'disparaging' song. She merely remembered a skit about Liberace, but could not remember whether it was flattering or unflattering: 'It was a burlesque,' she said. She didn't think being reminded of the words would mean anything after all this time. She remembered the sketch had been a big success but was unaware it had been on television. She didn't know whether 'a great number of people' would have seen it. Even if the show ran for a long time, she had no way of knowing whether the theatre had been full. She had not seen the performance at the Festival Hall, so she could not say whether she agreed with the criticisms of it.

John Jacobs, a practising lawyer in Hollywood, told the court he had been the plaintiff's lawyer and business manager since 1949.

He told Milmo his client and the Liberace company had made nothing from the two publications, *Liberace* and *The Liberace Story* or from the serialisation of one of the books in *TV Mirror*.

GARDINER: You do not agree with Mr Liberace, apparently, that when he gave people authority to publish things of this sort, he received part of the proceeds? – A: In this article particularly they wanted to write the thing in the first person, and insisted upon it. Because Mr Liberace did not have the time to write it himself, they wrote it over in this country, and we had a very difficult time because we wanted to approve the article, but we could not get it back from them. The fact of the matter is that it almost got into the question of a law suit over it, but we did not receive one cent.

–It was published and advertised as being a true story? – A: It was so published.

–'The following story of my life, written by my friend Anton Burney… is accurate in every detail', and it purports to be signed by him? – A: I heard his testimony, and it was quite accurate.

–This was being put out on his authority? – A: This was put out because he was coming over here. Mr Liberace did not have time to read it and approve of it, and it was done, one of those hectic things, to get it over here; Mr Liberace did give implied authority.

–Are you familiar with his life, written by a gentleman called, I think, Whitehead? – A: Just to the effect that we did not receive any money. I am familiar that it was done.

114

–It was authorised? – A: This is my recollection; I have really gone through my files. It was more or less authorised by George Liberace, Lee's brother, and by Seymour Heller, his then personal manager.

–Without asking for any royalty from it? – A: It would not have been my policy, not to have asked for any royalty, I can assure you.

–Do you know… just think… one way or the other whether any royalty was obtained for it? – A: I would say that approximately three to four million dollars came through my books for Mr Liberace and the corporation during the time I have represented him; and I was unable to find one penny to him on this story… I have been looking for the past year, since I was over here last year...

–Many things in it are untrue? – A: There are a lot of things which are grossly exaggerated, as they always are in this kind of paper.

–Is any step being taken to stop the continued sale of this publication, with his signature 'Sincerely yours, Liberace', to the British public for money? – A: No stop by me.

The next witness, Mrs Helene Boisot, said she was professionally known as Helene Cordet and was owner of a club called the Maison de France in Hamilton Place, where Liberace held a press reception on his arrival in England in September 1956.

Milmo asked how long the reception had lasted. – 'It started about four o'clock in the afternoon. First of all, may I say that I went up to Southampton to meet Mr Liberace because the reception was being given in our restaurant. I saw him facing the cameras and the people there. It seems he was on the go since seven in the morning. We got to London about two o'clock where he was again faced with cameras and a lot of people. He then went to his hotel to change. He was in the restaurant at four o'clock. He had an enormous crowd of photographers, to start with, falling over each other, taking pictures of him; and after that the press came, and they started firing questions to him, which he answered one after the other without faltering, right to, it must have been, about eight or nine o'clock in the evening, when it finished. Even then he stayed on, and more people came and worried him for autographs, and I never saw him falter once.'

She said she had seen his shows on stage, on TV and at the Festival Hall.

–Would you describe it as being a sexy show at any time? – A: No.

–Was there anything suggestive at any time? – A: Certainly not.

GARDINER: Is it right that you had the plate glass doors taken off for the occasion at your restaurant... You knew a fair crowd of women would be there? – A: There was an enormous crowd – not only women, everything; children, full of children.

–Men, women and children –A: Yes.

–Because Mr Liberace has a universal appeal? A: He must have, if an artiste is popular.

–Miss Cordet, I am sure you would be the first to agree that, if artistes have sex appeal, they are entitled to use it? – A: Well, I think they are entitled to use it to a certain point, if they have, but I do not think he ever does it.

–If you are singing a love song there is no reason why you should not use what sex appeal you have got, obviously? –A: I see a lot of this winking on television.

–Have you seen some of his television films... Do you remember the one in which he sings *I'm in the mood for love*, with a tall, fair girl who looks longingly at him? It is quite a well-known song, is it not? I forget whether it is one of the old Berlin songs. – A: I heard it very often, I did not see it. I cannot recall it.

–There is nothing wrong, is there, in an artiste who has got sex appeal putting all the sex appeal he has got into the song? – A: There is nothing wrong in having some sex appeal come over.

–Different people are visited with different quantities. – A: Yes, I agree.

–You went to the Festival Hall performance... Did you read any of the notices about it? ... You probably remember that, rightly or wrongly, it got unfortunate notices. – A: I was there; it was very successful.

–I do not know what paper you read. Do you read *The Daily Telegraph*? – A: I read them all.

–Would it be right to say that there was shrieking, that hysterical adulation and no less hysterical distaste have quite obscured his qualities by now? Would you agree with that? – A: Yes. It did not impress me much because I see on television shows where this shrieking continues every week for different performers. It did not impress me when I heard this shrieking. I have heard it before.

–You probably would not agree with the view that the voice cannot be judged with the use of a microphone, because practically nobody living now can sing without a microphone? – A: Well, I cannot. It is not the voice.

–We have had the great pleasure of seeing you many times on television... Perhaps you can tell me this: are two of the television times which have the largest viewing public *Sunday Night at the London Palladium* and *Chelsea at Nine*? – A: Well, I watch them, yes.

–Are they regarded as about the top spots from the point of view of the number of viewing audience on television? – A: I have read that it is so.

–Did you see in London the revue *For Amusement Only*, either at the theatre or on television? – A: I did not.

116

Robert Alan – Bob – Monkhouse told the court he had been a professional theatrical performer for about 12 years and on the day of Liberace's arrival at Waterloo station had gone there with the official interviewer from Associated Television to greet him and help with the commentary and interview which was to be televised over their network that morning.

BEYFUS: It is common ground that there was a very large crowd, a very considerable hullabaloo and so forth? – A: Yes, it was a tremendous reception.

–Have you been present at Waterloo Station or other stations when other well-known entertainers have arrived? – A: I would say only one was comparable, and that was outside my experience. It happened before I was born, but I have seen a newsreel of Charlie Chaplin's reception at Waterloo Station. That I believe was comparable, I do not know whether it is going to be suggested that he depended on his sex appeal or not!

–Were you present when Mr John Ray arrived? – A: I was present when there was a demonstration in his favour... Outside the London Palladium.

–Were there considerable scenes on that occasion? – A: Yes quite impressive; a little depressing.

–I think actually at the time Mr Liberace arrived you were performing at the Savoy Hotel... In the cabaret... And one of the things which you were doing was to give an impression of Mr Liberace himself. – A: It was because of this impression which I had given in the theatre and on television that I was associated with Liberace, and I was therefore asked to greet him at Waterloo.

–At some stage or other, after he arrived, did you discuss with him the impression which you were giving? – A: It was a part of the cabaret act which I was doing at the Savoy at that time, and Liberace was in the audience two nights after he arrived, and saw the impression of him which I gave, which was exactly the same as I had been doing on television.

–Did you later discuss it with him? – A: He invited me to his table after he had seen the act. He was extremely complimentary about it. He made several suggestions to improve the satire. Some of them I thought were too generous. I wanted my impression of him to be in the nature of a purely satirical act.

–I do not want to go into detail. He endeavoured to be helpful to you in that respect? – A: Enormously helpful.

–Although a satire, I suppose it poked at least gentle fun at him. – A: Yes, it was a fairly broad burlesque.

–You have seen his performances on television... in cabaret, Café de Paris and at the Royal Albert Hall... In your opinion was there ever anything suggestive about his performances? – A: Suggestive of what?

–Suggestive of impropriety in any sort of way. – A: Good heavens, no.

117

−Was there anything improper about his performance... Was there anything which you would call sexy, designed to stimulate the sexual appetite, anything of that sort? − A: Not with that definition.

FAULKS: When you say 'Not with that definition', what exactly do you mean? − A: I mean that any artiste with reasonably good looks, who is masculine, will give an entertainment which is not necessarily sexy, but we know that he is the male sex and so he is bound to get more fan letters from girls than he does from men.

−That is exactly what I thought you meant. If you are a really able artiste and happen at the same time to be physically attractive your performance will attract a good deal of sexual interest from your audience irrespective of whether you are trying to stimulate it or not? − A: Yes, to the extent of Charlie Drake as well as Liberace.

−Do I gather from what you say that when the newspapers say that Mr Liberace had the biggest reception since Charlie Chaplin arrived, at the same station, Waterloo, on September 12 1921, you at any rate would not quarrel with that statement? − A: Indeed, I would not,

−In fact you would think it was pretty accurate? − A: I would imagine so, although I have not had the opportunity of seeing other receptions afforded to American artistes arriving at Waterloo Station.

−I think we all agree, because it has been conceded several times by Mr Gardiner but the plaintiff has found it necessary to call about seven witnesses to say it, that Mr Liberace is not what you call a 'blue' artiste; he is not a vulgar man who deals in smutty jokes or anything of that sort? − A: No.

−I am afraid I do not understand those theatrical technical adjectives. When you say that you give a fairly broad burlesque of Mr Liberace, what does 'broad' mean? − A: It is not an intimate satire. This is a burlesque which can be offered on the stage of a variety theatre as distinct from an intimate revue theatre.

−It would go down better at the Penge Empire than it would... − A: I wish it could. Unfortunately the Penge Empire has closed down. Let us say it was more successful at the Winter Gardens Theatre, Blackpool, than I would have expected it to be at the Criterion Theatre, Piccadilly Circus.

−I was going to ask you whether you could draw a distinction between the fairly broad burlesque of which you are speaking, and the burlesque which Mr Jimmy Thompson put on in the Apollo Theatre in *For Amusement Only*. − A: I would draw the widest possible line between the two burlesques.

−You did see it so that you are able to draw that line? − A: Yes; I saw the item in which he burlesqued Liberace; I did not see the whole show.

118

–You have been here all the morning... You heard me rather unsuccessfully attempt to persuade Miss Courtneidge that, if a play ran for a year and three-quarters, it would be reasonable to assume that a lot of people had seen it? – A: I did miss that testimony

–Let me put it to you and see if I can strike virgin soil... Would you agree with me that, if a play ran for a year and three-quarters, it is reasonable to assume that a great many people have seen it? – A: The public goes to theatres and they see television.

–But still pressing pathetically in the hope of an answer, you would agree that if a play has run for a year and three-quarters it is a reasonable deduction that a lot of people had seen it? – A: I would not know... certainly more people than if it had run for a year and less people than if it had run for two years.

–What was put to me was, 'Oh, no, maybe a backer wanted to keep it on'. That is a possibility, but a fairly remote one, is it not? – A: Some shows do run half empty. Some programme productions draw a line and say this is the lowest figure at which we can budget. They can run with half empty theatres.

–You know about these things, and I do not, but when you say a show runs half empty is it not the practise to 'paper' it? Do you not give a lot of free tickets, commonly known as 'paper'? – A: That depends on the policy of the management. They may feel that it will get around the town that you can get in for nothing, and that will harm the show more.

–It is always difficult to take on an entertainer! –A: It is quite tricky from the legal side too!

–You are very kind. Mr Monkhouse, is it not the fact that members of the theatrical profession can generally get in to any theatre? –A: Oh, yes. That is often possible, provided the theatre is not doing exceptional business.

–Would it not be reasonable for me to suggest that, when *For Amusement Only* ran for a year and three quarters there can have been very few members of the theatrical profession who had not had an opportunity of getting in there? – A: Opportunity, perhaps. Most members of the theatrical profession are out of London. That seems very odd... For the legitimate theatre, yes, in London, I would say they would have had the opportunity, unless they were working.

–Shall we just come to some agreement? During the year and three-quarters that it ran it will be reasonable to assume that all the members of the theatrical profession in London had the opportunity of seeing it? – A: They probably had the opportunity.

–It would be more than surprising if the terms of this satire sung by Mr Thompson about Mr Liberace had not come to Liberace's notice? – A: Oh no. I would not think he would have heard of them... There are an enormous number of shows running in London, as there are in most major

119

cities. An enormous number of jokes are made on every topical subject, and Liberace is a topical subject, and has been since he achieved fame, and it would be quite impossible for him, I imagine, to read all the jokes, all the burlesques and all the lyrics written and performed about him.

–Do you know any other performance about him, besides yours and Mr Thompson? – A: I have seen a great many burlesques. Harry Jacobson does one of the best I have seen. Victor Borge does it rather well, I think, too.

–In this country? – A: Yes, he performed at the Palace Theatre. He gave a most amusing moment in his impression of Liberace, to whom he paid tribute.

–Members of the theatrical profession who may have been to the Apollo Theatre to see *For Amusement Only* would not be limited to those who were resting, necessarily? – A: No.

–The words of this particular skit by Mr Thompson did come to your attention, so that you do draw this tremendous dividing line? –A: I do, indeed.

–It is helpful and interesting, because I put to Miss Courtneidge that it was not a favourable burlesque of Mr Liberace, and she would not have it. She said that it was a burlesque. Do you take the view, having heard Mr Thompson, that it was unkind? – A: Ill-judged by the writer. I thought that Mr Thompson's performance elevated this material to a point where it was entertaining. Reading it coldly, I think it is a fairly careless piece of revue writing, not up to the standard of the rest of the material in the show.

–It would not be fair to read it coldly; it has got to be judged in... – A: It was written for the performance.

–After dinner at the Apollo Theatre one is perhaps in a different frame of mind from 11.15am in Queen's Bench Division, Court IV? – A: Very true.

–Looking at that lyric in the Apollo Theatre background, you would say it was ill-judged? – A: Yes. If you are going to write a burlesque piece you would put it on some comedy basis. My burlesque of Liberace was based on an exaggeration of certain characteristics. For instance, if I were doing a burlesque of Charlie Chaplin I would steal his props – the bowler hat and cane. In my burlesque of Liberace I would use a grand piano, wavy hair and include a reference to his Ma, because those are his theatrical props.

–I do not know if my Lord will allow it, because one must not use the court for advertising, but could you give us a few seconds of your burlesque so that we can see what you mean? – A: If you would undertake to bring in a grand piano, I would be delighted. [Laughter.]

MR JUSTICE SALMON: This is the Queen's Bench... [Laughter.]

FAULKS: I was only hoping so that the jury might follow what particular effects of Mr Liberace it had been found necessary to exaggerate. Perhaps you can tell us, Mr Monkhouse... The wink, did you do that? – A: Oh, yes, indeed, in the same way that, if I was doing Charles Laughton, I would do Captain Bligh, throw out my belly and purse my lips.

–Shall we stick to Liberace... What else, besides the wink, did you find it necessary to imitate? – A: I used candelabra; I used a grand piano; I used the music associated with Liberace's song, *I'll be seeing you in all the old familiar places*, and also his opening signature tune...

–*I do not care, so long as you care for me*... You did that. I expect you did that in a rather special voice? – A: Yes, indeed I did.

–That was a singing voice. We cannot have that here. You could not convey the effect by just saying it to us? – A: Yes, I think I could.

FAULKS: If that is permissible.

MR JUSTICE SALMON: Yes.

FAULKS: Mr Monkhouse, will you try? – A: Well, sir, the opening is finished. Then I would obviously give an impression of Liberace, which would be [Giving an impression of his speech] '*Thank you, ladies and gentlemen. Thank you very much indeed*'. This is a crude imitation; I am not an impressionist. I would then proceed with a short line of...

–I was hoping you would just tell us – I am sorry to spoil the show! – how you said *I don't care so long as you care for me*, his signature tune? – A: It is very long ago. Excuse me while I try it out myself.

–If you cannot remember we must not prolong the matter. – A: Forgive me for just taking a little time. I can assure you it was quite harmless.

–I have no doubt it was harmless; I was admiring you. What I am trying to do is give the jury an idea of what particular tricks of one expert entertainer strike another expert entertainer, that is all. – A: Forgive me; I failed to take your point.

–I am not suggesting you were singing bawdy songs or anything like that. – A: This was different from a performance given in an intimate revue... I was giving a performance which was calculated to be amusing to those who had seen Liberace and liked him, but not amusing to those who had seen Liberace and disliked him.

–That is fair enough. That is an excellent summary. This ill-judged script, including the words:

> But my fan mail is really tremendous;
> it's growing so fast my head whirls;
> I get more and more; they propose by the score;
> and at least one or two are from girls...

...is on the 'blue' side, is it not?... By that technical expression I do not mean anything to do with the Conservative Party! What I mean is something that is vulgar – right?... One can go on with this, ending with those rather odd words: 'When Momma and I wear our mink coats, Oh my, to tell us apart takes the vet'. That is the same point, is it not? – A: It is the same old point.

–At that point, which does make a suggestion of you know what, which has been played at the Apollo Theatre for a year and three-quarters, and on television, there cannot have been a soul in the British entertainment industry who did not know that allegation was being made, can there? – A: Yes there could.

–Not very many. Perhaps someone who had been in the Carlisle Rep. – A: No, quite honestly. The variety side is not interested in the more intimate revue, and the revue side is not interested in variety. Only people who are absolutely enthralled by what takes place in intimate revue are chosen to do revue.

–That is exactly what I wanted. One must not throw names about, but I quite understand that Dame Sybil Thorndyke would not go and see it; but anybody who is on the musical side of the entertainment world would have seen it, and if they had not seen it would have known about it. – A: I should think, after seeing that particular number, if they had known Liberace personally they might well have told him about it; but I do not know anybody who saw that show in London who had any knowledge of Mr Liberace, who had not yet visited this country.

–I will not ask you to give positive evidence about something you know nothing of, but after that long period of a run it must have been common knowledge throughout the musical side of the entertainment industry that that sort of thing was being sung about Mr Liberace by Mr Thompson. – A: I would say that is true, though in my opinion it is unlikely that word of that would reach Liberace himself.

–You give an expression of opinion about which you cannot base anything on fact. Did you see the performance of Mr Thompson's on television? –A. Not on television. This bewilders me. I am told he gave it in *Sunday Night at the London Palladium.*

–No, *Chelsea at Nine*… It was both; I beg your pardon. – A: That lyric that you have just been reading me was performed on *Sunday Night at the London Palladium*?

–I am going to call Mr Thompson in due course. He may tell us a lot of stories. Did you hear it on television? – A: No, I did not. I can believe that part of that lyric would have been passed for *Chelsea at Nine* where censorship is not regarded as vital if the entertainment falls within the standards of the producer; but I cannot believe it was performed on a family programme on Sunday night.

–Whether or not the censorship is adequate on *Chelsea at Nine*, the fact is that *Chelsea at Nine* commands a tremendous public, does it not? – A: No. It is not even in the top ten.

–Have you got the figure with you? –A. Not with me, but I can quote it from memory.

–You know you put your script down in front of you... –A. Not my script; the copy of the statement.
–Did you come up to the terms of your script? That is your proof, is it not, what you were expected to say? –A. Yes, this is a rough draft.
–Did you remember it all? – A: I really have only had time to read it on the car journey from Bournemouth. I do not even remember what it says.
MR JUSTICE SALMON: You should ask Mr Beyfus. [Laughter.] – A: I agreed with everything it said. I was perfectly prepared to read it.

BEYFUS: I do not want to ask anything in re-examination, but there is one thing which I forgot to put in chief. May I put it now, subject to cross-examination? I do not think it arises out of cross-examination... Did you read the article which is complained of? – A: I did, yes.
–Did you come into contact with any consequences of that article to Mr Liberace? Did you have personal experience of any consequences of that article to Mr Liberace?
GARDINER: I object to the question because this can only be designed to lead to an answer 'I heard somebody say something', or words to that effect.
MR JUSTICE SALMON: I am sure Mr Beyfus is not going to ask him whether he heard somebody say anything. I do not know what is coming.
BEYFUS: The answer to that question is either 'Yes' or 'No'. [To the witness]: I do not think you did answer it, did you?
MR JUSTICE SALMON: Did you understand it? – A: Yes, I did. The answer is 'Yes'.
BEYFUS: Were those consequences favourable or unfavourable to Mr Liberace? – A: Unfavourable.

Beyfus then told the judge that he had only one other important witness, the musician Mantovani who was travelling up from Bournemouth but had not yet arrived. There were other less important witnesses he could call, he said, but he felt they would be wasting time. Would it be possible to interpose Mr Mantovani at some later stage, when he eventually arrived? Mr Gardiner said he had no objection.
BEYFUS: Subject to that, that is my case.

At the end of the plaintiff's case Gerald Gardiner must have been thinking that his clients' case was looking pretty good. Beyfus had produced only one witness that mattered: Liberace himself. And he appeared welded only to the idea that the simple words 'He, she and it' somehow implied that he was a homosexual. Beyfus had said that, following the Cassandra article, somebody had shouted 'Fairy' and 'Queer' in the concert hall at Sheffield – but if anybody other than Liberace himself had heard that, they had not

123

been brought to court to say so, and Liberace had referred only to the one word, Queer. He had said himself that, since the article appeared, he had continued to top the bill at the most prestigious venues and was about to star that weekend in a Royal Command performance, so he could hardly suggest that his reputation or his career had suffered.

The other witnesses on the plaintiff's side had been basically called to confirm that Liberace's show had not contained any sexually offensive material; but nobody had suggested that it did. Bob Monkhouse, in his brief impersonation, had exaggerated the pianist's smaltzy stage voice, but the jury had heard the real voice in court, and would no doubt have all heard for themselves, anyway, how he spoke when performing. And the witnesses who appeared to have read the offending column had not said they were in any way influenced by it.

Connor would now be able to assure the jury that there was no actual malice in his mind when he wrote the offending article, but merely that he thought the entertainer went over the top with his sugary act, to the extent that it made him feel sick. Beyfus had learnt the art of argument in the debating society at Harrow and honed it in the Oxford Union; Connor was the expert in the pithy phrase, he would be able to hold his own corner.

Thereafter, there would be witnesses to prove that most of what had been quoted in the Cassandra column was true, or at least fair, and that much of it had come from Liberace himself. That left only 'He, She and It,' a phrase that nobody could really take seriously, even if they could understand it.

Gardiner opened, as he felt obliged to do because Beyfus had given the jury one explanation of it, with his own version of the law.

I have at this stage to submit first that the subject-matter of this article is one of public interest, and I apprehend I need not say anything further about that, and secondly that the words complained of are not in their ordinary and natural significance capable of meaning that the plaintiff is a homosexualist. Every plaintiff who brings an action of libel can either complain of the words in their natural and ordinary meaning or can say that they have a hidden meaning known to lawyers as an innuendo.

Order 19, Rule 6, sub-rule (2) says: 'In an action for libel or slander if the plaintiff alleges that the words or matter complained of were used in a defamatory sense other than their ordinary meaning, he shall give particulars of the facts and matters on which he relies in support of such sense.'

From having seen the Statement of Claim, there is no innuendo here alleged. It does not suggest that these words have a hidden meaning that the plaintiff is a homosexualist, and the position, in my submission, is this: where it is being said that there is a hidden meaning it is either because

124

there is some word which is used in some special sense other than its ordinary sense or else there are facts known to some people which would lead them to draw a different meaning from the words than its natural and ordinary meaning.

Your lordship may remember (as indeed my clients do) *Cassidy v. Daily Mirror*, where the *Daily Mirror* photographer at the races, seeing a smartly dressed man and girl, took a photograph, asked their name and was given a name and told 'This is my fiancée'. So there was the photograph of Mr So-and-so with his fiancée; nothing on the face of it defamatory. The *Daily Mirror* were then sued by the gentleman's wife.

[The case, dating back to 1929, may have meant something to lawyers (although it might be difficult for even them to follow the point being made). Mrs Cassidy had claimed that the report suggested she must have been living in sin with her husband, if some other woman was his fiancée. She was awarded damages of £500, even though it was accepted that the newspaper had acted totally innocently. In fact it is a classic case for journalism as a benchmark for inadvertent, out-of-nowhere, unpredictable libel claims.]

But, of course, here that is not said. There is no claim in respect of any re-publication or causation of publication in America. I mention that because at one point the plaintiff said something about some special word – I forget whether it was 'chromium-plated' or 'fruit-flavoured' – having some special meaning in America. If a publication is to be complained of outside this country as resulting from a publication in this country, then, of course, it has to be specially pleaded because it depends to some extent on the foreign law and, of course, there has been no question of that. I would respectfully submit that the question whether these words in their natural and ordinary meaning bear this special meaning now suggested is one upon which the opinion of the jury ought to be taken, and I was not going to ask your lordship to rule on this point at all now. I have merely taken the point as I conceived it my duty to do.

BEYFUS: With regard to the first, I accept that this is a matter of public importance. With regard to the second, I understand my learned friend is not asking that this matter should be withdrawn from the jury, so there is nothing for me to say.

MR JUSTICE SALMON: No. It would obviously be convenient to postpone any ruling until after the jury have given their verdict.

GARDINER: The law might have been that everybody calls any evidence they like and then the jury does whatever it thinks right, and although it may seem to you there is a lot to be said for that, of course, the result would be that nobody would ever know what the law is or whether they were going to be liable or not. So the law has to be rather more precise than that. The law is that if somebody brings an action of libel the initial burden on the plaintiff is a very easy one because all he has got to do is first of all say that the words complained of are defamatory – and there is no question here that the article as a whole is defamatory – secondly that the defendants before the court are the people who published it, and, of course, that it refers to the plaintiff. Then it is for the defendants to consider what their defence is.

There are many situations in which the law gives to a defendant a defence which lawyers call privilege. There are innumerable occasions in life in which, not for the benefit of people who defame others but because it is in the public interest that people should feel free to say what they think, what they say is protected by the law, even if it is defamatory and even if it is untrue. But this, of course, does not apply where something is broadcast to everyone. Another complete defence is: 'What I said was true, and I will prove it to be true'. Except in criminal prosecutions for libel, which are rare in this country, it is always a complete answer to say: 'What I said was true, and I will prove it to be true'. You may say: 'If that is so, why should there be any additional defence, this defence of fair comment?', because, of course, the defence of fair comment means that although what you have said is defamatory and although you are not saying 'it is true, and I will prove it to be true', you nevertheless ought not to have to pay any damages. The answer is that the defence of fair comment is the reason, and the only reason, why there is free speech in this country. It may be that many people do not realise that.

Many people again may think that there is some special right in the newspapers to comment on public affairs. It is not so at all. If the dramatic critic of *The Times* goes to see a play, it may well be, and probably is the case, that he sees about two plays a week. So he has an enormous experience to draw on to compare one play with another. He is probably a considerable student not only of English drama of the days of Shakespeare and restoration actors but of foreign drama or classical Greek drama; but with all that experience he writes his opinion of the plays. If you have never been to a theatre before and know nothing about drama and you go and see a play, when you are in the bus on the way home you are entitled to say at the top of your voice: 'I have just been to see such and such a play. It is the biggest drivel I have ever seen, and I strongly advise everybody not to see it.' If that is what you honestly think, you are entitled to say it, and your position in law is exactly the same as that of the dramatic critic of *The Times*. This is not a thing on which a newspaper has any special rights at all; it is your right and my right and everybody's right in this country to say what we honestly think on any matter of public interest.

If you come to think of it, you will realise that a democracy cannot really work in any other way, because where decisions have to be taken public

126

opinion has to be formed, and public opinion grows out of expression of differences of opinion. That is why there is free speech in this country, not because there is any Act of Parliament which says 'There is to be free speech in England', but because the common law – that is the law as worked out by the judges – has provided, not for the benefit of libellers but in the public interest, that in wide fields anybody is entitled to say what they honestly think. Of course, in some sense they are questions of fact; but within these fields they are treated as matters of opinion.

If you say: 'I think this Chancellor of the Exchequer is the worst Chancellor we have had for 20 years', you are entitled to say it. I suppose in some sense it is a question of fact whether he is or not, and I suppose if he is a politician earning his money by being a politician he may be aggrieved at that; but it does not matter; anybody in this country is entitled to express that opinion if that is their opinion. If they say: 'This is the worst Budget of the last six', there are jolly few people saying that who could face an examination as to what was in all the last six budgets; but it does not matter; you are entitled to say that if you honestly think it. You are not, of course, entitled to do it with malice. If you go and see a play and you think it is a good play, but because you have had a private row with the playwright you slang it in order to get your own back on him, that, of course, is not your honest opinion. You are then doing that, in the eyes of the law, with malice and you can quite properly, of course, no longer rely on that defence.

You will appreciate from what I have said that it is of great public importance, not to newspapers but to all of us, that in these fields of public interest on which opinions differ strongly – religion, politics, art, and particularly, of course, any form of public entertainment – everybody in this country is entitled to say what they think although it may be defamatory and although they do not rely on the defence that it is true and they are going to prove it to be true. The reason is simple enough. Where there are matters of opinion the fact is that honest people hold widely different opinions, and if you could never express an opinion without being liable in damages, unless you could get a jury to say 'This is the opinion we agree with', then nobody could safely say what their opinion was in these fields.

Judicial language is always better than that of counsel. May I just put it in the words of a Lord Chief Justice in a case on a subject on which there was considerable controversy? A man who felt very strongly against contraception made some very strong remarks indeed about a lady who was in favour of it. It is set out in *Gatley* as the classical direction. It is *Stopes v Sutherland*, and it was approved in the House of Lords. This is the way the Lord Chief Justice put it to a jury in that case:

127

What is it that fair comment means? It means this - and I prefer to put it in words which are not my own; I refer to the famous judgment of Lord Esher, Master of the Rolls, in *Merivale v Carson*: 'Every latitude', said Lord Esher, 'must be given to opinion and to prejudice, and then an ordinary set of men with ordinary judgment must say (not whether they agree with it, but) whether any fair man would have made such a comment... Mere exaggeration, or even gross exaggeration, would not make the comment unfair. However wrong the opinion expressed may be in point of truth, or however prejudiced the writer, it may still be within the prescribed limit. The question which the jury must consider is this - would any fair man, however prejudiced he may be, however exaggerated or obstinate his views, have said that which this criticism has said.'

Again, as Mr Justice Bray said in *Regina v Russell*: 'When you come to a question of fair comment you ought to be extremely liberal, and in a matter of this kind - a matter relating to the administration of the licensing laws - you ought to be extremely liberal, because it is a matter on which men's minds are moved, in which people who do know entertain very, very strong opinions, and if they use strong language every allowance should be made in their favour. They must believe what they say, but the question whether they honestly believe it is a question for you to say. If they do believe it, and they are within anything like reasonable bounds, they come within the meaning of fair comment. If comments were made which would appear to you to have been exaggerated, it does not follow that they are not perfectly honest comments.'

That is the end of the quotation. Then he added to the jury:

'That is the kind of maxim which you may apply in considering whether that part of this matter which is comment is fair. Could a fair-minded man, holding a strong view, holding perhaps an obstinate view, holding perhaps a prejudiced view - could a fair-minded man have been capable of writing this? - which, you observe, is a totally different question from the question: Do you agree with what he has said?'

So you see, members of the jury, the question which you have to decide is not in the least whether you agree with Cassandra or not. The sole question is: Was this Cassandra's honest opinion?

Now, the plaintiff has conceded from the start that his performances have excited the greatest controversy to a quite remarkable and extraordinary extent, because here he has had these enormous audiences, this adoring public of all ages and all sexes on the one hand and on the other hand the critics in America and in this country have been almost unanimously hostile. On the one hand you have people saying he has great charm, sex appeal. There is no doubt at all his performances arouse enormous enthusiasm, screams, lipstick on the television set and so on. He plays divinely, he sings divinely and he has a particularly wide appeal. On the other hand you have people to whom his performances are anathema, who

128

cannot stand him, who do not like all this sort of mock humility and his patter and his always introducing his mother and God, sugar and treacle; and nearly all the critics have said substantially the same thing. We have in this country, have we not, more than one pianist, formerly concert pianists, who, for financial reasons no doubt, are now to be found either alone or with bands playing sometimes classical music interspersed with modern music, from *Oklahoma* to *My Fair Lady*, with no similar criticisms of them as artists? I will not mention names, but we have all heard them and everybody would agree that they are beautiful pianists; but, of course, their fame is very small indeed compared with that of the plaintiff, and their earnings are obviously minute compared with those of the plaintiff. Now, why is that? Nobody suggests that that is because they do not play the piano as well, but they are artists who do not make use of sex appeal. There is nothing wrong in that if you are singing as well as playing the piano. They do not bring their mother on the stage. There is not any reference to God at all in their performance. They have not got fine clothes and they have not got this vast publicity build-up. That is the real difference, is it not, between the two? This is a subject on which Cassandra feels very strongly, and as Mr Beyfus told you something about his client, I suppose that I should tell you something about Mr Connor, Cassandra.

He was educated at Albury Primary Secondary School. His father intended him for the Navy, but he failed on an eyesight test and started as a messenger boy at Derry & Toms. Then after three or four jobs he found that he could not help writing, and he got a job with some advertising agents writing advertising material. It was there when he was about 26 that the then managing director of the *Daily Mirror* who had seen some of his material got him to join the *Daily Mirror*. Not long afterwards he started this daily column Cassandra.

He did not choose the name; the editor chose the name. I am not quite sure that I agree altogether with Mr Beyfus's mythology. I think he said that Cassandra prophesied evil. She was a prophetess and a bit on the gloomy side, certainly, but her two specialities were first that she was always right (though Mr Connor I am sure would not claim he was always right) and secondly, which one may hope is equally untrue, that the Gods had put a curse on her as a result of which nobody ever believed what she said. I think she even warned them about the wooden horse, but owing to the curse nobody believed her. From what Mr Beyfus said you might have thought that Mr Connor was hiding himself under some pen name. There are, of course, columns in journalism written under a pen name, some of the articles being written at one time by one person and at another time by another person; but for something over a quarter of a century we have had this daily column. Nobody has ever written under the name Cassandra except Mr Connor. When he has been away, unless he sends material back the column does not appear.

When the war broke out he tried to join the air services, but was excluded because of his eyes. But he got into the Royal Armoured Corps as a private, worked his way up, got a commission and he served in North Africa, Italy, Greece and elsewhere. He was not demobilised, I think, until 1946. He came back again in November 1946, beginning with a rather famous article which began 'As I was saying when I was interrupted...' He has been contributing this daily column ever since except when he has been abroad. I say 'abroad', because he has been a *Daily Mirror* war correspondent in Malaya, the war in Korea, I think in Indonesia, I think he covered the Spanish Civil War before the great war and, of course, he covers the world. He goes to America and other countries.

Now I should tell you something of the materials which were before him when he wrote this article. It may be that some of you have seen one or two of his articles before. If so, you will probably appreciate that he is a very serious man, taking perhaps a slightly gloomy view of life, very conscious of all the cruelties and sufferings of the world which he is anxious to put right, usually standing up for the poor and downtrodden, sometimes praising, sometimes blaming, never being afraid to blame merely because the person in question is in a high position, taking a serious view – as, indeed, he does of this action, naturally enough.

You have heard a good deal of the plaintiff's record. Perhaps I should say with regard to Cassandra, who has written articles, often very trenchant, for over a quarter of a century, that his record is that he has never had a verdict given against him by a judge or jury. There have been four occasions on which the *Daily Mirror* has been involved in actions through what he has written. In two of them I think he was a party and in two he was not. I think a sum of £50 was paid to Sir Oswald Mosley on one occasion. There was an action by a Soho gentleman who gave the action up, and there was an action by a property dealer whose actions have been very much criticised in the press, and he gave his action up. There was one other action which the newspaper settled for £250. You may think, in view of the fact that his style is undoubtedly a trenchant style and that he is not afraid to attack people when he thinks they ought to be attacked, that after 25 years that is a pretty good record. Of course, there are occasions on which he is wrong, naturally, being human. If he finds he has written something and he is wrong, he then writes and says so.

The materials which were before him in this case were these. In 1953 he was in America and it was then that he first heard all about Mr Liberace. The *Daily Mirror* has a New York office and is in touch – I think it is the same office – with the *New York Daily News*. He discussed him with the dramatic critic of the *New York Daily News*, and, as I expect you know, the

130

hub of every newspaper is the library. In the library there is always available everything that has been written in all the papers, not only that paper, about any public figure, and he read everything about Mr Liberace that there then was in the library of the *New York Daily News*. He was in America again in 1954, about three weeks before the Madison Square Gardens concert when everybody was wondering whether Mr Liberace could possibly fill it. So when he got back here naturally enough Mr Connor was interested to read what the papers had had to say about that performance. He is a regular reader of several American papers, both daily papers and *Time*, which is a weekly paper with a very large sale indeed. Indeed, it would be right to say that he spends most of his day reading, as in the case of English newspapers, several of which he reads from cover to cover. In 1955, when he was in America again, he again discussed the plaintiff with American critics, read some more about him and saw two of his television films. As you have heard, they are about half an hour each. He does not, of course, pretend to remember at this date which were the particular songs which he was singing or the particular items which he was playing. When, at the beginning of 1956, the films were shown here, he saw 1½ of them. I say '1½' because he saw one all the way through and as much of another as he could stomach.

Each day he has to choose a particular subject, and the arrival of Mr Liberace in London made it clear that there should be something about him. His original intention in fact was only to write part of that day's article about Mr Liberace, but when he had talked to those who had been to Waterloo, when he had seen the unsubbed material, that is to say the reports put in by the reporters (they are here; they have been produced, of course, to Mr Liberace's solicitors) from which what is actually put in the paper is taken, and when he had talked to press photographers, some of whom had met every visiting American celebrity for over 30 years, he decided to devote the whole of it to it and he then sent for everything that there was in the library. I am certainly not going to trouble you with any of these newspaper cuttings, but you have probably heard enough of them already to observe that, subject to the opening paragraph, which, of course, I am going to deal with, there is not really anything that Mr Connor said from beginning to end that has not been said before by practically all the newspapers.

It is a curious thing. You sometimes get an artist, do you not, where the press critics – and, after all, they are used to seeing innumerable performances and being able to judge – are divided; some critics are in favour of a performer and others do not like his performances so much? The remarkable thing about this is that it is literally true to say: name any newspaper in England and whatever the newspaper is there is very strong criticism of an artist who, on the other hand, there is no doubt has an

131

enormous public following. As you have heard already, the substance of all these criticisms is very much the same. I forget what the *Daily Telegraph* or *Manchester Guardian* called it now; 'technical indifference', or something of that sort. Nobody apparently thinks very much of his piano playing as piano playing. There is a good deal of criticism certainly from the music critics – criticism because he speeds things up and alters them. Indeed, the publication which he himself authorised, you remember, says that if it is complicated he simplifies it; sort of potted classics, which the critics apparently do not like. There are many people, it is evident, who do not like the professional charm. This, of course, is entirely a question of degree, is it not? ... 'Good evening, ladies and gentlemen. It is so nice to see you all. I see when I smile at you, you smile back at me. All I want is to be loved', then his mother and his early days, what his mother did for him, kissing his mother, 'I give my applause to my mother', and then they all clap his mother, and these frequent references to God, make some people feel rather sick. That is the way a lot of people have put it. .

What Mr Connor feels rather strongly is that what he does is to make use of emotions. Ordinary love with his sex appeal there is nothing wrong about at all. I made it perfectly clear to Mr Liberace that nobody was suggesting that that was in any way improper. He is not a blue artist. He does not tell dirty jokes. He does not make suggestive remarks. Nobody has ever suggested that. You have heard some of his criticisms. Mr Connor has in none of these criticisms suggested it. The plaintiff said there were a few double meanings, but nobody has suggested that he is a purveyor of dirt or anything of that sort at all. If he sings a love song, perfectly properly he uses all the sex appeal he has got. But what Mr Connor has felt throughout is that apart from that what he does is to play on the finest of the human emotions to an illegitimate extent.

Mother love is perhaps in a sense the highest form of love because it is completely selfless, and it is, after all, on this love that the future of the world depends. While it is very proper for a man, even if he is an unmarried man of 40, to be fond of his mother, this, in Mr Connor's view, is really exploited by the plaintiff, having his mother on the stage, kissing her, singing to her 'I shall always call you sweetheart', and so forth. In reference whether it is to God or his mother, the human emotions are really exploited.

The paragraph of which the plaintiff particularly complains is the opening paragraph, that he is: 'The summit of sex – the pinnacle of everything that is masculine, feminine and neuter. All that he, she and it can possibly want', and he says that this means that he is a homosexual. The peculiarity of this in the first place is that until Mr Beyfus got up and suggested this the day before yesterday no such suggestion had ever been officially made. I say 'officially', because, as I pointed out to the plaintiff
132

– I do not want any misunderstanding about this – I am not suggesting for a moment that rumour had not reached the *Daily Mirror* that this was what he was going to say; but the extraordinary thing is that the Writ in this action was issued without any letter before action saying 'You published this, and I want you to withdraw it'. The Writ was endorsed with a claim for an injunction; that is to say for an order that the *Daily Mirror* should not repeat what they had said, and, of course, you can apply to at once issue a Writ. No such application was made. They delivered their Statement of Claim. There is not a word in it to suggest that the real complaint is that he is a homosexual.

Of course, there would have been a furore from Mr Liberace if the *Daily Mirror* had suddenly published a statement saying: 'We agree he is not a homosexualist', because the word had never been mentioned at all. But he has never asked them to withdraw it, nor was there any letter from his solicitors all the time this action has been going on saying 'This is my real complaint'. That, you may think, is in itself a very odd thing.

How the whole thing started, we do not quite know, though if the evidence I am going to call is right it was really Miss Ambler who first suggested that he should sue the *Daily Mirror*. As you have heard, after the publication he went very happily as the guest of the *Daily Mirror* on this pub crawl. It is useless, in my submission, to say that he was in some way bound to do that. The suggestion had come from him, not the *Daily Mirror*. When Mr Doncaster was in America Mr Liberace had said that one of the things he would like to see in England was 'some of your English pubs'. Mr Doncaster said when he came over he would see if he could arrange it. There was no obligation on Mr Liberace to do it at all. There he is, a few days after the article has been published, accepting the hospitality of the *Daily Mirror*.

You have heard the evidence about the Jimmy Thompson skit in *For Amusement Only*, and you will consider for yourselves whether you believe the plaintiff in what he says about this, which had been televised before he came here, at all. I think when we get the evidence you will hear that it was because it was so successful on television that it was put into the review. It then ran for a year and three-quarters, and then in April 1958 Mr Liberace comes back, again sees Mr Thompson and again they are photographed together, Mr Thompson sitting at the piano. The plaintiff accepted what I also accept, which was that on the back of the photograph it says that he is watching Mr Thompson doing his impersonation 'and which he will be giving to ITV viewers in a programme called *Chelsea at 9* next Tuesday, April 22.' Mr Liberace has told you he was in this country at that time. He had just finished, I think on April 21, a fortnight's engagement. He has told you he was here till the end of April. He sees Mr Thompson and this photograph is taken a few days before Mr Thompson is going to do it on television. Do you think that at no time at all had he either the curiosity to watch it, or do you think that nobody ever told him what the nature of Mr Thompson's performance was? ...The lady who was engaged in publicity for whoever was presenting him must obviously have known of it, and those who were presenting his performances. He had his own London theatrical agents. He had his own theatrical agents and at the time when this photograph was taken he had got his London solicitors. Do you suppose for one moment that with his London solicitors, with his London theatrical agents, going into people's dressing rooms and all his fan club, he did not know what was going on?

He has told you how all his fan club always rally to his defence when he is attacked, and, as you have heard, the *Daily Mirror* itself received letters which they published, very properly, expressing the hope that Cassandra would fall down dead. They obviously rushed to his defence in England as they do there. Here was this thing first televised in 1956, and then again at this time in 1958, and for a year and three-quarters played in this review. You will have to consider whether it is possible that he did not in fact know what was going on. You will have to judge that, of course, in the light of the whole of his evidence and of the evidence which you heard him give with regard to the publications which are sold for 1/6d or 2/6d. You remember how first of all, when he was asked whether Anton Burney was a friend of his, he said: No, of course he was not; he had never met him. Then, when he realised (because, having heard the plaintiff, you will appreciate how quick-witted he is) that that was an admission which was going to end in difficulties – because to allow a statement which is not true, apparently signed by you, to be sold for money is not an easy position to be in – he then changed his evidence and said; Yes, Mr Burney was a friend of his and the statement was true because he often came on to the platform and said 'Good evening, my friends'; therefore, the fact that he had not met him did not mean he was not his friend. It is in the light of that sort of evidence that you will have to decide whether to accept his evidence or not.

Now, of course, the performances on which, among other things, Mr Connor was commenting cannot really be satisfactorily described in words, and when I have sat down in a few minutes I am going to ask my lord to allow arrangements to be made that you should see some of the performances of the plaintiff which were given not in the Café de Paris after the article was published, and still less anything he is doing during his present tour, but which had been shown at the time. I understand that will be opposed by Mr Beyfus, but that will be a matter for my lord to decide.

If you have a love song to sing, the extent to which you make use of all the sex appeal you have is a thing which can really only be determined by looking at the performance. That is really the only way. Therefore, I

134

express a hope that you will see it. Mr Liberace, it is only right to say, himself said he had no objection, but it may be if we each choose half an hour's worth, so to speak, you would then have a fair range. I have made it quite plain, I hope, that I am not suggesting from beginning to end that there is anything whatever wrong in his using all the sex appeal he has. All that was in Mr Connor's mind was that he has a considerable quantity, that he makes use of it quite legitimately but extremely successfully, and, indeed, in publicity put out in his name there are the stories of the lipstick on the glass and the publication which describes him as the hottest thing on wires, or words to that effect.

Mr Connor also felt rather strongly this, but it may be he is getting old; a good many of us are getting rather old. There used to be a time, though most of you members of the jury are probably too young to remember it, when people could sing without a microphone. If any of the members of the jury are old enough to remember artists like Marie Lloyd and others, they will remember that she did not wear a £2,000 dress, she had no elaborate scenery, she had no fan club, she had no high-pressure American salesmanship; she just walked on the stage, and she depended on herself and her own ability. Today we have seen what a lot of people are quite entitled (because these are all matters of opinion) to regard as a considerable improvement, and that is young men or people of both sexes who cannot sing without a microphone, cannot dance, in comparison with good dancers, cannot act; but they have got a very good photographer and a very good publicity agent. In the case of a girl there may be something peculiar about her vital statistics, but, after all, a very large bust is really just a physical abnormality, is it not? You may have somebody who has no inherent talents, but suddenly their photograph appears in all the papers and everybody begins talking about them. A fan club is laid on (there may be no technical difficulty in laying on a fan club) and everybody feels that this is the person they want to see because this is the person that everybody is talking about.

You may regard that as a great improvement, and it may be a sign of old age that there are some people who feel that it is an undesirable sign of our times that you should have some young man, who is very good looking and may be a very nice chap, but who can only sing with a microphone, cannot really do anything else, and there is this vast publicity build-up, and wherever he goes there are screaming bobby-soxers producing the kind of scream which the *Manchester Guardian* described as being like 40,000 Persian cats having their tails trodden on at the same time. That is not, in the view of some people, a pleasant thing to hear and possibly not a very healthy sign in our society. This was the first occasion really on which we were having the full American treatment.

The people I referred to here may have a good English publicity agent and photographers and so on, and what one might call a rather amateur fan club compared with the really high-pressure American ones; but this is the first time on which an artist was landing and we were going to have the full treatment. The publicity before he arrived had been enormous. You would think from something somebody said that there is a press conference because all the press suddenly decide to go there. You may have thought when Miss Cordet was giving her evidence, perhaps, that all the reporters suddenly said to themselves 'Let's all go along to Maison de France, in case by any chance Mr Liberace should be there'. But you will hear in fact, of course, that there are always what are called press handouts put out by the plaintiff's publicity organisation, as, of course, there are in relation to his present visit. I mention the present visit because those can be produced. By now the others would have been destroyed; there is nothing improper in that. Then you have this special train, the advance publicity, the fan club going down there to meet him and all the hullabaloo, which I am not attacking.

What they do in America is entirely their own affair; but Mr Connor thought, and he may not be alone in this, that the time when those who felt that this phenomena to which I have referred ought not to be extended had come, and that someone ought to say so and say so strongly. You quite appreciate I am not asking you to agree with any single thing that Mr Connor has written in this article at all. You may entirely disagree with the whole of it. Most of it has been said before in America and in this country by innumerable critics, just the same sort of thing, perhaps not put so concisely. That perhaps is why Cassandra is Cassandra.

He had no thought at all of suggesting that the plaintiff was a homosexual, and it was an amazement to him to hear that anybody could possibly think that. Mr Connor will not like my saying this at all, but really when you come to read it, 'Everything that he, she and it can possibly want', is it not in substance one of those things which sounds awfully good when you read it, but really, when you come to analyse it, it does not mean very much? Perhaps that is the art of journalism; I do not know.

He does not know how anybody can get a homosexualist out of this. All Mr Connor is drawing attention to is the fact that he uses his sex appeal and the fact that he is a man who receives adulation from all sections of the population. It is the universality of his appeal. Eventually the plaintiff did agree with that. It took a long time, but when I sat down – and you may all have been very thankful when I did – I sat down because he had agreed with that. How Mr Beyfus is going to go on suggesting that Cassandra obviously meant he was a homosexualist after what his own client said, I do not know. It may not stop him.

May I just remind you of what it was? I reminded him of his own statement about the secret of his success which he made and which was published in the same issue of the *Daily Mirror* as the article complained of. I was suggesting to him that all this 'The pinnacle of Masculine, Feminine and Neuter. Everything that He, She and It can ever want' refers and refers only to the universality of his appeal. I referred him to the article; 'It is in the issue of September 1956, on the front page, in which you sum up for yourself what you describe as the secret of your success', and this was it:

'The secret of my success? It is a very simple thing – everyone in this world wants to be loved and I express that love to my viewers and listeners and they seem to respond to it'. Your viewers and listeners include men, do they not? (A) Yes. (Q) When you said they respond to it, you did not mean that in any improper sense? (A) No, I did not. I was speaking of love, humanity, brotherly love, the love between peoples. That I feel is sadly lacking in this world.'

...That, I suggest, is exactly what Cassandra was obviously referring to when he was describing the universality of his appeal. Then there was a long pause and he said: 'Yes, I believe he was referring to that,' and that is right – that is exactly what he was referring to.

These, of course, are all very much matters of opinion. In my submission it is rather fantastic to say that this reference to the universality of his appeal means that he is a homosexual or that anybody in this country had got such an idea in their heads. You may well think it is much more likely to have come from words which I won't read again, you have heard them read before, in the review, running over a year and three quarters, but Mr Connor knew nothing of it, he had not seen it.

All I say is that if anybody did have any such idea about the plaintiff, 99% of people forget 99% of what they read day after day. Therefore the defence in this case is simply this: some of this is fact; what was said about the reception at Waterloo is fact; what the plaintiff said to the press reporters at the press conference as is set out in the article is fact; but he has in substance agreed he did say those things; the rest are entirely matters of opinion and, in substance, there is nothing which Mr. Connor has said which has not been said in either exactly the same words or in other words by numerous other critics both here and in America, and the plaintiff agrees that the critics both in America and here have been almost unanimous. I will now call the evidence. As my lord has ruled, this is a matter of public interest on which anybody, whether he is Cassandra, or whether he has got anything to do with newspapers or not, who sees a performance of Mr Liberace, is entitled to say afterwards in strong terms, if he feels strongly about it, what he feels about it – it may be exaggerated, but if he honestly believes what he says, if that is his honest opinion, then he is entitled to say it.

I will now call Mr Connor.

But he would not. Gardiner was fully into his stride and knew exactly what he was going to do and say next, but he was interrupted – brilliantly, some might think – by his legal opponent. In addition to being a skilled advocate, Beyfus was an expert tactician. He now stood up.

BEYFUS: Mr Mantovani is now here, my lord.

MR JUSTICE SALMON: It will probably be more convenient to have Mr Mantovani first.

GARDINER: Yes, my lord.

Composer and conductor Annunzio Paolo Mantovani who, like the plaintiff and the pianist Semprini, was internationally known by only his surname, was the next star in the spotlight. Again, his evidence-in-chief was brief and to the point.

He told Beyfus that he had been a professional musician for more than 30 years, had his own orchestra and had appeared on television and in concerts all over Europe and the United States and had seen Liberace perform on stage and on TV.

BEYFUS: How would you describe the nature of his performance? – Well, he is an excellent pianist, a first-class entertainer, and a most charming person.

–Have you ever seen anything sexy or improper about any of his performances... Or anything suggestive in any of his performances? – A: No, never.

That was it. That was the evidence for which Beyfus had interrupted Gardiner in full flow. The defence counsel hoped that he might be able to salvage some benefit from it.

GARDINER: You are speaking as a musician... You sometimes read the papers, I expect... And you have observed, have you not, that as a whole the music critics do not appear to entertain a very high regard of Mr Liberace as a musician... Haven't you noticed that, in general, both in America and in this country? – A: They do not criticise so much his playing as what he does.

The witness was handed the cuttings book and led to an article by Francis Martin, music critic of the *News Chronicle*, headed: 'Enter Liberace, wriggling, winking and wooing. The man who plays in the key of love.

GARDINER: Then do you see Mr Martin says:

> Once in a while Liberace turns from slop songs and hoofing routines to the keyboard classics. No longwinded nonsense for him. When Liberace

138

has finished with it any forty-minute piano concerto looks like the front page of a New York tabloid.

I have been listening to some of his feats on record. As printed, Tchaikovsky's first piano concerto, the popular one in B flat minor, runs to 153 pages. Liberace's version gives thirteen pages of first movement and eleven pages of finale, the two fragments being linked by four bars that belong elsewhere.

Or take the Grieg piano concerto. Of this he throws away two movements, takes the stomach out of a third, re-orchestrates what's left and has the piano playing at one point when it should be resting.

...Have you heard him do that? –A: Yes.

–Beethoven's *Moonlight* sonata is hacked to four minutes, lest American womanhood should yawn. Chopin, like Rachmaninov, becomes a stew of popular keyboard bits with orchestral effects impertinently added.

...Would you agree with that or not? – A: Yes.

–The manner of playing matches the matter. Schumann's *Träumerei*, Liszt's *Liebestraume*, anything, in short, about dreams and amour, drip from his fingers like treacle, with lots of wistful lingerings and, to compensate for these, coy little scurries.

...Do you think that is a fair account or a view which some people may take? – A: In this case is the critic criticising him as a concert pianist or an entertainer?

...As a pianist. – A: He criticises him because he cuts pieces; he is not criticising him as a pianist.

–He is apt to go at loud, double-octave runs like a bull at a gate, pedal down. The lustre candelabra on his outsize grand, one of his innumerable talismans, vibrates sympathetically, although its flames, being electric, give never a wink. The cumulative resonance is as thick, though not as nourishing, as aldermanic soup. His bravura stuff sometimes sounds sketchy or laboured.

...Do you agree with that? –A: I still say Mr Liberace as an entertainer and not as a great concert pianist does extremely well and much better than the average entertainer on the piano. I would like to say as a pianist there are very few who could even do as Mr Liberace does.

–At seven, according to a worshipful biographer, he was told by Paderewski: 'Some day, when I have gone, you will take my place.' Things haven't quite turned out that way. Great pianists are not necessarily great prophets. In the shades Paderewski must be kicking himself. Not that we need worry greatly. Music is not Liberace's true cause. Love is the thing. Mention of it brings that faraway, solemn look into his eyes. 'When I do a show,' he explains, 'I exude Love'... 'I try to sparkle. That is something people like... I shall never be satisfied until I make people happy on an international scale.' What is the worth of international happiness based on a wink, a smile, a hairdo and a cosy voice? Precious little, I should have said. But then, my own line is Music.

139

…What expert critics may think of a particular performance in the musical field is very much a matter of opinion, is it not? – A: Once you classify in what grade and what he is playing.

–He has tried to criticise this man here as though he was playing… – A: As though he was playing at the Festival Hall in front of a classical audience. In that case he is perfectly right to say that, but he was not playing before a classical audience; he was playing to an ordinary audience who would not understand classical music at all.

Beyfus directed the witness to the next page in the book, 'where a favourable notice seems by some accident to have strayed into the defendants' documents'. This cutting was also from the *News Chronicle*: 'A little earlier I had met Mr Coward in the ship's library'. That is Noel Coward. 'Liberace,' he said, 'played for an hour and a half, but it seemed only ten minutes to me.'

GARDINER: Will you read the next paragraph?

BEYFUS: Of course I will: 'Perhaps Mr Coward's delight is explained in part by the fact that Liberace played two Coward numbers, *Zigeuner* and *I'll See You Again.*' Mr Francis Martin says: 'No long-winded nonsense for him. When Liberace has finished with it any forty-minute piano concerto looks like the front page of a New York tabloid.' Mr Liberace has explained that his television performances were confined to 24 minutes… Would it be possible in 24 minutes to give more than extracts from a 40-minute concerto? – A: You cannot do it.

Mantovani was then allowed to leave the witness box and return home to Bournemouth. Gardiner was still unable to continue his opening with the introduction of his star witness, Cassandra. First, there was the on-going matter of the TV performances for the jury's benefit.

GARDINER: In my submission it would be right for the jury to have an opportunity of seeing some of the films which were the subject matter of this article. As I have indicated, Mr Connor cannot remember at this stage which were the precise pieces which were being played because in most cases, as your lordship has said, they are short numbers, short things rather than long ones, and I would submit your lordship should allow the jury to see them and perhaps the right course would be for each party to have a certain length of time, say half an hour, as the case may be, and each party can produce whatever film they think proper.

MR JUSTICE SALMON: This is on the question of fair comment?

GARDINER: Yes.

MR JUSTICE SALMON: Because you are saying that the comment was on the television and other performances of the plaintiff which Mr Connor had seen?

140

GARDINER: Yes. He cannot specify the actual ones because he does not remember them, but where you have got somebody singing a love song whether he uses sex appeal or not, although it is no part of my case there is anything wrong in it, if the jury see them they could judge for themselves whether somebody might honestly take that view.

MR JUSTICE SALMON: That is the point; will it help them to form their judgment as to whether anyone could honestly form the view Mr Connor expressed?

GARDINER: Yes, and the plaintiff, your Lordship will remember, said he had no objection; rather he said he would like them to.

MR JUSTICE SALMON: Yes, he said he did.

GARDINER: If the jury can afford the time.

MR JUSTICE SALMON: How long would it take?

GARDINER: I would suggest about half an hour each. I think they could be made available at almost any time. I hesitate to suggest Friday because the members of the jury have probably made their own arrangements.

MR JUSTICE SALMON: I think probably tomorrow it should take place.

GARDINER: Yes, my Lord, if it is to be done, I should think perhaps sooner rather than later.

MR JUSTICE SALMON: I agree. Mr Beyfus, I do not see how that can possibly hurt your client.

BEYFUS: No, I am not objecting, but I would like it to come after I have cross-examined Mr Connor in the first place, my lord. Although he may not be able to identify the precise television show which he saw he will probably be able to identify when and where, and we may be able to be helpful there because it would be best that the members of the jury should see one which he saw, or a similar one.

MR JUSTICE SALMON: Yes, certainly. I think that is right, Mr Gardiner; the jury shall see these films then as Mr Connor in evidence may be able to help us as to the type of film he did see, so that the jury will be seeing the right type of film.

GARDINER: Yes, my Lord. Then I will now call Mr Connor.

Much as his counsel had outlined it in his opening speech, William Neil Connor told the court he was a journalist employed by Daily Mirror Newspapers Ltd and when he was in London he wrote a column five days a week under the pen name of Cassandra. He was born in 1909, had a general elementary and secondary education and had been rejected by the Royal Navy on account of defective eyesight. He started work as an office boy in Derry and Toms and later became a copywriter in an advertising agency. In 1935, when he was about 26, he was asked by the managing director of the Daily Mirror to join the staff and started writing under the name Cassandra within a matter of days. The pen name had been chosen for him by the editor, Cecil Thomas. He continued writing until the outbreak of war when he volunteered as air crew but was again turned down because of his eyesight. Subsequently he volunteered for the Royal Armoured Corps and enlisted as a trooper. He gained a commission and served in North Africa, Italy and Greece and was discharged in 1946 with the rank of major, after which he returned to the *Daily Mirror*. Apart from writing his column he was an accredited war correspondent of the *Daily Mirror* in Malaya, Korea and the Indonesian war, and under government accreditation had been present at the hydrogen bomb explosion near Christmas Island in 1957. He had also studied the rise of Hitler in Germany 'very closely'.

He had visited strategic air bases in the United States and lectured at Harvard, Columbia University and also at the University of California. He had first visited the US in 1935 and had returned many times since. When he was working abroad the Cassandra column appeared if he sent material for it, but nobody else had ever written under that name except himself.

He said he first heard of Liberace around 1952 or 53. He had discussed the plaintiff with people in New York and read a great deal about him. The *Mirror* kept 'tremendous volumes' of cuttings about people in the public eye and he also read reports from America about what people said about Liberace. He said that for more than 20 years he had read *Time* magazine practically cover to cover. He also had subscriptions to the *New York Herald Tribune*, the *New York Times, Life, Atlantic Monthly*, and a paper called *The Reporter*.

He went to America in 1955 and again discussed Liberace 'with dramatic critics and others qualified to judge'. He watched two of his television films, but had no recollection of what he played or sang. When his films were shown in Britain he saw two more. Again, he could not remember the specific melodies, except that he did remember *Ave Maria* being played.

GARDINER: When ordinarily do you decide what is to be the subject matter of your daily article? – A: I decide after I get to the office in the morning, which is about half-past nine, and then I generally discuss this with my colleagues, to make sure we are not all writing on the same subject, so although the primary decision may be in my mind it may well go on to two o'clock before I have decided and it may be later than two o'clock before I start to write it.

–Which British newspapers do you ordinarily read, if any? – A: I have a fixed routine on this and I will tell you the order in which I read them. I read the *Daily Express* first, then the *Daily Mail*, then the *Manchester Guardian*, then *The Times*, and I read those in the train coming up where I have an unfortunately long journey. When I get to the office I read the *News Chronicle*, the *Daily Herald*, the *Daily Telegraph* and I then look at the *Financial Times*. I only glance at the *Financial Times*.

He had decided to write about Liberace fairly early one morning, about 10.30. He had not intended to devote the whole article to him, but then he saw the accounts and photographs of his arrival at Waterloo. It was the photographer, Mr Howe, who told him it had been the biggest reception since Charlie Chaplin's. He said he had not seen the Ed Murrow interview, but had read reports of it in the English papers.

GARDINER [reading from the cuttings book]: The *Daily Express* says: 'Astonishing broadcast on US television. Liberace links name with...' and then it says who. Then it says:

> The hennaed, perfumed TV entertainer was being interviewed by Edward R Murrow on a coast-to-coast telecast titled *Person to Person*. The paunchy, 35-year old piano thumper (as several critics have labelled him) made his presumptuous and distasteful remarks as he showed millions of televiewers around his garish piano-strewn house in Sherman Oaks, California, near Los Angeles.

...Then it sets out what he said, as we know, at the interview. And says:

> Liberace is famous for his white fur coat, his scent, his sequin-covered suits, and his fetish for pianos. There are 190 real and toy ones in his house... Liberace himself was too busy with other matters to do any explaining.

...Then the *Observer*, one of the papers which has not been mentioned:

> Liberace, in pantoufles, was beyond one's wildest expectations. The highspot came when he made a fairly formal proposal of marriage... He introduced us to his wonder-Mum... He thanked God for her and for America - because only there could the son of a poor first-generation emigrant have got such a break. He ended archly by contradicting the misapprehension that the appeal of his art was restricted to the higher age brackets, the Mums and Aunties. Compulsive he certainly was. I found my ambivalent reaction to him stronger than ever; that night I dreamed of a thrush being chased by a sailing water-moccasin.

Connor said that he had asked the *Daily Mirror* library for all the cuttings and all the comment available on Liberace, and read them all before writing his column.

GARDINER: Was your article your honest opinion of his performance? – A: It was.

–It begins: 'He is the summit of sex – the pinnacle of Masculine, Feminine and Neuter'. Would you tell us what you had in mind when you wrote that? –A: What I had in mind was that by reason of his sex appeal he was the greatest exponent in the show business who had received audiences of world record.

–'Everything that He, She or It can ever want'? – A: That was a reference to the nature of his technique which was designed to apply to the whole community, the whole show.

–Have you read what he had said to the press on that actual morning and which was published in the *Mirror* itself? – A: I have read that.

MR JUSTICE SALMON: Have you seen any of the pictures? – A: I had sent for all the pictures from the art library.

GARDINER: What effect did the plaintiff's performances have on you when you saw them? – A: A feeling of astonishment to begin with and then a feeling of nausea... Because of the flamboyant nature of his appearance, the actual spectacle of the man, and then because of the cloying sickening nature of what he was singing and what he was trying to put across.

–In what respect? It has been referred to by many critics in newspaper articles, but can you explain to the jury in what respect? – A. Cloying? Sickly, over-sentimental with a note of calculated commercialism behind it.

–Had you at any time any intention at all of imputing any homosexuality to him? – A: None at all.

–Had you seen or heard anything about the sketch which had been performed in *For Amusement Only*? – A: I knew nothing about it.

–In relation to your article, as a follow up from the first paragraph, had anything which you said not already been said in several newspapers? – A: No; I think it had been said by most of the papers,

–I want to ask you about these from that point of view because there is a question as to whether you could honestly have believed what you said...

But first, Gardiner suggested to the judge that it might be a good point to adjourn for lunch.

When the trial resumed Beyfus wanted to say something: 'Before my learned friend continues with the witness, my learned friend told your lordship and the members of the jury that not until this case started were the defendants officially notified of the fact that we were alleging that the meaning of these words was that my client was a homosexual. I am told by Mr Helenus Milmo that on several occasions on interlocutory applications before Masters he made that perfectly clear. Of course, Mr Gerald Gardiner was not present on those occasions and therefore it would be the case that he would not know it, at any rate at first hand; but it was made abundantly clear by my learned friend on a number of occasions quite officially on applications before Masters. I thought I ought to tell your lordship and the members of the jury that.'

FAULKS: Perhaps I should say that, of course, I was present on all these interlocutory occasions, and although I have personally no recollection of it I unreservedly accept everything that Mr Milmo says.

Gardiner then continued his examination, directing the witness to another despatch, one [by Donald Zec of the *Daily Mirror*] that had not previously been read:

–On the Queen Mary (shaped like a boat)...

With a song in his heart, a fixed dimpled smile, and fragrantly perfumed with toilet water, Liberace, the flashy Casanova of the keyboard, arrived here today. I doubt if a more extraordinary piece of human cargo has ever been carried on this historic ship.

Liberace greeted me in his flower-decked cabin with a podgy handshake. It was murder on the eyes. From points all over his comfy frame diamond pianos flashed, silver keyboards glinted, two beautiful rows of wide-screen dentistry gleamed, and one brown eye winked.

But wait. His hair was fashioned into silken greying waves and curls. His nails were too genteel for scratching. He wore a violet shirt with white horizontal bars. A flashing diamond and ruby button needed to be dipped for safety. His £125 suit (he called it typically English) was silk tweed with gold thread right through it.

Then, seated next to his dear old Mom, and his brother, George, Liberace spoke. I still can't believe my ears. Listen:

'There is no-one like Liberace. What the people want of me they want from no-one else'... 'I am a missionary. It is an inspiration to know that I am able to reach all the people of the world'... 'I think I have a stabilising effect on family life. Middle-aged women love me because I give them a love that many of them cannot enjoy'... 'I am the answer to the drab realities of life.' He paused to beam his smile around the ship's lounge.

'Sex appeal?' He fluttered his long lashes, purred his dimpled smile full on me, winked at me and said: 'If people notice it I am happy.'

He said he would like to marry. 'Who knows,' he said with a mischievous wriggle of his hips. 'I might meet the right girl in England.' (I've heard this somewhere before.) 'The girl I would like to marry? Her physical attributes must be secondary to her charm and personality.' He said he would like to meet Marilyn Monroe.

Beside him throughout it all his violinist brother George said not a word. He looked pretty drab compared to his piano-happy brother. His cuff links were only half crown size. But they did have violins on them.

At last George had to speak. 'People are surprised when they hear I can talk,' he said excitedly, while Liberace took a three bars breath. But that was as far as he got. Liberace took over the chorus, and his voice, the smile and the dimple remained on throughout the day...

...Then did you also see the next page about his candelabra and so on and his sequins? Then:

...The interview was stage managed in the best candelabra style. His manager said 'I would like Liberace to sit between his mother and George on the other, so that he can be kissed from both sides'.

Connor said he could not identify that despatch specifically, but he had read a lot of messages that day. He was also shown copy submitted by Peter Harris and Angus Hall, two *Daily Mirror* reporters who had been at Waterloo station. One of them quoted a Miss Bacon, founder of the fan club, and Mr Gardiner read it:

–'We have saved for weeks and weeks for this trip - about £10 each. But every penny has been worth it. It is the most exciting moment in our lives. And we are not stopping now. We have tickets for every one of his concerts throughout the country and will get there if we have to hike.'

Another fan, a 15 year old girl, had 'I love Liberace' embroidered across her black sweater. Around her neck she wore a 16-shilling necklace dangling a tiny silver piano. On her wrist she had a gold bracelet with a picture of Liberace on it.

She had stayed away from school - all for Liberace. 'I don't care what happens to me. They can expel me for all I care,' she cried. 'I've met him, touched his hand – it went all through me – that's all that matters.'

A pretty blonde clerk from Islington said: 'My boss thinks I'm ill, so I daren't give my name. If he knew I had gone to see Liberace I would get the sack. Like so many stupid men he doesn't seem to like him very much.'

Then she added: 'But we would never tell Liberace how some of us got to see him. He's very sensitive you know, and it would only hurt and worry him.'

The witness was asked to identify a number of photographs admitted as evidence. He said he remembered seeing some of them but thought he should explain the newspaper process to the court:

'When you are in a newspaper office and the event is being covered you will receive at least 100 photographs, an enormous stack, which are taken by agencies and which are taken by our own particular firm. So when you ask for the photographs you receive certainly, on an occasion like Mr Liberace's arrival, at least 100 photographs; so if I am asked specifically to identify any specific photograph, I am at a slight loss because after a long period like this you cannot. But I can tell you the photographs in which I was interested and which directed the thought and meaning of my article.

'I divide those into two classes. One was the photographs of Mr Liberace and his mother, and Mr Liberace kissing completely unknown strangers through the window of the railway carriage. That interested me greatly. The second was the photographs which were of the crowds outside. I cannot specifically identify the ones about the crowds outside, but I can tell you that I was most interested in them because it seemed to me a form of mass hysteria which had been raised by this particular occasion.'

GARDINER: I think the passage particularly complained of in the article has been picked out at the top and preceded by the words 'Cassandra says'. Did you in fact do that yourself? – A: Normally I do so. There are occasions when I do not. But on this occasion I think that I did, and I take complete responsibility for it.

–Was the picking out of a passage and putting it on top preceded by the words 'Cassandra says' special to this occasion, or is that done every day? – A: Every day.

–I want you to deal with the facts first. The article complained of starts with an account of what you say happened when you were in Berlin a week or ten days before the outbreak of war in 1939. Are the facts there stated true? – A: They are.

–Then there is the arrival at Waterloo. You told us about that. And here are various statements which are said to have been made to press reporters on the Queen Mary, and of course if any of them are in dispute they must be called to tell my lord and the jury what they said. I merely want to ask you questions on the footing as to whether you were acting honestly in writing the article. Would you look at some articles which have not yet been referred to and tell me whether or not you had seen them? The first of them is the *Daily Mail*. My lord, I am sorry about this, but I do not see any other way of doing it, as his honesty is in question and whether he had reason to believe that these things had been said. This is the *Daily Mail*:

> With wink and all. From Stanley Bonnett: Aboard the Queen Mary, Cherbourg, Monday.
>
> With the candelabra's sparkle making the piano glisten like an outsize cash register, the Liberace Armada went up the Channel to Britain tonight. But the booty this astonishing keyboard buccaneer hopes to capture with sequins, music and a Deanna Durbin smile is not money.
>
> 'I can't expect to make a million dollars on this trip', said Liberace, as the gold thread in his tweed suit winked at the September sunshine. 'But I can make fans. A million fans in England would be very nice.'
>
> Two cakes for 2,000 fans.
>
> To make sure that the fans 'on later trips' will make sure of the money Wladziu Valentino Liberace already has his fifth column ashore. There are 2,000 Liber-Ah-Chee admirers whom his exotic talents hypnotised into fan clubs long before his candelabra cavalcade was ever planned.
>
> 'I've two cakes for them,' giggled Liberace, his impeccably waved grey hair nodding as he spoke. 'They have been baked aboard.'

...I do not think I need read the whole of it. All this is preceded by the words:

> Everything about Liberace has a piano theme. Or almost everything. His platinum knuckleduster ring is adorned with a miniature piano carved in ivory. Proudly he showed the gold and platinum cufflinks in his shirt. Four pianos. His gold watch-strap turned out to be another piano keyboard.

...Then there is a heading: 'Nine cents. All this and mother too.'

> By his side smiling contentedly tonight was his Mom - 61 year old Mrs Frances Liberace, the Polish girl whose marriage to an Italian French horn player was to give Britain its nine Liberace concerts.
>
> Liberace kissed her cheek, fondled her wavy brown hair, and talked of the trials of earning $1,000,000 a year.
>
> 'You see', he said, parting his lips around his milk-white, almost-too-perfect teeth 'I get only nine cents out of every dollar I make.'

147

...Then in the next column under the heading 'On marriage':

What sort of a wife does the 36-year-old Liberace want? Now almost dead-pan, he answered: 'Physical attraction would be secondary to charm, personality and faith.'

Still more seriously: 'I happen to be a religious man and I want my marriage to be blessed by my faith.'

...I think those and the million dollar income and the references to the nine cents were among these which you quoted. Now this is the *Daily Express*, also from the Queen Mary, from John Lambert. I think one of the things you had quoted were these words:

'Do you really enjoy wearing such clothes?' I asked. 'Yes, I do', he said. 'I think people love lovely things - and they are deductible from income tax.'

A music critic started to attack a Liberace habit of cutting classical scores down to popular tunes. He smiled and said: 'I am no Rubenstein. But then Rubenstein is no Liberace.'

He said his mission in life - at £2,000 a concert - was to whet the appetites of uneducated musical minds. 'My fans prefer pieces to be short.'

BEYFUS: My friend is reading that, and reading it rather fast. The way you read it, it suggests that he put in the words 'at £2,000 a concert'. I think it is quite clear, is it not, that it is the sarcastic interpolation of the critic?

GARDINER: Yes, certainly. 'He said his mission in life – at £2,000 a concert – was to whet the appetites of uneducated musical minds. 'My fans prefer pieces to be short', he added. Then he started to give details of two piano-shaped cakes which were baked for him aboard ship.

'They will be my present to my fan club in England,' he said.

I asked him why he attracted middle-aged women. He said: 'I think it is my mother love which so many of them do not get from their children.'

...That, I think, was one of those you quoted. 'I think it is my mother love which so many of them' – middle-aged women – 'do not get from their children.' Then would you look at the *Daily Telegraph*: 'Liberace strikes a popular note. Success afloat. From J F A Frost, *Daily Telegraph* Shipping Correspondent. Queen Mary, at sea.' The only things I think to which I need call attention are in the fourth paragraph:

The pianist, who is on his way to Britain, assured me that he has had the 'wink and the smile', which he frankly admitted are 'gimmicks' that help him to earn anything up to £357,000 a year in America, since he was a little boy, and one cannot help believing him. His second Christian name is Valentino.

...And so on. Then it says:

For 30 years I have interviewed people in the public eye and seldom have I had more admiration for a man's handling of sometimes awkward questions. Liberace is a showman with a plus something.

148

...Then below the heading 'Million a Year', you see: 'Individualist's earnings.'

Someone said: 'Why the black tie?' 'Goes with the suit, and I've got 50 more with me,' Liberace replied. 'It cost me $400, but to be able to pay that I have to earn $4,000. I earn about a million a year and could earn more if I tried harder; but I only manage to keep nine cents out of each dollar I earn.'

...I think there is another passage you quoted in the middle of the next column:

I am a religious man, and a great believer in family life. That is my theme all the time. Mom is my inspiration, George, my brother, my colleague and my musical director, and we have a perfect telepathy.

...Then the *News Chronicle* from 'The Channel, Monday', you see at the bottom of the first column:

Peeling off his gorgeous dressing-gown, Liberace put on what he playfully calls his 'English suit' – a cuffed and chic creation of silk tweeds with glittering interweave of gold metal thread. Cost: $400.

On their concerts in the United States the Liberace outfit, including brother George and band, gross from $10,000 to $60,000 a concert, he claims. 'Sounds a lot, I know; but how much do you think I keep from every dollar I earn? Not more than nine cents.'

...Then at the top of the next column you see:

Afterwards Liberace explained to us that his love for Mom helps strengthen Mom love the world over...

...So much for the quotations. You say after the quotations: 'On the occasion in New York at a concert in Madison Square Garden when he had the greatest reception of his life and the critics slayed him mercilessly, Liberace said: 'The take was terrific but the critics killed me. My brother George cried all the way to the bank.' The plaintiff accepted that that is right. Had you read that in the American notice? – A: I did.

–'Nobody since Aimee Semple McPherson has purveyed a bigger, richer and more varied slag-heap of lilac-coloured hokum'... Who was Aimee McPherson, for those members of the jury who do not remember? – A: Aimee Semple McPherson was an evangelist who hit Los Angeles and Hollywood, where Mr Liberace lives and has a considerable following. She was a woman who may have sincerely believed in her opinions, which I do not question; but she brought the same methods of proselytising the gospel to her business, such as a million dollar temple, private radio stations, supporters dressed up as angels. She brought this to carry on what she thought, or may well have thought, was religion. Part of the technique, I suggest, has been followed by Mr Liberace to exploit first of all what he gets out of it, secondly religion and thirdly love and affection and friendship, which I think that he has prostituted.

BEYFUS: I did not hear a lot of that. May I have it repeated?

149

MR JUSTICE SALMON: If you did not hear, the shorthand writer will repeat it. [The shorthand writer then read the previous answer.]

GARDINER: And was that the opinion which you held? – A: That was the opinion which I held when I wrote the article, and that is the opinion which I hold now.

–In relation to Aimee McPherson, you use the phrase 'a bigger, richer and more varied slag-heap of lilac-coloured hokum.' You have observed the word 'hokum' used in relation to the plaintiff by others. Would you look at the *Sunday Express*? I do not think we have had it before. In the third column he was asked what the critics had said. It says: 'They were beastly,' said Liberace. 'But then, they're always beastly. When people ask me what I thought of the notices I always say: I cried all the way to the bank.' Then he said it was an insult being offered £200 for appearing at the Palladium. Then lower down, you see:

> 'Is anyone impersonating me in London at the moment?' he asked. I told him he was featured in a revue on Shaftesbury Avenue. 'Oh goody.' he said. 'I must get tickets. I love to watch myself being impersonated.' At the door I said: 'Mr Liberace - you have a wonderful line in hokum. You ought to write a book.'
>
> 'But I am', he said, 'I am.'

…I had not observed, as my friend points out, that in the last article I referred to, the words in the heading are: 'And the matrons delight of Miami who shows just how far you can go on hokum.' If you look at the *Evening News*, you see, just above the words 'Tom Dowries' Column':

> Liberace - half-Italian, half-Polish - has few fans among the bobby-soxers. He is derided by serious critics. He is the butt of most TV comedians. But millions of middle-aged women here think he is the greatest heart-throb since Rudolph Valentino.

…You observe the heading is 'Candlelight Casanova... Dimples and hokum? Maybe – but America's latest TV idol appeals to middle-aged women and will strum £357,000 out of his grand piano this year.' In relation to what you said about religion and Miss McPherson, I think you said that your recollection was that among the films you had seen was a film in which he played the *Ave Maria*? – A: That is so,

–He told us about that. Now would you look at the *Daily Herald*:

> So simple, so sincere, so lucrative... The screams of his adoring fans drown the small, quiet voices of the critics – who say that he is not an outstanding pianist - and the moans of nauseated husbands.

…Dealing with his films, in the right-hand column you see:

> In one of his recent films - the first the family and I have ever seen - he showed us his home in Hollywood. Not alone. While Brother George played *Home Sweet Home* on the violin Liberace walked into his living room, squeezed between two grand pianos, and showed us his collection of miniature pianos – 188 of them.

150

'Do you like my home?' he asked us at the end of that piano-strewn tour. 'Mom and I live here' - he isn't married - 'along with my cute French poodle. But Somebody Else lives here, too'. And he started to play *Bless This House*. I shall watch the British reaction with interest when Liberace arrives soon.

...Then if you turn over to the *News Chronicle*, you see:

For months Liberace has been pipelined to Britain every Sunday afternoon. On ITV we have come to know his smile, that triangle of sugar-icing. We have been stroked, smoothed and patted by his astute eyes. The balding have madly envied his ornate, greying hair.

We have listened to that cosy, hugging voice. Sometimes, startled, we have listened to what the voice was saying. To this, for example, about his home in California: Mother and I are vurry, vurry happy there. (Smug twinkle). So is my little French poodle who lives with us. (Eyes slide sideways, face goes solemn).

And there is Someone Else who dwells with us and to whom I speak. (Lights dim. Liberace sings). *Bless this house, Lord we pray, make it safe by night and day*. Little touches of this kind are splendid for beer and soap sales. Incidentally, they help to explain such things as Liberace's reputed income (£350,000), the dress suit in cream mohair, the dress suit in black velvet and gold lamé, the piano-shaped swimming pool and wrist-watch...

...And so on. Had you read those two references to that particular film? – A: I had.

–In relation to those and your own opinion of the *Ave Maria* film, did you consider that they were profane or not? These things are matters of opinion. – A: I did, yes.

–Will you explain to the jury why? – A: I think that they were profane, and I think that Mr Liberace's constant references to God might well be true; but they seem to me to be introduced to prove or to insist that he is a very sincere person. I do not happen to be a Christian; I happen to be an agnostic, and wish I were a Christian. The reason for that is this, that I cannot swallow the simple act of faith which gives you Christianity and which is such a great comfort in life. When Mr Liberace constantly refers to God when he does these performances, such as he does with the *Ave Maria*, out of which he gets money, I am revolted.

–With regard to all these adjectives, in what sense did you mean deadly? – A: That it overwhelms one. It is a kind of lethal attack on the senses.

–As to 'winking, sniggering, snuggling', I do not want to take this at great length; a number of these things have already been read; but were there a number of references in what you had read both here and in America which contained adjectives of that nature? – A: I had indeed, and I had observed him on television doing this very thing.

BEYFUS: I just remind your lordship that these adjectives are not supposed to be true as facts but are set out as comment in the defence.

151

GARDINER: They are, of course, matters of opinion.

BEYFUS: Comment.

MR JUSTICE SALMON: It will be for the jury to say.

GARDINER (to the witness): 'Chromium plated'? – A: Chromium plated means to me a bright light-reflecting surface, and in the performances which Mr Liberace does he takes great care to have light-reflecting surfaces such as a completely white suit of tails and candelabra, which reflect light, and an enormous ring on his finger. So I would say that Mr Liberace, regardless of what he may say of himself, was a light-reflecting surface.

–'Scent impregnated'? Mr Liberace agrees he uses scent...

BEYFUS: I am so sorry; he does not agree anything of the sort. He agreed that what he used was after shaving lotion and colognes, and in the article which is put forward for his approval the word 'perfumes' was struck out and 'colognes' substituted.

GARDINER: 'Scent' is wrong. I should have said that he uses scented toilet water, or whatever it is. I will look it up so as to be sure I have got the right phrase.

MR JUSTICE SALMON: My recollection is scented cologne and scented deodorant.

GARDINER: That is quite right. I did not mean 100-per-cent scent, but either after-shave lotion or toilet water, or whatever it is, which is in fact scented. I think I had referred before the adjournment to a *Daily Express* article. [To the witness]: Would you look at another article in the *Express*? I think you only had many of these a day or two before you wrote your article.

BEYFUS: My Lord, this I must object to. This is said to be fact as well as comment. I have no objection, of course, to the *Daily Express* reporter being called to say that in his opinion he was close enough to say that he was scent impregnated. It would be a perfectly proper thing to do; but I object very strongly to some article by a *Daily Express* reporter being read when I have no opportunity at all of cross-examining the reporter. Inasmuch as it is alleged to be true as fact, that, in my submission, is the only way in which it can be proved.

GARDINER: Of course, I am not tendering this as any evidence that he used scent or, rather, that he used scented toilet water; but there is not, as far as I know at the moment, any dispute about it; if there were, of course, I would have to call the reporter to prove it. This is no evidence of what he did at all, but if the question is asked 'You cannot possibly have honestly believed this because you had never met him', Mr Connor is, in my submission, entitled to say 'I know my journalist colleagues and how far they are reliable on questions of fact. I had read several entirely

152

independent and different accounts in different papers drawing attention to the fact that he uses something scented'.

MR JUSTICE SALMON: Will you remind me; is the defence on this point that 'scent impregnated' is fact, or that it is comment, but if it is fact it is true?

GARDINER: The defence is that it is comment, but that if it is fact it is true. I think my learned friend Mr Faulks took the view that there might be some doubt whether 'scent impregnated' was fact or comment. Therefore it is pleaded that the whole of this paragraph is comment, but that if the expression 'scent impregnated' was fact, it was true.

BEYFUS: I would ask your Lordship to rule that the words that somebody is 'scent impregnated' cannot be a question of comment; it must be a question of fact, just as though it was said that he was wearing black clothes or he was wearing white clothes. Scent impregnated must be a question of fact, and I object to this form of trying to get in an article by a reporter. There is no reason why the *Express* reporter should not be called if they want to call him.

MR JUSTICE SALMON: I think whether it is fact or comment is a matter for the jury, and I shall allow this; but I shall warn the jury at the appropriate time that it is no evidence on the facts, that it is merely evidence which they have to consider, if they think it is comment, as to whether he honestly believed it.

BEYFUS: Very well.

Gardiner still had more cuttings to back up the references in the Cassandra column.

–Quietly, diffidently even, and with many an ingratiating wiggle of his silken-draped shoulders, Liberace told me of himself, just before he sailed. We met in an hotel room high above New York's Central Park. A blast of scent preceded and gave warning of the maestro's entrance.

...That is Mr Rene McColl of the *Daily Express*. Then had you read the article of Mr Zec?

MR JUSTICE SALMON: Have you told us; had you read that article of Mr McColl? – A: I had indeed, yes.

GARDINER: That was the article, was it not, in which Mr McColl quotes Mr Liberace as saying, and he agrees he did say: 'People who have never walked before start walking because I ask them to. At my request, people leave their iron lungs. Why, only the other day, in the Hollywood Bowl two cripples arose and walked at my command'... But had you read this: 'From Donald Zec aboard the Queen Mary. With a song in his heart, a fixed dimpled smile and fragrantly perfumed with toilet water, Liberace, the Casanova of the keyboard, arrived here today on his way to England'... And this, where the *Evening Standard* refers to 'A grey-haired, fragrantly perfumed American piano player'.

Connor said he had read them all.

GARDINER: 'Fruit-flavoured'... What did you mean by that? – A: I meant that that was part of the impression of confectionery which Mr Liberace conveys to me; over-sweetened, over-flavoured, over-luscious and thus sickening.

–I am not going to read them now. Are there other references to confectionery in the writings of other critics? – A: There are.

–'Heap of mother-love'. I think, in view of what I have already read, I need not go into this in detail. What did you mean by 'heap of mother-love'? – A: I meant that Mr Liberace was dealing with what I think is the closest bond which exists between human beings. It seems to me that the relationship, or rather the positive relationship, between human beings begins with friendship, then develops to affection and then comes to love. When it comes to the question of love, I think there are various degrees of love. I think there is sexual love, which provides its own immediate pleasures, and indeed is the basis of how we carry on; but I was thinking of something which was much more tender and important, which is the love for a mother and for the child. I think it survives the disagreements of the parents who made it; I think it survives poverty; I think it survives war, and I think it is the most sacred thing of all; and when I see this done on the stage of the London Palladium by a 40-year-old man in the company of his mother, who he may well love highly, I regard that as a profane and wrong thing.

–Are you a family man with children yourself? – A: I am.

> –This appalling man - and I use the word appalling in no other than its true sense of terrifying - has hit this country in a way that is as violent as Churchill receiving the cheers on VE Day. He reeks with emetic language that can only make grown men long for a quiet corner, an aspidistra, a handkerchief and the old heave-ho...

...Was that your honest opinion? – A: It was.

–Is there anything you would like to add on that? – A: Yes. I would like to tell you why I used the words appalling and terrifying. I am always suspicious of people gathered together in large quantities. I did see the Nuremburg rallies. I did see people there who were persuaded by propaganda, by searchlights, by violent speeches by Goering, who were all driven to that most dangerous thing of all which is the herd instinct of people thinking and feeling together. I happen to think that is a bad thing, and when I see these young and impressionable people gathering outside Waterloo station or, rather, saw the photographs of them, I do not like to see that, and I particularly do not like to see the most impressionable and the most susceptible of these people, who are the 17-year-olds, the 18-year-olds and the 22-year-olds.

–He has told us that when women came up to the platform to feel his knee and touch his clothes it used to result in a prolonged scream. Do you think that sort of thing is healthy? – A: I think it is unhealthy. It happens to be also unwise, but also it is wealth to Mr Liberace.

–You take the view that this is a subject on which other people are, of course, entitled to have entirely different views from yours? –A: I do.

BEYFUS: Please do not lead, him, putting the words into his mouth.

CONNOR: May I answer that question? From my long experience in journalism a very large proportion of the people in this country have views which are strongly opposed to mine. I welcome that, for the simple reason that it is not people thinking together, being guided together and subjected to wrong propaganda.

GARDINER: 'Without doubt he is the biggest sentimental vomit of all time. Slobbering over his mother, winking at his brother, and counting the cash at every second, this superb piece of calculating candy-floss has an answer for every situation.' You told, us, having seen his performances, about his mother. Why 'counting the cash at every second'? – A: I think that that is an exaggeration. I do not think he counts the cash at every second. I think he probably counts it once a month just to see how many millions are there.

–Had you observed in the articles which you say you had read his own references to his earnings? – A: I had, yes. Mind you, if I may say so, I do not object to people being rich. I rather like people being rich, and I would quite like to be rich myself; but I think it can be pursued through legitimate channels and ordinary honest jobs, but I do not think it should be pursued through the channels in which Mr Liberace affects the things which appeal most deeply to us, such as affection, friendship, love, God, religion.

–Why 'calculating candy-floss'? – A: Again, a reference to his sugary appearance and his sugary performances.

–'Nobody anywhere ever made so much money out of high-speed piano-playing with the ghost of Chopin gibbering at every note.' I am not going all through them. Had you read articles which have been referred to, dealing with his method of playing and what may be called potted classics? – A: I have.

–Chopin, candelabra and so on. Then: 'There must be something wrong with us that our teenagers longing for sex and our middle aged matrons fed up with sex alike should fall for such a sugary mountain of appalling claptrap wrapped up in such a preposterous clown.' You have told us your age. Can you tell me when the teenagers and bobby-soxers and fan clubs started? – A: No, I cannot. I have no objection to bobby-soxers; I have no objection to fan clubs at all; but I object to them when they are exploited and misguided for commercial purposes. I remember in my own time when I was a bit younger when people used to wear Oxford bags; I do not

155

object to jeans; I do not object to all these manifestations of youth. If they like to dress in jeans, jolly good luck; let them do so; but I dislike seeing them all together en masse and used for commercial and what I regard as base purposes.

–Do you remember a visit from a Miss Ambler... Is it true that that took place on October 26? – A: Yes... It was on a Friday morning... My memory on this is not precise, because when I heard the name Miss Ambler I had forgotten all about it; but I did receive a telephone call from *Picture Post* and it was a woman. I am not sure whether it was Miss Ambler or not. She said 'May we come down and take some photographs of you and your cat, to whom we understand, you are deeply attached, because we are running a series on well-known people and their pets?'... The reason I said 'Yes' was that when people of my own profession ring me up I always like to see them because we are all in the same trade or craft or unfortunate predicament together. I said: 'Would you come down on Friday, which is my day off?' and I think I said: 'A good time is about 11 o'clock in the morning.' On the morning at 11 Miss Ambler, who I had never met before, arrived. She was accompanied, rather to my surprise and to my pleasure, by Mr Hayward McGhee, who I had not seen for many years and who I had seen in the Army and came down to take some pictures when I was at Tidworth in the Royal Armoured Corps. I was pleased to see Miss Ambler, and I was doubly pleased to see Mr Hayward McGhee. What happened then was that we sat down. I think I offered them a drink to start with; I do not know; I may well have done. Then we had the problem of photographing the cat. The cat does not like strangers, and he took a bit of an alarming view of Miss Ambler, which I subsequently confirmed was right; it must have been a perceptive cat. We then tried to catch the cat and to photograph it. He rushed upstairs, my wife went upstairs; we all went upstairs. I lay on the ground, to get these pictures, and all the rest of it. I also appear to have upset the cat. So then my wife, who is able to handle cats much better than I do, said: 'Leave it for the moment while it calms down.' I went downstairs with Miss Ambler. We were not there for much time together. I said: 'I have got a jolly good idea... Why not have an article for *Picture Post* in which Cassandra writes about his cat and the cat (who was called Smokey Joe) writes about Cassandra, so that we can have two swift examinations of each other, both from the cat and also the columnist?' Then, having given her the idea, I wrote the piece. I did not write it on the spot, but I was anxious that this should appear. She agreed with this and then the subject of Liberace was raised by Miss Ambler in the presence of my wife. Again, I will not be precise. This is a long time ago, and as I have already said I had forgotten about Miss Ambler, who I had never seen before and have not seen again. She said then that she had been at a party with Liberace and that the matter

156

had been raised about who Cassandra was. But I do not want to be precise on this matter; I just cannot remember precisely. Then the fact emerged that I knew that he was going to sue me, and I then said – indeed I did say it – in a jocular way (it may be one of the jokes which I will regret): 'It will be interesting to see who is the biggest buffoon in the box.' My wife came down and I then talked to Hayward McGhee about old friends we had met in the Army. My wife then took her upstairs, showed her round the house, and showed her round the garden. The whole operation occurred within, say, 35 minutes, and then Miss Ambler left my life and did not enter it until I saw her in the box.

–Is it true that you made any of the further statements which she attributed to you? – A: It is absolutely untrue.

–Can you produce, if my friend wants it, 'Smokey Joe by Cassandra' and 'Cassandra by Smokey Joe'? – A: I regret I cannot produce Smokey Joe because he died a week ago.

–I mean the article which he wrote. You told us about your service in the Army. I would just like you to deal with this. When you were in North Africa, had you as part of your duties to edit an Army newspaper? – A: Not to edit it, but to assist in the compilation of this journal.

–Have you been a witness on many occasions? – A: I have never been a witness before, in any action.

–Is it something over a quarter of a century? My arithmetic is always wrong. – A: 24 years.

–In all that time how many actions have been brought for things which you have written; do you know? – A: I have never been in court before, but I remember disputes with Oswald Mosley, when I was writing about Oswald Mosley before the war, which were many. I believe these were settled for – I am not sure of the sums, I think about £50. Another one which I recall is something which I wrote about Lester Piggott, who is a jockey, and I believe there was some settlement out of court.

–Those the only two, as far as you know, which have involved legal action? Have there been occasions on which you have been wrong? – A: There have been quite a number of occasions.

–On such occasions have you apologised? – A: I have.

–There is no dispute about it; had you ever met Mr Liberace? – A: Never.

–Had you had any personal disagreement with him? Or any reason for saying anything against him otherwise than on these performances which you have seen and everything which you had heard and read about him? – A: No reason at all. All I was criticising was his appearances on the stage.

Gardiner had no more questions and Beyfus, taking over quickly to cross-examine, picked Connor straight up on his last words: '…His appearances on the stage which you had never seen?' – A: That is quite true.

This might have been the point to which Gardiner could reasonably have expected the plaintiff's side to have kept back Mantovani. But the defence had lost the advantage, lost the flow, and the Old Fox had brilliantly thrown them off balance.

Although he had delayed it, Beyfus had been eagerly anticipating confronting Connor 'on the cross'. He didn't like him much, but he admired and respected the columnist as a consummate professional wordsmith. He may even have admitted a small professional jealousy – a frustrated writer himself, Beyfus had started a book about his experience as a prisoner of war, and had tried writing a play, but both works lay unfinished in a drawer. Nevertheless, wordplay was what they had in common: each man at the top of his own tree of verbal argument. They were separated by only a narrow divide: one made his living sitting and writing while the other did it standing and speaking. But they were in the standing-speaking arena now: Beyfus's own home ground. It was his court, he knew the rules, and it was his advantage. Whatever the witness would say, the barrister could be assured of having the last word.

–Would you agree that you have achieved the reputation in Fleet Street of being a violent and vitriolic writer? – A: No. I would not.

–Do you think it would be wrong to call you a violent and vitriolic writer? –A: I would indeed.

And Beyfus winked at the witness. It was no more than the counsel's (allegedly) irrepressible and involuntary nervous twitch from his old riding injury. But to Connor it appeared as 'a real how's-yer-father wink' as if saying: 'Don't worry about it; I have to ask these questions; it's not personal.' He quickly realised it was not a matey wink. As the cross-examination continued, the spasm would appear less frequently, but it discomforted the witness all the time he was in the box.

–Would it be right to say that the *Daily Mirror* is normally known as (I think it is a slang word) a tabloid? – A: Yes, it is rather loosely applied, but I certainly agree with that.

–Is a tabloid an expression usually used to denote a paper which depends upon sensationalism? – A: No. It is a paper which compresses and uses strong display to express the views which it holds and the views which it reports.

–Would it be right to say that the *Daily Mirror* is a sensational newspaper? – A: No. It is quite wrong.

–You are on oath, are you not? – A: I know I am on oath.

–Are you a comparatively close friend of Mr Hugh Cudlipp... Did you both join the *Daily Mirror* together in about 1935... Is he now the head both of the *Daily Mirror* and the *Sunday Pictorial*? – A: That is right.

–Although they belong technically to different companies, they are associated newspapers... And both published from Geraldine House... With Mr Hugh Cudlipp as the head of both. – A: That is correct.

–You have been intimately associated with Mr Cudlipp for 24 years... And are not only constantly with him in Geraldine House but constantly with him socially... Drinking together in bars in Fleet Street. – A: 'Associating' is the word I would like.

–And it would be a common sight in Fleet Street to see you and Mr Cudlipp drinking together in bars. – A: It would be a reasonably common sight, yes.

–You have not in the last few years in any way fallen out with Mr Hugh Cudlipp. – A: Mr Hugh Cudlipp and I quarrel so violently almost every day that you would never believe it.

–Is that a fair indication of your character, then, that you quarrel violently nearly every day with one of your closest friends? – A: That is quite true.

–In 1953 Mr Hugh Cudlipp wrote a book which is a history of the *Daily Mirror*, did he not... With some assistance from you, which he greatly acknowledges in the preface? – A: That is so.

You wrote in the *Daily Mirror* of Monday, September 7 1953 a review of that book... In which you did not complain or suggest that any part of it was untrue. – A: I did not, not in the review.

–That is all I am saying; not in the review. You did make one reference to what Mr Cudlipp said about you. You said this: 'The book sparkles and flashes... It has everything – even the damned impudence to include disrespectful and distasteful details in the worst possible taste about myself.' – A: That is true.

–Then I think you set out quotations. 'Cassandra says the uninhibited author is the guest who is seldom invited, twice'... Is it not a fact that Mr Cudlipp not only admits that this newspaper the *Daily Mirror* is a sensational paper but boasts of it? – A: I am not aware of that.

–Then let us have a look at the book. You reviewed the book. I can give various passages. It is quite clear, is it not, that the story told of the *Daily Mirror* was that from 1935 onwards, from being a decorous and gentlemanly paper it was changed into a sensational tabloid? You will not have the word 'sensational', into a tabloid. – A: That is true. Actually, it was re-changed in 1910.

–I do not mind; re-changed from a decorous and gentlemanly newspaper into a tabloid. It boasts, does it not, now, of the biggest circulation on earth of any daily newspaper; is that right? – A: It says that.

–Is that not right? – A: It says that.

–I am asking you whether you think it is true or not. – A: I happen to know that it is not quite true, because the *Ashaki-Shirnum*, which is published in Tokyo, has a few hundred or a few thousand more copies. There happen to be more Japanese in Japan than there are intelligent Britons in England who buy it.

–The largest circulation in Europe, in the western world; is that right? – A: That is quite true.

–What does it run into now; 5,000,000 or more? – A: We do not want to give away secrets to our competitors, but I think it is 4,560,000. I am not sure about the 60,000.

–I think in the review which you wrote you suggested you had 11,000,000 readers. – A: I think it is 13,000,000.

–Before I forget it, I want to go on to something quite off the topic. Evidence has been given that at Sheffield my client was greeted with cries of 'Queer, go home'. You know that? –A: I have heard it said in court, but I have not heard of it before.

–You have heard it suggested, have you not, that that might be due to the fact that a gentleman Jimmy Thompson playing at the Apollo theatre sang a song which would suggest that my client was a homosexual? – A: Yes, I have heard that.

–Which do you think more likely, that a boy or boys in the gallery at Sheffield had come to London and been to the Apollo theatre or that they were one or more of the 13,000,000 readers of the *Daily Mirror*? – A: I should have thought they were one or more of the 13,000,000 readers of the *Daily Mirror*.

–You have sworn that in your opinion the *Daily Mirror* is not a sensational newspaper. Would you look at this book you reviewed without suggesting it was inaccurate? This is Mr Cudlipp. What was he at that time, 1953, when he wrote the book, editor? – A: No, I think that he was editorial director, but I am not sure.

–Time and experience, and the trials of the conflict, had tempered its brashness. It regained and still remains a popular sensational newspaper, but its sense of purpose became highly developed; it regarded itself as a paper with a mission and it was accepted as such.

...You see there it is being described by the editorial director as a popular sensational newspaper; do you regard that as wrong? – A: I regard it as wrong. One of the strengths of the friendship with Mr Cudlipp is we have disagreed continually. I draw a line between sensation, which means exploiting something for commercial matters, and forthright and strong opinions well held.

–You see, at page 250, Mr Cudlipp is dealing with the evidence given before the Royal Commission on the Press... Who was Mr Bartholomew at that time? Was he the head of both papers? – A: He was. Technically I think he was the managing director, but in effect he was the head of both papers.

–Let us see what happened:

> In evidence to the Royal Commission on the Press the frankness about sensationalism became positively brutal. Cecil Thomas and I, representing the *Mirror* and *Pictorial...* accompanied Bartholomew to the session held on February 19, 1948. The volcano did not take lightly to being kept waiting in the corridor. 'Why don't we go,' asked Bart. 'It's not a court of law.' We were also a little concerned at how he would react to the solemnity of the proceedings inside, for he was notoriously not susceptible to schoolmasterly cross-examination.

–That is Mr Bartholomew, is it? – A: That is Mr Bartholomew, and in view of the proceedings which are occurring here I have every sympathy with him.

–I dare say, but at any rate he did not write libellous articles as you admittedly have. – A: I have not admittedly written a libellous article.

–The article which you have written is admitted to be defamatory. – A: You said libellous.

–Defamatory. – A: You said libellous; I do not admit to it.

–A defamatory article, so it is libellous, although there may be a technical...

MR JUSTICE SALMON: There are two legal views about that.

BEYFUS: I am not going to argue that point now. [To the witness]: What happened...

> Bart charmed them all with his bluntness. When Mr Herbert Hull endeavoured to ascertain how and why the *Mirror* allocated its space in the way it did he was treated instead to a homily on sensationalism. Said Bartholomew: 'If you will look at the *Daily Mirror* every day next week you will find we will be more sensational than we have ever been for six days running. You will think we have gone mad.

...That was Mr Bartholomew. Do you still say on oath that the *Daily Mirror* is not a sensational newspaper? – A: I still say that on oath. What I say is it expresses what it feels in a strong, powerful, simple way and that is my way and there is a difference between strong opinion and sensationalism, in that commercialism corrupts one and the other is lively treatment.

GARDINER: Would you read the next paragraph?

BEYFUS: 'The Commission smiled, but Bart was referring to the *Mirror*'s bold plan to teach the economic facts of life to the public at large; the campaign received much praise.' Then a little lower down...

> Any doubts, if they still existed... were dispelled by Silvester Bolam who succeeded Thomas in the editorship from 1948 until February, 1953. Bolam expressed himself thus in a front-page manifesto:

The *Mirror* is a sensational newspaper. We make no apology for that. We believe in the sensational presentation of news and views, especially important news and views, as a necessary and valuable public service in these days of mass readership and democratic responsibility.'

...Do you disagree with that? – A: I disagree with that on the explanation which I have given between the expression of strong views and sensationalism and, Mr Beyfus, I would like to tell you that one of the difficulties I have had and one of the crosses I have had to bear for 24 years is disagreeing with my employers who pay me more or less every day.

–I suggest not only was the *Daily Mirror* – did it become a tabloid? – a sensational newspaper, it was violent and vicious, vitriolic, and you were one of the instruments employed to turn it into a tabloid and a sensational paper. – A: I have never taken part in the editorial management, with the policy. I have a very difficult position on Fleet Street which is to write what you please and what you think and I have never been any part of the editorial direction or the executive administration of the paper.

–I think you should do me the honour to listen to my suggestion. What I suggested was that you were from 1935 onwards one of the instruments used by the editor to turn this decorous and gentlemanly newspaper into a violent, sensational, tabloid. – A: We say what we did was we revived something which was limp, dead and flaccid into something which is alive, strong and true.

–Turn back to page 64:

In Geraldine House, where the *Mirror* was produced, nobody cared what the rivals published; we were living dangerously. A different type of newspaper was being evolved, and the mounting circulation established beyond all question that the public adored it.

–I want to ask you about: 'We were living dangerously'... – A: Would you like to ask me some specific question?

–I suggest you were living dangerously in that you were behaving in a manner, the paper was being conducted in a manner, which raises the very great danger of court action. – A: No, I do not think so at all.

–Why do you think those responsible for the paper were living dangerously? – A: I will tell you. When you are connected with a concern which is dying you are then trying to rectify the situation and put all your heart and soul and mind into the job.

–I suggest that the danger was not of dying but the danger of getting into trouble with the authorities. – A: No, not any more than the normal way. We are always worried about getting into trouble with the authorities.

–You have, of course, in the last 20 years, been in great trouble with this newspaper, have you not? – A: We have been in serious trouble many times as indeed has every other newspaper.

162

–You have been in serious trouble over the manner in which the newspaper was conducted? – A: Would you be more specific?

–Cannot you say yes or no to that? – A: Will you kindly repeat the question?

–I would rather have an answer to my question before I go on. The paper has been in grave trouble on several occasions within the last 20 years? – A: The paper like every other paper in Fleet Street and indeed in the provinces is often in trouble, often in grave trouble, and it is not selective to the *Daily Mirror*; for instance there was grave trouble last week with *The Times*.

–That is what you call grave trouble? – A: *The Times* evidently did; I read their limp explanation today.

–Some few years ago was the *Daily Mirror* fined £10,000 and did the editor go to prison for three months for contempt of court? – A: Quite true, but please don't try and saddle me with the responsibility of the editorial duties; I sympathise in what he does but please don't pin that on me. I had nothing to do with it and I regarded it as sad and regrettable.

–You realise you are only one of the defendants in this case? – A: I have realised that only too well by the multiplicity and length of these proceedings.

–The other one is Daily Mirror Newspapers Ltd and at the moment I am cross-examining you with regard to the newspaper rather than with regard to yourself. – A: I wish you would make the distinction very clear, whether you are asking me in my capacity as an employee and not on the board of directors of Daily Mirror Newspapers.

–Are you on the board of directors? –A: No, I have never been given this privilege.

–All these questions are with regard to the newspaper with the exception of the one I put that you were one of the instruments with your vitriolic pen of turning this paper into a sensational tabloid. Most of the questions were directed to the *Daily Mirror*. – A: May I say I am trying to do the bravest thing in Fleet Street to say in my own column what I believe and what I think and I am no part of the executive administration of the newspaper; they pay me.

–What I suggest you were trying to do was to hack out a good living for yourself by making yourself extremely useful to the newspaper. – A: In the same way as distinguished advocates of the Bar do the same thing in the law.

–Quite right. I am going to refer to your rudeness in a moment but perhaps you have just given a good illustration of it. In the war was the *Daily Mirror* nearly suppressed? – A: It was threatened with suppression.

–By Mr Morrison as Home Secretary... Was that owing to a cartoon to which you supplied the caption... You having suggested that the

cartoonist's caption was not adequate and you would supply a better one?
– A: I supplied the caption; I take the responsibility.

–You have written on sex in this article. Would you turn to page 272 of this book? Mr Cudlipp deals with Lord Rothermere severing his connection with the newspaper. He was not the original owner but shortly before 1934 and 1935 he was the owner of it? – A: He had a strong financial interest.

–Look at this paragraph: 'Foolishly, the *Mirror* never told the public the facts'; that is with regard to the dealings in the shares in the *Mirror*.

> Two references only to its ownership and control appeared in that newspaper since the death of Northcliffe. The first was in 1936, briefly stating the severing of Lord Rothermere's connection, though not disclosing the reason for his action: he was, quite simply, appalled at its new racy policy and outraged in particular at its attitude to sex?

…Have you seen that... Have you read it... Do you think that is right? – A: I do not think Lord Rothermere, this particular Lord Rothermere, was the best adjudicator on morals and sex.

–I did not ask you that. Do you think it is right that he was appalled in particular at the newspaper's attitude? –A: He may well have been appalled.

–Now let us come to yourself. You say you do not think that you have acquired the reputation of being a violent and a vitriolic writer? – A: I do not know; I do not think so. I think I have acquired the reputation of a man who is prepared to say strongly, very strongly, what he feels and what he believes.

–What I put to you was violent and vitriolic. –A: I disagree.

–Let us see. This is what your close friend writes: 'William Neil Connor, already famous as Cassandra when war began and soon, to his critics, to become infamous, is a stronger, headier brew than Richard Jennings'… he was later editor? A: Yes, and a very good one.

> –Four-star instead of Tio Pepe. Psychiatrists might linger over the titbit that he was born a dissimilar twin, or make heavy weather with the plausible theory that a man so aggressive must be concealing a whopping inferiority complex, or cherish as a material clue his rejection by the Royal Navy on leaving school as 'not up to optical standard'.

…Do you suggest you had not acquired the reputation of being aggressive? – A: At which time?

–At any time while you were employed on the *Daily Mirror*? – A: I will not say aggressive because there is a French saying: 'This dog is a bad dog, because it defends itself when attacked.'

–I was not asking you about that. We have all heard that. Do you suggest the description of you by your close friend Mr Cudlipp as aggressive is inaccurate? – A: Can we deal with it sentence by sentence?

164

–I am asking whether you were aggressive. – A: Anybody who believes strongly, either rightly or wrongly, and defends it can be accused of being aggressive, so I will accept that, in the circumstances in which I feel indignant against things which are wrong.

–Then a little further down:

> Yet the biographical details shed little or no light. The measure of the matter is that Cassandra is a medical and mental problem; physically and spiritually he suffers from blood pressure.

...First of all, I do not know... – A: Do you want me to tell you if I suffer from blood pressure?

–No, not physically; I do not want to know your medical details. – A: But I am prepared to supply them.

–I am not cross-examining on them.

MR JUSTICE SALMON: Just answer the question, Mr Connor.

And there, at that moment, may have been the first hint that the judge was finding Connor's responses not to his taste, or perhaps not what he was used to hearing in cross-examinations by esteemed advocates. Maybe, like Beyfus, he was offended by the witness's suggestion that distinguished barristers, like journalists, 'hack out a good living for themselves' by making themselves useful to the people who pay them. Whatever, here was the learned judge instructing a witness to answer a question when none had actually been asked – the question about 'aggressive' having already been answered twice. But clearly the witness was getting impatient, too.

BEYFUS: The suggestion of your close friend and colleague working with you for 25 years in the same office with you is that spiritually you suffer from blood pressure; do you think that is an accurate description of you? – A: I hold very strong views.

–Do you think that is a fair description of you? – A: Well, I will accept that; I mean I will accept I have very strong views – the phrase is spiritual blood pressure, if you say I am angry, of course I am.

–J Walter Thompsons, they are advertising agents, aren't they? –A: They are indeed.

> –He learnt a lot in that spirited American-influenced concern, for they were the pioneers of consumer-research, high-pressure marketing, point of sale, and all the rest of the paraphernalia of convincing the public they cannot possibly do without something they have never previously heard of, or needed. Some of Connor's best stories concern this black art, for it was in advertising that he grasped the power and the value, though not the danger, of words.

–Do you think that is right? – A: What?

–'Grasping the power and the value of words' but you did not grasp their danger? – A: Walter Thompsons I regard as the best and the most logical

165

advertising agency in the country and I was taught many things. And one of the things was brevity and the second thing was a close marshalling of logical terms as applied to selling material and...

−I want to ask you this question: do you think you have never appreciated the danger of words? − A: Mr Beyfus, I used to be a close student of a paper called *Völkischer Beobachter* run by Dr Goebells and I knew then and I know now what happens when words are wrongly used, when propaganda machines are used as in that case.

−Words can be terribly dangerous? − A: They can indeed.

−And terribly harmful? − A: They can, and they can be terribly encouraging, and terribly good.

−There is a poem, if I can think of it; do you remember Shelley wrote a poem on the death of Keats? − A: No, but I agree that he probably did.

−And he wrote a preface addressed to the Edinburgh reviewer, as the review was supposed to have hastened his death: 'You did not use daggers but you spoke them.' Do you know that? − A: What is the operative phrase?

−I have asked you... − A: Please, sir, I did not quite hear.

−I said: do you know Shelley... − A: If you turn the volume control up I can hear you.

−Do you know Shelley wrote in his preface to the poem on the death of Keats these words, addressed to an Edinburgh reviewer: 'You did not use daggers but you spoke them.' Have you ever heard of that? − A: No, but I have heard it now; a very good phrase.

−Do you agree words may well be daggers? − A: I have already said, sir, I have given an example of the complete adulteration of the words used by the propaganda machine controlled by Dr Goebells and that is one of the things that led this nation which I saw into the greatest calamity that has come in our time which was World War Two.

−I am going to suggest that you have developed the art of vituperation more strongly than any other journalist in Fleet Street? − A: I reject that.

−Would you agree that your strong point is vituperation? − A: I would not.

−You would not? − No, I would not.

−Let us see how this description of you goes on... I suggest this sums you up:

> He would have been content to run a lucrative bookmaker's agency, but the fact is, for good or ill, he drifted into journalism and swiftly progressed in the only profession where big-scale, incessant rudeness (skilfully written) is highly paid.

...Do you see that? − A: I do... I now see I have to sue Mr Hugh Cudlipp for writing this book. I disagree with it.

166

–Very well. – A: It is an interesting legal action when Cassandra sues the *Daily Mirror*.

–You have remained for the last six years on the same terms with him, as I asked you, as the preceding 19 years, having violent quarrels with him and then having drinks with him in Fleet Street. – A: Yes, but the quarrels have increased and the frequency of the drinks has been reduced.

–Let us see how he looked at you...

> When I first met Connor I felt that I was involved in an extremely unpleasant motor crash; even the exchange of orthodox civilities, the casual Good Morning, was accompanied by the awful din of screeching mental brakes. It has never been a question of What Makes Connor Tick, but What Makes Connor Clang.

...Do you think that is a good description of you? – A: I think that Mr Cudlipp's timidity on meeting me on the first occasion when he thought he was involved in a motor-car accident has been substantially reduced in the passage of time.

–Then he praises you.

FAULKS: You do not want to read that!

BEYFUS: Of course, I do. I am not selective, like your side! Let us see your virtues now:

> He is industrious, no doubt of that, and a well-informed sort of cove. For he has an appetite for newspapers, magazines and books; he does *The Times* every day from the first personal ad to 'printed by' at the foot of the final page...

...I do not suppose you wholly accept that? – A: That is an exaggeration,

> –...studies the American political columnists, keeps an eye on *Pravda*, an ear to Iron Curtain radio, and masticates *Hansard* before meals in the evenings. He remembers every point of detail...

...This is rather interesting; this is among the praiseworthy part apparently:

> ...to the slightest disadvantage of the victim he picks up on the tip of his pen for public scrutiny in his column.

...Is that a fair description of you? – A: It is not a fair description, and when I had the task of reviewing this book I objected to this, and I said he was wrong, but in view of that democratic principle of listening to what your enemies have to say I allowed it to go without legal action.

–There is no complaint in the review except to say that he has 'the damned impudence to include disrespectful and distressing tales in the worst possible taste about myself'. – A: That is my view now.

–Your close colleague and superior, Mr Cudlipp, says that you remember every point of detail to the slightest disadvantage of the victim you pick up on the tip of your pen for public scrutiny in your column.

> When memory fails, and the enormity of a politician's early misdemeanour temporarily escapes him, Cassandra taps his head and says: 'My private librarians are looking it up.' The value of the man is

that he writes superbly, is a born journalist, means what he writes, and writes without fear.

CONNOR: I would like you to read that again, I rather like that.

BEYFUS: I am sure you do:

...The value of the man is that he writes superbly, is a born journalist, means what he writes, and writes without fear. According to subject and the state of his liver, he can make his column purr or bark, nuzzle or bite, canter or gallop, soothe or repel. And, a rare gift, his words appeal alike to men and women, young and old, intellectuals and ignoramuses, priests and atheists, judges and old lags, heterosexuals, homosexuals and hermaphrodites.

CONNOR: Would you care for me to comment on that?

MR JUSTICE SALMON: Just listen to the question.

And there was the judge intervening again. But where was the question?

BEYFUS: That was the view expressed by Mr Cudlipp in his book, and no complaint of it in the very favourable review you wrote of the book. – A: I would like to explain that; Mr Cudlipp made these further remarks at the end because I think he felt that he had been doing me serious damage in the first place, and he was making amends for an unwarranted attack.

–Where was he making amends? – A: In the last paragraph, in which he says that.

–You think that is making amends? – A: I think his first judgment was wrong, and his second judgment was right.

–Godfrey Winn wrote a column for a couple of years, did he not? – A: I think it was for more than that. He certainly wrote a column.

–Godfrey Winn referred from time to time, like my client, both to his mother and his dog... Did you take a profound dislike to the fact that he referred to his mother and to his dog? – A: I am a bit suspicious of mothers being introduced in newspapers, and on television.

–You dislike anybody who writes about mothers or dogs in a journal? – A: I do not. It depends on how you write about them. It is quite possible to write about mothers in a strong powerful way, and it is quite possible to write about dogs.

–Look at page 134. There were present apparently Mr Godfrey Winn, Mr Cudlipp and yourself.

'Winn', said Connor, 'how do you like being a performing clown in Cudlipp's Feature Circus?'

...Is that right? Did you say something like that?...

'The charm of the host withstood the remark. He smiled and ordered another cocktail. The second and fatal rip came with the entree. 'Godfrey', said Connor, warming to his task, 'you know I don't like your column. It's not my sort of stuff. Dogs and mothers - I don't write about them and I don't like reading about them.'

168

If Connor had been as thorough in his library research on the people he would face in court as he had been on Liberace, he might have wanted, might have been wise, to expand a little on that point and – having already insisted that he thought mother-love was 'the most sacred thing of all' – to have emphasised that he had nothing against dogs, maybe even to have claimed that he liked them. For Beyfus also had a mental library; when he had spotted the mention of dogs he had wracked his memory and recalled seeing a newspaper photograph of the judge, the day after sentencing nine youths for their part in the Notting Hill race riot. He was walking his dogs. And Cassandra had already established himself as a cat man. Now, he was quoted as saying he didn't like reading about dogs.

–That is right, is it not?... And at the bottom of the page: 'Cassandra is the guest who is seldom asked twice.' Now look: January 1941, when the *Daily Mirror* was being threatened by the government... And Mr Cecil H King was the editor of the *Daily Mirror*... – A: No, he was not.

–He was head of both of them. He wrote, 'Dear Prime Minister', and he said, 'Cassandra' – that is you – 'is a hard hitting journalist with a vitriolic style.' You disagree with that? – A: I disagree with that, certainly. This is my employer writing behind my back, without my permission.

–'...but I can assure you his attitude to neither you personally nor to Mr Eden is in any way malevolent'... 'The Prime Minister has also noticed the enclosed cutting... He wishes me to say that it is a pity that so able a writer should show himself so dominated by malevolence.' Do you see that? ... Those extracts from that book at any rate show the opinions which various people who have worked with you have formed? –A: Yes, with which I do not agree.

–I do not think unfortunately this book contains many samples of your writing, but it does contain a little one... I suggest this is typical of what you wrote and of your vitriolic style. 'Cassandra dealt with the medical profession'. Do you see that?

> 'Of course I'm biased', he wrote, 'I'm agin doctors. I don't like 'em. For one thing their mumbo-jumbo, their smooth, lying inefficiency, and their blunt assumption that the disease laden clients have the mentality of sick cattle. They are traders in the most valuable commodity we have - life itself. And they give poor value for money.'

...Do you agree that is a piece of quite wicked, vitriolic writing? – A: I do not, but I think that I was entirely wrong, and I regret having written it.

–It went on:

> Cassandra opined that the General Medical Council was 'unparalleled in bigotry and autocracy' and described the ordinary doctor as a man with 'neither the wit nor the means to break into the big money'...

CONNOR: I think I was wrong to write that, and I regret it.

169

BEYFUS: Indeed, that is rather a shocking thing, is it not, to attack the ordinary GP, the general practitioner, because he is content to earn a modest income doing his duty to his clients on the basis that he had neither wit nor means to break into big money? – A: Mr Beyfus, I have already said that I regret that. In the one million words which I have written and in the six thousand columns which I have written I do not pretend to be right, and I will admit when I was wrong, and when you read those words back to me they seemed foolish and stupid and wrong, and I am sorry I wrote them.

–And shocking and vitriolic? –A: No, I will not agree that. I said I am sorry for them; I will not defend them anyway.

–Do you agree that they are shocking? – A: I have said I am sorry, and that I regret writing them.

–I am not content with that. I am not the medical profession. You need not apologise to me. Do you agree that they are shocking? – A: I agree that they are wrong.

Beyfus shook his head. The National Health Service was only ten years old; doctors were liked and respected by the public, and there were twelve members of it on the jury. He tried again:

–I did not ask you that. Do you agree...? –A: Yes, I agree they are shocking.

–Do you agree they are vitriolic? – A: I did not think they were particularly vitriolic, but I will agree they are vitriolic.

It had taken Beyfus slightly longer than even he had anticipated – 13 pages of transcript – to get Connor to shift from his words being 'not vitriolic at all' to 'not particularly vitriolic' and finally, in the very same answer, to 'I will agree they are vitriolic.' But the Old Fox had done it.

A lesser advocate might have rubbed the point in and repeated the response: '... "I will agree they are vitriolic"... You finally accept that you are a violent and vitriolic writer...' But that was not Beyfus's style. He contented himself with peering over his spectacles to ensure that the jury had got it, as those sitting on the press benches and in the well of the court and the amateur lawyers on the public seats certainly had. He marked his notebook with two large crosses in blue pencil to remind himself for his closing speech where that admission had come. Then he slowly clipped his pencil back on its chain, replaced it in his waistcoat pocket and pressed on. He still had a long way to go.

–The only other instance I have, apart from the one about which you told us, which I cannot find at the moment, is where you attack the Church. You remember that just before the Abdication you wrote an article, which

170

was entitled 'I Accuse', a translation of Zola's famous article. Do you see that? ...

> I am writing about what I regard as the biggest put up job of all time. I accuse leaders of the Church of England of putting our King in a position from which it was almost impossible to retreat.

...There you say the leaders of the Church are guilty of the biggest put up job of all time. Do you want to apologise for those words? – A: No; I think there was a great deal of manoeuvring on that.

–Do you think they were...? – A: I think there was a good deal of manoeuvring over and above the Church.

–...Vitriolic? – A: The words...?

–Yes. – A: No.

–'The biggest put up job of all time'. –A: No; I do not think they are.

–Everybody has heard the words. Now, do you know Mr Richard Dimbleby personally? – A: No.

–Is he a well-known performer on television for the BBC... A very popular figure... Did you write an article about him... Before I read any part of it, would you agree that it was violent and vitriolic? – A: No.

–It was in the *Daily Mirror* of June 12 1956. I am taking this as a sample of your writing... What I am suggesting to you throughout is that these violent articles were written by you as part of the policy of the *Daily Mirror* in presenting views in a sensational manner... You remember I read the passage that it was the policy of the *Daily Mirror* to present both news and views in a sensational manner. I am asking you beforehand: was this article written as part of that policy? – A: It was written as part of the policy which I have. I write what I think, what I feel, and what I believe in.

–I will ask the question once more. Was it written as part of the policy of presenting news and views in this sensational paper in a sensational manner? – A: No, because there is no direction given to me on policy.

–Let us see what you write about poor Richard Dimbleby: 'Richard Dimbleby OBE, by Cassandra', and the heading is: 'Such Condescension. Such Affability'. Then it says:

> In *Pride and Prejudice* there is a magnificent, thick skinned character called the Reverend William Collins who in the presence of his social superiors - and especially Lady Catherine de Bourgh - was overwhelmed by them.
>
> When in the company of these people who were all unknown to him, doing their damnedest to snub him, he cried with real admiration at their none-too-subtle rebukes: 'Such condescension! Such affability!'
>
> Curate Collins would have loved Richard Dimbleby. He would certainly have applauded him with the same respectful cry of 'Such condescension! Such affability!'
>
> I have spent a good deal of time this last weekend listening to Richard Dimbleby reporting the movements of the Queen in Sweden.

The man shimmers in his own unction. He swells in a glycerine respe
for his subject that makes the Royal Family look like an advertiseme
for an immensely costly hair tonic - for which Mr Dimbleby may sign
the advertising rights at any moment.

Mr Dimbleby is the object of the Reverend Collins' admiration bo
again. He is one of the select Praetorian Guard around the Palace. Th
belong to a chosen company of photographers, radio commentators a
magazine biographers who, with a greasy cocoon of adulation, make t
Queen and the Prince almost an unknown pair to the British public. Th
are drowned in honeyed words and over-lit pictures. Around this guar
but not within its closest precincts, are the long-eared nurses of the Roy
kindergarten and the lesser biographers.

−Would you tell me what you mean by 'long-eared nurses of the Roy
kindergarten'? − A: I was referring to Nurse Crawfie, Nurse Crawford.

−Were you referring to her personal appearance? − A: I was not, indeed

−To what were you referring? − A: To the fact that she collected all t
keyhole secrets of the royal family carefully over many years, wrote the
took money for them, and exposed the royal family to one of the greate
indignities to which they had been exposed for many years.

−Around this guard, but not within its closest precincts, are the lon
eared nurses of the Royal kindergarten and the lesser biographe
Scratching like tired but acquisitive journalistic hens they can build up
intimate memoir of things they have never seen and persons they ha
never known - except from a bunch of faded cuttings.

But Mr Dimbleby is none of these. He is a man who has been there
often that he ought to know better. He is the Royal Radio Pussy Cat. F
purrs from the Coronation to the Polo Match, from a Ducal Household
a Country Fair. And still the result is the same - glossy pap soused wi
the mayonnaise of unlimited unction.

−Do you think that is about the height of vituperation? − A: No; I think
is sharp, fair comment.

−You can do better than that! Do you seriously say that you can do bett
than that? − A: I think there is a good deal further to go, if I wanted to go.

−It is pretty vitriolic. − A: No, I do not think it is vitriolic. It is what
thought and wrote at the time. There was a certain amount of indignatio
behind those words. I think the royal family has been badly served b
Nurse Crawford or Crawfie, and by Mr Richard Dimbleby who puts
gloss...

−You have only to hear half a dozen of his carefully modulat
syllables to know that there is nothing more to learn. He stands
attention with cushioned respect. He is like Mr Michelin, the symbol
French motor tyres.

...That is an extremely fat figure composed of motor tyres, is it not... Ar
that is a reference to the fact that poor Mr Dimbleby has the misfortune
be rather fat. − A: We share the same burden.

–I suggest you do not. – A: I did at the time I wrote that. I was two stone heavier.

–That is a reference to the fact that Mr Dimbleby is not exactly a lean person... It is a reference to his personal appearance... Making fun of the fact that he is rather fat. – A: Not making fun of it, referring to his well-known...

–It was not making fun of the fact that he is rather fat... What else then? You say it is not making fun of him, by saying 'He is like Mr Michelin'? – A: I do not think so.

–Do you think it was intended to be pleasant? – A: No.

–'...To listen to Mr Dimbleby describing a Royal occasion is like tuning into an oily burial service.' [Laughter] Do you think that is almost the height of invective, or can you do better than that? – A: No, I could not. It is what I thought and what I believed.

–That is just about the vitriolic height? – A: No.

–'There is nothing more to be said and done about it.' Have you ever seen any vitriolic writing in your life? – A: I have seen some magnificent stuff.

–You have? Have you modelled yourself on it? – A: I have not; I have not endeavoured, but I admire their strong, powerful expressions.

–Eighteenth century? – A: It was, indeed.

–Dean Swift? – A: It was, indeed, wonderful stuff. It was in the great age of the pamphleteers in which people could say much more what they thought than now and less rigidly controlled.

–It was the age of the vitriolic pamphleteer, was it not? – A: It was the age of men who had the power to express themselves with great fury and force.

–It was the age of the vitriolic pamphleteer? – A: I will not accept the word 'vitriolic'.

–I thought you said that you had read vitriolic writings, and had accepted my suggestion that was in the early 18th century. – A: I draw a distinction between being vitriolic and people who feel enormously deeply about what they think and are not afraid to say what they think.

–I asked you if you had ever read vitriolic writings, and your answer was Yes... Do you remember? ... And I asked you whether that was early 18th century, and you said Yes... I suggested Swift to you, and you said Yes... Have you tried to model yourself on the vitriolic writers of that period? – A: I am not by nature a vain man, and I would not presume to do so.

–I did not say you had succeeded. I asked if you had tried to model yourself on the vitriolic writers of that time. – A: No.

–The man is there and what he will say is the same as he has said a score of times before - platitudes coming hushed, honeyed from their author, standing at waistcoated attention. It so happens that the Queen

173

and Prince Philip are vivid personalities. But buried beneath the Dimbleby quilt they are reduced to scented flock.

...That is pretty offensive. – A: I regarded it as one of the wisest and sensible things I have said for a long time.

–Do you think it is offensive? – A: I do not think it is.

–To say that Her Majesty and Prince Philip are reduced to scented flock? – A: I do not think it is offensive.

–What is 'flock' – the cheap stuff which is used in cheap mattresses? – A: Padding material.

–The cheapest form of padding material? – A: I am not aware of the cost of padding material.

–Are you seriously saying that you use words without knowing what they mean? – A: I endeavour to know the exact meaning of every word I use, but I am not always successful.

–The cheapest form of padding? – A: I know it is padding. I do not know its economic value.

> –With his immense talents for the inevitable mental bow at the hips and with his genius of affability and condescension he moves around the Throne Room purring with more than accustomed ease.

...You do not like affability very much, do you? –A: I do not like it?

–I am putting a question. Affability in other people is a quality which brings out the worst in you? – A: Are you asking me whether I like affability? I rejoice in it.

–You do not seem to rejoice very much in the affability of Mr Richard Dimbleby? – A: I do not.

> –In his way, Richard Dimbleby is the greatest and most accomplished radio butler that Broadcasting House has even seen. He rules above stairs.

> He is one of the few select men in the British radio and television set-up who have made their names inevitable, and often unbearable at the receiving end. They rule the House of Radio and they dominate the Tower of TV.

...Then you drag in poor Wilfred Pickles. Is it right that it was not sufficient for you to be offensive to one person in the article? You had to be offensive to another as well. Here you are saying that Mr Dimbleby rules above stairs, and then you say:

> Below stairs Wilfred Pickles roars with homespun laughter with those whose business is near the kitchen sink. There, with the sick and the impoverished, no one can approach his genuine concern and his guffaws.

> But on the floor above, in the vestibule, with an eye on the ancestral hearth and a sharp word for the third footman who dares to let the fire go down, is Mr Dimbleby - very much master in somebody else's household. His talent for putting most people slightly ill at ease and preventing them from interrupting is very useful when it comes to conducted tours around the Stately Homes of England.

174

He does this extremely well and leaves the viewers grateful that they have not muddied the hall with their boots or knocked against the carefully laid out bric-a-brac on the period Chippendale table. The only recent occasion when the technique skidded was when Mr Dimbleby visited Arundel Castle, He was quietly sizzling and gently bubbling like an over-rich Welsh rarebit...

[Laughter.]

−It would be difficult to think of a more offensive description of a man than to describe him as quietly sizzling and gently bubbling like an over-rich Welsh rarebit? [More laughter.]− A: I can conceive of no more healthy corrective to the person concerned.

−I did not ask you that. It would be difficult to think of a more offensive description. − A: I do not think it would.

Beyfus knew that it was usually a good thing to make a jury laugh, albeit while pretending that the words being quoted were actually wicked, and now the jury members were laughing out loud. When he used the expression a third time one of the ushers, sombrely calling out 'Silence, silence' risked choking himself by trying to stifle his own laughter with a handkerchief stuffed into his mouth. But while Beyfus was getting the laughs, it was Connor's words that he was using. Professional observers in Court Number Four were unsure who was actually scoring the points, here.

−You say: 'Quietly sizzling and gently bubbling like an over-rich Welsh rarebit.' − A: That is what I thought; that is what I meant.

−You think it would be quite easy to think of a more offensive description? − A: Well, you will have to give me a long time.

−...When the Duke of Norfolk burnt the edges by putting him smartly in his place and indicating that a television interviewer, no matter how good at his job, was still not the Premier Duke of England. He is the Master of the Notable Occasion - and can reduce it into an inconsequential event quicker than any other man on the air. His business is Deference. His trade is Over-Respect.

One of his greatest triumphs - and it was a notable achievement of the first magnitude - was his handling of the Grace Kelly Affair.

To this prodigious skylark, to this ear-splitting eye-searing romance, Mr Dimbleby switched on what might be called his 'York Minister' treatment. Undaunted in this maelstrom of ballyhoo, he seated himself at the organ, pulled out the stop *Vox Humana* to the full and played the hymn of reverence with surpassing skill.

It was masterly. Where Pickles reeks of free tripe and onions given away under the privacy of a searchlight...

−Do you think that is pretty offensive? − A: No, I think it is fair comment on preposterous behaviour by the person whom I am criticising.

−Mr Wilfred Pickles? − A: And Mr Richard Dimbleby.

175

–…Dimbleby softly deprecates the price of red carnations under a chandelier. Where Pickles and his Mabel pound the old pianner and get well publicised cripples shouting the *Gin-Mill Blues*, Dimbleby is coughing discreetly at Covent Garden with a gardenia in his buttonhole and an old appraising eye on the Royal Box.

Pickles slays you with vociferous kindness. But Dimbleby puts his arm round the Archbishop of Canterbury and makes the Primate of All England wonder what the hell would happen if he brushed off the discreet and all too friendly arm.

…While I have read that the court has been roaring with laughter. You do not think it very funny to Mr Richard Dimbleby or his family, do you? – A: No.

–It was intended to hurt, and it was intended to hurt very much. – A: It was not intended to hurt.

–Let us see. You knew that it was bound to hurt, did you not? – A: I thought it might offend.

–Is that as far as you go? – A: Yes.

–You thought it might hurt? – A: That is right.

–You did not know for certain it was bound to? –A: No.

It was getting towards the end of what had seemed to be a long day. Before the adjournment the judge asked the jury about the suggestion that it might be helpful if they saw a film, or films, of Liberace performing on television. A juryman told him: 'Only two of the jury have not seen them, and they do not consider it will be necessary.'

The judge sent them all home for the night.

Buffoon in the box

Like a dog with a bone – or perhaps more appropriately like an old fox with the neck of a chicken between its teeth, Beyfus was not prepared to let go of his idea that the entire plot was based on the need for 'sensationalism' with increased newspaper sales as the motive in this case. As the fourth day started he returned to the article attacking Richard Dimbleby. It would be right to say that this was an example of a tabloid paper expressing its views in a sensational form and had been written 'for the same reason you write all your vitriolic articles, in order to boost the circulation of this newspaper,' he suggested.

No, said Connor; it was written because it was what he had thought at the time and he was allowed to write what he thought.

BEYFUS: Is it right that since what Mr Cudlipp calls a tabloid revolution the circulation of the *Daily Mirror* has gone up from a million to about four and a half million... As he suggests as a result of a tabloid revolution? – A: As a result of the change of policy.

–And the change of policy can be summarised as the tabloid revolution. – A: I prefer to summarise it as the change which resulted in the paper saying strongly what it felt and what it believed which was very different from a tabloid revolution.

–Very well. Now there is another small example perhaps of your style of writing. You hate poodles, do you not? – A: I hate poodles but I also like poodles in the same way as I hate human beings and I also like human beings.

–Did you take an opportunity quite recently of expressing your detestation of poodles... Did you find it impossible to express your detestation of poodles without dragging in prostitutes? – A: I do not remember the phrase.

–I will read it to you. It is quite recent; Friday, May 22 1959:

> Of all the breeds to debase the coinage of animal and human self-respect, the poodle, now prancing round the West End in hordes, and significantly being found mincing and prancing in attendance on the fancier Tarts of the Town, is the worst.

Connor replied: I not only wrote it but I believed it and meant it when I wrote it.

–This is a small example of your style; you cannot express your detestation for poodles without dragging in references to prostitutes? – A: If I dislike a poodle it is because it is a dog which is often found in the company of people who I dislike... Found in the company of prostitutes who use it as advertisement... It is indeed, a dog which is simply being

177

used as an advertisement for prostitutes to take round with them; that may be why I dislike poodles, but I have been since favoured by my readers who tell me that the poodle is a very tough, courageous dog.
–Does that mean you want to withdraw the defamatory observations you made about poodles? – A: It does not; it seems to me on this occasion that poodles were being exploited by their mistresses and were therefore being subjected to great indignity.
–So any woman who owns a poodle is obviously suspect as regards her morals? – A: No; you know that is not true and I reject it wholeheartedly. I have friends who own poodles and I can assure you they are not prostitutes.

But the point had been made, and scored. Connor almost certainly did not know that the judge was a dog man; Cyril Salmon actually kept dachshunds but, like the poodle, that breed was basically a hunting dog before becoming a family pet (and sometimes a fashion accessory). Edward Marke, managing clerk in the solicitor's office, had spotted the reference to poodles and been offended by it; his wife owned one. And David Jacobs, his boss, had two, Tio Pepe and Gilbert, gifts from the broadcaster and newspaper columnist Gilbert Harding, who was one of his clients. Liberace owned a poodle.
Mrs Beyfus had a poodle, too.
The British public liked dogs and they liked doctors. What might be the odds of there being a poodle owner on the jury?

–I want to ask you about another article which you wrote, do you remember, some years ago, writing an article around a picture of a number of women looking over a wall... And were the women supposed to be looking over the wall into a prison... Was it Dartmoor prison... And is this what you wrote? –

> As I stand by these wretched women and watch their gloating faces my heart despairs of human nature.

...And actually it is a fact, is it not, that the women were not looking over a wall into a prison at all... And the whole of the article which you wrote about these women with their gloating faces was absolute nonsense from beginning to end? – A: It was inaccurate, but I do not think it was wrong.
–It was completely untrue; they were not looking into a prison... They were not gloating... And there was no reason for your heart to despair of human nature. These women, or some of them, brought an action against the *Daily Mirror* in respect of it. – A: Mr Beyfus, I did not stand by these women, I was not at Dartmoor. I was shown a photograph...
–I was just trying to get the date. – A: I cannot remember the date.
–I am trying to help you. – A. I rather doubt it. [Laughter.]

178

–Mr Connor, I am sometimes more helpful than you can imagine. Listen to the question.

MR JUSTICE SALMON: Listen to the question.

But Connor wasn't sure what the question had been.

BEYFUS: Did these women bring an action against the *Daily Mirror*, or some of them? – A: You know, I do not think, to the best of my recollection, that they did.

–Did they not make a claim for damages? – A: I do not think that they did, but again I am speaking from recollection of events which I think occurred seven years ago.

–Just pause a moment. Did the defendants seven years ago have the same solicitors as they have now? – A: How should I know?

–I want to turn for a moment from you to the *Daily Mirror*. So far as you know am I likely to see any other senior representative of the *Daily Mirror* except yourself in the witness box? – A: You mean today?

–At any time in this action. You do not know? – A: No.

–Then we will try and find out who they may be. Who is the present editor of the *Daily Mirror*? – A: He is Mr Jack Stanley Nener.

–Was he the editor in 1956; September, 1956? – A: I think he was. In fact he was.

–Has he been in court in the course of this case? – A: He is, to the best of my knowledge, in the south of France.

–Who is the editor of the *Sunday Pictorial*? – A: They changed hands rather recently. The new editor of the *Sunday Pictorial* is Mr Lee Howard.

Connor presumably wondered what the editorship of the *Sunday Pictorial* had to do with anything; he painstakingly explained that the newspapers were jointly owned, but were not editorially associated; they had different staffs and he did not accept that one was a 'Sunday comparative' of the other. What he accepted was that both were under the editorial control of Mr Cudlipp. And, yes; both newspapers were tabloids.

–One of the highlights of your defence and that of the *Daily Mirror* is to the effect that my client made a jocular observation in regard to Princess Margaret in his interview with Mr Murrow... So much highlighted it is repeated twice in the particulars, the only matter specifically repeated twice... My learned friend called your attention to the *Daily Express*, 'Liberace links name with Princess', February 14 1956... Do you see next to it there is an extract from the *Daily Express* of the next day?... Let us read it:

> An apology and a hope came today from dimple pianist Liberace for his reference to Princess Margaret on US Television, 'I deeply regret that my remarks in regard to Princess Margaret on the Ed Murrow programme have been misinterpreted and misunderstood,' he said.

179

'I meant no offence and I did not refer to Princess Margaret in a light manner. I am an admirer of hers like millions of others.' And he expressed the hope that when he visits England in the autumn he will be introduced not only to Princess Margaret but to other members of the Royal family, as his friends in show business have been.

...Neither my learned friend nor you thought it right to call attention to that expression of regret, did you? –A. I am not in charge of the conduct of this case.

–You did not think it right when your attention was called to the paragraph of February 14 to say: 'But I know he apologised'? – A: Mr Beyfus, I did not mention Princess Margaret in my article and therefore there would be no occasion for me to introduce something which has not occurred in my column.

–You mention it here twice, in the particulars of defence, as ground on which you base your defence? – A: Yes, but I did not mention it in the article.

–In the first place you would not expect an American, the Americans in general, to treat our royal family with exactly the same respect as we do in this country? – A: I would not.

–I suggest, you know, that this defence of the *Daily Mirror* with regard to this alleged disparaging remark about Princess Margaret is utterly and entirely dishonest? – A: I would disagree with that.

–Some years ago did the question of Princess Margaret's possible marriage become discussed... Did the *Daily Mirror* conduct a poll amongst its 13million readers on that subject... What was the poll – as to whether in the opinion of the readers she ought to marry Mr Townsend or not? – A: I believe it was.

–Can you imagine anything in this world more distasteful to Princess Margaret and the royal family than that poll? – A: I do not think it was distasteful.

–You took a long time to express that opinion: you did not think it was distasteful. – A: I did indeed and I would like to ask your compassion in taking time to answer your questions.

–Are you now saying that you do not think that would be a distasteful thing to Princess Margaret? – A: No, I think it was a matter of public interest and a fair comment.

–And not distasteful? You have the *Daily Mirror* asking 13million readers what they thought she ought to do with regard to marrying or not marrying. – A: I thought it was lively and pertinent.

–Was the matter brought before the Press Council? – A: I do not recollect that, but it may well have been.

–Do you not know perfectly well that the *Daily Mirror* was censured by the Press Council because of that poll? – A: Mr Beyfus I do not recollect it, but I think it is right, since you remind me of it.

–If I remind you of it, it must have happened? – A: I am quite sure it did if you say it did.

–Let me take something else even more distasteful, again, you see, suggesting that the papers and associate papers controlled by Mr Cudlipp are completely reckless in what they do and particularly with regard to the royal family. – A: I do not think that is true, but I would like to point out I am not in charge of these papers.

–I am not cross-examining at the moment with regard to you as the defendant; I am cross-examining you with regard to the defence of the Daily Mirror Newspapers Ltd; I made that clear, did I not? – A: Yes, you have.

I am not likely to have the opportunity of cross-examining an editor so I must do the best I can with you. – A: You are doing very well, sir.

–I want you to look at the *Sunday Pictorial* of the Sunday before last. It is published at Geraldine House and is closely connected with the *Daily Mirror*. It is under the prime direction of Mr Cudlipp. One of the features of tabloid newspapers is they compress news in order to have room for strip cartoons... And so far as your experience as a journalist goes one of the things that your readers look at pretty quickly is a strip cartoon... You have got a whole page of strip cartoons in the *Mirror*... Now would you look at the *Sunday Pictorial*: 'Thousands may laugh at this, but we call it a stupid insult.' Let us see the excuse this tabloid has for publishing it.

> The strip cartoon reproduced above comes from an American magazine published in New York. The cartoon - entitled 'Bringing up Bonnie Prince Charles' - is no doubt intended to be smart and funny.

> We say that it is a cheap and contemptible insult. Copies of the magazine with this tasteless strip cartoon are unfortunately circulating in Canada as well as in America. A Canadian reader was so disgusted he sent it to the *Pictorial* with this comment:

> 'I feel that if you published this in your paper, enough people would complain to the magazine in question and discourage them from making further insults on the Royal Family.'

> We have our doubts about whether the American publishers of this muck will be influenced by appeals to their sense of decency. We are certainly not going to publicise the magazine by giving its name.

...So that the one reason for publishing it, suggested by a Canadian reader, is rejected; that is right?... This is a cartoon which quite obviously is unlikely to have been seen by anyone in England unless it had been republished in an English newspaper. – A: That is so.

–Owing to the action of the editor of the *Sunday Pictorial* this would probably have been seen by about 13million readers? – A: I think that is quite true.

–Have you ever heard it said that a man who repeats a libel or a slander is just as guilty as the man who originates it? – A: I have not heard the phrase, but I appreciate its significance.

–And this cartoon, if you look at it, is a most revolting attack upon Her Majesty both in regard to the caption and the drawing. – A: I would not have published that if I had been editor of the *Sunday Pictorial.*

–That is not an answer to my question. This is a revolting attack upon Her Majesty both as regards the captions and the drawings. – A: I think it is a bit of folly... I think it is unwise.

–Do not bother about it being unwise. Is it a revolting attack on Her Majesty both as regards caption and drawing? – A: No, Sir.

–Would you look at the last of those four pictures? Look at the second, the third and the fourth. Is that a picture of Her Majesty looking as sour as vinegar? – A: It is recognisable as being Her Majesty.

–Looking as sour as vinegar? –A: No, looking unhappy.

–I suggest that for the *Daily Mirror* to make a song and dance of this harmless little joke made by my client in an impromptu interview with Mr Murrow is obviously dishonest in view of the behaviour of the *Daily Mirror* in regard to Princess Margaret and Her Majesty in regard to the *Sunday Pictorial*... you do not agree? – A: I do not agree; I think it is ill-advised and had I had the opportunity which I did not have I would not have published this.

–I am talking of the *Daily Mirror*. – A: You must realise the *Daily Mirror* and myself, although I accept money from them, are often two different entities. When we disagree, my employers are free to say something and I am free to criticise my employers, so when you are dealing with me I do not see everything which goes into the newspapers, and we have other newspapers, we have newspapers in Ghana, and I have no responsibility.

–Do you remember the visit of an American entertainer called Bill Haley; it was sponsored by the *Daily Mirror*... Was he a rock and roll artist... And he came over with his band? – A: Yes, he did.

–Were there riotous scenes as a result of his appearance here? –A: There were scenes of enthusiasm.

–Scenes of enthusiasm, but were there riotous scenes? – A: I do not recollect it was in the nature of a riot.

–Were cinemas closed as a result of the scenes of enthusiasm to which you refer? – A: I have not the faintest idea.

–Did you ever write any review attacking him because of the herd instinct which was encouraged by his arrival? – A: I did not.

182

–I want to come to this article. As I understand it, you had seen Mr Liberace on two of his television performances in the United States; is that right... The year before you wrote your article... And you had seen two televised performances in this country... In your own home... You sat it out, did you, both of them? – A: I sat the first one out; I endured the second one but switched it off half-way through.

–As I understand it, the only song which you remember at all in those three and a half performances you watched is *Ave Maria*... You do not remember his singing: *You will always be my sweetheart* to his mother, or anything of that sort? – A: No, I do not. Mr Beyfus, the main thing I remember about this, and my recollection is not exact, was of the spectacle of the man rather than the melody which he was singing.

–You did not like his dressing up... Do you ever go to hunt balls? – A: I have never had that privilege.

–Let us take *Ave Maria*. I gather from your evidence that you object very strongly to his singing *Ave Maria*? – A: I did not; I objected very specifically to the accompaniment which was going on with his playing which was a woman dressed up as a nun in front of a Madonna.

–You know, do you not, that is a song which is constantly sung in the course of ordinary light concerts... Did you not know that it was a most popular item in the repertoire of Miss Gracie Fields? – A: I did not know, but it may well be... What I knew was that it was a song with a strong religious and sacred attachment and when I heard Mr Liberace playing this and when I saw the spectacle of a woman dressed up as a nun facing a Madonna and undergoing the agony of prayer which was portrayed by her, I thought a sacred occasion was being misused by Mr Liberace.

–Why do you talk about the agony of prayer? – A: Because to the best of my recollection...

MR JUSTICE SALMON: Just give the answer. Why did you say agony?

Interestingly, perhaps, here was the judge, again, intervening in the defendant's cross-examination; but this time he was interrupting an answer, in telling him to answer the question.

Connor started again: Because to the best of my recollection, it is such a long time ago, I seem to recollect that the woman in the picture dressed as a nun began to writhe in front of...

BEYFUS: What? – A: Writhe.

–...Now I want you to consider the article for a moment. It was written, was it not, to express your detestation of Mr Liberace? – A: Dislike.

–It is stronger than dislike... detestation? – A: I would say dislike.

–You call him, amongst other things, a terrifying man? – A: Indeed.

–What? –A. Indeed.

183

–But you say you did not seek to express your detestation? – A: I do not detest Mr Liberace. Mr Liberace is a person who is entirely unknown to me but I strongly dislike what he does on the stage, in the concert hall and on the television. I do not detest Mr Liberace; I do not know him.

–I am not suggesting that you wrote this article out of personal malice to Mr Liberace. – A: I certainly did not.

–I am suggesting you wrote it in accordance with the ordinary normal policy of the *Daily Mirror* of writing a sensational article in order to boost its sales? – A: I do not accept that.

–But at any rate one thing we are agreed about is that it is defamatory... And it was intended, was it not, to hold him up to hatred, contempt and ridicule? – A: I do not know whether it was; I just wrote what I thought about it and I cannot accept any legal interpretation. I strongly disliked what he did and I said so.

–I am not putting to you any legal interpretation. Was it not written with a view to holding him up to hatred? – A: No.

–What? – A: No.

–Was it written with a view to holding him up to contempt? ... Was it written with a view to holding him up to ridicule? ... – A: No.

–You say all those three answers – you say them on oath? – A: I do.

–Do you believe that any person reading this article and believing it to be true, that in his eyes Mr Liberace would be a hateful person? – A: No.

–What? – A: I think his act would be regarded as...

–Mr Liberace himself; if a reader read that article and believed it to be true, do not you think Mr Liberace would become a hateful person in his eyes? – A: Not hateful, no.

–Do you think he would become a contemptible person in his eyes, the eyes of the reader who read it and believed it to be true? – A: Yes, his act would be so interpreted.

–You do not think Mr Liberace himself would appear to be a contemptible figure? – A: I do not know about that.

–Well, I want you to think. Don't you think that in the eyes of any reader who read it and believed it to be true he would become a contemptible figure? – A: I would think he would be an unworthy figure.

–What? – A: Unworthy.

–And ridiculous? – A: Unworthy.

–That is one word. I am asking about another. Do not you think it would be ridiculous? – A: No.

–You swear that? –A. I do.

One of the effects of a constant barrage of repetitious questioning is that it becomes hypnotic to the witness. Professional interrogators and skilled advocates understand this; journalists – why would they? – do not. The

184

witness hears, and considers, only one question at a time and is determined, in cross-examination, not to agree with the questioner; but the audience, and this includes the jury, is listening to the questioning as a whole. One result is that the witness, unaware, starts to defend the indefensible. Thus, here was Connor denying that a consequence of describing a man as 'a preposterous clown' would be to make him appear ridiculous.

–I borrow a phrase from my learned friend. May the members of the jury judge the rest of your evidence, the truth of the rest of your evidence, on the basis of that answer? – A: Obviously they will.
–I hope so. Not ridiculous. 'There must be something wrong with us that our teenagers longing for sex and our middle-aged matrons fed up with sex, alike should fall for such a sugary mountain of jingling claptrap wrapped up in such a preposterous clown.' Do not you think that that would make him appear ridiculous? – A: I think it would reduce him to his correct proportions.
–And that this correct proportion would be that of a ridiculous person? – A: It would be those of a preposterous clown.
–Do you agree that a preposterous clown is a ridiculous person? – A: Yes.

Some rallies were shorter than others, but Beyfus had the mastery on this court.

–'Without doubt he is the biggest sentimental vomit of all time'. That is a pretty revolting phrase in itself, is it not? – A: It is a strong phrase, but it is a phrase which reflects and accurately reflects my reaction to Mr Liberace's public performances.
–Do you think it would make him appear contemptible and ridiculous? – A: I do not think it would increase his stature.
–Do you think it would make him appear both contemptible and ridiculous? – A: Ridiculous.
The QC's hand was cupped dramatically to the ear.
–What? –A: Ridiculous.

Beyfus had scored his point. Again. Connor had finally capitulated on 'ridiculous'.

–Not contemptible? [No answer]... Not contemptible? [No answer]... Vomit? Vomit! Have you ever heard any other person in the world described as vomit? Have you? [A pause...] – A: I do not know but...

–Can you remember any other person in the world ever having been described as vomit? – A: I can remember other phrases which have been applied to other...

–I did not ask you that. – A: I cannot.

–I know there is a phrase to the effect that his performance sickened you but I did not ask you that. Have you ever heard any other person in the world being described as vomit? – A: I cannot recollect one.

–Let us look at another phrase: 'They all say that this deadly, winking, sniggering, snuggling, chromium-plated, scent impregnated, luminous, quivering, giggling, fruit-flavoured, mincing, ice-covered heap of mother-love...' – do you think that would make him appear hateful in the eyes of the reader who believed it to be an accurate description? – A: I do not think hateful – distasteful.

–Contemptible? Ridiculous? –A: I would not say that.

–At any rate, the whole object of the article from beginning to end was to depreciate Mr Liberace in the public eye? – A: No, sir.

–It was not? Do you say that on oath? – A: I say that; it was to express my particular dislike of Mr Liberace; I was not concerned with what the public thought.

–If you were not concerned with what the public thought why publish it to 13million people? – A: You would be very surprised, you might be surprised what I write in my column is not conditioned or governed by what my readers want and what they want to read.

–It is governed by purely circulation motives. – A: It is not in the slightest. It is curious, Mr Beyfus, but I am not concerned with the circulation of the *Daily Mirror* in any way. I am concerned with the privilege of having this particular pulpit to say what I think and what I believe in and I do not care about the circulation of the *Daily Mirror*.

–You came into the office and employment of the *Daily Mirror* at the very beginning of the tabloid revolution... And you started writing for it in a style which would not have been permitted in the decorous and gentlemanly *Daily Mirror* which existed before the tabloid revolution. – A: It was the only style which I knew in 1935 and it was the only style which I used until 24 years later.

–I did not ask that. You have been writing in this style which you know quite well would not have been permitted in the decorous and gentlemanly *Daily Mirror* which existed before the tabloid revolution? – A: I do not know that. [–What?] I do not know that fact because I was not there.

–You know from your experience in journalism, do you not, that the type of article which you have been writing would not have been permitted before the tabloid revolution? – A: The situation then was that it was a complete disarray and nobody knew what was being written and what was being done.

–Are you unwilling to answer my question? Do you not know as a result of your journalistic experience the type of article you write would not have been permitted in the decorous and gentlemanly *Daily Mirror* which existed before the tabloid revolution? – A: I do not know.

–You honestly say that? – A: Yes, I do not know; I was not there.

–You do know it was a decorous and gentlemanly paper and not a tabloid? – A: I knew that.

–By the way, there is one thing which I forgot. You gave a description, did you not, of the *Daily Mirror* in your review of a book *Publish and Be Damned...* I will just read it:

> I have been in the middle of a typhoon for 18 years. It rose. It howls and the rain comes in horizontal spears. The surrounding scenery rolls up in a ball and disappears down the street. The gale shrieks, the sky goes black in the face, there is the crash of falling masonry and the barometer sways on the quivering wall pointing with tipsy scorn to 'set fair'. The only time in nearly two decades of this that I ever got a bit of peace and quiet was with the army in World War II. The bangs were more gentlemanly.
>
> Then it all started again. The tiles peeled off the roof upwards, the windows were blown in and once again it wasn't necessary to lock the front door. It was lodged in what remained of the upper branches of the old elm tree next door. The name of this unending hurricane, this non-stop cyclone is a tempest of a business called the *Daily Mirror*.

...That was your description of the *Daily Mirror* in your review of *Publish and Be Damned...* And, of course, it was written I concede and it is quite obvious, in a humorous vein, but it was intended, was it not, to describe the violence of the manner in which the *Daily Mirror* was conducted at Geraldine House? – A: No, sir... It was intended to convey something which goes on in a newspaper, a daily newspaper where there is constant disagreement, constant strife, as I said yesterday, and constant trouble.

–Now let us come back to this article. Whatever else may be true about it, it was highly depreciatory of the plaintiff; there is no doubt about that. You told us it was intended to be? – A: Of his public performance.

Beyfus then turned to the box of type at the top of the Cassandra column, what journalists call a pull-quote. Connor confirmed that he usually, though not always, selected the text that appeared in it, and had done so on this occasion. He accepted that it appeared in larger type to attract the attention of readers. He again denied that the words were intended to suggest that the plaintiff was a homosexual, but referred only to the universality of Liberace's appeal to people of both sexes and ages.

–What I am suggesting is that, using your very great skill as a writer, you deliberately, studiously, invented phrases which would convey to many

187

millions of your readers that my client was a homosexual... – A: I strenuously...

–Wait... while enabling counsel who appear for you, or who might appear for you, in court to say with wide-eyed innocence 'Where on earth do you find that meaning?' That I suggest is the motive behind your choosing these very curious words? – A: It was not.

–Let us see what your explanation of them is. If your explanation of these words is true, they were a very considerable compliment to Mr Liberace, were they not? – A: They were.

–And you are inviting members of the jury to believe that, having written this highly depreciatory article about Mr Liberace and his performances, you chose to highlight, to print in the box in larger print, words which were highly complimentary to him? –A. No, I am not saying that at all. May I say what I am saying? What I was emphasising was the totalitarian nature of his performance, which has been one of the most astonishing phenomena of our time, to say for instance that he gets 16,000 people in Madison Square Garden.

–I am going to ask to have your previous answer read by the shorthand writer. I suggest that you agreed with me that these words were meant to describe the universality of his appeal to both sexes, to people of all ages, and that would be a compliment.

The shorthand writer explained that the question and answer had been recorded by the writer who had just left the court. The judge read it back from his own notes. Mr Beyfus continued:

–In other words, what you are saying is that these words were intended to describe and convey to the public the universality of his appeal... That would be a compliment, surely? – A: Not necessarily. In the context of the article they could be read annexed to the caption; they could be read annexed to the views which I expressed.

–That is not a compliment. – A: Dissociated from the article it might well be so, but in association with the article it was not a compliment.

–Let us see, if we may so put it, your extraordinary state of mind on September 25 1956, if your evidence be honest. You were writing an article in the strongest possible terms, expressing, as you say, not your detestation but dislike of Mr Liberace's performances. You select for the box at the top, for special attention, in larger print, words which in themselves would be taken to be a compliment? – A: I am not saying that at all. It is expressing my wonderment and my astonishment about the magic of this man's appeal, allied to commercialism, in which he can fill places like Madison Square Garden. It has never been done before, except on another occasion as a result of what was a resettlement fund.

–'The magic of his appeal?' If you are not careful you will end like Balaam, making a curse and end by blessing. We are now talking about the

188

magic of his appeal? Are you seriously suggesting that this article was intended to describe the magic of his appeal... Why use the phrase when you are giving evidence on oath? – A: What I am referring to is the astonishing effect of the attraction which he has for enormous sections of the community, which in my view, in the entertainment business, I have never seen before. I think it was done for commercial reasons, not for truth.

–Now let me put the way in which I suggest you intended these words to be understood by many millions of people. First of all, the words in the box start 'He is the summit of sex'... Quite clearly, from the words in the box, the subject which you are dealing with is sex. – A: Sex and sex appeal.

–Sex. 'The pinnacle of Masculine, Feminine and Neuter. Everything that He, She and It can ever want'... sexually? – A: I object to the sentence being chopped up and divided. Sentences have a total meaning.

–You may object to it, but I am afraid you are going to suffer it. 'He' in that context means another man or men, does it not... You are saying that he is everything for something or other? – A: In the nature of his performance men are strongly attracted.

–There is nothing in that paragraph about the nature of his performance, is there? – A: No, but there is in the rest of the article

–I know there is. He, Liberace, is everything that another man can ever want, sexually? – A: No; I do not agree 'sexually'.

–That is what you are saying? – A: I did not say 'sexually'.

–The word 'sex' at the top quite obviously governs what is in that box, does it not? – A: In that box? Yes.

–That is what I am saying. Then we can take it that the next two phrases are used with a sexual connotation. – A: They are designed to draw attention to the fact that Mr Liberace is the most successful exponent of sex appeal in the theatre.

–Everything that another man can want sexually, that is to say a body willing to participate in sexual practices with any man. – A: I entirely disagree.

–I suggest that is the obvious meaning which you intended... – A: I did not...

–...millions of people to understand? – A: I did not, and it did not occur to me.

–You agree with me that it is a most offensive piece of writing? – A: It is not as clear as it might have been.

–It is quite different in style from your usual very clear, if strong, style? – A: No, I do not agree.

189

–Let us see what the word 'It' means and the word 'Neuter'...
'Everything that He, She and It can ever want'... 'It' was just thrown in for
confusion? – A: No, it was not.
–It might refer to animals, but it does not mean that. It could suggest that
the poodle sits up, the cat purrs and the budgerigar calls 'Tweet, tweet'
when the television is turned on and Mr Liberace's face appears. It is not
meant to convey that. – A: No, it was not. It is part of the continuity of the
theme of the totalitarian appeal of Mr Liberace, which transcends anything
which any other entertainer has done. He sits down in a great barn-like
place as Madison Square Garden, unarmed with anything else except a
piano and candelabra...
–There are two... – A: Can I go on? May I finish?
MR JUSTICE SALMON: I think he wants to finish, Mr Beyfus.
BEYFUS: I am sorry, I thought he had.
CONNOR: He then goes along to a place like Madison Square Garden
where there are 16,000 people, a most hostile and unhomely place, and
thus armed with nothing except a piano and candelabra, and possibly his
mother – I think she was there on this particular occasion – this man can
attract the whole community, defy all the critics, and get everybody there
of every age and every sex. That is what I meant. I was referring to what is
Mr Liberace's secret of this business, that he commands the whole of the
audience.
–Have you finished... You have had the opportunity of making a long
speech. Would you tell me what on earth it had got to do with the word
'It'? – A: This is the continuity...
–I understand. – A: Mr Beyfus, I would like to answer.
GARDINER: Let him finish his answer.
BEYFUS: I understand what you are saying.
CONNOR: 'It' is the continuity of the particular phrase 'Masculine,
Feminine and Neuter', which is put in to emphasise that he appeals to one
and all, and there is no sexual imputation in that, and no imputation, when
I wrote the words, of homosexuality.
–That is exactly what I am suggesting. You are now telling the jury that
'it' means continuity, and therefore his appeal was not only to men and
women but also to animals. What else does 'it' mean? – A: It is a phrase
which means that he has supreme command, dominating the whole of
mankind when he goes into a place.
–You told my lord and members of the jury – perhaps you now want to
go back on it – that the word 'sex' at the top there obviously governed the
rest of the words in the box, and that the next two sentences must be read
with that context. Do you remember telling us that... I suggest that, on
your reading of it, the word 'it' and the word 'Neuter' are completely
meaningless? – A: I am sorry, I may have been unsuccessful.

190

–You are not suggesting, are you, that you had no idea, when you came into court, that the plaintiff's complaint was that he was being described by you as a homosexual? – A: I had learnt that there was, and I was astonished.

–Do you know that one of the documents which have been disclosed in this case by the secretary of the *Daily Mirror* was the programme at the Apollo Theatre? – A: I know nothing of that programme, as I say. Let me say this. In the consultations which I have had with my lawyers, which have been very close, I did not know of what happened at the Apollo Theatre until three days ago.

–It was a joint affidavit which you swore on oath a long time ago now, more than eighteen months ago. On November 11 1957 you, together with the secretary of the defendant company, swore this: 'The defendants have in their possession or power the documents relating to the matters in question to this suit...' and one of the documents which we find is the Apollo Theatre programme *For Amusement Only*. That is what you were swearing? – A: I do not recollect this, and I wish to tell you the exact truth of this matter. What happened was that three days ago I said to my colleague...

–I do not want to know what three days ago you said to someone. I am asking whether you had not by November 1957 acquired a programme of the Apollo Theatre for the show *For Amusement Only*? – A: I have never seen it. It may have been in the possession of my solicitors and advisers, but three days ago I said to Mr Phillips, who is here in this court, 'What is all this about the Apollo?' I did not know it. I may have been a party to the signature, but I assure you I did not know.

–You did not know about it? – A: I did not know, not for one second.

–Did you not read the affidavit before you swore it? – A: I think I read it. I may have read it, but if this point was in it, it escaped my notice entirely. I am completely in the dark. 'What is all this business about the Apollo Theatre?' I said; I did not know what was going on. I said to Mr Phillips 'What is it all about?'

–Do not tell us what you said to someone else; it is not evidence.

MR JUSTICE SALMON: Did you read the document set out in the schedule, before you swore it? – A: I think I read it, but I read it with the rather desultory care with which one reads legal documents.

BEYFUS: Do you remember saying that nothing was said in the article which had not been said before? ... Where do you find anybody who has said before that my client was 'appalling', in the very literal sense of the word, namely, 'terrifying'? – A: I am not claiming, although I may have said it, that everything which is said in my article was said by someone before.

191

–That is just what you did say. – A: Then I disclaim that. I say that is untrue.

–Nothing there which has not been said before? – A: I have not said that.

–You retire from that position? – A: I do not. What I say is that most of it has been said before. I do not say identically, because I am not in a position to copy an article by another journalist.

–Nothing like 'terrifying' has been said by anybody else? – A: He was terrifying to me.

–You knew that he had come over to this country to give public concerts... Live concerts at the Festival Hall and the Albert Hall... Why did you not go and see him before writing an article? – A: Because I had seen Mr Liberace in the most revealing of all mediums, which is television, which is better than the front row of the London Palladium. It is more revealing than any other.

–You think that seeing a man on television for 24 minutes, with an interruption for commercials, is better than seeing him live for three hours? – A: I do; I will tell you why. Television is the greatest lie detector. It is the greatest exponent of falseness and synthetic appeals. On television, in two or three performances, and in this particular case four performances, they did indeed give me an extraordinary revealing picture of Mr Liberace which I could not have obtained in the front row of the London Palladium.

–That is what you tell the members of the jury... you did refer to his appearing at the Palladium with his mother. Do you remember that, in your evidence in chief? –A: Yes.

–Do you know that he never appeared at the Palladium with his mother... You are a little reckless, are you not, not only in what you write but also in what you say on oath? –A: Not reckless, but wrong.

–The expression 'fruit-flavoured' is a somewhat remarkable one, is it not, even for a man with your vocabulary? – A: It is associated with the rest of the confectionery adjectives.

–One of the things you knew quite well, did you not, was that it was virtually certain that your article, or important parts of it, would be reproduced in the United States of America? – A: That is always a contingency with which one is faced.

–With regard to anybody with the fame, or you would probably put it 'notoriety', of Mr Liberace, it was a virtual certainty that your article, or large parts of it, would be reproduced? – A: Likely.

–You have been in the United States quite a lot... You know, did you not, that 'fruit' is slang in the United States for homosexual? – A: I did not, for one moment. Mr Beyfus, I am well acquainted with many hostile words, including implications as to homosexuality, but I did not know that 'fruit-flavoured' in the United States was an imputation of homosexuality. It came as a bit of a surprise to me.

–Are you sure? I have here the *American Thesaurus of Slang* by Berrey & Van den Bark. Would you look at it?

GARDINER: I am not clear, with respect, how this book, whatever it says, can be relevant, in view of the absence of any allegation.

MR JUSTICE SALMON: It may be that the witness is going to be asked whether that book is among his bedtime reading.

GARDINER: It may be 'winking' in America means something awful.

[Laughter.]

MR JUSTICE SALMON: I do not think Mr Liberace was cross-examined on his evidence that the word 'fruit' or 'fruit-flavoured' had a homosexual connotation in the United States. I do not think that was challenged.

GARDINER: I did challenge that.

MR JUSTICE SALMON: Then I am wrong in my recollection.

BEYFUS: I am putting this on the issue of malice, as suggesting with regard to the words in the box that they were carefully contrived to have a double meaning. Was this very carefully put in for American readers?

CONNOR: Not so. I have read the paragraph.

BEYFUS: It is right, is it not, that if that dictionary be right, 'fruit' is one of the slang words used in the United States as designating a homosexual? – A: This dictionary says so, but I have never heard it before.

–I am only saying, if the dictionary is right? We assume the dictionary is right. That is all I am putting to you, if the dictionary be right... Your case is that it is pure coincidence that there happens to be in this article of yours this very curious expression 'fruit-flavoured'. – A: It is, indeed. Mr Beyfus, I know all the naughty words, and most of the implications, and I have never heard of 'fruit-flavoured' in connection with homosexuality.

–I was not suggesting that the word 'fruit-flavoured' is used. I was suggesting the word 'fruit' by itself indicated... – A: I did not know. I am very sorry. I am getting ignorant of these things.

–Have you ever heard anybody in this wide world previously described as 'fruit-flavoured'? – A: Not to my knowledge.

Counsel then asked about the 'sad but kindly men on this newspaper' to whom he had spoken. Connor said one of them had been Henry Howe, a photographer, who was 'very kindly'. He knew nothing of his opinion of Liberace, but he had described the reception at Waterloo. And he had spoken to other reporters who went down there. He had spoken to Donald Zec later.

–You would not call Donald Zec a kindly man, would you? – A: I would call him one of the nicest guys I know.

–A man who apparently likes Mr Liberace, but wrote an article knocking him as hard as he could... You may like unkind men? – A: As a matter of fact, I do. I happen to like unkindly men, wrong men, people who are weak, as well as people who are strong, brave and courageous. You may

193

not believe it, but it is quite true... I spoke to Mr Harris and other reporters. There was considerable commotion in our office, as you can well imagine.

–This long list of insulting epithets, most of them insulting at any rate, which you chose, was based on what you saw on television and on what you read in the newspapers? – A: And conversations with people whom I have mentioned.

–You still do not think it would have been better to have seen him in a live show? –A: No, I do not, and I will tell you why, Mr Beyfus.

–You have told me once. – A: I am sorry.

–Then 'this terrifying man'. What you find terrifying about him is that he was collecting crowds, and you do not like the herd instinct. – A: I do not like the herd instinct.

–I want to see if I have got your case correctly. The reason he is terrifying is that he collects crowds, and you do not like crowds because of the herd instinct. – A: Because that was motivated by things which are false. I suggest the false effect of a young unknown girl kissing Mr Liberace through the window of a railway train. I have never seen that done.

–You know quite well that no young girl kissed Mr Liberace? – A: I remember looking...

–Would you look at the photograph? It is quite clear, is it not, that the young girl kissed the glass? – A: I quite agree.

GARDINER: He said, through the window.

BEYFUS: Let me cross-examine, please.

GARDINER: I do not think my learned friend heard the end of the answer. Mr Connor answers, and lowers his voice at the end of his answer. He said she kissed through the window.

BEYFUS: I know. If I kiss someone through a window, I expect to kiss them. I do not expect to kiss a bit of glass.

GARDINER: The lady apparently did it with the glass up.

CONNOR: May we settle for a proximity of osculation? [Laughter.]

BEYFUS: What a horrible word! One of the things which you tell us caused you to write this article was a young woman kissing the glass of the carriage from the platform? A: Yes, indeed.

–And he put his lips to the corresponding part of the glass on the other side... You tell us you are married, but if you were a good looking young man and you were unmarried, do you not think you would have done the same thing? – A: My passion, although it always has been strong, has never forced its way through plate glass.

[Laughter.]

–Do not let us be too jocular about this serious matter. Are you seriously saying that the fact that when this girl parted her lips on the glass and he jokingly put his lips on the other side of the glass, that is one of the things on which you relied in writing these comments? – A: As a matter of fact I do.

–I like to try to find out. That gives you justification for saying that he is the biggest sentimental vomit of all time? – A: It is a contributory cause.

–You do not normally in your articles repeat yourself very much, do you? – A: I am addicted to adjectives.

–I read a very long article about Mr Dimbleby yesterday, and there was no repetition of abuse there, was there? You managed to find a different offensive epithet in every paragraph... Did you notice that you are so overcome with the desire to be offensive to Mr Liberace that you have to refer to being sick in two successive sentences... Do you realise that... No, it is three times, altogether, 'He reeks with emetic language'. That is the sort of language which makes you sick.... 'He reeks with emetic language that can only make grown men long for a quiet corner, an aspidistra, a handkerchief and the old heave-ho.' Such language that the only thing to do is to go in a corner behind an aspidistra and be violently sick... Remember the next sentence – you are so pleased with it that you repeat it in even more offensive terms: 'Without doubt he is the biggest sentimental vomit of all time'? – A: That is right.

–One of the things on which you base these sentences is this pretty girl putting her lips to the glass and he putting his lips to the other side... That was honest comment? – A: It was.

–Nothing to do with boosting the circulation of the paper? – A: No.

–'Slobbering over his mother, winking at his brother, and counting the cash at every second'... 'Counting the cash every second' even on your view was a most offensive exaggeration, was it not? – A: It was an exaggeration.

–If it was an exaggeration, it was a very offensive one... Indeed, it is a reference to what you said yesterday, that he was over-sentimental, and then you brought in the words, 'There was a note of calculated commercialism'. Where did you find in his television performances, not having seen the live performances, anything which brought in a note of calculated commercialism any more than any other singer who gets a large salary for singing? – A: I think he has been particularly successful. When I said 'calculated commercialism' the reason I said that was that his act applies to things which I hold quite sacred, such as mother love.

When you say 'mother love' you do not mean mother love at all, do you? You mean love of mother. Mother love means the love of a mother for her children. – A: The relation is a two way one, I believe.

–You are a master of words. Does not 'mother love' normally mean the love of a mother for her children? – A: It means also love of the children for the mother.

–I suggest it does not. – A: I suggest it does, with great respect.

–Whether it does or does not, at any rate are you saying that the fact that he sang to his mother *You'll always be my sweetheart* introduced a note of calculated commercialism? – A: Yes.

–I suggest that, so far from your evidence on this point being true, your real complaint about his performance was that it was over-sentimental... Did you not say cloying? – A: That is one of the complaints.

–Yesterday you used the word 'over-sentimental'... How can an act at the same time be cloying and over-sentimental and at the same time have a note of calculated commercialism? – A: I think that unfortunately both those qualities are combined in Mr Liberace's public performances.

–They are absolutely opposite qualities, are they not? – A: I do not agree.

–Then you say: '...this superb piece of calculating candy floss'. Most of your writings I suggest are vitriolic, but what you set up against my client is this: 'On the occasion in New York at a concert in Madison Square Garden when he had the greatest reception of his life and the critics slayed him mercilessly, Liberace said: 'The take was terrific but the critics killed me. My brother George cried all the way to the bank!' Do you think that is a very humorous observation? – A: I think it is very revealing.

–You think it is humorous? – A: I would prefer the word 'revealing'.

–The answer to my question is either 'Yes' or 'No'. Do you not think it is a very humorous observation? – A: Not very humorous.

–Leave out 'very'. Do you think it is a humorous observation? – A: No.

Mr Beyfus kept trying: Do you think it is the observation of a man making a joke against himself... Do you think it is jocular... You obviously do not think that 'The take was terrific but the critics killed me. My brother George cried all the way to the bank' was jocular? I am not saying a good joke... I agree that opinions may differ on what is a good joke, but it is quite clearly jocular? It just shows how he can take a joke against himself?

It was the hypnotic rabbit-in-the headlights syndrome again; the repetitious, relentless questioning and the automatic denial. However Beyfus put it, Connor could not agree that it was meant to be funny. He was doing himself no favours in the eyes of the courtroom audience.

–'Nobody since Aimee Semple McPherson has purveyed a bigger, richer and more varied slag-heap of lilac-coloured hokum.' The first suggestion in that is that Aimee Semple McPherson purveyed a big, rich and varied slag heap of lilac coloured hokum. That is right?... And that suggests falsity? – A: Humbug.

–Did you tell the members of the jury yesterday that when you wrote that you were not suggesting in the very slightest that this deceased lady was anything but completely sincere? – A: She may have been in what she thought but what I thought of her performance was that it was humbug.

–Your favourite American paper is the *Daily News*? – A: No, it is not. My favourite one in America is the *New York Herald Tribune* for daily journalism.

–The office to which you resort, when you are in New York, is the office of the *Daily News*? A: That is so.

–That is about the lowest tabloid in New York? – A: No, it is not, as a matter of fact.

–It is about the most sensational daily paper in New York? – A: It is not, actually.

–It is tabloid? – A: Yes. What other tabloids are there in New York? – A: *New York Post*.

–Is that more sensational than the *Daily News*? – A: It is more violent.

–Does the *Daily News* come next? A: I think the *New York Daily Mirror* comes next.

–...It is one of the three most sensational tabloids in New York? – A: Yes, Mr Beyfus.

–That is where you go the moment you arrive in New York, so far as business purposes are concerned? – A: I go there for the very simple reason that we have our office there.

–That is exactly what I thought. Then we go on. 'Nobody anywhere ever made so much money out of high speed piano-playing with the ghost of Chopin gibbering at every note.' This last bit was meant to add a little offensive note, 'the ghost of Chopin gibbering at every note'? – A: They are meant to reflect and to convey what I think of Mr Liberace's piano playing.

–Do you think the ghost of Chopin does come down and gibber at every note? – A: I hope that he does come down and gibber at every note, and returns to the Shades from which he came.

–Are you a musical critic? – A: I am not a musical critic.

–Have you ever heard Mr Liberace play Chopin? – A: I cannot positively identify that.

–At any rate, if you ever heard him, it did not make any impression on you that he played it badly? – A: No. I have seen other performances on the piano.

–You have heard people like Mr Mantovani say that in his opinion he is a first class pianist? – A: I thought Mr Mantovani was a rather bad musical critic.

–I did not think he was a musical critic at all; he is a conductor. – A: He was invited here to give his opinion on the technical excellence of Mr Liberace's playing.

–At any rate, you heard him express the opinion that he was a highly competent musician... You chose to write this about 'high speed piano playing with the ghost of Chopin gibbering at every note' without having heard him play Chopin... Certainly without any knowledge that he played Chopin badly? – A: Yes; Chopin.

–'There must be something wrong with us that our teenagers longing for sex and our middle aged matrons fed up with sex...' – you have left out the men, the children, the dog, the cat and the budgerigar, all of whom seem to have, according to you, fallen for Mr Liberace. It goes on, '... alike should fall for such a sugary mountain of jingling claptrap wrapped up in such a preposterous clown.' Was that endeavouring to wind up on as offensive a note as you could? – A: Not at all. You have to finish some time, as indeed I hope these proceedings will finish.

–I am not sure of that. The whole of that article, from beginning to end, was bound, was it not, and I give you one last opportunity to deal with it, to cause Mr Liberace to be looked upon with great hostility by millions of readers? – A: That was not the primary purpose. The primary purpose...

–I did not ask you that. – A: Then the answer is 'No'.

–I did not ask you the primary purpose. I am not suggesting it was the primary purpose. My suggestion is that the primary purpose was to boost the circulation of this tabloid. – A: No.

–It was bound, was it not, to create grave hostility towards Mr Liberace and his performance? – A: That was not my purpose.

–I did not ask you that. Did you not think that it was bound so to do? – A: No.

–You say that on oath? – A: I do.

–You say the same thing in your article about Mr Dimbleby. That was bound, was it not, to hold him up to the most complete and utter ridicule? – A: No.

MR JUSTICE SALMON: If people accepted the opinions you expressed in this article, it would not be likely to endear Mr Liberace to them, would it? – A: I would agree with that.

BEYFUS: The second article is October 18. You were so anxious, were you not, to keep on this fertile field that you had another go at Mr Liberace on October 9? Apparently a number of my client's admirers – when I say 'a number', it was not very many; four or five – from the United States sprang to his rescue and wrote letters to you... Letters which, of course, were not published anywhere; just received by you privately... I suppose a great many of the articles which you write produce correspondence; is that right... And you thought it right to write a special article dealing with these four or five private letters which you received? – A: Yes.

–I suggest this shows how intensely malicious you were in this case. 'Liberace's Disciples'. Again we have got a box. 'From Maxine Ducray: president of the Liberace Club, Broadview, Illinois, USA:

'We of the Talent Club, demand an apology from you for the insulting remarks you made about Liberace... The people love Liberace! Go ahead and live with your ulcers and your headaches – be a grouch. We love Liberace'... From Vicki King, Nashville, Tennessee: 'I have just read some very uncomplimentary remarks on Liberace by Cassandra. How can you have a grouch like that? Such terms he used on the wonderful, nice Liberace! I am a very devoted fan of Lee's – and resent this jerk and his vicious talk against the most wonderful of men. A big boo and drop dead to Cassandra.'

...Obviously a humorous observation; do you think so? – A: So far I have not obliged.

–It was obviously a humorous way of expressing her disapproval of you:

From the Senior Liberace Fan Club of New Orleans, Louisiana: 'Portions of your column in which you degraded Liberace appeared in our local newspaper... Liberace is a great favourite here in New Orleans, not just as an entertainer, but as a person and as a friend. You not only hurt Lee, but hundreds of thousands of other Americans. However, honeychild, you just hurt your own English entertainers when you did it because every Liberace fan in America will boycott the English entertainers from now on.' Then there is a letter from another lady who lives in Kansas: 'One of the Ten Commandments says very definitely to Honor Thy Neighbour. Well, do you think your remarks about Liberace were observing this commandment? Liberace is a very definite improvement on some of the trite entertainers you send over here supposed to entertain us. Why in hell don't you keep them in England?'...

...That is more your style, is it not?

We'd gladly keep Liberace here in the US. We all miss him terribly. The kindest thing I can say to you is – drop dead.

...Then you go on:

'It was Wladziu Valentino (Lee) Liberace who said: 'I want to spread the World of Love, the 'World of Family Love, Love of God and Love of Peace.' But of these four disciples the first wishes me diseased, the second wants me dead, the third is a blackmailer and the fourth, like the second, longs to dance upon my grave. It seems a poor sort of philosophy that depends on a grimacing Messiah like this candlelit, leering, heaped-up ball of syncopated saccharine.'

...Were you there endeavouring to outdo the Cassandra of the preceding month... You almost succeeded, did you not? – A: Probably you are a better judge than I am.

–Perhaps the jury will be a better judge than I am; but 'a grimacing Messiah'; can you imagine anything more offensive than that, particularly coming from an agnostic? He may not have known it, but now that we

199

know you are an agnostic do you think you could possibly have chosen a more offensive phrase to use about a devout Roman Catholic? – A: They were strong words.

–Do you think it would be possible to find a more offensive phrase? –A: I do not know.

–'...But such is apparently the New Liberace Society. It is made up...'
...this is what you say about people who apparently like and defend Liberace:

...of the exponents of throb and thump and slush and smile. It is led by the pathfinders of the rootless, the aimless, the gutless, the lost, the bewildered and all the rest of the bemused plankton who in a ferocious world are prepared to cling to any smirking, winking, predatory jellyfish like Liberace who drifts their way.

...That is your description of the people who, liking and admiring Liberace, spring to his rescue by writing letters complaining of your article. ... And, indeed, so pleased are you with it that you repeat it in the box:

I suppose it was always thus. But the lost, the lonely and the truly bewildered in days gone by sometimes stood for better causes than that hoisted by this globule of glistening syncopated pride. And I think they were more right than, say, the President of the Liberace Club, Broadview, Illinois.

...Those last words you thought sufficiently important to repeat in the box in larger print... Is that truly your view of people who like and admire Liberace and spring to his rescue by writing letters of protest against your article? – A: I have a very low opinion of people who are misled by him; but I recognise their misfortune.

–Will you sometimes try and answer my question? You see that sentence 'It is led by the pathfinders...' My question is a very simple one: is that really your true and honest opinion of people who, resenting your article about Liberace, come to his rescue by writing letters of protest to you? – A: Yes.

Connor would have been unaware of the real motivation behind this line of the counsel's questioning. Beyfus had calculated that, so popular was Liberace generally, it was highly likely that among twelve people picked at random for the jury at least one would have been an admirer of the pianist as a performer and possibly even as a person.

His attention had already been drawn to one juror, a middle-aged woman, who arrived daily (this was the fourth day) in a different outfit and appeared to exchange supportive smiles with his client. He had now contrived to cause Connor to attack not only his client but also his supporters.

And he needed only one determined juror on his side to win the case.

200

–On October 18th, without any, shall I say, provocation or anything of the sort, you thought it right to abuse Liberace again; is that right? – A: Yes.

–Absolutely refusing to leave the poor man alone. It is in the big headline 'Calling all Cussers'. You say: 'I am not by nature much of a cusser. The four-letter words – all three of them' – I will not ask you which they are – 'are admittedly useful but they are grossly overworked and are often blind and meaningless spots in any intelligent denunciation.' Then you say, quite truly, as you have shown by your own writings:

> The ammunition dumps of vituperation in the English language are so wide, so diversified and so abundant that the fastidious denigrator hesitates to use ordinary bad language, for the traditional words are so threadbare that their meaning sometimes becomes an endearment.

...Are you really thinking of yourself when you use the phrase 'the fastidious denigrator'? – A: No.

> –It is now possible to call somebody an old ---- and to make it quite clear that you have a great deal of affection for the one over whom you have just heaped a major obscenity.

...Then you deal with tea. Then you deal with the wonderful denunciations by Isaiah. Then you say:

> I think we should return to these greater and more sonorous maledictions. For those were the days when a cussword was a cussword and, when well and truly laid, the recipient knew that what had been said was no term of endearment but a prayer that his liver should be devoured by maggots and that his children should be fatherless before nightfall.

...In these more modern days you have endeavoured, have you not, to return yourself to these greater and more sonorous maledictions? – A: No.

> –In their daily programme of events called Today's Arrangements *The Times* was yesterday at its impassive, unsmiling best. It said...

...Then there are a number of announcements of religious services. Then:

> ...Albert Hall: Liberace, 7.30. Rarely has the sacred been so well marshalled alongside the profane.

...You thought it right, did you, to accuse Mr Liberace of profanity? – A: Yes.

–One of the reasons being that he played Liberace with the background of a nun praying? – A: That is right.

–The *Daily Mirror* has disclosed, and most people in this court have seen, the book of press cuttings. It is right, is it not, that substantially speaking the press cuttings which have been disclosed by the *Daily Mirror* are adverse ones, highbrow musical critics and so forth? – A: Yes.

–Why has not the *Daily Mirror*, and why haven't you, disclosed the favourable ones? – A: I cannot answer that question.

–I am going to ask you. – A: I do not know. That is the answer.

201

–I am going to ask you about yourself. There are to be found quite a number of favourable ones, are there not? – A: There may well be.

–For example, one of the best known papers dealing with the entertainment industry is *Stage*. I just want you to look at it:

> Mollie Ellis reports on The Legend that is Liberace. Seldom has there been so much excitement over one show business personality as there has been over American pianist-entertainer Liberace, who has become a legend in his own life-time. Never, as far as we can remember, has any one person been the subject of so much organised abuse from the vast majority of the British Press. The newspapers, on the whole, tried, by cheap insinuation, to prejudice the public against this top-line artist before he had a chance to give his opening concert.

–That would be a good description of you, would it not? – A: No.

–Perhaps you are right. It would not be cheap; but it would be expensive insinuation; is that right? – A: I think it would be wrong.

–On that, have you steadily progressed during the last 20 years that you have been with the *Daily Mirror*? – A: Do you mean financially? Yes, I have.

–So that by now you are, would it be right to say – I am not asking for details, because it is not my business to pry into your personal affairs – one of the highest paid columnists in Fleet Street? – A: I am highly paid.

–One of the highest paid? – A: Yes.

> –…The public, on the other hand, have shown exactly what they think of the abusive headlines which have been flashed in front of them every day for weeks by booking Liberace's tour solid, and on each and every occasion showing how miserably the campaign of the press has failed...
>
> Accustomed though they are to critics who regard the event of someone falling out of the balcony as far more important than the play under review; the décolleté of an audience more interesting than the opening performance of the Bolshoi Ballet, and the statistics of otherwise undistinguished young ladies as the most important aspect of present-day show business, neither public nor artist has been quite so disgracefully treated as it has in the recent reportage on Liberace.
>
> Glitter and glamour being synonymous with show business, Liberace has made use of obvious physical advantages of good looks and an ability to wear dazzling suits. He has used an undeniably magnetic personality to help him bring good music (not necessarily classical) to people who would otherwise remain ignorant of it...
>
> At the Davis, Croydon, on Sunday, he played for two and a half hours to a tightly packed audience of men as well as women, intelligent-looking adults and youngsters as well as squealers. His technique in handling them was an experience never to be forgotten. He made it perfectly clear before he played that he would be introducing his own arrangements and extracting the highlights of the works of Debussy, Chopin, Brahms and Strauss, rather than playing the entire work. Interspersing his programme (which he introduced himself with flashes

of humour, patter and information about the next item) with songs and a dance, he played a variety of numbers including Latin American mambos, boogie (with 16 beats in a bar) and a religious number.

It would have been possible to hear the proverbial pin drop whilst he was actually playing, so great a hold did he have over his cross-section audience. Once the piece was finished, a great roar of approval and appreciation filled the theatre.

Liberace's fingering is magnificent, his timing impeccable and his talent abundant. He puts into classical waltzes a gaiety and feeling that would delight their composers, we suspect, far more than the funereal pace and expression accepted by too many as 'correct'.

...Then in the *New Musical Express* of October 5 1956, the headline is: 'Doug Geddes reviews last Monday's Royal Festival Hall concert and says: 'As an all-round entertainer, Liberace is fabulous.' Is it just a coincidence that neither you nor the defendants happen to have any of the newspapers with favourable notices, or did you have a bonfire in the office? – A: We have many bonfires, but we do not make bonfires of documents which may not assist us.

–What has happened, do you think, to *Stage* of October 11 1956, and the *New Musical Express* of October 5? You have an abundant library, have you not, at Geraldine House... You sent, as I understand it, for the papers... I quite agree – I do not want to make a false point – that those particular ones would not be in existence when you wrote the article of September 25; don't think I want to deceive you or make a false point. But when the time came to make an affidavit of documents, one would have hoped, would one not, to see included in it the good notices as well as the bad notices? – A: I should have thought so.

–These two sound pretty good, do they not? – A: The critic which you last read out seems to me to be somewhat unperceiving, but certainly they are favourable to Mr Liberace.

–It does seem a little unfortunate, does it not, that neither of them appear? Let us look at the very day after your first article and before you wrote the second one in which you called him a grimacing Messiah. I do not want to carry this too far. This is the *Manchester Evening News* of September 27 1956. This deals with his press conference:

A top performance when Liberace faces a grilling... Women in the North, they tell me, are too hard-headed to fall in love with Liberace, not like their Southern sisters, who sentimentalise his TV image. I wonder what Manchester mothers would have thought - and said - had they been at his reception in a candlelit restaurant run by Helene Cordet the other night. I went along because I wanted to see this phenomenon in the flesh, and there was the plump piano player, his back to the wall, facing the most hostile press I have ever seen - and I've seen quite a few. The top TV and film critics brought out their choicest ammunition as battle commenced.

...I suppose there were some representatives of the *Daily Mirror* there, were there not? – A: It is possible, but I do not know.

–For almost two hours the grizzled, curly-locked personality, whose second name is Valentino, held court. And I had to hand it to him for withstanding that blistering barrage. Most characters I know would either have wilted under the strain or gone fighting mad. Some of the questions were unprintable - but they all rolled off a back smooth with a suit that cost every penny of £100. Liberace parried - and sometimes thrust - with the weight and sincerity of a great showman. Quite a performance. Better than on television.

...You have relied on his answers at press conferences. That would appear to be a very high compliment to him on his handling of a press conference... And we do not get it, do we? I will take one more. This is the *Melody Maker* of September 29 1956:

Liberace. Like him; loathe him: The show's the tops. Let's face it; whether you like or loathe Liberace, you cannot deny the superb skill with which his TV programmes are presented. The judicious blending of light classics with polite jazz; the alternating shades of comedy and sentiment; the swift cutting; the camera movements; the occasional speciality dancers; the dressing up; the cosy piano-stool chats. The achievement of variety in both sound and sight in what is, after all, merely a programme centred around a man singing and playing the piano.

...That again would appear to be pretty high praise. That again does not appear in the list of papers disclosed by you or the *Daily Mirror*... You can take it from me that it does not. Can you account for it? – A: No.

–It does seem, does it not, on any view a most unfortunate coincidence that you and the *Daily Mirror* should only have disclosed unfavourable cuttings and no favourable cuttings... Can you not give an opinion as to whether it is a most unfortunate coincidence? Does it seem to you unfortunate? – A: I should have thought that everything that one side wanted to disclose to the other would have been probably disclosed; but I do not know about these legal matters.

–Does it seem to you unfortunate that you and the *Daily Mirror* should have given a list of cuttings from newspapers virtually all of which were unfavourable and none of which were favourable? – A: I had no control over the selection of cuttings or documents in this business whatsoever.

–I do not know how far you took any part in the preparation of your own defence; but did you not ask anything at all about the cuttings being disclosed? – A: No. I saw all the cuttings which were in our library, and I did not know anything about the procedure in which cuttings were disclosed. I read a very large number of cuttings.

–I could go on and on. I will read only one more: the *Record Mirror*. I only want to read one sentence from it:

204

Liberace's last TV night at the Palladium. The crowds cheer... inside and out for a grand guy. Liberace played *Auld Lang Syne* to millions of viewers in last weekend's *Sunday Night At the London Palladium* television show - his second within three weeks and his last before preparing to return home. I was present at the Palladium right from rehearsal time that Sunday afternoon, from 4 o'clock onwards, and I can only confirm what I went at length to say in our Liberace Special edition - Liberace is a grand all-round guy, a grand all-round entertainer and a grand all-round trouper.

...Again, not disclosed by you... I am reminded that I did not challenge your evidence with regard to Miss Ambler. I had forgotten that. I think one of the things you said was that you told her that you thought a writ was going to be issued against you. – A: I do not remember that, but it might be true.

–I thought that is what you said. After dealing with the proposals with regard to the two articles about the cat, you go on: 'Then the fact emerged that I knew that he was going to sue me, and I then said – indeed I did say it – in a jocular way (it may be one of the jokes which I will regret) "It will be interesting to see who is the biggest buffoon in the box".' In fact you had already been served with a writ on October 26, had you not? – A: I am not aware of that, but I accept it.

–It was issued on October 22, and I suggest served on the same day. – A: I do not know.

–Is that the only observation that was made between you and Miss Ambler with regard to this action? – A: Yes. There may have been a passing reference – I am not sure of this – to a Mr Lucius Beeby, who I had seen in New York. That might well have been so.

–Apart from that, nothing? – A: No.

–You saw her in the witness box? – A: I did, yes.

–She swore not only that a longish conversation took place but that she had made notes about it within two hours when going up in the train. – A: I observed that.

–And she produced them... You say the whole of that story is untrue? – A: Yes.

–In which case the notes must have been obviously forgeries? – A: Yes.

–But the bit about Mr Beeby, which is not very important (or I do not know how important it is) is true? – A: I am not sure. I believe that Miss Ambler mentioned this and it is possible that Mr Beeby was mentioned. He sends me a copy of his paper every week, so I am quite uncertain on that; but it is possible.

–Who is Mr Beeby? Is Mr Beeby an American who had re-published part of your article? – A: No. Mr Beeby is a contributor to the *New Yorker* and also the proprietor of a paper called the *Territorial Enterprise* which is published in Carson City, Nevada. He had written an article about Mr Liberace.

–You did not say anything at all about 'He will take a lot of money off us'? – A: I did not; nor would it be likely, if I may make this observation, that to a complete stranger I would make such a comment.

–Prima facie it would be unlikely, but you say to a complete stranger it would be interesting to see who is the biggest buffoon in the box? – A: It was raised, and she raised it.

–And you said that? – A: I did say it.

–Is that what you meant? – A: It was a jocular remark which I have since regretted.

–I dare say you do. Which of you, do you think, now has appeared the biggest buffoon in the box? – Or perhaps you would rather not answer that. – A: That is a most embarrassing question.

–I said I would not press it. This lady, therefore, according to you, in her devotion to my client, invented this story, forged notes and has come here to commit perjury with regard to that matter? – A: I think that she was a deliberate spy.

–You know that she did come down from the *Picture Post...* With a *Picture Post* photographer? – A: Yes, with Mr Hayward McGhee.

–Who eventually, despite the lack of co-operation on the part of the cat, did apparently take a photograph... Did the photograph appear in *Picture Post*? – A: Yes, and the article. In the end, by a curious circumstance, I wrote the article, because when I was with Miss Ambler I said: 'Look, I have got a good idea. Let me write a piece, Cassandra by the cat, and The cat by Cassandra. So in the end I found myself writing the article, for which I was not paid, though I do not mind that because I enjoyed the occasion. Indeed, I enjoyed Miss Ambler's visit; otherwise I would not have given her drinks, I would not have shown her round the house and taken her out in the garden and spent time, which I would normally spend working in the garden, seeing a colleague from the same profession.

–You liked Miss Ambler? –A: I was friendly-disposed towards her. That is why I asked her to sit down and have drinks.

–You poured out drinks... And took her round the house... And chatted about other matters than cats. – A: Very little. We stuck to cats most of the time. Most of the chattering was done with Mr Hayward McGhee who was an old Army colleague of mine.

–At any rate, chattered to a mild extent about this action? – A: Yes, to a very mild and a very short extent. I did not say these things which Miss Ambler says that I said except for the phrase about the buffoon and the possible reference to Mr Lucius Beeby.

Beyfus then turned to the judge: My lord, I am in a little difficulty. I heard only this morning of a book called *The Street of Disillusion*, which I

206

understand deals, I will not say very largely because I do not know yet, but deals in part (at any rate one whole chapter) with the *Daily Mirror*. I did want, if possible, to cross-examine Mr Connor on it, but I have no further questions to ask him apart from that.

The judge took the hint from counsel: it was a convenient point to break for lunch. When the trial resumed Beyfus did not mention the book.

BEYFUS: There are one or two questions on another matter. You have told us you saw one and a half of the television performances in this country of my client. Were they produced by a company known as Associated Television? – A: I do not know.

–Do you know the London Palladium Sunday performance is televised by this company, Associated Television? – A: I do not know that.

–Do you know Daily Mirror Newspapers Ltd are interested in Associated Television? – A: I did know that.

–Do you know Mr Hugh Cudlipp is a director of Associated Television? It is the fact, is it not (I do not know whether it is calculated commercialism or not), but do you know that this very Sunday night the *Daily Mirror* through this holding in Associated Television Ltd is going to help to produce Mr Liberace? – A: I do not know that.

–On television.... You have no idea of that? – A: None at all.

It was the end of Mr Beyfus's cross examination. Clearly he could have asked those few short questions before the lunch adjournment, but he preferred, when possible, to be the first person the jury would hear after any break.

Gardiner picked up the line of questioning.

–If the *Daily Mirror* had any control of the matter, do you think it would be right for them because of the action which has been brought against them by Mr Liberace to try and stop his performing anywhere he wanted to perform? – A: I am sorry – would you repeat that?

–Well, it is perhaps a rhetorical question. I gather Mr Beyfus was suggesting because Mr Liberace had brought an action against the *Daily Mirror* they ought to have tried to stop his performing at the London Palladium.

BEYFUS: No.

GARDINER: May I deal with the suggestion I understood to be made – if I have misunderstood it Mr Beyfus will tell me – that somewhere in the library of the *Daily Mirror* there is a cutting favourable to Mr Liberace.

BEYFUS: *Cuttings*. Cuttings in the plural.

GARDINER: So far as you are aware does it contain every cutting relating to Mr Liberace whether favourable or unfavourable which was in the

207

library at the time when you wrote your article? – A: I think so but I am not positive because the number of cuttings ran into hundreds.

–Does it include the *Daily Express*, the *Daily Herald*, the *Daily Mail*, the *Daily Mirror*, the *Daily News*, the *Daily Sketch*, the *Daily Telegraph*, the *Daily Worker*, the *Evening News*, the *Evening Standard, Everybody's*, the *New York Herald Tribune, Illustrated*, the *News Chronicle*, the *Observer*, the *People, Reynolds, Reveille*, the *Star*, the *Sunday Dispatch*, the *Sunday Express*, the *Sunday Graphic*, the *Sunday Pictorial*, the *Sunday Times, TV Mirror, The Times, Time* and the *Woman's Sunday Mirror*? – A: Yes, that seems highly likely.

MR JUSTICE SALMON: Mr Gardiner, does it include the *Manchester Guardian*?

GARDINER: I did not include the *Manchester Guardian* because, so far as I am aware, there was no reference in the *Manchester Guardian* prior to this report at the Festival Hall. That, of course, was after the first article was written. The one of the Festival Hall is included.

BEYFUS: Of these other papers you have mentioned a very great number are after the September 25 and 26.

GARDINER: I do not think so, Mr Beyfus.

BEYFUS: *Daily Mirror*, September 26, October 1…

GARDINER: I asked whether they included all the ones in the library at the time when he wrote his article. I said included because there are a certain number which were written or which were published afterwards. [To the witness]: They included, did they, all the ones so far as you know which were in the library at the time when you wrote your article? – A: Yes, so far as I know, but I cannot be positive.

–It is said that while none of these papers contained any article favourable to Mr Liberace, there were favourable articles in the *Melody Maker*, the *Record Mirror*, the *Musical Express, Stage* and the *Manchester Evening News*… Does the *Daily Mirror* library include either trade papers or provincial papers? – A: I should have thought not.

–So far as you know does it include… – A: It might include the *Manchester Guardian* which may be thought to be a provincial newspaper.

–I should not have thought you would call it that, however. You were asked about Mr Cudlipp's book *Publish and be Damned* and I think there was reference made – my Lord, I do not know whether this was put in – you wrote an article about the book in the *Daily Mirror*… You say this: 'This book sparkles and flashes like a welder's arc. It has everything – even the damned impudence to include disrespectful and distressing tales in the worst possible taste about myself.' – A: Yes,

–You were asked about an article on Mr Dimbleby. I rather think the members of the jury were given a transcript of that article and I think your lordship has a copy of it. Do you observe the last photograph and
208

'Dimbleby puts his arm round the Archbishop' – your Lordship sees there is a photograph and Mr Dimbleby in an attitude which I won't venture to describe with the Archbishop?

MR JUSTICE SALMON: It is not in the copy I have.

GARDINER: May I hand up my copy because your lordship will see Mr Dimbleby has his arm round the Archbishop who, if I may respectfully say so, is looking extremely like Dr Fisher.

MR JUSTICE SALMON: I think all the jury have is the typescript.

BEYFUS: I have only seen a typescript of it.

GARDINER [To the witness]: Would you also identify an issue of October 29, in which you wrote an article about the broadcast on the opening of parliament. – A: Yes

–You were asked about your recollection of an *Ave Maria* item in the film you saw. Does that agree with your recollection of the item? – A: Yes.

–Would you look at your affidavit of documents which is a joint affidavit of documents between the secretary of the company and yourself? Does that include 110 different documents, or thereabouts?

MR JUSTICE SALMON: Look at the schedule.

GARDINER: It is a matter of arithmetic really... Was this prepared by your solicitors? – A: I think so; it seems so.

–Does the document show a theatre programme *For Amusement Only* without any reference to Mr Liberace... Did you pay any special attention to that at the time or ask any question about it? – A: None at all.

–You were asked whether you read the American *Daily News*. Where is the New York office of the *Daily Mirror*? – A: On the second floor of the *New York Daily News*, 42nd Street, New York City.

–Had you any choice in deciding where the New York office of the *Daily Mirror* was to be? – A: None at all.

–It is suggested the article was bound to create great hatred among millions of people. Did you find in your correspondence your readers usually agree with you or not? – A: I am very glad to say...

BEYFUS: Is that an admissible question? With great respect, in my submission it is wholly inadmissible.

GARDINER: He was asked a question what he thought was likely to be the effect of the article and he can only judge from the letters he received.

BEYFUS: The question I put on every occasion was if the reader read this and believed it to be true would it not have this that and the other effect. That is the question I put and I prefaced it by if he believed it to be true.

MR JUSTICE SALMON: I do not think, Mr Gardiner, you had better pursue that topic. I would leave it there.

GARDINER: [To the witness]: How free are you to say what you think in your column? – A: I have a complete free hand to say what I like. The newspaper also, my employers, I give them a free hand to say what they

209

think about me and there are frequent differences between what I think, for instance in the matter of commercial television which I happen to be against, I am right against this and quite frequently it is in a leading article of the paper as so effective are my words against commercial television that they write in a leading article saying this man is a chump.

–What is the *Daily Mirror* policy about Germany? – A: Divided; they have one view, I have another, one which is strongly opposed to the *Daily Mirror*'s view about Germany.

–Do the *Daily Mirror* in their leading articles publish their views about Germany? – A: They do.

–Do you in your column publish your view? – A: I do.

–What is your object? It has been suggested that your object when you write is to increase the circulation of the *Daily Mirror* to please your employers or something. What is in fact your object when you write articles? – A: My object is to write to say what I feel. I have no interest in the circulation of the *Daily Mirror*. I would be glad if it did not go bankrupt but I rejoice I have this particular pulpit in which to say what I think and I write what I feel.

–How far in writing do you try to please your readers? – A: I do not try to please my readers. I have no fan clubs and in point of fact I do not care what they think. If they do in fact write letters to me flattering me or praising me I do not mind but in this particular case I have been fortified that…

–You cannot tell us what is in the letters you have had. – A: I am sorry.

–You say you write what you honestly think. Was that what you were doing in this particular case? – A: It was.

That was the end of Connor's evidence. He had been under no illusion, when stepping up to the witness box, about the toughness of the grilling he would face under the master of the craft, but he thought he had acquitted himself fairly well. He was, of course, in no position to judge. While he felt that he had held his own under questioning, the jury had seen the big picture. His experience was in writing copy and sometimes dictating it over a telephone, not in addressing a court. Halfway through his longer answers his voice would drop and the jury would strain to hear what he was saying. Perhaps theatrically, Mr Beyfus from time to time cupped his bad ear, to emphasise the witness's lack of projection and possibly, with that, imply a lack of sincerity. Bill Connor felt that, behind the tough façade, the QC probably quite liked him. But who in the end had appeared the bigger buffoon in the box? The question worried him.

Roy Perrett, a reporter on the the staff of the *Manchester Guardian* was the next witness for the defence. He said he had attended a Liberace concert at

Belle Vue, Manchester, on October 8, 1956 and that the reception had been 'extremely warm' with plenty of applause and cheers 'and even a few screams'. That atmosphere continued throughout the performance and he heard no interruptions.

Cross-examined by Beyfus he said he had seen no hostility outside the venue, nor any groups with placards, only groups of teenagers waiting for autographs.

He said he was not a music critic and could not comment on his competency as a piano player, but – 'I thought the showmanship was excellent and the audience was perfectly held, captured. The audience were enthusiastic all the way through and they were obviously devoted to him from the start so I cannot sort of pick out the degrees of enthusiasm.' There had been 'a great ovation at the end', he agreed.

Kenneth Tossell, from the *Daily Mirror* Manchester office, said he had attended the same concert and noticed about 30 teenage girls waiting outside. Liberace received a 'very excited' reception. He guessed that the audience comprised about four women to every man, or possibly more than that. 'The applause got more fervent during the performance' and he heard no hostile interruptions.

During the interval he spoke to Mr George Liberace and after the performance he spoke to Mr Liberace. He and a colleague had introduced themselves as reporters from the *Daily Mirror* and had been received quite cordially. Nobody had made any complaint to him about the newspaper.

Allan Cassell, a freelance reporter in Sheffield, said he had been asked to cover the concert at Sheffield City Hall for the *Daily Mirror*. He had watched the show while standing at the back of the hall. The reception had been warm, but there was a party of students present and 'when Mr Liberace came on the stage you could hear squeals in mock ecstasy and cat calls and wolf whistles and then there were a few cries: Where's Mum? I think, and things of that kind.'

Mr Gardiner asked whether he had heard anyone saying either 'queer' or 'fairy'; Mr Cassell said no, but he would have heard, if anybody had. One or two students had been asked by attendants to leave the theatre, he remembered.

George William Edwards said he was a reporter employed by Odhams Press which had no connection with the *Daily Mirror*. In October 1956 he had been working for the *Sheffield Star* and had covered the Liberace concert for that newspaper. The performance had started quite ordinarily and then some students had thrown paper darts and when Liberace started to dance there had been shouts of 'Where's Mum?' Some students had

211

been shown out and one of them had shouted: 'Mr Liberace, they are throwing me out.' It had been 'quite an orderly sort of exodus,' he said. 'A few went and the rest followed.'

Mr Gardiner asked whether he had heard anybody use the words 'queer' or 'fairy'. He said he hadn't heard, but he would have heard it, if anybody had.

–If they had been loud enough to reach Mr Liberace on the stage would you have heard them? – A: I should think so; I was probably nearer to them than Mr Liberace... because the students were on my left, and Mr Liberace, of course, was in front of me on the stage.

There were no other interruptions during the performance, he said: 'Afterwards I asked him whether the interruptions had thrown him off and he said they had momentarily but he soon recovered. That is all I remember.'

James Edward Thompson said he was professionally known as Jimmy Thompson and told Gardiner that in January 1956 he had performed a skit on Liberace on television in a late night revue called *Here and Now*, and in June that year started in a revue at the Apollo Theatre called *For Amusement Only*, in which he also performed the sketch, which had been altered slightly. When he left the show the following year to go to America another actor continued to perform the same sketch for about four or five months.

He said he had read an article in a Sunday paper in which Liberace had said he understood he was being impersonated. When he arrived in London Thompson had sent him flowers in the shape of a dove of peace and then went to meet him at the Café de Paris. He said: 'My wife and I had been taken up specially to meet him, and Mr Liberace came out of his dressing room, and with great good humour he just sort of said the kind of remark – obviously I cannot remember the exact words – 'What about you?', you know, that sort of remark, and I said: 'I do not know how I have the nerve to shake your hand.'

The following year he had performed one night in *Sunday Night at the London Palladium*. Then in 1958 he had met Liberace at the Savoy Hotel, the night before appearing in his revue on TV in *Chelsea At Nine*. He did not remember whether any reference had been made to the programme he was due to perform the following night.

'The Granada television publicity people decided that it would be a good idea for us to meet, to be photographed together... He was in quite a hurry to get to the Palladium... We chatted, and we were taken to the piano by the photographers and we were photographed.'

212

Cross-examining the witness, Beyfus asked: 'In the Television Act 1954, as I daresay you knew, it says that it shall be the duty of the authority to satisfy themselves so far as possible that the programmes... comply with the following requirements, that is to say, nothing is included in the programmes which offends against good taste or decency?' – A: That is right.

–*Thank you, ladies and gentlemen. Thank you very much indeed.* That is a perfectly proper satirical opening. *The name's Liberace; Each Sunday quite archly; You're exposed to my dentifrice grin. I'm a sort of a Winifred Atwell Combined with all the nice aspects of Vera Lynn.* That is comparing him with two ladies? – A: Could I explain why that line is in there?

–Can you? You did not write it? – A: No, but I do happen to know why it was in... It was actually originally intended, as Winifred Atwell was a pianist, that she was a natural parallel, and there was another line which, instead of Vera Lynn, said 'Godfrey Winn' – I am not trying to be funny – because at that particular time Godfrey Winn was doing a sort of 'homey', if you will forgive the phrase, programme on television which was of the same ilk, chatty and that sort of thing, as Mr Liberace did. Godfrey Winn objected to being used in the revue, and so at the last moment the line had to be changed, and the only rhyme with 'dentifrice grin' was 'Vera Lynn'.

–You compared him with Vera Lynn because you needed a rhyme? – A: Vera Lynn also does a sort of 'folksy'...

–*My sequin dress suit is a bit of a brute; But it does take your mind off disasters; That occur it is true; When I'm leering at you; Instead of the piano, when I play the Masters.* Then you played a bar of the *Rhapsody in Blue.* The next part is important. *But my fan mail is really tremendous; It's growing so fast my head whirls; I get more and more; They propose by the score: And at least one or two are from girls.* That is about as offensive as anything could be? – A: Well, sir, if I may be permitted to say so, having naturally thought a great deal more about this thing than I did at the time, that is actually a very old traditional music hall joke which I personally heard at the Halifax Palace 25 years ago. It also is intended to reflect the person who makes the proposals and not the recipient of the proposals. When I first heard it, I believe it was aimed at Gary Cooper.

–Do not let us beat about the bush. It was intended to suggest that the rest of the proposals were from men? – A: Yes.

–*I'm so coy with Tchaikovsky; I mince through Moscovsky; With Albinez I'm so light and airy; But my fans all agree: That I'm really most me; when I play the sugar plum fairy.* That is a double entendre. You know that the word 'fairy' is slang for a homosexual? – A: In America.

–In America? – A: I did not know it was here.

213

–Did you not... Are you standing there in the witness box and saying that you never knew before that the word 'fairy' was a slang word in this country for a homosexual? – A: Well... 'sugar plum fairy'.

–I did not say 'sugar plum fairy'. I said the word 'fairy' is a slang word for a homosexual. – A: I do know now, but at the time I honestly think, I did not know.

–You do not think you knew then... You know now, do you not? If it was modified to 'sugar plum fairy', it was obviously a double entendre. – A: The author would be able to tell you that. I was ordered to read the lines.

–You were half singing them? – A: I am compelled to, by my contract.

–I daresay you were, but quite obviously it tended to have a double entendre meaning to the audience. – A: The author would be able to tell you that, quite definitely.

–Let us see how it goes on. *And my programme is very artistic; On the stage and the cheers and the noise; In a frenzy of bliss I made two children kiss: In spite of the fact both were boys.* Again, something about as offensive as there could be? – A: That was inserted not as a joke. That version was inserted there because in the original version the author had written something which I thought was inexcusable bad taste at the time, about cripples.

–To your idea, this is an improvement. – A: I just asked them to remove the joke about cripples.

–*In a frenzy of bliss I made two children kiss, in spite of the fact both were boys.* You thought that was an improvement on the previous version? – A: No, it is not an improvement. I see that now.

–You thought so at the time. *As I sexily render the classics; I've caused many a happy divorce; I send thrills down their spine; Playing Beethoven Nine; Cut down to two minutes of course.* What do you mean by 'caused many a happy divorce'? – A: I have never thought about that line before. It is a rhyme.

–It is not a very good rhyme, is it? Oh, yes, I see: rhymes with 'course' at the bottom... *I've a piano shaped bar; And a piano shaped car; In the piano shaped house where I dwell; I've a piano shaped hearth; And a piano shaped bath; And a piano shaped piano as well.* That may be a little 'blue', but it is all right from my point of view. *I've a Chinchilla coat; And a dress suit that's stoat; And a tail coat of new marmoset...* That is all right so far, a satire. *When Momma and I wear our mink coats, Oh, my! To tell us apart takes the vet...* Again, about as offensive as you could imagine. – A: I am compelled to confess that it is.

–You realise that now... The sort of thing which, if anybody wanted to describe it to Mr Liberace, he would properly describe as vulgar and embarrassing? – A: No, I feel very strongly about that. It was never

214

described by the many people who came to see the show as vulgar and embarrassing. I have never been a vulgar and embarrassing artiste. Those lines were written down, and I was compelled to sing them. Mr Jack Benny himself came to my dressing room and congratulated me several times.

–I do not mind what Jack Benny said. Do you agree that if anybody wanted to describe this song to Mr Liberace… – A: Not my song. I did not write it. I was merely performing it.

–If anybody wanted to describe the song which you were singing to Mr Liberace it would quite properly be described as vulgar and embarrassing? – A: I can only speak for my performance, which so many people said was not embarrassing. It was described as stylish, witty and those sort of phrases. I do not want to brag, but I am…

–Do you not think it would have been very embarrassing to Mr Liberace to come to the Apollo Theatre and listen to it? – A: Yes, I do think it would have been embarrassing for him.

–We have reached that at last. You sent this floral tribute in the form of a dove of peace, with a telegram, to the Savoy Hotel. With regard to the Café de Paris, you had a publicity agent… who looked after your publicity affairs… It is quite clear, is it not, that you arranged to go to the Café de Paris because you wanted to meet Mr Liberace? – A: It had been arranged, so far as I understand, between our mutual press representatives.

–I suggest it was you who wanted to meet him… Eventually did you have to wait until the very end, after all the autographs were signed? – A: Yes, he signed hundreds of autographs. He saw everyone.

–I know he did. Did you have to wait until they were all signed? – A: We stayed on at the table. We were taken up when Mr Liberace was ready to meet us.

–That is exactly what I was putting. He signed autographs, and then, after he had finished, you were taken up… You were taken to be introduced… Was there a cameraman there? – A: There was. Mr Liberace called the cameraman over, and asked him to take our photograph.

–…In 1958 I gather you went to see him again… Who took you? – A: The Granada Television press representatives.

–They wanted to get you photographed with Mr Liberace? – A: Yes.

–And he said he was in a great hurry… He consented to be photographed? – A: He did.

–If he was in a great hurry I assume that you did not have much conversation. – A: We did not, very little… Apart from talking about Bob Monkhouse, the fact that he was looking well and that I was delighted to see him again.

–That is all? –A: Very little else.

215

–You did not broadcast this version – A: Yes, I did... I do not know what date... It would be April or May.

–This is what you say was the final form. I suggest you could never have been allowed to broadcast it, even for Granada. – A: There should be a camera script somewhere with those words down on it.

–Where is the original version? – A: What do you mean by the original?

–The first. – A: If Associated Rediffusion keep files, again there must be a camera script on the files of Associated Rediffusion.

–When did you type this? – A: I do not know when I typed that. It was asked for by Mr Robert Tee of the *Daily Mirror*, because he said he wanted it. He told me he was a friend of mine, and he asked...

–You typed it last week? – A: No, no, two years ago probably, eighteen months ago.

–All I am trying to get at the moment is this... You were approached some two years ago or eighteen months ago by someone on behalf of the *Daily Mirror*? – A: Yes; I am sorry I did not remember that.

–Do not bother about your sorrow. Who was it who approached you, a reporter or solicitors? – A: His name was Robert Tee. He does not work for the *Daily Mirror* now, but at the time he was their dramatic critic.

–He approached you some eighteen months ago? – A: Well, sir, it is almost impossible to know when he approached me.

–A long time ago? – A: Yes.

–Eighteen months to two years ago, something like that? – A: Yes.

–Did you then and there type this out? – A: He said he wanted to read it at a party. I typed it out for him, and he gave me his word of honour that he would not read it otherwise. I never expected to see it again.

–You produced it out of your pocket today? – A: I was given it in court this morning.

–That is what I wanted to know. That was all play acting? – A: What was play acting?

–You were asked if you produced this, and it has been in the hands of the defendants for two years. –A: Yes, but I did not know at the time...

Daily Express reporter John Lambert told the court that on September 24, 1956, he had joined the Queen Mary at Cherbourg and attended Liberace's press conference on board. The conference had been long and involved and lasted more than an hour with 'a whole swarm of reporters', about ten from London and others from the continent.

He no longer had his notes '– but Mr Liberace said that he was coming to London and hoped to find one wonderful woman here. We also discussed his clothes, and he was wearing a rather vivid suit which had a gold thread in it. I asked him why he wore those sort of clothes, and he said "I love lovely things, and they are deductible for income tax, too." Also, I think I

216

asked him what he thought the secret of his appeal to middle-aged women was, and – this may be out of context – he indicated that he could give them the love which their husbands and sons might not do.'

BEYFUS: Of course, if you were to say to him: 'Do you hope to find a lovely woman in England?', or something like that, and he said 'Yes', you would put it down as 'I hope to find a lovely woman in England'? – A: Indeed I would not, no... Mr Liberace was quite loquacious without any prompting from myself or the other journalists... I gathered from what you say that I would put something to him, that he would agree and then I would quote him as having said that. That is something I would not personally do.

–But it is commonly done in these courts. If one asks a man whether he was in Sheffield last Wednesday and he says 'Yes', one would say he said he was in Sheffield last Wednesday. – A: Yes; but there is a difference in journalism between prompting a question and suggesting something and then quoting the person as having said this merely because they nod assent or something like that.

–With regard to his clothes, he was quite obviously dressed for a press conference? – A: It was a very, I dare say, flamboyant suit.

–There is nothing the matter with it for a public entertainer having a press conference? – A: No, except that I would say it was rather more flamboyant than is usually worn by celebrities meeting members of the press.

–One of the features of his entertainment is that he wears rather gorgeous clothes... And he was obviously dressing up for the press conference. There is a photograph of him... What is the matter with that? You or I would like it, except that we cannot afford it. – A: I do not think I would personally like it. I do not think I could afford it, either.

–There is nothing the matter with it worn by an entertainer on a public occasion, an entertainer who goes out of his way to wear elaborate clothes. – A: No, I would not say so, except it was comment-worthy. It was worthy of commenting on as not many entertainers would dress that way.

–It was with regard to that suit and clothing, was it, that he said he loved lovely things and the lovely things which he wore for the purpose of his entertainment were deductible from tax? – A: He did not exactly say it that way. He said: 'I love lovely things and they are deductible from income tax, too.'

–It was in answer to a question dealing with the clothes which he was wearing... No man with any sense at all would say, would he, that all lovely things were deductible from tax? – A: I just know I asked the question.

–I know. That is precisely it. You take the answer out of the context. The answer was in the context of suits which he wore for the purpose of his entertainment and for the purpose of public occasions like press conferences. – A: He had already described this suit, I believe, as his conservative suit.

–The context of saying that lovely things were deductible from tax was dealing with the clothes which he wore? – A: That may be, yes.

–You are not making now a suggestion anything so ridiculous as that all lovely things are deductible for tax? – A: Indeed not, no.

–The other thing that you remember his saying is that he would like to find some wonderful woman in England... A very natural expression of opinion for any bachelor coming over from the United States. – A: Yes, I suppose so.

–The other thing I suggest is that he said that he gave or tried to give the love which women did not always get from their sons. – A: Yes, I did say I did not know if I had the context right when I was just saying it to you.

–It is right, is it not, that what he said was that he tried to give middle-aged women the love which they did not always get from their sons? – A: From their children, I think.

–That is right; and 'husbands' is wrong? – A: I think 'husbands' must be wrong, yes. I was speaking out of context there because I was not referring to anything else.

Reporter Murray Sayle told how, while on the staff of *The People* in July 1955, he met a friend called Feeley, from the *Sunday Graphic* during a flight to Paris. Mr Feeley had been going to interview Liberace for his paper, but when he arrived at his destination he discovered that his passport had expired two days earlier and he was unable to enter the country. Sayle had volunteered to do the interview for him – 'because there seemed to be no other way in which he could carry out his job'. He found the entertainer had checked out of his hotel and eventually ran him down at Orly airport where he was awaiting a return flight to America.

He had interviewed him for something like an hour and a half.

'I had not been told very much about Mr Liberace by Feeley from the *Graphic*, and he was at that time not known to me, at any rate. I did not know what he did, except that he was an entertainer of some kind. I had been asked by Feeley to ask Mr Liberace – it had just been announced that he was going to appear here – what he did and what kind of a man he was and so on. They wanted an interview about his work and about him himself... He told me that he played the piano, and then he went on, much in the style of the article in front of you, to explain. He said the keynote of his work was sincerity. He asked me a number of questions about what I thought the British public would think of him. He asked me whether they would take a sincere man to their hearts, I think he said. He told me that his programme was based on a great variety of material, that he did the

218

Ave Maria and then he swung into the *Beer Barrel Polka*. I think I have written just that. But I asked him if people did not find this offensive, and he said No, they did not. He told me that he was a religious man. It was a lengthy interview, you understand. It went on for more than an hour. We covered a great deal of ground in that time.'

Gardiner asked him whether he said anything about the sort of audience that he found his performance appealed to. 'Women, he said,' Mr Sayle replied.

–Was anything said about his earnings? – A: I do not remember that he said how much he earned. I got the impression that they were large.

Beyfus professed to be confused by the article that appeared in the *Sunday Graphic* as a result of that interview, which had been credited as 'by Roger Lawrie'. No, said Sayle; that was not his name, nor was it his nom-de-plume: 'Murray Sayle is my name. To the best of my knowledge Roger Lawrie does not exist... It relates to the preamble of what I have been saying. I at the time was employed by *The People*. I was helping out another journalist who was in distress because the French customs would not let him into the country. Although it is customary under the circumstances to assist a colleague in this way, because it would have been embarrassing to *The People* had my name appeared in a rival publication, they have attached to it – quite properly – an invented name for the occasion, Roger Lawrie.

–That is all bunkum; it was really written by you? – A: Exactly.

–This is rather funny. One learns and learns and learns. The Master ordered my client to answer this interrogatory, 'Did you not speak to one Roger Lawrie in Paris, on or about July 30', certain words. And there is no such person. – A: I do not know that such a person exists, no. I should object if there had been one, because in fact I am the author of the piece... but surely you see that the *Graphic* could hardly put on the heading of this story 'This was written by a reporter from another newspaper because ours could not get to the job'.

–What are your names? – A: Murray Sayle.

–Is there any reason why it should not be by Murray Sayle? – A: Yes, because I was at the time employed by *The People*, which is an opposition paper.

–*The People* would not have liked it? – A: *The People* would not have liked it. They would not have objected to my doing this providing my name did not appear on it. The names of the reporters are considered to be an asset – a small one, admittedly – by the people by which they are employed.

–This is another insight into the ways of newspapers. You introduced yourself to this man when he was waiting, I suppose, impatiently for his plane? – A: Yes, I did. I do not remember that he was impatient. He had a large retinue with him... At the time Mr Liberace was being greeted and being saluted by his fans, or by people I took to be his fans, and he seemed to be having quite a good time.

–Are you completely reckless as to accuracy when you write newspaper reports?... Let me look at the third sentence of your article: 'I expected surprises when I met him yesterday in his luxury Paris hotel. I got them.' – A: I did not write that sentence.

–It got into the article. – A: It did indeed, yes. I should perhaps have made clear that my contribution begins from the next word, 'Sincerity', and ends with the word 'sincerely'. Everything between those two words is written by me. The three lead paragraphs were added, I presume, by a sub-editor in the *Graphic* office on the Saturday night.

–I suggest that it is quite impossible for you to say whether this is the original article written by you or whether it has been altered by some editor. – A: By no means impossible. You must remember this was a fairly special occasion.

–That which is completely untrue you say is not your part? – A: You mean the reference to the hotel? I did not write the first three paragraphs.

–You did not write this: 'It had to happen... A male Monroe (or so he says)'? – A: I did not write that, of course.

> –Look out you women of Britain - you're in danger of being mown down by the million dollar work at the keyboard of America's fabulous hymn-to-swing pianist Liberace (say Leeberarchy). Plump and cuddly heart-throb No.1 of American TV - 'I appeal to women exactly as Marilyn Monroe appeals to men' - will soon be seen on British commercial screens.

–That is 'By Roger Lawrie'. The whole of that is completely imaginary? – A: I did not write it. I do not know where the author got his information from.

–At any rate, you apparently were being described as Roger Lawrie, were you not? – A: The name of Roger Lawrie was attached to this piece. I do not think I was trying to pass myself off as Roger Lawrie.

–I am not suggesting you were, but the *Sunday Graphic* were describing the person who was writing the article under 'I' as Roger Lawrie... The *Sunday Graphic* was pretending that Roger Lawrie had written those first three paragraphs... And it is completely untrue. – A: William Hickey is not employed by the *Daily Express*. Surely this is a convention that is known to anyone.

–I am talking about the truth or untruth of the first three paragraphs. – A: It does not seem to me that any deceit is involved. If you want to use the word 'untruth', certainly; but there is no deceit.

–I do not mind what you think of deceit on the part of the *Sunday Graphic*, but those first three paragraphs are completely untrue? – A: I do not think they are untrue at all. I say I did not write them.

–They are completely untrue in so far as they suggest that those words were used by my client to Roger Lawrie which temporarily was your nom-de-plume? – A: Which words, 'I appeal to women exactly as Marilyn Monroe appeals to men'?

–The first, second and third paragraphs, that is right. – A: Is it stated there that Mr Liberace has said 'I appeal to women exactly as Marilyn Monroe appeals to men'? Is it said that this has been stated by Mr Liberace to me or Roger Lawrie?

–Listen: This was put to my client in interrogatory No.6; 'Did you not speak to one Roger Lawrie' – your temporary nom-de-plume – 'in Paris on or about July 30 the words 'I appeal to women exactly as Marilyn Monroe appeals to men'? It has been suggested by the defendants that that second paragraph is true and that my client said to you under that nom-de-plume those words, and there is not one word of truth in it. – A: He did not say those words to me, no. That he is plump and cuddly, I should think there is some truth in that, if we are indeed arguing.

–Inasmuch as you knew nothing at all about him, you must have asked him a whole series of questions... Is that the sort of way that he told you; he was a pianist, and that his keynote was sincerity... And that his programme was based on variety... As an instance of variety, he told you, did he not, that he played *Ave Maria* and the *Beer Barrel Polka* in the same programme? – A: Yes.

–I suggest that is as far as he went in dealing with these two pieces of music, saying that he played them both in the same programme. – A: I asked him whether people found this offensive, and he said 'No'.

–What are you? Are you a musical critic? – A: No.

–You are a journalist of some sort... You seem a little doubtful. Have you any speciality? – A: I have done gardening notes and horoscopes and court cases.

–Have you ever heard Miss Gracie Fields sing? – A: Many times, yes.

–At concerts? – A: No, never at concerts... On the television, I think, and, of course, on the radio innumerably.

–Have you heard her sing *Ave Maria*? – A: No, not to my knowledge.

–Have you heard her record, *Ave Maria*? – A: No, not to my knowledge. I am not one of her fans, I might say.

–I am sorry to hear that. Then I suppose you asked him if he was religious and so forth. – A: I did, yes, and he said he was sincerely and deeply religious. He may have used the word 'sincerely' 30 or 40 times during the course of the interview. You see my piece is built around the word 'sincerity'. It begins and ends with the word 'sincerely', and so on. This, of course, is because this is what I think he has not got.

–What did you add? – A: I was trying to explain that it should be obvious from a reading that this is a tongue-in-cheek piece, and what I mean is...

–Where am I to find that it is a tongue-in-cheek piece? – A: I would hope that this would be obvious from the way it reads and that what I am trying to cast doubt on – this is the point of the interview from my point of view – is precisely upon his sincerity in this.

–Good heavens; you had only seen the man for half an hour... And talked to him when he was in a hurry to catch his plane... And because he said that sincerity was the keynote of his programme, you did not think he was sincere? – A: How does one form the impression of a man's sincerity? I take it by what he says and the way he comports himself.

–One of the things is that you might watch his programme. – A: Indeed: although when I subsequently saw it I was confirmed in my view.

–He told you apparently that he was completely unknown until 1952, and then he went on TV and so forth... Did you ask him who principally attended his concerts and that sort of question? – A: I did, yes... He certainly said they were women and, as I remember, he said they were middle-aged... Yes. He told me that he tried to give his audience some of his faith in God and so on.

–I suppose you saw this article, did you not, in the *Sunday Graphic*? – A: In the *Graphic*, yes. I was in Paris, you remember, at the time. I saw it on the subsequent Monday.

–Did you see a photograph with, in large letters, 'I appeal to women exactly as Marilyn Monroe appeals to men' repeated?... Did you protest to the *Graphic*... Let me finish my sentence... at the complete misrepresentation to the effect that Mr Liberace had used those first three paragraphs? The answer is 'Yes' or 'No' Did you protest? – A: It is not complete misrepresentation. The answer is: No, I did not protest,

–But you have already told me that it is a complete misrepresentation. – A: I have not. If you ask me as a journalist my view of this, this is very proper. This is frequently done in newspapers. I do not know where they got the phrase 'I appeal to women exactly as Marilyn Monroe appeals to men' from. I assumed they got it from the clippings.

–It is a complete misrepresentation that it was said to you? – A: It is not stated in this piece that it was said to me, surely.

–It is a complete misrepresentation that it was said to Roger Lawrie? – A: Is that stated in the article?

–Is it not, in effect? – A: I do not think so.

–Did you not think that was the meaning of it? – A: No, I did not, certainly not. People have catch phrases associated with them. I assumed this was one associated with Mr Liberace.

–I am interested, and the jury may be interested, in the morals of journalism as they are practised today. I am suggesting that those first three paragraphs make it abundantly clear to the reader that my client said to Roger Lawrie, whoever he may have been: 'I appeal to women exactly as Marilyn Monroe appeals to men'. That is so, is it not? – A: It is not. I do disagree with you. It never at any time seemed to me that they were saying that this derived from my copy.

–Do you realise that not only did you quite clearly deceive the public but you deceived the defendants and the defendants' solicitors and the defendants' counsel? – A: At what time have I deceived the public?

–In allowing this to go without any protest. – A: Allowing what to go without any protest?

–Those first three paragraphs. – A: The name was used with my permission. They told me that they would put some phoney name.

–I am not complaining of the name. You can call yourself by any nom-de-plume you like. What I am complaining of is those first three paragraphs, all of which are quite untrue, if my client is supposed to have used those words to Roger Lawrie. First of all, did you realise that you and the *Sunday Graphic* between you deceived the defendants, their solicitors and their counsel? – A: We did not.

–Do you realise it now? – A: No, at no time did I deceive them, I have told the defendants' counsel all along that my contribution to this begins at the word 'sincerity' and ends at the word 'sincerely'.

MR JUSTICE SALMON: Were those first three paragraphs ever submitted to you? – A: No, they could not have been in the circumstances. The interview was phoned through from Paris on Friday and this was running in the paper on Saturday night. There is no way in which it could have been.

BEYFUS: Somebody added those first three paragraphs... And you made no protest. – A: No. Otherwise a journalist would protest every time he wrote anything. Introductions are always being added by sub-editors. This was added by a sub-editor.

–I am only suggesting that a journalist should protest when he is misrepresented. – A: I have not been misrepresented. To this day I do not feel that I have been misrepresented. If there had been some consequence to this I might well have been involved myself in a legal action. This is something which a journalist does all the time. Naturally when I read the piece in the *Graphic* I read it to see how they had handled the story and whether they had made any improper, from my point of view, changes or additions, and they had not.

–Are you seriously saying that on oath? – A: Yes, with the greatest sincerity.

–Listen: The defendants in this case, in case you do not know it, first of all delivered a defence and then they delivered, as they were bound to do, particulars. In that they said: 'To one Roger Lawrie in Paris on or about July 30 1955 the plaintiff said: "I appeal to women exactly as Marilyn Monroe appeals to men".' That is what the defendants thought that my client had said to you. That is right? – A: It would seem from that, yes, indeed.

–And the place from which they would have got it would have been the *Sunday Graphic* of July 31? – A: Yes, indeed.

–And they would have got it because of what is written in the second paragraph and the words 'By Roger Lawrie'... And the fact that the *Sunday Graphic* thought it so important that they reprinted it in heavy type with a photograph of my client... Quite obviously – let us leave the public for the moment – you deceived the *Daily Mirror*. – A: But is this such an extraordinary thing for Mr Liberace to have said? It comports exactly with everything else he said to me. That is why I do not understand why I should have been, as you suggest, very annoyed or offended about this. I assumed that they got this line – I do not know that they did...

–I do not know that he is very offended about it. I am protesting about lies being told by journalists and published in the press... – A: I have not told any lies or published them in the press.

–...And not protesting at any rate when a newspaper gives an inaccurate account of what was said. – A: The offensive phrase, or the phrase to which you take offence, occurs between walls, that is to say between dashes, and in quotes. Is there any suggestion there that this is not merely a catch phrase which has been associated with Mr Liberace's name?

–I just made it quite clear to you that you deceived the defendants, their solicitors and their counsel from what was just read. – A: They have made a mistake about this. I myself am not employed by the *Sunday Graphic*.

MR JUSTICE SALMON: He did not write that, Mr Beyfus.

SAYLE: You are reflecting on my reputation.

MR JUSTICE SALMON: It is the *Sunday Graphic*, or whatever the paper is. – A: The *Sunday Graphic*, yes,

BEYFUS: At any rate, I have got your ideas as a journalist. You thought there was nothing in that which needed any sort of protest by you? – A: Nothing whatever.

–And you allowed it to continue, and you allowed the readers of the *Graphic* to be under such an impression as those words might convey. – A: Yes, the same impression conveyed by the rest of the article, I should suggest. I do not think that anybody reading this phrase gets any other idea than the one which I was conveying in the rest of the story.

–Either my client used those words or he did not. – A: He did not use them to me. I do not know where they got them from.

224

–That is the only thing I am interested in.

GARDINER: You have nothing to do with the *Daily Mirror*? – A: Absolutely nothing.
–There is one thing I missed. You said you were concerned with gardening, horoscopes and... what else?
MR JUSTICE SALMON: Law reports.
SAYLE: I have covered many cases.
GARDINER: Law reports. Now we really are learning something.

A year later Sayle would write his highly acclaimed novel, *A Crooked Sixpence*, about his experience writing for *The People*. In it his protagonist – an Australian reporter, like himself, who had previously written gardening notes and horoscopes and covered court cases – found himself in court giving evidence in a libel case and being questioned by an eminent barrister about an article appearing under a name other than his own.

> ... it seemed to him that a man who opened his case by contending that a reporter's by-line was a fraud on the public had departed far from the issue of truth or falsity and converted the hearing into a childish debate, with so many points for matter and so many for manner, pick your side out of the hat and to hell with the rules of argument...
>
> 'He doesn't know much about newspapers, does he?' he whispered to a colleague.
>
> 'As much as you or I do,' was the reply.

It was late Thursday afternoon and the end of the court's week. Adjourning the case until Monday the judge told the jury: 'You will remember what I said to you about speaking to anyone or allowing anyone to speak to you about this case, I am sure you have that well in mind. I think it probably would be a good thing if you did not see the television performances that the plaintiff is giving on Sunday night, because it is long after these matters which are now in issue, and it might convey quite a wrong impression in your mind. I think it would probably be better if you did not see it.'
In those days the *Daily Mirror* carried news on both front and back pages. The headline on the following day's back page would be: 'Don't watch Liberace on TV on Sunday, judge tells jury.'

As he collected the papers from the table in front of him Gardiner told Hugh Cudlipp that he needed to speak to him in his chambers. There, among the leather bound law books and collection of ancient cases in his room in the Inner Temple the old Harrovian former Coldstream guardsman said that he intended to recall Connor on the Monday to re-examine him on the matter of the Dartmoor photograph; he believed that Beyfus had misquoted the report when he had related it to the jury, and that he had not properly explained the background to it, nor had he dealt fairly with the newspaper's apology.

But that was not the most important thing he wanted to discuss. His professional opinion, having listened by this stage to the most important elements of the trial, was that Cassandra and the *Mirror* were going to lose. He advised Cudlipp that the company should cut its losses and settle out of court.

Cudlipp could not accept that suggestion: he felt it would be cowardly and would cause serious damage to the reputations of both the newspaper and its principal columnist. He knew that three of his prominent staff – Paris bureau chief Peter Stephens, show-biz writer Donald Zec and entertainment reporter Pat Doncaster were due to give evidence on Monday about their own encounters with Liberace; the editorial director suggested that he should give evidence himself. Nobody had been listed to give evidence, nor to accept responsibility, on behalf of the company and he thought he should do that, both as a director and as editor-in-chief.

In any case, he had already been referred to often enough, as author of *Publish and Be Damned*. He did not wish to be damned personally as the author too scared to face the music.

So be it, said Gardiner. Cudlipp must expect to face a mauling when he confronted Beyfus; but the Old Fox, although still on great form, was showing signs of a lack of his usual alertness as each day wore on, so he would ensure that he played Cudlipp as his last ace, some time after lunch on the final day of evidence.

Publish and Be Damned

When the trial resumed on Monday William Connor – Cassandra – was recalled to the witness box. His counsel, Mr Gardiner, produced a ten-year-old photograph and documents to which the plaintiff's QC had referred during his cross-examination and which might have mystified the jurors when Connor said he had been wrong about the situation and had apologised for it at the time. The picture, which had been published in the *Daily Mirror* on August 1 1949, showed people purportedly watching convicts at work on Dartmoor. And the accompanying story, headed 'A Commentary By Cassandra', said:

> You who are now reading this newspaper are looking over the shoulders of fifteen people and a dog... The fifteen people are, in their turn looking at seventeen other people.

GARDINER: Let me just ask you this. It was put to you on Thursday that what you wrote was this: 'As I stand by these wretched women and watch their gloating faces'... Do any such words in fact appear in the article? – A: No.

–Is there anything in the article to suggest that you were or you had been there? – A: Not in my opinion.

–When you wrote the article, had you been supplied with the photograph and a statement by the *Daily Mirror* staff photographer? – A: Yes, I had.

Gardiner read a memo from the photographer to his picture editor:

> Driving on the main Princetown Road past the prison yesterday, I came across numerous parked private cars, and one motor coach. The occupants were in the road and looking from the vehicle windows, all gazing intently at the prison. Convicts engaged on farm work could be clearly seen. With them were prison warders. The tourists were very interested in the scene, and some had binoculars and cameras, which they used. The driver of the motor coach, in my picture, was explaining the scene to his passengers. Although I was unable to hear his words, it was evident he was discussing the prison and the convicts and telling the story to the tourists. It is quite usual for many coaches, each day, to pull up at a wide portion of the otherwise narrow road at this point, so that passengers can study the scene. While I was there, warders beside the working convicts some one or two hundred yards away could be seen waving the spectators to go away, but they all ignored this gesture. Some of the tourists came from as widely different places as London and Glasgow. When I approached them with a camera they got out of the coach and stood beside other spectators already standing by the prison boundary wall viewing the scene.

...Did you accept that as being true? – A: I accepted that as being entirely true, especially as it was from one of our own staff.

–When the article had been published and complaints were received, were the facts investigated... What were the facts found to be? – A: The facts were found to be that the photographer did in fact pose the photograph.

Gardiner then showed the witness a photostat from the *Daily Mirror* of August 6, and read it to the court:

DARTMOOR PEEPSHOW: AN APOLOGY

An injustice has been done to a group of holiday makers. The *Daily Mirror*, having received and investigated their protests about the 'Dartmoor Peepshow' story we printed on August 1, wishes to apologise to them. The photograph of sightseers from a motor coach lining a wall at the roadside overlooking Dartmoor prison and watching prisoners at work in the fields misled the *Daily Mirror* as well as misrepresenting the people in it. A number of them inform us that the party left the coach at the invitation of the photographer and were asked by him to stand against the wall facing the prison. It was not, as the *Daily Mirror* was led to believe, a spontaneous picture, but was posed, at the express request of the photographer. We hasten to repudiate his action and we offer our full apologies to all those people in the picture who have been embarrassed by its publication and the accompanying commentary. Every endeavour was made by us to establish the authenticity of the situation about which Cassandra commented on August 1. When the photograph of the sightseers was received - with every assurance that it was a genuine picture - a photographer, a reporter and an independent witness were sent at once to the spot to check the situation. The reports of these witnesses clearly show that a situation does exist which in our view is to be deprecated and with which the authorities appear to be unable to cope. The *Daily Mirror* acted in good faith and in the public interest. It is to our great regret that these people were embroiled in the scene by the photographer.

...What action was taken by the *Daily Mirror* in relation to the photographer? – A: I think he was discharged, but I am not certain.

Mr Beyfus asked him: Was the photographer's name Lewis? – A: It was.

–Is he not at the moment in the employment of the Daily Mirror Newspapers Ltd? – A: I do not know.

–I suggest he is. – A: It may well be, but I do not know.

–I want to ask you about this. Even on this report which has been read from Mr Lewis there is a terrific amount of exaggeration in your article, is there not? – A: Well, it expressed the indignation which I felt at the time.

–You only see the backs of the people, and you say: 'The fifteen have every appearance of being on the gloat'? – A: That was the impression I got. If people are watching other people's unhappiness then I assume they are getting satisfaction from making an outing to do so.

228

–It may be they are merely interested to see what the prison conditions are like? – A: I would not agree with that.

–Why suggest from the backs of the people they are gloating? – A: I suggest they were. The impression I got from this is that they were out on an outing, making an outing to see the spectacle of other people's suffering.

–The article goes on,

> Gloat. A horrible sounding word, well matched by its ugly meaning. But it fits this spectacle. These holiday makers would prefer to call themselves sightseers. But the scene which lies before their curious gaze is the shame and misery of their fellow men. And they are not alone. There are many more of them. By the coachload, by cars by bicycles and on foot they travel from miles around to get a kick out of such scenes. With binoculars - even with telescopes - and with their own sharp prying eyes, some of these sightseers get their sordid little thrills from convicted men whose punishment, severe as it is, should not include this wretched indignity. It is all part of 'having a good time'. A dirty part without pity and without decency. A filthy peepshow that degrades and reduces convict and freeman alike into creatures in a human zoo.

...Let us consider what the facts are. The facts are – and these facts I suggest reflect very much on the *Daily Mirror* – that, these being dull days, Mr Lewis, wanting copy, stopped a coach as it was coming along... Asked, the persons inside to get out and pose for a photograph for the *Daily Mirror*? – A: I believe that is true.

–And, as many people enjoy having their photographs published in the press, they got out and posed for the photographer in the way in which we see... The suggestion that there was anything improper in their conduct was wholly wrong... The illusion of it was brought about by the action of the *Daily Mirror* photographer? – A: Yes.

–...Quite obviously, on any view, a shocking libel on those sixteen people, or whatever the number was, was brought about by the action of an employee of the *Daily Mirror*? – A: Yes.

–Plus, I suggest, your own exaggerated version of the photograph. – A: I felt deeply angry about it. I had been misled by this. I felt shocked, and did, later on, when I met Mr Lewis; I expressed my disgust. I felt I had been gravely let down.

–How much later did you meet him? – A: I cannot remember. I should think it was a year, and it was purely by accident.

–Was he then in the employment of the *Daily Mirror* – A: No, he was not, to the best of my knowledge.

–You do not know whether he is now? – A: No, I do not.

Stanley Bonnett had covered the Queen Mary press conference for the *Daily Mail*. He told Neville Faulks, representing the defendants, that he no longer had his notes, but he had read the published version and it accurately represented what he had telephoned to his office, and he had sent what he had heard said.

Faulks read a paragraph headed 'Nine cents':

> All this and mother too. By his side smiling contentedly tonight was his Mom – 61 year old Mrs Frances Liberace, the Polish girl whose marriage to an Italian French horn player was to give Britain its nine Liberace concerts.
>
> Liberace kissed her cheek, fondled her wavy brown hair, and talked of the trials of earning $1,000,000 a year. 'You see,' he said, parting his lips around his milk white almost-too-perfect teeth, 'I get only nine cents out of every dollar I make.'

...There is a dispute in this case whether in fact those words were used. Can you help us whether the actual words were used or not? – A: Yes, Those words were used. They have never been disputed with me or, to my knowledge, with my newspaper.

–...There is a heading 'On marriage':

> Liberace, the matrons' delight, crossed one tweed-and-gold-thread trouser leg over the other, lit a cigarette and called for a whisky and soda. Fresh smiles from the entourage as he talked of marriage: 'It is not quite my express purpose for coming over here, but you never know.' And he winked.
>
> What sort of a wife does the 36-year-old Liberace want? Now almost dead-pan, he answered: 'Physical attraction would be secondary to charm, personality and faith.'
>
> Still more seriously: 'I happen to be a religious man and I want my marriage to be blessed by my faith.'

...Pausing there, you know that in this case Mr Connor and the *Daily Mirror* are being sued for having written certain things about Mr Liberace? – A: Yes.

–The sort of thing that Mr Connor lifted from your article was the passage which we have dealt with, about nine cents out of each dollar. He also lifted this from your article: 'I happen to be a religious man and I want my marriage to be blessed by my faith' – lifted it in its *ipsissima verba*. Mr Bonnett, it is of importance in this case to know whether what he ascribed to Mr Liberace there is what Mr Liberace actually said or not. Can you help us as to that? – A: Yes. What I mention there, what is reported in the *Mail*, is what Mr Liberace said.

–You have not any doubt about it? – A: No doubt whatsoever.

–Did you just go off and telephone and report it to the *Mail*, or did you take notes at the time? – A: Yes, I took most comprehensive notes, but unhappily, as this was two and a half years ago, I no longer have those notes.

–I am not surprised at that. What I am getting at is this. When the words were uttered they went down in your notebook... Then you go off and telephone, or whatever it is. – A: What I did in this case was the thing one normally does. I sat down and transcribed my notes, wrote the story, and then dictated it over the telephone.

–These words which Mr Connor subsequently put in his article agree with your shorthand note and what is in your transcript? – A: Yes.

–Had you got any desire to injure Mr Liberace on that occasion? – A: None whatsoever.

–Were you in the hire of the *Daily Mirror* in any way? – A: Not at all.

...'No desire to injure him...' said Mr Beyfus getting to his feet for the cross-examination.

–...But a very considerable desire to have a good knock at him... Let us just look. 'You see', he said, 'parting his lips around his milk white, almost-too-perfect teeth'... What is that but having a good knock at him? – A: Well, that is obviously part of the way in which I endeavoured to describe how he looked, and his very white teeth struck me as astonishingly white.

–Obviously an attempt to have a good knock at him? – A: No, I would not say so.

–Do you regard these words 'almost too perfect' as complimentary? – A: Well, I wish I had almost-too-perfect teeth.

–I daresay you do. I am only asking you, is it not quite clear that by that phrase you were seeking to have a knock at him? – A: No, I would not say so.

–Were you suggesting that they were not genuine? – A: No. I was suggesting that in his teeth, as in the whole of him, as I saw him, everything was very, very, deliberately perfect.

–He cleans his teeth? – A: Very much.

–'...His platinum knuckle duster ring is adorned with a miniature piano carved in ivory'... Is that accurate? – A: Yes.

Beyfus said: 'Look at it!' And the ring was shown to Mr Bonnet, who told him: 'Clearly it is not an accurate description.'

'How comes it that you should write or telephone to the *Daily Mail* that he had a ring carved in ivory, when quite clearly the piano is represented by small diamonds? It does not look a bit like ivory, does it? – A: No, it does not.

–You are here, as I understand it, to vouch for the accuracy of your article. – A: Yes, and in that part I am clearly wrong.

–Quite clearly. With regard to his marriage intentions he was quite clearly cross-examined by you and the other reporters. Is that right? – A: Yes.

–He was also cross-examined, was he not, with regard to his views on religion? – A: Yes, I think so.

231

–Do you see anything wrong in those answers... 'Physical attraction would be secondary to charm, personality, faith'... Do you see anything wrong in that? – A: No, I think it is very proper.

–And still more seriously, when he is asked about religion, he says, 'I happen to be a religious man and I want my marriage to be blessed by my faith.' Do you see anything wrong in that? – A: No. It is one of the reasons I reported it.

–With regard to '9 cents on the dollar', how did that come about, do you know? – A: I think we had been asking how much his clothes cost. And he gave us an answer about the cost of the clothes and income tax, and then said that.

–As, of course, actors and actresses in this country do in respect of their stage clothes that they pay for... And you say you cross-examined him as to the tax, and so forth... And your recollection is that he told you that he only received 9 cents in the dollar? – A: Yes.

–...And, so far as you know, the only dispute as to what took place at all is as to whether he said '9 cents in the dollar'; as far as you know, that is the only dispute? – A: Yes. This is mentioned here; no one ever disputed that to my knowledge with my paper.

–Not terribly easy for either him or for you to remember the precise phrases used? – A: Yes, except, I did write it down at the time and transcribed it into this report exactly.

Francis Arnold Frost, inevitably known to his Fleet Street colleagues as 'Jack', had been a journalist for 45 years and was shipping correspondent for the *Daily Telegraph*, a job that included interviewing celebrities who arrived in England by sea. He had also gone to Cherbourg and had taken a shorthand note of Liberace's Queen Mary press conference. Mr Faulks referred him to the cuttings book and his published article:

> Liberace strikes a popular note. Success afloat. From J FA Frost, *Daily Telegraph* Shipping Correspondent. Queen Mary. At sea, Monday.
>
> It is said of a television artist, described in the passenger list of this liner as 'Lee Liberace', that husbands in the United States hurl things at their television sets when he appears on the screen, while their wives swoon in ecstasy. I confess that when I first saw him on television in Britain when he was little known I felt as the husbands did. But it was not my set.
>
> Yet after listening to him during a 90-minute press conference in the garden lounge as we lay alongside at Cherbourg's Gare Maritime, I relented. The pianist, who is on his way to Britain, assured me that he has had the 'wink and the smile' which he frankly admitted are 'gimmicks' that help him to earn anything up to £357,000 a year in America, since he was a little boy and one cannot help believing him. His second Christian name is Valentino, and an excellent choice it is. Liberace seems to have

232

the same appeal to matrons as the great film lover had, judging by the enthusiasm of the women in the biggest audience the Queen Mary's lounge has known at a concert last night.

As a special privilege Capt O H Morris invited tourist and cabin class passengers to join the first class, and Liberace, sequin suit, candelabra and all, entertained them for three hours. It was his third concert on the five-day voyage, in addition to several private parties. For 30 years I have interviewed people in the public eye and seldom have I had more admiration for a man's handling of sometimes awkward questions. Liberace is a showman with a plus something.

…Is that your view? – A: Yes.

–We had to wait while he shaved and had his wavy hair trimmed, and then he came in wearing a grey, metallic cloth suit, a grey striped shirt and black tie with two bars of piano music on it. He had a piano on his cuff-links, a piano on his outsize signet ring, and candelabra inscribed on his white silk handkerchief.

'A million a year individualist's earnings,' someone said; 'Why the black tie?'

'Goes with the suit, and I have got 50 more with me,' Liberace replied. 'It cost me $400, but to be able to pay that I have to earn $4,000. I earn about a million a year and could earn more if I tried harder; but I only manage to keep nine cents out of each dollar I earn.'

…Is that what he actually said? – A: He did, sir.

–Then there is a further reference to that; and then:

He was asked: 'Do you like wearing these clothes?' Liberace replied: 'Of course, I do; and also they are deductible.'

…Did he also say that? – A: He did, sir.

–And then in the next paragraph, about the middle, do you see this passage:

'I am a religious man and a great believer in family life. That is my theme all the time. Mom is my inspiration, George, my brother, my colleague and my musical director, and we have a perfect telepathy. My love of family life I try to inculcate into my viewers and listeners, and especially the children.

'If I appeal particularly to middle-aged women, it is because they want to mother me, and they see in my act my love for my mother. George and I believe that people enjoy our love of family-life. But believe me, the breakdown of my fan mail of 100,000 a year is 38 per cent from men.'

And then someone asked George to speak, and George said: 'People think I am deaf and dumb and mute. They are amazed I can talk.'

Then he referred to the people he wanted to meet in England: 'I am surrounded too, you know, by such happy married couples, and there are so many things that I can do that they can't.' And he grinned. Truly a great showman, a great artist, and a man with a great sense of humour, and a great belief in himself.

...And then you deal with this wandering round. Are the quotations which you gave in your article quotations of what Mr Liberace in fact said? – A: Yes, sir.

–Were there some subjects, do you remember, which he introduced and some subjects which were brought up by questions by reporters? – A: I think he introduced religion. I am not sure. I do not quite remember, because there were a lot of us; there were more than 14, a lot of photographers, and they were asking questions too. It is unusual for photographers, but they were.

You cannot remember which subjects were first mentioned by them and which first by him? – A: I have an idea that religion was mentioned by Mr Liberace; I think so.

BEYFUS: At any rate, it is quite clear from your article that you were very much impressed by the way in which he answered the questions? – A: I was, sir.

– And said so in no uncertain words? – A: Yes.

–Indeed, having gone with an unfavourable impression, to use your own expression, you relented and ended with a favourable impression? – A: Not unfavourable, a very open mind; because there is one mistake in this article: I saw Mr Liberace in America, not in this country; and there my impression was very bad. It was some years ago.

–At any rate, having started either with an unfavourable impression or an open mind, you came away with a favourable impression? To which you gave expression? – A: Yes. I did.

–And the only dispute, so far as you can see, is whether on that occasion Mr Liberace said that he only got nine cents in the dollar? – A: I am certain of that, sir.

–You appreciate, do you not, that he was answering questions on that occasion for something like an hour... – A: An hour and a half, yes.

–...To about 14 reporters, and you realise that he is continuously having press conferences... I mean, it is one of the features of his life ... And it would not be extraordinary, would it, if in 2½ years he forgot that particular observation? – A: I quite agree, Sir.

Peter Stephens, head of the *Daily Mirror* Paris bureau, said he had met Liberace at Le Bourget airport on September 27 1956. Asked by Faulks what was most noticeable at that encounter, he replied: 'We discussed a perfume he was wearing. He said it was American toilet water.'

He had met Liberace on the tarmac after his aircraft landed and accompanied him to the airport dispensary for treatment for a wasp sting on his thumb.

–Where did the discussion about toilet water take place? – A: In the dispensary.

–A dispensary normally smells of antiseptics? – A: It does... in fact, it overpowered the antiseptic.

–What was the discussion, as far as you can remember? – A: The discussion was general, really. We discussed what he was doing in Paris, how long he was going to stay, if he would put on his act in Paris, perfume, his clothes...

–Let us limit it to that part of the conversation which related to the perfume. Can you remember what you said and what he said? – A: Yes; as I mentioned just now, I asked him what it was. He told me it was American toilet water. He also added he had heard that they made very good perfume in France and intended buying some there.

–Did he say anything about his own possible future purchase of perfume? – Yes, he said he would probably buy some French perfume because he had heard it was rather good.

–In fairness to him, had he said that it was his intention to buy for other people? I take it he did not indicate for whom he wanted to buy it. – A: Well, I think we all assumed it was for his own personal use.

–You assumed that; he did not actually say so? – A: He said 'I intend buying some.'

–Well, I will leave that to Mr Beyfus.

Indeed. And Mr Beyfus was ready for it.

–You know that most men who have wives, mothers and sisters and go to Paris are expected to buy some perfume there for their mothers, wives or sisters, if they can afford it... But you, of course, immediately assumed the worst; is that right... that he intended to buy it for himself? – A: That is the impression he gave.

–Because he said 'I am going to buy some perfume'? – A: Yes. Well, normally one says: 'I am buying some for my wife, sister or daughter.'

–Just tell me: he immediately said whatever he had on him was toilet water, did he? – A: Yes; American toilet water.

–Would you tell me what was the aroma which you smelt? – A: It was a very scented aroma... I am sorry: I cannot identify it.

–You see, toilet water may be quite strong. – A: Yes, but I assume he had been travelling for about three hours and I do not know a toilet water that would keep its perfume for that time.

–I dare say. For all you know, he may have washed and put it on on the plane? – A: He could have.

235

Re-examined by Faulks, Stephens said there had been one other reporter present from Reuter's agency, and 15 to 20 French and continental reporters and photographers present.

–And were you the only one to discuss the perfume matter? – A: No; the French were treating it rather lightly.

–Do you know whether 'toilet water' in America means the same as 'toilet water' in England? – A: Well, I happen to use some myself, I believe it does.

Charles Stuart Reid, a music critic for more than 30 years, previously on the *Observer* and the *Evening Standard* and currently with the *News Chronicle*, had also attended the press conference on the Queen Mary. He said he used his own name when dealing with serious music, and the name Francis Martin for lighter topics.

Gardiner referred him to the cuttings book and the article he had written.

–I just want to deal with a statement about money first. You see at the bottom of the first column:

> Peeling off his gorgeous dressing-gown, Liberace put on what he playfully calls his 'English suit', a cuffed and chic creation of silk tweed with glittering interweave of gold metal thread. Cost: $400.

...Do you see at the bottom of the first paragraph:

> On their concerts in the US, the Liberace outfit, including Brother George and band, gross from 10,000 to 60,000 dollars a concert, he claims. 'Sounds a lot, I know, but how much do you think I keep from every dollar I earn? Not more than 9 cents.'

...Is that what he actually said? – A: That is what he actually said.

–Then you deal with the photograph of him and his brother kissing his mother:

> Never have I witnessed a bout of filial osculation like the one that followed. Afterwards Liberace exclaimed to us that his love for Mom helps strengthen Mom-love the world over. When is he going to found a family of his own? Has he come to Europe with the hope of marrying? Not with that express purpose, it seems. 'But', he coyly added with a smile as sweet as candy floss, 'you never know.'

...'Candy floss'? You thought an appropriate expression to use in relation to it? – A: In relation to the marked sweetness of Mr Liberace's smile.

–Had you, a few days before, written an article on his films: 'Enter Liberace, wriggling, winking and wooing. The man who plays in the key of love'? – A: Oh yes, on the basis of records.

–About how many films had you seen? – A: I saw two.

> –On Tuesday Liberace will be on the boat at Southampton, all set to wriggle, woo and wink his way more deeply into British hearts. In America his smirk and smarm act at the piano rivets 35,000,000 viewers...

236

...Then you deal with the Los Angeles Bank: 'You appeal', they chant, 'to all that is loveliest, deepest and purest in American Womanhood', and so on. And then you deal with the film which he made in which he showed people round the house:

> 'Mother and I are vurry, vurry happy there. (Smug twinkle.) So is my little French poodle who lives with us. (Eyes slide sideways, face goes solemn.) And there is someone else who dwells with us and to whom I speak...' (Lights dim, Liberace sings.) *Bless this house, Lord, we pray, make it safe by night and day.* Little touches of this kind are splendid for beer and soap sales. Incidentally, they help to explain such things as Liberace's reputed income (£350,000), the dress suit in cream mohair, the dress suit in black velvet, and gold lamé, and so on.

...Then you turn to the classics and you say:

> Tchaikovsky's first piano concerto, the popular one in B flat minor, runs to 153 pages. Liberace's version gives thirteen pages of first movement and eleven pages of finale, the two fragments being linked by four bars that belong elsewhere. Or take the Grieg piano concerto. Of this he throws away two movements, takes the stomach out of a third, orchestrates what's left and has the piano playing at one point when it should be resting. Beethoven's *Moonlight* sonata is hacked to four minutes, lest American Womanhood should yawn. Chopin, like Rachmaninov, becomes a stew of popular keyboard bits with orchestral effects impertinently added. The manner of playing matches the matter. Schumann's *Träumerei*, Liszt's *Liebestraume*, anything, in short, about dreams and amour, drip from his fingers like treacle, with lots of wistful lingerings, and, to compensate for these, coy little scurries.

...And then you deal with the further technical side of piano playing; and then you say:

> Not that we need worry greatly. Music is not Liberace's true cause. Love is the thing. Mention of it brings that faraway, solemn look into his eyes. 'When I do a show,' he explains, 'I exude love. I try to sparkle. That is something people like. I shall never be satisfied until I make people happy on an international scale.' What is the worth of international happiness based on a wink, a smile, a hairdo and a cosy voice? Precious little, I should have said. But then, my own line is Music. Perhaps I don't see Liberace straight.

...Was that an honest expression of your view? – A: Entirely honest.

BEYFUS: One thing which is quite obvious is that as a music critic you do not think very much either of Liberace's playing or his selection of extracts from music to be played? – A: 'Selection of extracts' is hardly the phrase I would use. I do not think much of his playing, certainly. I think even less of his treatment of the classics.

–And you realise, of course, that, whatever you and other music critics may think, the general public have quite a different view of his performances? – A: Of his performances? They appear to do so.

237

–Tell me, is this article written on seeing the live performance or seeing a film? – A: On seeing two of his television films, typical ones I was assured, of his performance.

–I assume that; and they lasted about 24 minutes... And he usually gives about six different pieces of music. That would leave about four minutes for each? – A: Yes.

–It would be quite impossible to play Beethoven's *Moonlight Sonata* in four minutes, would it not? A: Indeed it would.

–And what he gave was an extract from the first movement? – A: I cannot recall the nature of the extract, whether it was a straight extract or whether it was re-written, whether it was re-phrased, as it may well have been, on his practice.

–Is Beethoven's *Moonlight Sonata* a beautiful piece of music? – A: Exceedingly.

–Do you think it is better the general public should have a little of it, than none? – A: Not necessarily.

–You have heard the expression: half a loaf is better than no bread? – A: Unthinkable, sir.

–In your view as music critic, that does not apply to music? – A: Most decidedly it does not apply.

–You were trying, were you not, in this article which you wrote for the *News Chronicle* to be as sarcastic as you could? – A: I was trying to make a series of strong adverse points against Mr Liberace's practice. If that includes sarcasm, I think it was justifiable.

–Were you trying to be as sarcastic as you could? – A: As sarcastic as the situation merited.

–All television in the United States is commercial, is it not... And the viewers hear them between advertisements... The soap and beer? – A: Yes.

–And every performance on television in the United States, of every type, whether it be opera or whether it be clowning is heard between advertisements... And the better the performances at any rate from the public point of view, the more people will hear the advertisements? – A: That depends on what is being played.

–...I did not say from the music critic's point of view. The better the performance, from the public point of view, the more people will hear it? – A: From the public point of view, yes.

–More people will hear it, and will hear the advertisements? – A: Yes.

–And yet you think it right to slip in this as though it only applied to Mr Liberace, that little touches of this kind are splendid for beer and soap suds? – A: I do not slip it in as though it would apply only to Mr Liberace, I repudiate that idea.

–Do you not slip it in? –A: Certainly not. I do not see how you can derive that from the expression.

–If it applies to everybody in the world, what is the necessity for putting it in? – A: Not to everybody in the world. It applies only to a limited series of performers who in my estimation are prostituting art, as Mr Liberace does treat it.

–It applies to everybody whose performance on television is successful? – A: You say 'everybody in the world', which is very comprehensive.

–I said everybody in the world whose performances on commercial television are successful? – A: Then my condemnation applies equally to them, in that case.

MR JUSTICE SALMON: In what case? – A: If it is the case that high art is treated as Mr Liberace treats high art in television, my condemnation applies to them equally. That is the point he is making.

BEYFUS: Your condemnation applies to all high art which appears on television between advertisements? – A: Not necessarily.

–That is what is suggested by that sarcastic phrase? – A: Not at all.

–It is a matter for the members of the jury to decide, if it matters. With regard to the interview and this matter of the nine cents, whether he said it or not, at any rate your version of how he came to say it is quite different from the last witness. Do you realise that? – A: Is that a reference to the nine cents?

–Yes. Let us look at yours. – A: Yes, do.

–I quite agree that he may have forgotten. He may have said it, but if we are going to consider accuracies, let us look at it. You say this: 'On their concerts in the United States the Liberace outfit, including brother George and band, grosses from 10,000 to 60,000 dollars a concert, he claims. 'Sounds a lot, I know, but how much do you think I keep from every dollar I earn? Not more than nine cents'... That is how you say it came about? – A: All that is how I say it came out.

–Look at the other version, which is something quite different. It refers to a suit. 'It cost me $400, but to be able to pay that I have to earn $4,000. I earn about a million a year and could earn more if I tried harder; but I only manage to keep nine cents out of each dollar I earn.' At any rate, your version and the *Daily Telegraph* version of how he came to say that are quite different? – A: Not quite different. The effect is the same.

–And what preceded it, how he came to say it, is quite different? – A: It sounds a lot, I know. You are referring to my quotation. There is one quoted paragraph.

–Look at what the *Daily Telegraph* says... where it is introduced by reference to a suit: 'It cost me $400, but to be able to pay that I have to earn $4,000; I earn about a million a year and could earn more if I tried harder; but I only manage to keep nine cents out of each dollar I earn.' Your version is that it arose out of the 10,000 to 60,000 dollars a concert? – A: May I observe here...

–The two versions of how it came about are utterly and entirely different, are they not? – A: I do not purport to quote Mr Liberace in the first paragraph to which you referred, I would stress that. It is not a quotation.
–Is it not? – A: It is not a quotation. The quotation itself starts, 'Sounds a lot, I know.' It is quite different...
–Listen: 'On their concerts in the United States the Liberace outfit, including brother George and band, grosses from 10,000 to 60,000 dollars a concert, he claims.' – A: He claims.
–That must have been something he said? – A: Something he said; but not on this occasion an introduction to the following paragraph necessarily.
–Is it not? – A: Not necessarily... 'He claims'.
–Mr Reid, you realise you are on oath? Look at what follows, 'Sounds a lot, I know'... Is that not a reference to the preceding paragraph? – A: It has a bearing on the preceding paragraph. It has a reference to the preceding paragraph.
–'... but how much do you think I keep from every dollar I earn? Not more than nine cents.' It is quite obvious, is it not, that whatever may be the truth, whether he said these words or not, and I am suggesting it does not matter twopence, your version and the *Daily Telegraph*'s are quite different about how he came to say it? – A: I cannot agree.
–You think these two versions are the same? – A: I do not think these two versions are the same. I am using material in the first paragraph which is derived from other parts of Mr Liberace's general publicity material
–...'Sounds a lot, I know', I suggest must refer to the 10,000 to 60,000 dollars a concert? – A: He had referred to his substantial earnings. It all...
–Listen. This is two and a half years ago? –A: Yes.
–This is what the *News Chronicle* reported in their paper after they had received your telephonic account. Is that right? ... It is quite obvious, is it not, that 'sounds a lot' refers to the 10,000 to 60,000 dollars a concert? – A: It does here, I agree with you.
–The *News Chronicle* was seeking to reproduce what you had telephoned... All I am saying is that, if we are here to consider the accuracy of reporters, the two accounts given as to what preceded 'It sounds a lot, I know' and what led up to it are quite different? – A: They are quite different.
–That is all I have been asking. Just another matter; the fact that my client kissed his mother in front of reporters is mentioned by you, and I think by others, in a derisory manner. That is right, is it not? – A: You find it so, sir... I think not. 'Give Mom a kiss'... All very amiable, I thought.
–'Give Mom a kiss,' bade a cameraman. Liberace complied beamingly. 'Now the other cheek,' commanded other operators... It moved Mr Heller with an astute idea to put things right. Wouldn't it be a good thing, he
240

suggested, for Mom to sit between Liberace and brother George so she could be kissed from both sides simultaneously? No sooner said than done'... The whole idea came from you reporters? – A: No, Mr Heller was not a reporter.

–The whole idea of kissing Mom came from you reporters. – A: Certainly not from me.

–I did not say you, but from some of the bunch of fourteen reporters, of whom you were one. – A: I was one, but I did not put forward that suggestion myself; I forget who did put it forward.

–I am not asking you that. I am not interested in whether it was Brown, Jones or Robinson, but it was these reporters who suggested the kissing? – A: I am telling you I cannot remember who suggested the kissing.

–...You cannot remember. I am sorry. I thought you were here to vouch for the accuracy of your report. – A: So I am.

–You are. 'Give Mom a kiss,' bade a cameraman... – A: A camera man, yes.

–I am including amongst cameramen reporters, or do you distinguish between cameramen and reporters? – A: It is certainly not the professional practice to include cameramen in the general term 'reporter'.

–I am wrong about a reporter. It was a cameraman who suggested it. Is that right? – A: A cameraman.

–The whole idea came from the cameramen? – A: It came from a cameraman, as I say here.

–Not suggested by one of the other operators, I do not know whether 'operators' are reporters or cameramen, one or the other? – A: Cameramen.

–Other operators commanded him to kiss the other side... The whole idea came from the newspaper side. – A: Sir, to the best of my recollection all those activities were encouraged or agreed to by Mr Liberace himself, and also by Mr Heller who, if I remember, had charge of publicity. There was no reluctance but a good deal of co-operation.

–Of course there was co-operation. All I am suggesting is that the idea of this kissing came from the newspaper side. – A: Sir, with the best will in the world... I cannot say yes to that, because the whole publicity came over in a sort of publicity parcel from America.

–I know. It is quite clear you are not prepared to say anything in favour of Mr Liberace or anything against the newspaper. It is quite clear, is it not, that according to your own account the suggestion that he should kiss his mother came from the newspaper side? – A: In this case, yes, in the case of the cameraman who said 'Now give Mom a kiss'.

–It is you who had met Mr Noel Coward... He told you that Mr Liberace had played for an hour and a half and it seemed only ten minutes to him. – A: Yes.

241

–Then let us see how far you were determined to be sarcastic. 'Perhaps Mr Coward's delight is explained in part by the fact that Liberace played two Coward numbers, *Zigeuner* and *I'll See You Again*... That was in an endeavour to score, wherever you could, off Mr Liberace. – A: It reflected my view that a man of Mr Coward's taste and sophistication could not really have been so engrossed with Mr Liberace's act as he suggested.

–You thought Mr Coward was wrong? – A: Not at all, I think it was a misuse of language on your part.

–You think he was telling the truth? – A: I think he was being polite.

–Going out of his way to say how he had enjoyed it. Is that right? – A: Yes.

–You knew, did you not, that Mr Liberace had given concerts for nothing on board ship? – A: I seem to remember that.

–Which had been tremendous successes... And here were you anxious to write an article which would depreciate Mr Liberace in the public view, his performances rather than him. – A: I was most anxious to write an article which should depreciate his maltreatment of the classics, which I regard as a matter of conscience.

–Do you know that the result of his performances has been an enormous increase in the sale of pianos in the United States? – A: How gratifying. I was not aware of that.

–And that it has also resulted in an enormous increase in the number of people learning to play the piano? – A: But to play what?

–To play the piano. – A: Yes, but I trust they do not maltreat the classics as Mr Liberace does.

–The ordinary amateur would have more time? – A: He would have a great deal of time to maltreat the classics as Mr Liberace does.

–Most classical pieces take not less than a quarter of an hour to play. There are very few important pieces of classical music which could be played wholly in fifteen minutes. – A: That is true.

–An artiste who has four or five minutes only on television, it is quite clear, cannot play more than short extracts. – A: Why does he try? If he cannot play more than very short extracts, what bewilders me is why he should try.

–That is because you will not accept the basis that in music either half or a quarter of a loaf is better than no bread. – A: I will not accept that.

Satisfied that he had managed to bring into doubt the accuracy of journalism as a whole, Beyfus sat down and Gardiner endeavoured to shed light on the difference between the *News Chronicle* and *Daily Telegraph* reports.

–Will, you help me because the jury have not got copies of those cuttings. Are the words in your article, 'Cost: $400... On their concerts in

242

the United States the Liberace outfit, including brother George and band, grosses from 10,000 to 60,000 dollars in concert, he claims' not in inverted commas? – A: They are not in inverted commas.

–Then in inverted commas is the phrase 'Give Mom a kiss'; and then you say: 'All this time brother George, who is Liberace's band leader, twiddled his thumbs and looked rather out of it. In moved Mr Heller with an astute idea to put things right. Wouldn't it be a good thing, he suggested, for Mom to sit between Liberace and brother George so she could be kissed from both sides simultaneously?' It was Mr Heller who had this idea. – A: Mr Heller, whom I have not seen since the case started, as I understood it was from the American side handling Mr Liberace's publicity.

–Will you assume that Mr Beyfus is right in saying that on commercial television you cannot play anything for more than four minutes? You have heard his long playing records. When doing his long playing records did Mr Liberace play the full item? – A: Never. Excuse me, not the items which I have examined, the classical items.

–He has played substantially the same extent as he does on television? – A: That is my impression, remembering the television films as I do.

Show-business reporter Donald Zec was yet another who had attended the press conferences in Cherbourg and on board the Queen Mary. He confirmed that he had heard the *Daily Telegraph, Daily Mail* and *News Chronicle* evidence.

FAULKS: Are you the *Daily Mirror*? – ZEC: I am the *Daily Mirror*.

–Let us get one thing out of the way first of all. You have heard Mr Beyfus getting rather cross with the *News Chronicle* about this photograph, when the lady was being kissed... Did you take down your notes, and send them by radio to the *Daily Mirror* on the same evening? – A: No. To be accurate, the first part of my story I sent by telephone from Cherbourg because there was still time to phone my office. It was subsequently that I phoned over the radio the additions from the boat while it was at sea.

–We know that your article eventually appeared in the *Daily Mirror*. Have you also preserved the items which you sent by radio or telephone, from which the final article was prepared? – A: If you mean the actual notes I took, no. We only keep notes for perhaps eighteen months in a newspaper office.

–What we have then is headed: 'Zec. From the Queen Mary, Liberace story...' – A: That would be the telephonist's copy of what I phoned. The story is taken down on a typewriter by copy telephonists.

–Splendid. Would you look at your last note but one. '10.29pm September 24. Zec, from Queen Mary... Please insert in Liberace story...
243

The interview was stage managed in the best candelabra style. His man said 'I would like Liberace to sit between his mother and George on the other, so that she can be kissed from both sides.

ZEC: I remember that very vividly.

FAULKS: In order that we can put the matter beyond any doubt, would you look at the photograph in your actual article? There is a picture of the actual kiss, at the bottom of the page... There we have the lady in the middle, being embraced by both her sons. You say you remember that well. Do you remember who it was who suggested it? – A: It was the manager who suggested it, and the manager had been suggesting most of the posed photographs at that time.

–You are satisfied about that? – A: I am, indeed.

–We will leave Mr Beyfus to deal with that then, I think perhaps the fairest way of going through this is to look at your notes and then at your article. This was telephoned at 6.20pm. It starts with 'On the Queen Mary (shaped like a ship).'

Monday: With a song in his heart, a fixed dimpled smile, and fragrantly perfumed with toilet water, Liberace, the flashy Casanova of the keyboard, arrived here today.

...What caused you to telephone the words 'fragrantly perfumed with toilet water'? – A: Because I was close to Mr Liberace throughout the whole of the interview, and also later in his cabin, and I was struck by the strong perfumed aroma which surrounded him.

–Did you at any time have an opportunity of going to his cabin? – A: I did, indeed. He in fact invited me down after a fairly long press conference. He said 'Come down. Perhaps we can have another little talk.' I went down to his cabin immediately after the press conference ended.

–What did you see relating to perfume, if anything? – A: The bathroom door was open, and I noticed the shelf was stacked with bottles of toilet water. I assumed it was toilet water. I cannot say I saw bottles of perfume, but I was struck by the fact that the whole cabin seemed to carry that same kind of perfume which I associated with Mr Liberace.

–Now you are saying 'perfume'. You tell my Lord that you must not say 'scent', but it is all right to say 'toilet water'. What is the difference? – A: I did not mean to imply that Mr Liberace was necessarily wearing perfume as such, but that his toilet water, or whatever preparation he uses, was very heavily perfumed.

–Later on in your note, you say:

I still can't believe my ears. Listen: 'There is no one like Liberace. What the people want of me they want from no one else. I am a missionary. It is an inspiration to know that I am able to reach all the people of the world. I think I have a stabilising effect on family life. Middle-aged women love me because I give them a love that many of them cannot enjoy. I am the answer to the drab realities of life.

244

...Was that, which was telephoned, a product of your imagination, or was it something which was in fact said: – A: As far as I can say this is a completely accurate account of what Mr Liberace said to me and to the others at this press conference, and it is exactly that I telephoned to my office.

–Then it goes on: 'Sex appeal? ... Fluttered his long lashes, purred his dimpled smile full on me, winked at me and said "If people notice it. I am happy"...' – A: He said that. I should add he had in fact said that to me once before, but he repeated it at the press conference at Cherbourg.

–He said that he did not say it. You took it down at the time? – A: I most certainly did.

> He said he would like to marry. 'Who knows?' he said with a mischievous wriggle of his hip, 'I might meet the right girl in England.' (I've heard this somewhere before.)

...That I suppose is a reference to his unfortunate remarks, for which he apologised? – A: No. The point of that reference is this. It is an unhappy coincidence that many visiting stars, who are either bachelor men or bachelor women, feel that it is the right thing to imply they might perhaps find a match whilst they are in England. It has been in fact said by dozens of visiting celebrities.

–You go on: 'The girl I would like to marry? Her physical attributes must be secondary to her charm and personality'... Those are the exact words which Mr Bonnett had in his article, and you took them down too? – A: I did, indeed.

–'He said he would like to meet Marilyn Monroe...' The rest of that I do not think helps very much. The remaining remarks attributed to him do not really play any part in this action. I think it is best to come to the actual article now. You know that Mr Connor had seen your material when he wrote the article complained of here? – A: So I understand.

–Let us go through them again to see whether you say the article was true. It says; 'Sparkle! Flash! Liberace's here – in a £125 suit with gold thread. With a song in his heart, a fixed dimpled smile and fragrantly perfumed with toilet water' etc... that is the same as in the original telephoned copy? – A: Yes.

– 'From his comfy frame diamond pianos flashed, silver keyboards glinted, two beautiful rows of wide-screen dentistry gleamed and one brown eye winked.' You heard the *Daily Mail*, I think it was, get into trouble because he said that the knuckleduster ring was made up of ivory and not, as Mr Beyfus points out, of diamonds? – A: Precisely.

–What did you mean when you said the phrase 'From his comfy frame diamond pianos flashed'... you got it right? – A: It was the diamond piano on the ring, but Mr Liberace was wearing so much jewellery carrying the

245

piano motif that it was very difficult to be absolutely accurate, I thought it accurate when I wrote it.

–'But wait', it goes on. 'His hair was fashioned into silken greying waves and curls'... It was grey in those days? – A: Yes.

–'His nails were too genteel for scratching. He wore a violet shirt with white horizontal bars.' That appears in the notes we have got. Then the suit we have heard about before. Then there is the bit about I still can't believe my ears. This is what he said: 'There is no one like Liberace. What the people want of me they want from no one else', taken exactly from your notes on the telephone? – A: Yes. It is a part of the things that he said, but those are some of the things which I wrote of what he in fact said.

–At the foot he said, 'I hope England will love me as much as I love England.' – A: Exactly.

–How long have you been a show columnist? – A: For the *Daily Mirror*, for about ten years.

–How many times previously have you met Mr Liberace? – A: I had met him once before at his home in Hollywood.

–He says he remembers that meeting, and in point of fact, as a result of it, he put his arm around you at the Cherbourg meeting and called you by name? – A: He did, indeed. That was the first demonstration he made. He put his arm round my shoulder, and in fact warmly thanked me for the article which I wrote about him in Hollywood. I recall it astonished me.

–Why did it astonish you? – A: This article was a very satirical one.

–We have read it to the jury. It ends with the words, 'In spite of his enormous ego, his piano crazy home and his frilly, foppish wardrobe, I like him. With his smile (and the dimple).' – A: Yes, Perhaps if I might just develop the answer I gave, what struck me about his thanks for the article which I wrote in Hollywood was simply this. Since it was very satirical, to thank me very warmly for it, if he had read it, suggested to me that he perhaps put a greater value on publicity than he does by touching on his personal feelings; and if he had not read it then to thank me warmly again for an article which he had not read seemed to me to be palpably insincere.

–I am sorry to say that that part of the article where you refer to yourself playing *The Rustle of Spring* he tells us is untrue. What do you say about that? – A: All I can say is that Mr Liberace must have a very short memory or he is simply not telling the truth, because it is precisely what I did do to illustrate a particular point I was making during the conversation.

BEYFUS : Well...

FAULKS: I hear noises. If Mr Beyfus is going to object I think he is entitled to object, but I am only asking these questions because he said several times that he does not want to leave anything out.

246

BEYFUS: I was discussing the matter with my learned friend, quite clearly this evidence is not admissible, but I have decided not to object although it is inadmissible. We were discussing the matter...

MR JUSTICE SALMON: I think you can be assured, Mr Faulks, that Mr Beyfus will not be shy about interjecting.

FAULKS: What were you saying about *The Rustle of Spring*? – A: Well, I say that Mr Liberace is wrong. I told him quite frankly that I personally found his performance unpleasant. In fact I recall using the word 'nauseating', although I recognised that there were many people who might, indeed, enjoy it. In order to illustrate the sort of demonstration which I particularly found unpleasant I sat down at one of the two pianos in the room and I played the first few bars of *The Rustle of Spring*, and turning upon him the smile and the wink in what had become a fairly well known part of his act. He then sat down at the other piano, seemingly singularly unaffected by my demonstration, and also played *The Rustle of Spring*. He played it better than I did.

–That is not really surprising. – A: No. I think I said at that time I found him unquestionably a competent pianist.

–He was asked by the learned judge to indicate to my lord and the jury what parts, if any, of the article he said were false, and I think they came to four in number, if my recollection is correct. One of them was this business about *The Rustle of Spring*. Somewhere in the article there is a statement saying that he went round the piano. He said that was quite impossible because the piano was up against the wall. Is it possible that that is so, or do you not remember? – A: He got up and did a springy little walk round the pianos in what I would describe as an arc of about 180 degrees and not a full circle around it.

–That is exactly what you meant? – A: That is exactly what I meant.

–Then there is a paragraph about his parakeet. 'He introduced me to his white parakeet, learning to screech 'Liberace'. He says he has got a parakeet but that it will not screech 'Liberace', and it is not learning to do it either. What do you say about that? – A: If I may say so, what I thought I heard Mr Liberace say was 'My parakeet cannot say, and does not say Liberace'. But then I did not say it did. What Mr Liberace said to me in his home was that he was teaching the parakeet to screech 'Liberace'. At the time I must confess it did not do it while I was there.

–The jury have not got this, but I expect you will be asked some more questions about it by Mr Beyfus. Taking it quickly, is it right that the cushions were shaped like pianos, the ashtrays were shaped like pianos, and the coffee tables were shaped like pianos? – A: There were so many things of Mr Liberace's which were shaped like pianos that one would have to spend hours to take an inventory of them. The whole home was

247

scattered with bric-a-brac shaped like a piano, or carrying that motif. It was even carried into the bedroom and bathroom.

–Let me just read you the next two paragraphs, because I seem to remember this was something about which he was cross. You can tell us what you meant:

> 'Liberace,' I said, stubbing my cigarette out on F sharp, 'I'd like to have a straight talk with you. Are you sensitive?'
>
> 'Only to beauty,' he said pianissimo. 'The sight of a lovely ballet dancer brings me out in a cold sweat.'

–He says that, when you say you stubbed your cigarette out on F sharp, which shows you were maltreating his piano, he would not have that. – A: I find that very surprising. Whether in my article I say I stubbed out my cigar or cigarette on F sharp, if I recall in the two preceding paragraphs I was referring to ashtrays shaped like pianos. It may have been put a little clumsily, but clearly I meant I put my cigarette in an ashtray which was shaped like a piano.

MR JUSTICE SALMON: I do not suppose the jury attach very much importance to that.

FAULKS: I am obliged; I will say no more about that article. I will only ask you about one other thing. You have been a show columnist for a long time. Have you in the course of your duties attended at the Café de Paris? A: I have, indeed.

–What sort of clientele goes there? – A: Well, the Café de Paris was a place of entertainment frequented mainly by rich business tycoons and visited by celebrities and the like.

–Would you say it was heavily attended by readers of the *Daily Mirror*? – A: I would think most unlikely.

–Have you experience of first night audiences at the Café de Paris cabarets? – A: I have, many times.

–I think it was the practice always to have the greatest possible names? – A: It was. It has not proved very successful.

–I said it was. I was speaking in the past. What was the nature of the reception generally, on the occasions you have been there at a first night? – A: The audience at the Café de Paris was a notoriously hostile one, in the sense that unless they got top entertainment for the very expensive tickets they had to buy they gave short shrift to most artistes who failed there.

BEYFUS: Mr Zec, we have had the evidence of the *News Chronicle* reporter who said this was accurate. 'In moved Mr Heller with an astute idea to put things right. Wouldn't it be a good thing, he suggested, for Mom to sit between Liberace and brother George so she could be kissed from both sides simultaneously? No sooner said than done.' Is that right? Look at it, if you want to. – A: As far as I can recall, it was.

–You heard the witness give evidence that it was correct... It did not strike you as incorrect? – A: As far as I recall, that is what took place.

–Now would you look at what you reported from the Queen Mary and see what was before Mr Connor we are told when he wrote his article. – A: I have.

–I will read it. This is from you, from the Queen Mary:

> Please insert in Liberace story: The interview was stage managed in the best candelabra style. His manager said: 'I would like Liberace to sit between his mother and George on the other, so that he can be kissed from both sides.'

–Do you see that? – A: I do.

–Yes; you reporting from Cherbourg that the idea was that he should sit between the two, so that he could be kissed by his mother, a woman, from one side, and from George, a man, on the other; do you see that? – A: I do indeed.

–That was an utter and complete lie, was it not? – A: No; this was an unfortunate mistake over the radio telephone. I never meant...

–Utterly and entirely incorrect? – A: As it reads there it is certainly incorrect, sir.

–And you vouched for it this morning when you gave evidence in chief, did you not? – A: When I read it I actually assumed it was the way you had in fact read it to me. I am actually surprised that I had not noticed it, but clearly when I identified the picture about Liberace's mother being kissed by her two sons...

–My friend Mr Faulks read that to you this morning when you gave evidence in chief, did he not? – A: I agree, Mr Beyfus, but...

–And you did not take the opportunity of saying 'That is an unfortunate mistake', did you? – A: No; I regret now that I did not, now having read it, but I...

–And you vouched it as correct, did you not? – A: Only because I myself misread it when it was sent to me, when it was put to me.

–But there is no reason to think, as far as you know, that Mr Connor misread it? – A: I do not know whether Mr Connor...

–Have you any reason for believing that Mr Connor misread it? – A: I am quite certain that Mr Connor put the correct interpretation upon that paragraph, and I regret that I did not when I read it a few moments ago.

–And you are quite certain that Mr Connor took it as meaning the opposite of what it said; is that right? – A: Since it was accompanied by a photograph showing who was kissing, I assume that Mr Connor could not have been misled by it.

–So you think; but there it is, completely inaccurate and never corrected until I got up to cross-examine? – A: Well, I must agree entirely that I should have drawn attention to it. When I read it I assumed that that was precisely the way in which they were to be grouped. It was merely a matter of grouping when I misread it.

–May we assume that the rest of your article is likely to be about as accurate as that? – A: I am on oath to say the truth, and everything that I wrote in my article and telephoned is the truth.

–Except this. –A: Except this, which is a simple mistake, and which I readily agree is a mistake.

FAULKS: My lord, I have handed the original to Mr Beyfus. It can be put in. Your lordship may think there has been a mistyping.

BEYFUS: Yes. Let us look at the original. There it is. [Handing it to the witness.] That is the original, and in the original there have been corrections, have there not? I would like the members of the jury to see the original. In the original there have been corrections. There have been crossings out by a series of Xs? – A: The crossings out are meaningless since this was taken down over the radio telephone and very often words are mis-heard.

–All I am saying is there have been corrections in the original, no doubt owing to mishearing or something like that; but there have been corrections in the original. –A: No, sir, I cannot accept that the word 'correction' means what I take it you mean. When a person types something sometimes he mistypes; therefore he types the word again. In that sense a word has been typed wrongly, if you mean there have been alterations.

–Let me ask you about newspaper practice. When a newspaper reporter reports from Cherbourg, through the telephone, an article, the telephone operator at the other end types it as he receives the message, does he not... And at the end he reads it over in order to be sure that he has typed it correctly; that is the ordinary practice? – A: No, not normally. It rather depends upon the pressure of work at the time, and certainly there is never an opportunity for it to happen when one is radio-telephoning from a ship.

–At any rate, that sometimes happens? – A: That a telephonist will re-read and check?

–Yes. – A: I suppose that if he had all the time in the world, he might; but under pressure in newspaper offices, if he hears wrongly, he hears wrongly.

–In this particular case it is quite clear that he had taken down something wrongly and crossed it out? – A: No; it may be he typed something incorrectly and has crossed it out.

–He has typed something incorrectly? – A: Yes, that I would accept.

–And the easiest way for him to find out that he had typed something incorrectly would be for him to read it out to the person telephoning at the other end? – A: I agree entirely, except that the opportunity never arises for him to do so.

–At all events, as my learned friend wanted the original to be seen, the word 'he' is absolutely clear, is it not: 'So that he'. – A: Yes. This is quite wrong. It certainly was not my intention.

–Wrong from beginning to end. Now, you are the gentleman who purported in your first article to declare that you liked Mr Liberace. Was that true or not true? – A: At that time, when I wrote that article, before the incidents, it was true. I held the opinion then.

–You liked him... You found him a competent pianist. And you found him a very pleasant person. – A: He was indeed a pleasant person.

–He was indeed a pleasant person. You heard him playing and he seemed to you a very competent pianist and you liked him; and the result of your entertainment by him, as a pleasant host and your feelings of liking was that you wrote this article with the big heading 'At home with the golden boy of syrup', in which you just tried to knock him as hard as you could, did you not? – A: That is quite wrong, Mr Beyfus.

–Do you seriously say that in this article 'Golden boy of Syrup', you were not trying to knock him just about as hard as you could? – A: Not at all. I went to his home with a completely open mind, and merely reported what Mr Liberace said, what Mr Liberace did, and how Mr Liberace appeared to me then. At that time I felt it preposterous and at times ludicrous, but not necessarily evidence of character. At the end of it all, although I had my doubts, I decided to cast them in favour and I said then that I liked him.

–You liked him; and what do you think you would have written if you had disliked him; can you imagine? – A: I do not normally permit my personal feelings to enter into an article of this kind. I went there to report upon a few hours in an extraordinary home with an extraordinary personality.

–Let us see whether you were trying to knock him: 'Come in,' he said at the door with a smile... and then you said in parentheses, 'and the dimple'. A dimple is a thing with which we are born or not born, as the case may be, is it not? – A: It is a thing with which we are born, but do not necessarily project.

–Well, it comes into existence when we smile, whether we like it or not, does it not? – A: Yes. Well, of course; but we were dealing with a special smile and a special dimple.

–I am asking you a simple question: if you are born with a dimple, it comes into existence when you smile, whether you like it or not? – A: I accept that as a fact, if you say so.

–Just let us see how sarcastic you can be.

> 'Come in', he said at the door with a smile (and the dimple). You have read in the *Mirror* before about this outrageous home with pianos thrown at you wherever you stand, sit or lean.

251

...In fact, there were only two pianos in this house, were there not? Pianos, I am not talking about models, only two pianos. – A: There were only two real pianos at which people sit and play.

–In one room there were getting on for 200 models? – A: I assume there might have been quite that number.

–A great number of models in glass cases? – A: The ones I saw were not in glass cases.

–But it is conveying a completely wrong impression, is it not, to say 'pianos thrown at you wherever you stand, sit or lean'? – A: I disagree, Mr Beyfus, if you read the subsequent paragraph which talks about every conceivable object shaped like a piano.

–Just stopping there for a moment, I am not talking about ashtrays which are shaped like pianos. To say there were pianos thrown at you wherever you stand, sit or lean is completely wrong? – A: If you are suggesting that I am saying that grand pianos are thrown at me from every corner of the room, certainly that would not be true.

–Then you go on: 'Now it's even worse. The cushions are shaped like pianos. The ashtrays are shaped like pianos. The coffee tables are shaped like pianos. – A: Precisely.

–Were you in court, did you hear Mr Liberace say that all these things were gifts from admirers and friends? – A: I did not hear Mr Liberace, but I think it quite likely that it is true.

–Then you say you are not trying to knock him. 'Liberace was dressed in a black monogrammed sweater with ivory trousers (like the pianos). It was a relief to see all his teeth were white, and not blacked alternatively (like the pianos)'... Trying to be funny at his expense? – A: Mr Beyfus, first I must reject your suggestion that there was sarcasm in this, because I never intended to be sarcastic. There is a certain amount of irony, because any visitor to this home would be struck by the extraordinary appearance of the place. This was merely a jocular reference to my own reaction.

–An attempt to ridicule him? – A: No, not at all.

–All right; I just want to get your idea. Then you say: 'Liberace', I said, stubbing my cigarette out on F sharp...' All you say about ashtrays is that they were shaped like pianos? – A: I said that ashtrays were shaped like pianos.

–It was not the note of the piano on the ashtray? – A: So far as I recall, he had an ashtray with a keyboard motif, and when I said I put my cigarette out on it, as a person interested in music, I seem to recall that the actual note was F sharp; but I am not absolutely sure.

–...'Cannot please everybody,' he said with a smile; and then again repeated (and the dimple). Is that right? – A: Yes.

> – 'You discovered that with your film, *Sincerely yours*,' I said, leaning against a treble clef. 'Wasn't that a big flop?'

The smile (and the dimple) on his chubby face faded. 'The tragedy was the film came two years too late.'

...'And the dimple', again. That was making fun of him; is that right? – A: No; I was drawing attention to what had now become a famous part of Mr Liberace's act: the smile, the dimpled smile, and this was merely a description of it.

–Then: 'It's doing very well in the Philippines though.' I suggest he said abroad? – A: I could not possibly know how Mr Liberace's film was doing in the Philippines unless he himself told me.

–Unless you were in an inventive state of mind? – A: No, that is quite untrue, Mr Beyfus.

–'He introduced me to his famous mother, a quiet homely lady, wearing a blue apron and pendant diamond earrings'... You were there obviously trying to draw a distinction between an apron, on the one hand, and diamond earrings, on the other? – A: I was describing Mrs Liberace as I saw her.

–She wore other things besides the apron and earrings did she not? – A: The two things I noticed was the fact that...

–You were trying to make fun of the fact that here was a lady somewhat incongruously dressed with apron and diamond earrings. – A: No, I was certainly not making fun: I was merely recording the picture as I saw it.

–Would you accept that they were rhinestones? – A: I accept unreservedly that what I saw from a distance looked like diamonds may in fact have been rhinestones. I may be wrong on that one small point.

–'Then he showed me round the house, which was like a nightmare in the Royal Albert Hall'... I suggest, apart from the fact that the piano motif appeared constantly in the decor, it was a normal house. – A: Mr Beyfus, if I slept on a bed with the back made entirely of a piano keyboard, I can imagine my having a nightmare.

–I expect you could, but you are not a pianist. I am suggesting it was quite a normal house except for the piano motif in the decor? – A: No, I would say not. There were things about it which made it a most unusual home. I would say that apart from the decor, particularly because on almost every wall there were pictures of Liberace.

–I said apart from the decor and the furniture, the house itself was a normal house? – A: If you except the things that I have mentioned in this article, yes.

–I do not want to go all through it. You go on with your joke: 'How can you sleep nights with eight octaves hanging over you?'... 'It was given to me,' Liberace explained with a smile (and the dimple) 'like most of the things in the house.' That is the fifth time, I think 'and the dimple'. And then again: 'He sat down at the piano (shaped like a piano) and sang it to me with a smile (and the dimple).' Do you seriously say that in that article you were not seeking to knock him as much as you could? – A: No. I am afraid, with great respect, Mr Beyfus, I do not attach the importance you seem to to this reference to the dimple. It was merely a key phrase which I confess I used throughout the article, but merely as a key to each phase of the piece which I wrote.

–Always trying to make fun of him? – A: I think that much of what happened in this house when I was there was exceedingly amusing. I do not think Mr Liberace needed much assistance from me.

–I see; and, much as you appreciated his hospitality, and though you liked him, you thought it right to write this article on the 'Golden Boy of Syrup'? – A: When Mr Liberace began to dance to me and carry out other of the sort of posturing remarks and behaviour, at that time I saw it as amusing, extraordinary but harmless and therefore at that time I said I liked him, but Cherbourg at that point had not taken place.

–I suggest to you he never danced to you at all. – A: Mr Liberace was doing a show at Las Vegas, and he illustrated one of the numbers which he himself was going to do there. He played a song called *A Girl's Life*. He sang that song, and then told me that he does a soft shoe shuffle at the end of it, which he did.

–I am suggesting that that is inaccurate. Supposing it were accurate, it would be helpful to a reporter if he gave a sort of idea of the show he was going to give? – A: I did not find it particularly helpful, Mr Beyfus.

–You were out for copy? – A: Not at all. I was there to see with an open mind what Mr Liberace is like at home, and this is a very faithful and a most accurate account of what took place from the moment I arrived to the moment I left.

–Mr Zec, do you seriously say you were not out for copy? – A: Well, if a writer is invited to interview a personality, naturally one is out for copy, but I do not quite know what you mean by 'out for copy'.

–You went to the house to get material for an article for which the *Daily Mirror* would pay you? – A: Yes.

–That is shortly described as 'out for copy'. – A: Well, that expression has an innuendo about it which I cannot accept.

–After this action was started, were you employed by the *Daily Mirror* in connection with this case? – A: I must confess, I do not follow the question, Mr Beyfus.

–Then I will repeat it and see if you can follow it if I repeat it. After this action was started, were you employed by the *Daily Mirror* in connection with this case? – A: Not at any time, Mr Beyfus.

–Did you visit hotels at which Mr Liberace had stopped? – A: I did not visit any hotel. In fact, after my last article which I telephoned from Cherbourg, and apart from the press reception at the West End restaurant in the evening, I have had no connection whatsoever with this case or with Mr Liberace personally.

–Had you not made any enquiries about him at all? – A: None whatsoever, Mr Beyfus.

–Neither in the United States nor in this country? – A: I personally have not been asked to make any enquiries in any shape or form in connection with Mr Liberace or this case.

–Do you know nothing at all about enquiries which have been made? – A: I know absolutely nothing at all about any enquiries which may have been made subsequently.

–I have forgotten to ask you about the Café de Paris. Were you there on Mr Liberace's first night? – A: I was not, Mr Beyfus.

–Were you there at all when he was performing? – A: No.

–You are just speaking about the Café de Paris generally? – A: I was asked a question about a first night audience at the Café de Paris from my own experience.

–Do you normally go to first night performances? – A: I frequently go. When performers are important I usually go.

–I suggest that people like Miss Marlene Dietrich received an ovation, when she first came? – A: I remember Marlene Dietrich, since you mention her, as being in a state of terror and remarking to me that…

–You must not tell me what she said, but I am suggesting she received an ovation when she appeared? – A: If I remember, I think that is not quite so.

–Did Mr Steele receive an ovation when he appeared? – A: Mr who?

–Steele? – A: I do not know; I was not there; I do not know.

–One other little point on that: you told my lord and the jury that you did not think that many of the people at the Café de Paris would be readers of the *Daily Mirror*? – A: I said that of the first night audiences who go there I should be surprised that large numbers of them read the *Daily Mirror*.

–We are told it has some 13million readers? – A: That is so.

–I suppose that would be more than one in three of the adult population of this country? – A: Precisely, but very much a provincial and country readership.

–Do you seriously think that a great number of persons at the Café de Paris would not have read the *Daily Mirror*? – A: It is, of course, very hard to answer your question.

–Yes, but you put yourself forward as an expert on that matter? – A: No, I put myself forward as a person who knows something about audience reactions who visit stars at the Café de Paris.

–You were not being asked about that. On the basis that more than one in three of the adult population read the *Daily Mirror*, it is pretty certain that a good number of the people at the Café de Paris must have read it? – A: I

255

cannot accept that because it is a very small audience at the Café de Paris compared with the population.

–I said a good many people at the Café de Paris must have read it? – A: Well, one can only express an opinion, and I should have thought only a small part of the audience at the Café de Paris would be, as we understand it, *Daily Mirror* readers.

FAULKS: There are only two points. Mr Beyfus emphasises that in the house, apart from the decor and the furniture, it was an ordinary house? – A: Exactly.

–That, of course, just leaves the house itself, which was not actually shaped like a piano. –A: No, except that, if I recall, a swimming pool was shaped like a piano.

–A swimming pool was shaped like a piano, but not the house itself? – A: Yes.

–Now may I perhaps be allowed to put in the article this gentleman wrote on September 25.

BEYFUS: My Lord, I do not know how my learned friend can put it in in re-examination.

FAULKS: Perhaps I may be allowed to do that which I should have done in chief.

MR JUSTICE SALMON: It has been read I think more than once.

BEYFUS: Yes.

MR JUSTICE SALMON: I think we can consider it in.

FAULKS: I can help my friend as to why I want to put it in now and did not want to burden the jury with it in chief. It is for this reason: Mr Zec, your attention has been drawn to this what you call a typist's mistake... Which says, it is quite true, that the manager said: 'I would like Liberace to sit between his mother and George on the other hand, so that he can be kissed from both sides.' Now, supposing that came to Mr Connor's attention on the same day, the 24th, he did not write his article until the 26th, and on the 25th he would have seen the final article which is now being handed to the jury? – A: Yes.

–It has a photograph at the bottom of it which makes it completely clear to a person of the slightest comprehension that it is the lady who is in the middle being kissed by her sons on each side? – A: Yes.

BEYFUS: My Lord, that is in question; and, secondly, it does not make it clear that that suggestion was not made. It only makes it clear that the suggestion was not carried out, which is something quite different.

MR JUSTICE SALMON: Anyway, it is before the jury, and what it means and does not mean is a matter for them and for argument hereafter.

FAULKS: Yes, my Lord. [To the witness]: I was only emphasising that your report may or may not have been before the next day? – ZEC: Yes, that is exactly what happened.

Questioned by Faulks, Mr Sydney Leonard Drewe said that he was a qualified chartered secretary and was secretary of the Apollo Theatre Company. From the weekly receipts he could say that the revue, *For Amusement Only* ran at the theatre for 698 performances from June 1956 to February 1958. There had been good houses throughout the run, he said, of between 500 and 600 people in the audience each night. A total of 350,000 would be a fair estimate of the number of people who had seen it, he agreed.

Beyfus had no questions.

Patrick Doncaster, a feature writer with the *Daily Mirror*, said that in July 1956 when he was in America he had telephoned Liberace and in the course of conversation he had said that when he next visited England he would like to see some London pubs. Doncaster said it would make a good feature for the paper and followed up that suggestion with a letter on October 1, and consequently the visit was arranged in the company of another feature writer, Tony Miles. In answer to Mr Gardiner he said that the two writers had paid for the various drinks that people had that evening.

He said he had also been in pianist Winifred Atwell's dressing room at the Palladium on Wednesday October 10, in the presence of Liberace, Miss Ambler, and several reporters and photographers.

He said: 'There was a small piano there and it was suggested by one photographer that it would be a good idea if there was a picture of Liberace and Miss Atwell at this piano. In a jocular mood Mr Liberace said "Let's have one with Cassandra while we are at it." A short while afterwards Miss Ambler was talking rather loudly and she said: "If Randolph Churchill could get £5,000 from the *People*, Liberace should get something from the Daily Mirror."… I then approached Mr Liberace and I said to him "Are you really going to sue us?" He said No, he was not.'

GARDINER: Did he make any reference to your public house story in the *Mirror*? – A: He did; he said he had just read it and he liked the idea.

–Was there anything else that you remember at that interview? – A: No, nothing more that I can remember.

Gardiner might have done better – far better – to have pressed Doncaster (and also Liberace, when cross-examining him) further on the truth about the pub-crawl story. For, far from it being a simple desire for the entertainer – as any foreign visitor might wish – to experience 'traditional

257

English pubs' during his visit, it was no more nor less than a cynical publicity stunt: in the jargon of the trade, a photo-opportunity.

Doncaster and his colleague Tony Miles had driven (in those days you could park anywhere in London) across the river to the south end of London Bridge and to an area so seedy it would be rejected in future years as a potential location for the Mirror headquarters. They found a down-at-heel pub with a battered upright piano that Doncaster – an accomplished pianist who numbered Errol Gardner among his close friends – tested to ensure that it was in tune, and they reported to features editor Colin Reed that they had chosen the ideal spot and he should send a photographer there to meet them. To ensure exclusivity for their story, they didn't tell the pub management what they were planning.

Reed shared the information not only with the picture desk but also with his neighbours from Surrey who turned up in force to meet the American star. Never had the pub landlord had such a big sale of gins and tonics, with customers wearing blazers and cavalry twill trousers demanding a slice of lemon, and ice, in their drinks and asking him where Liberace was. When the pianist and his entourage arrived, in two black limos, the minders took one look at the Hogarthian scene and beat a hasty retreat.

They quickly relocated to The George, which at least had the distinction of being London's only remaining galleried inn.

In spite of the story eventually woven around it, it was a quick in and out visit, lasting a matter of minutes – just long enough for Liberace to be photographed at the keyboard surrounded by loveable cockney characters.

But that totally cynical 'photo-op' was not the only point that Gardiner failed to follow through.

The question being asked in Fleet Street pubs was why, if Liberace was truthfully so upset about a story in the *Daily Mirror*, he agreed to go along with its journalists on a pub crawl. If he had been angry with the paper – if he seriously believed it had labelled him as a homosexual and damaged the health of his mother – he could have signalled this easily by offering the story to one of its rivals who, as Doncaster made clear in his letter, were vying for the same picture opportunity.

Was it simply that he could not resist the chance of coverage in the paper with 'the greatest daily sale on earth'?

It was a question that hadn't escaped the notice of the judge.

If Beyfus knew the facts of the pub crawl, he would be careful to skirt around them.

BEYFUS: I gather from your evidence the journalists and photographers had been invited by a gentleman who was acting for Miss Atwell? A: That is true.

–In order to get publicity for her? – A: I should think so.

258

–Well, obviously it would be, would it not? Try and be fair. A man acting for Miss Atwell would only be interested in publicity for her, would he not? – A: I could not really say; I do not know.

–It does not occur to you that someone who is representative or publicity manager to Miss Atwell would only be interested in publicity for her? – A: He would be interested in publicity for her.

–Yes; and then, as I understand, it was suggested that it would be a good idea if they were photographed together. –A. Yes.

–And your recollection is that Mr Liberace said: 'Let us have one for Cassandra.' – A: That is true.

–Well, he does not recollect saying that, but obviously a sarcastic observation, if he said it? – A: No.

–He said it... what? – A: He did say it.

–If he did say it, it would obviously be a sarcastic observation? – A: I should think so.

–If Mr Liberace said 'Let Miss Atwell and I be photographed together for Cassandra,' what else could it be but a sarcastic observation? – A: I have just agreed with you.

–What else could it be?

MR JUSTICE SALMON: I think he is agreeing... I think, Mr Beyfus, that he is agreeing.

BEYFUS: I am sorry.

DONCASTER: I have just agreed with you.

–You have agreed with me? – A: Yes.

–I am sorry. Then you say Miss Ambler, you know she has denied it, said to you: 'If Randolph Churchill can get £5,000, Liberace ought to be able to get' - what - something - 'from the *Daily Mirror*'? – A: She did not say it to me: she said it in a voice which could be heard all round the dressing room.

–How many people were there? – A: I think about a dozen.

–Who else was there besides those you have mentioned? – A: Mr Perrin; Miss Atwell's husband, Mr Lew Levinson...

–Who else? A: Oh, reporters and photographers; I do not know their names.

–You do not know the names of any of them... Or what newspapers they represented? – A: Some were from the *Daily Express*.

But you do not remember their names? – A: No.

–And are you saying that you asked Mr Liberace whether he was going to sue the *Daily Mirror*? – A: I did. I went up and stood quite close to him and said it to him.

–You know he has denied that? – A: I know that he has denied it, yes.

–Did you say it in such a voice that everybody in the room could hear it? – A: No, I do not think so, sir.

259

–Did you whisper it to him? – A: I should not say I whispered it to him: I just said it normally to him.

–Who do you think heard it: who would have heard it in the ordinary course? Would Miss Atwell have heard it? – A: I should think Miss Atwell would have heard it.

–Mr Perrin? – A: I could not say for Mr Perrin, whether he was near enough to hear.

–It was a risky thing to say, was it not, you being a *Daily Mirror* man? – A: I do not think it was risky at all; it was trying to get information.

–Do you say you spoke to him in California? – A: Yes.

–To whom? – A: Mr Liberace.

–To Mr Liberace? About what? – A: About his visit to England.

–About his visit to England? Where were you? – A: I was in Hollywood.

–You were in Hollywood and spoke to him on the telephone? – A: I telephoned, yes.

–You do not write under the name of Doncaster, do you? – A: Yes, I do.

–You are Patrick Doncaster, are you? – A: I am, yes.

–What is your real name? – A: That is my real name.

–I am sorry: I thought your name was Johnson. I am extremely sorry. You talked to him then about a visit to a London pub? A: That is true, yes.

–You suggested it, did you not? – A: Suggested visiting a pub?

–Yes. – A: No. I asked him what he was going to do in London. He said he wanted to see some of our pubs.

–Is that the only thing that he said he wanted to see in London? – A: No; it was not, no.

–What else did he say he wanted to see in London? – A: I think he said restaurants.

–Restaurants. Yes, what else? – A: I cannot remember any more.

–Then all you can remember of this conversation in California over the telephone is that he said he would like to see some of the London restaurants and pubs? – A: It is not all I remember. I remember it mostly because I wanted to do a feature on it.

–What else do you remember of what he wanted to see? – A: I cannot recall without reading my article: it is nearly three years ago now.

–All you can remember is that he told you that he would like to see London restaurants and London pubs; is that it? – A: I remember him saying obvious things, that he looked forward to the visit and bringing his mother with him…

–I only wanted to ask you… – A: I cannot remember.

–You said you asked him what he wanted to see in London? – A: The first thing he said was he wanted to see some of the old lovely public houses.

–You told the members of the jury you asked him what he wanted to see; is that right? –A: Yes.

–And all that you remember is that he wanted to see restaurants and public houses; is that right? – A: That is all I can remember.

–That is all you can remember? – A: That is not all I wrote though.

After the lunch adjournment Mr Beyfus returned to the arrangements for the pub crawl.

–You are the author of the letter of October 1? – A: That is so.

–That is a strong appeal to arrange for Mr Liberace to visit public houses with you? – A: It is a letter from me following on our conversation in Hollywood.

–Disagree with me if you like: was it not a strong appeal by you to Mr Heller to arrange that Mr Liberace should visit public houses with you? – A: Yes.

–You wanted to be able to publish an article in the *Daily Mirror* with photographs of Mr Liberace visiting public houses? – A: Yes.

–The reason for that being that you thought that it would help to sell the *Daily Mirror*? – A: I thought it would be a good, interesting feature. I did not know whether it would sell the *Daily Mirror*.

–Are not all these feature articles put in the *Daily Mirror* for the purpose of selling the *Daily Mirror*? – A: I suppose they are.

–To make it attractive to the public? – A: Yes.

–That was your object in trying to arrange this visit? – A: I suppose so.

–How long have you been with the *Daily Mirror*? – A: Seven years.

–Were you with the *Daily Mirror* at the time when the editor was sent to gaol? – A: No, I was not.

–That is less than seven years ago, is it not? – A: I joined just afterwards.

–Have you read *Publish and Be Damned?* – A: I have.

–Were you with the *Daily Mirror* when the *Daily Mirror* sponsored the visit to this country of Bill Haley? – A: I was, yes.

–Did you cover him at all? – A: I did.

–Did large crowds attend to try to see Mr Haley? – A: They did.

–Did some of the crowding to see Mr Haley result in riots? – A: I did not see any riots myself.

–Do you not know that there were riots in connection with the visit of Mr Haley? – A: Riots at his film. I do not know about any riots in connection with his personal visit.

–There were riots with his film? – A: There was a film called *Rock Around the Clock*, which was being shown. There were riots in cinemas. I do not recall any riots in personal appearances.

–While he was here his film was shown. Is that right? – A: I believe it was.

261

–I suppose he made personal appearances with a view to boosting the film? – A: I should think so.

–As a result of the riots were several cinemas closed? – A: I could not tell you. I do not know.

–Do you not? You have never heard of it? – A: I do not know.

–When was this? – A: It was either the end of 1956 or during 1957, I think.

–Very roughly the same sort of time as Mr Liberace's visit? – A: After.

–A few months afterwards? – A: Yes.

–What did you do in connection with Mr Haley? Did you follow him around? – A: To a certain extent, yes.

–Did he perform at all? – A: Yes. I reported him.

–To vast crowds? – A: Yes.

–Enthusiasm outside? —A. Some.

–Did he arrive at Waterloo station? – A: Yes.

–And crowds met him? – A: Crowds.

–Let us be quite frank: the same sort of hysterical welcome as Mr Liberace received? – A: I should think so. I was not present at Mr Liberace's arrival.

–On the other occasions when you attended his concerts were there crowds outside trying to get his autograph and so forth? – A: Mr Haley?

–Yes. – A: Yes.

–You did not read anything, did you, in the *Daily Mirror* about unduly promoting crowds or the herd instinct or anything of that sort? – A: I cannot remember reading that.

–I think there is only one other matter. Have you since this action started been deputed to make enquiries with regard to the plaintiff? – A: No.

–None of any sort? – A: None.

–Have you made any? – A: No.

–On your own? – A: For myself?

–No. Without being specifically asked to do so, have you made any enquiries? – A: No.

Mrs Gwynfil Mair Connor, wife of William Connor, said she remembered a visit about three years earlier by a Miss Ambler and a Mr McGhee.

Questioned by Gardiner, she said: 'I had just recently come out of hospital and I was not feeling particularly interested in entertaining strangers. This was the first time my husband ever had asked professional people into our house to write a story about him, so I remember it very clearly... I took them into the sitting-room. We had a problem, because we had a very antagonistic cat called Smokey Joe. Secretly he did not even like my husband; he just liked my daughter and myself. We wanted to get him pictured... Mr McGhee helped me most nobly. He spent most of the time taking pictures under great difficulties... I took Mr McGhee upstairs to find out where the cat had gone to, and then I came down, because Mr McGhee said that he wanted to take pictures of the animal and get to know it before he set to work.'

GARDINER: When you came down did you have some conversation with Miss Ambler? – A: I got a drink for her, which was in the sitting-room, because that is where we keep our drinks. It was a very friendly and chatty gathering. I gave her a drink, and we talked about the weather. We were all very friendly. There was a whole lot of talk. Then my husband went upstairs to join Mr McGhee to take pictures, because the idea of the whole thing was for him to take pictures with my husband.

–At some point did somebody (and can you remember who) mention Mr Liberace? – A: I think possibly it was Miss Ambler.

–Do you remember what she said? – A: I think it was a straightforward sort of boomerang to start me off. I was sitting in the sitting-room. She said to me that she had been to Miss Winifred Atwell's party and that the name 'Cassandra' had cropped up, and that Mr Liberace had said 'Who is this guy Cassandra? Is he one of those?' which I thought was such a funny statement. It was so, so ridiculous to me that I just turned the whole thing away with a laugh.

–At that time was there anybody else in the room? – A: I think that it was while Mr McGhee was downstairs, because he was talking to my husband about his wartime experiences. They had met in the past.

–Was there a conversation about wartime experiences? – A: Yes. They had been at Tidworth with Mr Frank Owen for a time, or with somebody.

–Was there some conversation about the action which Mr Liberace was bringing? – A: As far as I can remember none, though Mr Liberace was discussed in a slightly silly laughing way by Miss Ambler and possibly me.

–If a statement had been made that Mr Liberace was going to win the action and that the *Daily Mirror* was going to pay a lot of money because of what your husband had written, would you have remembered it? – A: I should have remembered it, but I did not hear anything of the sort.

BEYFUS: When the cat proved so antagonistic did you not accompany it upstairs? – A: I did. I had to try to discover under which bed the cat was hiding.

–Didn't you take it upstairs? – A: I did not take the cat upstairs, no. He ran upstairs. He does not like strangers.

–The moment he saw Miss Ambler, off he went upstairs? – A: Certainly. He does not like strangers.

–I gather that he is very antagonistic? – A: He was. He is dead now.

–At any rate, you went upstairs with the photographer? – A: Yes.

–Leaving your husband and Miss Ambler together? – A: For a very short time, because Mr McGhee said that he could produce better pictures of animals if he were left alone to deal with the animal than if I was around.

–At any rate you went upstairs and spent a little time upstairs with the photographer? – A: I should say two or three minutes at the most.

–Leaving your husband and Miss Ambler to chat? – A: That is true.

–Then the photographer wanted to be left alone with the antagonistic cat? – A: Yes. He had lots of gadgets and lights, and he was crawling on his stomach looking under beds for cats.

–At any rate, nearly three years afterwards, you would not pledge yourself to the number of minutes you were upstairs? –A: No, certainly not, but I was not feeling well, and I wanted to sit downstairs and be a good hostess to the company.

–Then you came downstairs and some conversation took place with regard to the action? – A: Yes; but my husband in the meantime had gone upstairs to have his picture taken with the cat.

–So that your conversation with Miss Ambler was quite independent of your husband's conversation? – A: It was the sort of conversation that all women can start when they first meet each other.

–That does not convey anything at all to me, as a man. At any rate, you started talking, and again the subject of this action came up, did it? – A: That is true, yes.

–You say that Miss Ambler said 'Who is this guy Cassandra? Is he one of those?' – A: I did not say that. Miss Ambler said it. I said that she had referred to some gossip which she had heard in Miss Winifred Atwell's dressing-room.

–Who is supposed to have said it? – A: I rather gathered it was Mr Liberace.

–You say that you rather gathered it. Are you not certain? – A: Miss Ambler was a very chatty lady, and I am inclined to shut my ears to lots of gossip which women tell me.

–I gather that you did not succeed in shutting your ears to this particular bit of gossip? – A: No, because it was such an outrageous bit of gossip reflecting on the sort of behaviour of my husband that it was so laughable that I remembered it.

–Apparently it was so laughable that it was not even put to my client when he was in the witness box, but perhaps you would not know that. Did you know that, or were you not here? – A: I have been here a good bit of the time, but I cannot remember if it was put to him.

–Did you hear my client cross-examined? – A: About half of it.

GARDINER: My lord, with great respect, can it be a proper observation to make in front of the jury for my learned friend to say that? It is no part of my case that Miss Ambler was telling the truth. I put the position quite clearly to the lady on the second day of the evidence. First of all I said: 'Did you say to Mrs Connor that you had met Liberace at a party? (A) No, I never mentioned Mr Liberace to anyone. It came from Mr Connor. (Q) At the party – I am not suggesting it was true – did you tell Mrs Connor that Liberace had asked 'Who is this guy Cassandra? Is he one of those?' and there being general laughter, and did Mrs Connor say 'What a ridiculous thing to say'? or something to that effect.

BEYFUS: I take it that it is not suggested in any way on the part of the defendants that it is true or that my client said anything of the sort.

GARDINER: I am not suggesting for a moment that anything which Miss Ambler said is true.

MR JUSTICE SALMON: I think Mr Gardiner did make it plain when he was cross-examining her that he was not accepting what she was saying as to what Mr Liberace said.

BEYFUS: It is a long time ago, and I did not want the members of the jury to be under any misapprehension. [To the witness] Is that all that you remember of the conversation with Miss Ambler? – A: Yes. I was much more interested, possibly, in the fact that I wanted to show the lady out. I wanted to show her the house and garden and bring the whole thing to a close, because I was not feeling well.

–I do not quite understand. Why did you want to show her the house and garden? – A: That is always a very tactful way of getting rid of guests. [Laughter.]

Mr Michael Rogers Ashburner appeared on subpoena. He told Mr Gardiner: 'In October 1956, I was merely one of the students at Sheffield University. I am at the present time the president of the students' hall of residence, and I am the president-elect of the Students' Union.'

In October 1956, he had gone with several friends from the hall of residence to see a performance by Liberace in Sheffield. The visit had been organised with only a couple of days notice.

GARDINER: Before you went had you read the issue of September 26 of the *Daily Mirror*? – A: I had not then.

–This is a very painful question for me to have to ask you, but is the *Daily Mirror* among the papers which are taken in by the hall of residence? –A: Most certainly not.

–Where were you and your friends sitting? – A: We were on opposing sides of the balcony. I should explain that this venture of ours was organised by two halls. There are three halls in Sheffield. There were two halls who participated in this, and our bookings were on opposite sides of this balcony.

–What happened during the performance so far as the students were concerned? –A: We went along feeling that we would have a fair rag. The

265

opening gambit on our part was to open souvenir editions of *The Star*, which had been published in connection with this affair. This, in a hall such as the City Hall, causes a great deal of noise. Any rustling of paper would do. If anybody knows the City Hall at Sheffield they would know what it would be like. Then Mr Liberace appeared. More accurately, Mr Liberace had appeared previous to this, and the reading of the newspapers continued. There was a certain amount of acclamation from the audience. We were rather intent on our own particular stunts. We had balloons which we blew up and allowed the air to exude through a tensioned part at the top. You understand the kind of noise that that would make.

–Fairly standard things I gather? – A: Yes, definitely. They were standard student pranks. I believe that when Mr Liberace appeared the shout went up 'Where's Mum?', 'Good old George!' and similar items such as that. Apart from that, we just continued to rag and make as much noise as we could. I think that was the general tenor of the whole rag.

–Were there any later developments? – A: Yes, there were some later developments. As soon as the City Hall authorities realised that the students were there in force, the whole body, so it appeared to us, were mustered on the balcony and appeared at all the doors, and unfortunately three of my friends were ushered out in a rather unfortunate manner. One of them on his departure shouted, and was clearly heard throughout the hall, 'Oy, Liberace, they are chucking me out!'

–When they were thrown out what happened to the rest of you? – A: That sort of noise went on for possibly three-quarters of an hour to an hour or so. This was all before the interval. After the three of them had been thrown out we decided that we had had just about enough, and we all left.

–Did anybody at any time shout out 'Go home, queer'? – A: Not to my knowledge.

–Or any reference to homosexuality or anything which could have been understood as such? – A: Nothing whatever as far as I could tell.

–If there was would you have heard it? – A: From my part of the hall if it had been anybody in the section immediately behind me I think I should have done, but in any other sections it is very difficult to tell. As I say, the acoustics of this place are atrocious.

–Was anything intended throughout except the rag? – A: That was the whole intention. We felt that Mr Liberace was, shall I say, a standard for a student rag. Numerous performers have had this treatment.

–Did you subsequently hear anything from Mr Liberace? – A: Yes. It was most interesting. This possibly did a great deal to stimulate his esteem amongst the students. We received a Christmas card from him.

–Can you tell me what happened to the Christmas card? – A: Yes. It has been destroyed, along with all the rest of our Christmas cards.

BEYFUS: I gather that there were two battalions of riotous students? – A: Yes. I suppose you could put it in that way,

–One from one hall and one from another... And one at one extreme end of the balcony and the other at the other extreme end? – A: Yes. That would be approximately correct.

–You carried on your misbehaviour separately? – A: It was not entirely separate, because you realise in a student body everybody knows everybody else within the union buildings.

–You went separately? – A: We went separately in the sense that we started from separate locations.

–You went to different parts of the hall, the extreme ends of the gallery? – A: Yes. It is not so extreme as one would imagine, though.

–You and your friends at one end kicked up a row for three-quarters of an hour? – A: On and off, yes.

–That is not very creditable behaviour, is it? – A: I agree entirely.

–Whatever you may think of Liberace, many hundreds of people had paid money to hear his show. – A: We realised that. I venture to point out that this is an unfortunate comment which occurs every time any student organisation holds any rag.

–You and your gang your side were yelling this, that and the other. Is that right? – A: Well, yes: anything we could think of virtually, I suppose.

–I changed the metaphor from 'battalion' to 'gang', which is perhaps more suitable. The gang the other side of the balcony were doing the same thing, shouting this, that and the other? – A: Yes. I do not take on myself to remember what was shouted. After all, we have various meetings within our own union building when things are shouted. There were such things as 'Good old Liberace!', 'Where's Mum?' and that sort of thing.

–You remember some things shouted and which were shouted from your side, but you would not undertake to say that you recollect everything that was shouted by the other gang the other side of the balcony? – A: I certainly would not. The babel of noise which was made was such that it would be impossible to tell what was shouted from the other side. I could only tell you what was shouted from my own immediate vicinity.

–That is exactly what I thought, and that is quite a fair comment. Then Sheffield University students received a Christmas card from Mr Liberace, I understand? – A: Yes.

–You probably thought that very amusing? – A: No, it was not very amusing. It caused quite a bit of a stir, and it was sent from the hall to residents. We were very pleased to receive it. We felt that it showed that Mr Liberace had a sense of humour.

–This was 1956. Since that time you have had the pleasure of commercial television in Sheffield? – A: Please, not commercial; BBC.

267

–Have you had commercial television in Sheffield since 1956? – A: I thought that you meant with respect to the University. Yes, commercial television has arrived.

–But you had not got it in October 1956? – A: No; I am pretty certain not.

–Did you at that time go to the Apollo theatre? – A: No.

–You never saw the revue *For Amusement Only*? – A: I personally did not.

–You are not suggesting that none of your fellow students read the *Daily Mirror*? – A: I am not suggesting that, but in our particular hall (as I said previously there are three halls in Sheffield) we do not take it. One does take it. We did have a newspaper poll within our own hall after these events, and the *Daily Mirror* was not there.

–But students do buy their own newspapers apart from reading the newspapers which are in the hall? – A: On the whole, I would say: No. That is my candid experience.

–You do not buy a newspaper yourself? – A: Yes. I personally have *The Times* delivered.

–You are amongst the top people.

Beyfus sat down to be replaced briefly by Gardiner:

–Neither of the two halls that did go to the Town Hall took the *Daily Mirror* at that time? – A: That is correct.

–Some students presumably have television at home? – A: Yes.

John Spitzer gave his address as the Grand Hotel, Sheffield and said that at one time in his career he had been a theatrical manager. He said he read the *Daily Mirror,* among many others, but not every day; he usually read the *Daily Telegraph.*

In October 1956 he had attended Liberace's concert at Sheffield City Hall, sitting in the stalls for a while and then standing at the back. He remained for only part of the first half, leaving before the interval.

Faulks asked him whether he heard any disturbance and he replied: 'Yes, quite a lot, from the gallery.'

–Did you hear any particular shout? – A: The only particular one I heard was 'Liberace, they are chucking me out!'

–You heard that quite clearly? – A: That was the only one I heard clearly.

–Did you hear anybody shouting 'Queer'? – A: I did not.

–Or 'Fairy'? – A: No.

Cross-examined by Beyfus:

–There was only one you heard clearly? – A: Yes: 'Liberace, they are chucking me out!'

–That is the only one? – A: That is the only one I heard clearly.

–That was quite obviously at the end of a disturbance? – A: Yes.

–No doubt there were a great number of that sort of thing which you heard but you did not hear clearly? –A: They were all together. There was nothing clear. They were all together.

–You were in a very bad position for hearing, at the back of the stalls, if the shouts were coming from the gallery two floors above you? – A: Yes; but this other one was very distinct.

–Have you anything to do now with independent television? – A: No.

–Do you know anything about it? – A: Yes. I watch it.

–You watch it, but you do not know anything about it? – A: No.

The defence had only one card left to play.

Answering questions put by Gardiner, Hugh Cudlipp said he was editorial director of the Daily Mirror Group of newspapers, a director of Daily Mirror Newspapers, of Sunday Pictorial Newspapers, and also of Associated Television. He had joined the *Daily Mirror* in 1935, became features editor of that paper and was then appointed editor of the *Sunday Pictorial*.

From 1940 to 1946 he served in the Army overseas and on demobilisation was reappointed editor of the *Sunday Pictorial*. From 1950 to 1952 he was managing editor of Lord Beaverbrook's *Sunday Express* and then returned to edit the *Sunday Pictorial*. In 1953 he was appointed editorial director of both papers and had written a book called *Publish and Be Damned*.

–How long have you known Mr Connor? – A: I met Mr Connor first in 1935 when I joined the *Daily Mirror*. He joined on the same day as myself, I think.

–Did you work with him when you were on the *Daily Mirror*? – A: That is correct.

–About how often do you see him? – A: I see him every day when I am in the office and he is in the office. That is if he is not abroad and I am not abroad we meet every day for a brief talk in the mornings.

–To what extent is he entitled to say what he thinks? – A: He has complete freedom to express his own views which appear under his own nom de plume Cassandra, unless the editor of the paper, Mr Nener, objects. Mr Nener has the last word in what he considers acceptable for publishing. Therefore nothing that Mr Connor wrote would be altered, and he has complete freedom to express his own views, but the editor, being an editor, would have the right to exclude it if he thought fit.

269

–How far in a paper like this is an article written in order to raise the circulation of the paper, or how far, in your view, can an article raise the circulation of a paper? – A: Mr Connor is not regarded as a circulation raiser by the paper. He is regarded as a specialist writer, a very brilliant writer whom we are pleased to have in the paper, but he is not regarded in any sense as a bringer-in of a huge audience by any means.

–Are you able to judge how far readers agree with him or disagree with him? – A: Occasionally we hold a poll of what the readers like and dislike in the paper, not very frequently. One was held perhaps about six years or seven years ago in which Cassandra's column endured this test, and it came out at about 50 per cent, meaning that 50 per cent of the readers of the paper read him regularly.

–We have heard that there have been occasions on which he has published a view which has been the opposite of the editorial view? – A: Very frequently.

–How usual or unusual is that in Fleet Street? – A: It is usual on the more progressive and better papers and very unusual on the others, but it does quite frequently occur. Another example is Lord Beaverbrook's papers publishing cartoons by Low, who for many years has been opposed to Lord Beaverbrook's own political policy. We are not the only newspaper which does it.

–What is a tabloid newspaper? – A: A tabloid newspaper is a newspaper of very small size. It is purely a technical phrase. If you fold *The Times* or the *Daily Telegraph* over into two, which some machines do, then it becomes a tabloid paper. The *Evening Standard* is a tabloid paper. It is a matter of size and not of style necessarily.

–I think you were a member of Sir James Grigg's Commission on Her Majesty's Services appointed by the present government? – A: I was.

Does the *Daily Mirror* bring out from time to time what is called *Spotlight*? – A: Yes, a pamphlet.

–On what sort of subjects? – A: The object of the *Spotlight* pamphlets is to convey a great deal of information which would not, on the whole, fit into the paper itself. We have a large number of specialist writers who gain a lot of information, and therefore they take time off, as it were; they take about six months to produce these papers. One was on Anglo-American relations. Another was on trade unions. These are distributed to people in industry and so on. Another one was on justice. There have been about 15 to date.

Cross-examined by Mr Beyfus, holding a copy of *Publish and Be Damned*:
–It is obvious that you realised that I would ask you about this book. Is that an honest book? – A: Of course it is an honest book. Yes, certainly.

–Did you endeavour to set out in that book accurately (1) what had happened and (2) your honest opinion? – A: It expresses not my opinion. It expresses what occurred. It is the story of a newspaper about which I was writing, but I was not employed by it, and in my opinion it is an accurate version.

–Is what you stated as fact true? Are these things which you stated as facts true? – A: They are the facts so far as I could ascertain them, and I think I ascertained them completely.

–Were the opinions expressed honest? – A: Most certainly.

–Would you agree that in or about 1935 those responsible for the *Daily Mirror* started to change it into a tabloid? – A: It was a tabloid already. They did not change its size. The word 'tabloid' indicates purely a matter of size.

–I suggest that that is quite inaccurate and that 'tabloid' refers to the nature of a newspaper? – A: I am sorry, but I cannot agree. The *Evening Standard* is a tabloid and the *War Cry*, produced by the Salvation Army, is a tabloid.

–How many pages has the *New York Daily News*? – A: I have not the slightest idea. It changes. It is probably three times as many as we have.

–You constantly go to New York? – A: Not constantly. I go there occasionally, but I do not count the number of pages. They are larger papers than ours.

–The *Daily Mirror* is in the offices of the *New York Daily News*? – A: Yes.

–What sort of size is that, 30 pages, or something like that? – A: Considerably more, I think. I have not counted up the pages.

–It is a very large newspaper? – A: It is the largest circulation in the whole of America.

–I am not talking about its circulation. It is in itself a very large newspaper? – A: Yes.

–In the same way the *New York Daily Mirror* is a very large newspaper? – A: Do you mean the number of pages?

–Yes. – A: All American papers are three times at least larger than ours and therefore by our own standard they are all large newspapers.

–It is a very large newspaper? – A: By our standards but not by American standards.

–At any rate it is very large? – A: By our standards, yes.

–I suggest that when you talk about a newspaper being a tabloid you are referring to the manner in which the news and views are expressed and to its size? – A: I do not. I refer to its size.

–In the first place is not the expression 'tabloid' generally regarded as a derogatory expression? – A: No, It is in fact a trade name held by a company which produces pills.

271

–I suggest to you that particularly in the United States, where it is more used, it is a derogatory term? – A: Not in my opinion. I am trying to answer honestly, and it is not so.

–You and those who were with you in 1935 started to turn the *Daily Mirror* into a tabloid, did you not? – A: I cannot answer that question because I do not quite understand what it means. Can you read the rest of the sentence?

–Did not you and those associated with you on the *Daily Mirror* start in 1935 turning the *Daily Mirror* into a tabloid? – A: That is correct.

–That turning of it into a tabloid continued over the years, did it not? – A: Of course.

–Will you take your book in front of you and look at page 66, Harry Guy Bartholomew was the head of both the *Daily Mirror* and the *Sunday Pictorial*, was he not, at that time? – A: That is so, yes, but I cannot see that on page 66.

–It is not on page 66. – A: I thought you were... I am sorry, referring me to a particular paragraph.

–So I am, but the question as to the position of Mr Bartholomew was not on page 66. I was asking you a preliminary question as to what he was. – A: He was at that time, 1935, editorial director of the *Daily Mirror*.

> –Bartholomew was getting around him a band of young journalists who had to be wide awake on their toes. Oddly enough, at their head was Cecil Thomas; cherubic, courteous and unobtrusive, he was the last man a Hollywood producer would cast in the role of the ruthless tabloid editor.

...Do you see that... Was that the role which he had to carry out? – A: That was the role which he did carry out.

–'The ruthless tabloid editor'... Will you now turn to page 115. I do not propose to ask you to look at it. That merely says in the second sentence:

> The *Daily Express* watched with some anxiety the rapid growth of the tabloid and began to be concerned about its own claim to being 'the world's greatest newspaper'.

....Then on page 119 we find the expression 'tabloid revolution' half way down. It says: 'The *Mirror* was curiously frank about itself in the years of the tabloid revolution and frequently printed vigorous attacks on its own technique.' So the tabloid revolution took place during a period of years. Is that right? – A: Yes, of course.

–Again we get the same phrase on page 215 in the last sentence of the first paragraph:

> It had still to declare its principles; the vague allegiance to a new sense of values which it had displayed since the tabloid revolution did not go far enough.

...You appreciate, do you not, that if the tabloid revolution took place over the period of years clearly it was not just a question of reducing the size of the newspaper? – A: No. I was not suggesting that. The size of the newspaper was not reduced. What was different was the phrase 'tabloid revolution'. That does not mean, with great respect, changing the size of the paper but changing what was done in that size.

–The tabloid revolution was turning what had previously been a gentlemanly and decorous newspaper into a sensational newspaper. – A: I think it would be less decorous but not less gentlemanly.

–Shall we say, then, turning what had been a decorous newspaper into a sensational newspaper? – A: We were not living in a very decorous age in 1935, and the newspaper changed its form and its approach to life to keep up with the changes which we thought were taking place in society.

–I am not sure whether you are agreeing with me or not. The tabloid revolution consisted of changing the paper from being a decorous newspaper into a sensational newspaper? – A: Yes; I would agree with that.

–Indeed you have given, I think, no less than three examples of three different high-ups in the newspaper who proclaimed and boasted that it was a sensational newspaper. Mr Bartholomew, for example, gave evidence before the Royal Commission to that effect? – A: You said that I boasted about it. I did not. I recorded in this book that others did.

–You boasted in this book that it glorified in the idea of being sensational? – A: The people who ran the paper. Mr Bartholomew, Mr Bolam and others and myself who conduct it now are proud of the paper.

–Proud of it being a sensational paper? – A: Proud of it being a sensational paper in the sense stated in this book by Mr Bolam in a paragraph about him. He defines the word 'sensational' very clearly, and that is the definition I accept when I use the word.

–Then may I put a definition. I suggest that it is a paper which presents the news and its views in a sensational manner? – A: No: a vivid manner.

–In a sensational manner? – A: That is what the word 'sensational' means and the way in which it is defined in this book. There are many definitions of the word 'sensational', but the definition is clearly given in this book. May I draw attention to it?

MR JUSTICE SALMON: Just listen to the question. Your own counsel will have a chance of dealing with any particular point later. – A: I am sorry.

BEYFUS: Will you go to the bottom of page 250. This is Mr Silvester Bolam:

> The *Mirror* is a sensational newspaper. We make no apology for that. We believe in the sensational presentation of news and views, especially important news and views, as a necessary and valuable public service in these days of mass readership and democratic responsibility.

–Do you accept that, that a sensational newspaper is a newspaper which presents both news and views in a sensational manner? – A: I accept that entirely.

–In order to bring about this tabloid revolution, to use your own words, I think, you had to live dangerously? – A: That is correct.

–'Live dangerously' means taking the risk of unpleasant consequences as the result of your presentation of news and views in a sensational manner? – A: No, I wrote the phrase 'live dangerously'. May I explain what I meant by it. By 'living dangerously' in 1935 I meant challenging some of the orthodox ideas of the day. I was one of the people who challenged them. I was features editor. I wrote the book. That is what I meant; I certainly did not mean challenging the law. No sane person would endeavour to do that. What I meant was challenging the conventions of the day; Britain was getting behind the times in the world, and I felt that we had to go on to other ideas. That was what I meant.

–Let us see what your sensational presentation of news and views led to. First of all did it lead to the imprisonment of the editor and the fining of the newspaper proprietors in the sum of £10,000? – A: I do not think the sensationalism of the newspaper did that; I think it was an error of judgment. That was agreed to by everybody on the newspaper. I was not on the *Daily Mirror* at the time.

–Do you say that that had nothing to do with sensationalism? – A: That was nothing to do with sensationalism in the form in which that word is understood in the office by all the people there.

–Was not the imprisonment and the fine based entirely on the fact that you were catering for sensationalism? – A: I was not on the paper at the time, but I read the material, and can express a personal opinion, but I cannot do anything else. I state the view in this book that every editor takes the risk that he may have under certain circumstances to endure punishment. Mr Bolam did so, and died three months after he came out of jail, so I think the price was paid. In this book I say that the law was a good law and that Mr Bolam took this punishment, and he did not complain. I did not defend the incident in any way, nor do I now.

–I am putting it on what is said at page 253. You made the most careful enquiries, did you not, before you wrote this book? – A: I did, indeed.

–On page 253 is this passage:

> Proceedings were taken before a Divisional Court presided over by the Lord Chief Justice, Lord Goddard, for contempt of court. They rejected the explanation and expressed the view that there had been a deliberate pandering to sensationalism. Bolam spent three months in Brixton and the paper was fined £10,000.

CUDLIPP: I...

GARDINER: Will you read the next paragraph?

CUDLIPP: I do not dispute that was the view of the court, but you did ask me what my view was, and that is given at the top of page 254, on the next page. It is quite a fair view.

BEYFUS: All I put to you was that the view of the court was that there had been a deliberate pandering to sensationalism? – A: Of course that view was stated by the court. I cannot dispute what the court's view was.

–I am suggesting to you that is one instance of 'living dangerously' to which you refer? – A: I do not think that was living dangerously. To me it has nothing to do with this case at all.

–I suggest that one of the instances of living dangerously is printing such an article as you printed about my client? – A: That remains to be seen; I have not heard the verdict.

–Take another instance. You were threatened by the Home Secretary in the course of the war with suppression? – A: When you say 'you' I do not know who you mean. I was in the Western Desert at the time. I have read the whole evidence, and in this book, again since it is mentioned, I do give my verdict on it. I do not think the paper was guilty of anything. Though I was not there, I am extremely proud of the part it played during the war.

–I apologise for saying 'you'. – A: You did say 'you'.

–The first defendants, the Daily Mirror Newspapers Ltd, were threatened with the suppression of the newspaper by the Home Secretary during the war? – A: That is quite correct.

–…Owing to a cartoon, and in particular to the caption written for it by the second defendant? – A: That is correct, in that Cassandra wrote the caption to that cartoon, I was not there, but he said so in the box.

–One of the excuses put forward by the then editor, or managing editor, whichever it may have been, was that the second defendant Mr Connor was a hard hitting journalist with a vitriolic style. – A: No, you have misread this letter from Mr Churchill.

–Have I? – A: The letters referred to a quite different incident altogether. The letters with Mr Churchill do not refer to the cartoon.

–Very well. – A: They are about Mr Connor's column. They are nothing to do with the cartoon at all.

–You saw it? – A: Indeed, that is correct.

–I am not going into details with regard to it. – A: It is not a matter of detail; that is untrue.

–In order to excuse the behaviour of the newspaper the editor wrote that the second defendant was a hard hitting journalist with a vitriolic style? – A: That is quite correct.

–Mr Cecil H King, I think at the time, was the head of both newspapers? – A: Mr Connor was wrong in his evidence there. It was an error of fact, Mr King was a director of the company. He was not the head of the firm.

275

—I do not know about members of the jury, but I am certainly a little puzzled. Mr Connor spoke of you, for example, as the head of both these newspapers, but technically they belong to different companies. – A: Mr Connor spoke of me in that way. I will explain precisely what I do.

—What are you in relation to both newspapers? – A: We have a chairman who is the chairman of both companies. We have a board of directors of each company. Each director is in control of a certain side of the business. There is a production director, there is a financial director. There are other directors. I am the editorial director, and therefore a member of the board of both companies. I am in charge of the editorial affairs, which means that I am responsible to the chairman and to the board for what we say.

—In both newspapers? – A: In both newspapers.

—That is what I thought. To that extent they are closely linked? – A: Each paper has an editor. The staffs are not interrelated. They are separate papers, but there is that link.

—A very considerable link? – A: I have explained that the editors are responsible for the contents, but I supervise the editorial activities. To that extent they are linked. I am not endeavouring to…

—With regard to your association with the defendant Connor, you mentioned that when you were both in London you therefore attended the office, and you met daily? – A: When I am not in Australia and Mr Connor is not in America, it is not a matter of attending the office. We know we have our duties there, and we do meet every day.

—You also, when you are both in London, may meet socially every day? – A: Not so frequently as Mr Connor hopes. We are friends. We do meet socially. We did formerly meet every day when we worked more closely together, but not, as he indicated, so often now, merely because we are doing different work.

—Up to quite recently it would be a quite frequent sight to see both of you drinking in a Fleet Street bar? – A: Most certainly, in El Vino, where barristers meet after their cases and where we meet after our newspapers.

—Since 1935 you would have had a very fair opportunity of judging Mr Connor as a journalist and his journalistic style? – A: Yes.

—Did you express your opinion of him honestly in this newspaper? – A: In the newspaper? I have not written about him in the newspaper.

—In this book, I beg your pardon. – A: I would reply 'No'. The chapter on Cassandra, as was known by everybody who read the book at the time, was an amusing profile. What it says of course is basically true, but there is a little leg pulling in it which was generally acknowledged in all the reviews I read, except Mr Connor's.

—Humorously written but basically true? – A: Yes.

—One realises that quite obviously it is not literally true because of what you say meeting him reminded you of… You deal with him, and you

276

describe him, you say this: 'He drifted into journalism and swiftly progressed in the only profession where big scale, incessant rudeness (skilfully written) is highly paid.' Is that your view of journalism? – A: That is a serious statement in a humorous vein. That is my view of writers, not only in newspapers but in most other companies, books and magazines.

–Here you are only talking about journalism... Indeed, you speak of it there as the only profession where big scale, incessant rudeness (skilfully written) is highly paid. Were you not implying there that he had drifted into just the right profession for him? – A: Well, I cannot say anything more than what I said there. I have said, yes, I believe what was written. There are other professions, but there I do not say it is the only profession. I say it is one profession.

–You do say it is the only profession. – A: I beg your pardon. If I wrote that I believed it. If I wrote it, I stand by it.

–All I am saying is this. Were you not implying that he had drifted into the profession which was eminently suitable for him? – A: I quite agree with that, of course. Mr Connor is one of the most brilliant journalists of our time.

–A brilliant journalist, famous for his big scale, incessant rudeness? – A: I can only say that Mr Connor has been quoted throughout the world, and has been invited by many newspapers to write for them. He was reviewed in the *Manchester Guardian Year Book.* It is not just a question of him being only rude. He has many other qualities.

–When you say that he is a most famous journalist and a most skilful journalist, he is famous, is he not, and has become so since 1935 for his big scale, incessant rudeness? – A: I do agree that Mr Connor is a very rude man on occasions, but a very kind man on others.

–I am talking of his writing. He may be an angel in private life. What he is famous for in journalism is his big scale, incessant rudeness? – A: I do not say that. I say that he came into a profession where big scale, incessant rudeness... you have the page in front of you. I do not say that Mr Connor's only quality is big scale rudeness. He has written some of the kindest material I have read. I remember twenty-five others he highly praised... Billy Graham, the Pope.

–The implication was that it was just the profession for him? – A: If that is the implication of what I am saying, that was incorrect. I do not say that is his only quality. He certainly has many other qualities. The one I am dealing with is rudeness, which undeniably exists.

–You have not followed me. I only suggested the implication was that that was just the right profession for him? – A: I think Mr Connor is in the right profession.

277

–Because of what you say in that paragraph? – A: Because he is occasionally rude, but frequently on other occasions displays other qualities, perhaps better qualities.

–On page 132 is what I agree is obviously meant to be humorous. 'When I first met Connor I felt that I was involved in an extremely unpleasant motor crash; even the exchange of orthodox civilities, the casual Good Morning, was accompanied by the awful din of screeching mental brakes. It has never been a question of What Makes Connor Tick, but What Makes Connor Clang.' – A: That, funny or otherwise, was intended to be humorous.

–The first half of it is quite obviously humorous, a humorous way of discussing the violence of his character? – A: Mr Connor on occasions is a very violent spokesman.

–...You were obviously giving a humorous view of the extreme violence of his character. – A: What I was trying to do was this, if I may explain this. If you meet Connor he is a man of great mental agility, and if you meet him early in the morning he has probably read far more about what is going on in the world. You do find yourself coming up against the immovable object. I describe it there humorously as the screeching of brakes. He is a very formidable character to argue with, and I am not intending to say more than that.

–What you wrote was that it is not what makes Connor tick but what makes Connor clang. What do you mean by 'clang'? – A: I think that can be filed as a bad joke. It is not meant to be anything frightfully sinister. Just a noise louder than a tick is really what I meant.

–Then you go on to deal with the bit which Mr Connor liked, as being complimentary:

> He is industrious, no doubt of that, and a well informed sort of cove. For he has an appetite for newspapers, magazines and books; he does *The Times* every day from the first personal ad to 'printed by', at the foot of the final page; studies the American political columnists, keeps an eye on *Pravda*, an ear to Iron Curtain radio, and masticates *Hansard* before meals in the evenings.

...The next bit in this item of praise is:

> He remembers every point of detail to the slightest disadvantage of the victim he picks up on the tip of his pen for public scrutiny in his column.

...You see that? – A: Yes, I do.

–That was meant really to be not a humorous but an accurate description of him? – A: That was meant to be an accurate remark, not humorous.

–'When memory fails, and the enormity of a politician's early misdemeanour temporarily escapes him, Cassandra taps his head and says: My private librarians are looking it up...'? – A: That is intended to be humorous.

–But the other part was meant to be serious? – A: The other part was meant to be serious.

–Do you see that the idea which it must convey to any reader is that here is a man who is always looking out for victims he can attack, and searches the newspapers for anything which he can find to their disadvantage? – A: No, I do not accept that. That statement says exactly what it is intended to say. As I say, it was a serious statement. Connor also, although I do not deal with it, spends a great deal of time remembering pleasant things about people. I have a long list here, which I can read out, if you wish.

–According to subject and the state of his liver, he can make his column purr or bark, nuzzle or bite, canter or gallop, soothe or repel. And, a rare gift, his words appeal alike to men and women, young and old, intellectuals and ignoramuses, priests and atheists, judges and old lags, heterosexuals, homosexuals and hermaphrodites.

...Cannot anybody in the *Mirror* write an article without dragging in something relating to sex? Why drag in 'heterosexuals, homosexuals and hermaphrodites'? – A: Is that a serious question? I am sorry I dragged them in. I do not write for the *Daily Mirror*. So there is no point in putting that question. I did write this book five years ago. That is what I wrote then. I am not denying that I wrote it.

–The whole of the *Daily Mirror*, when not devoted purely to sensationalism, is devoted to dealing with sex, is it not? – A: I refute that entirely. I think that is a ridiculous suggestion which just is not true.

–You wrote, did you not, that one of the things which caused the late Lord Rothermere to sever his financial relationship with the paper was the paper's attitude to sex? – A: Yes. In another part of the book you will find it was a good time to get out financially.

–There must have been something in the attitude to sex which appalled the late Lord Rothermere? – A: Of course there was. He was seventy-three. The people running the newspaper were much younger, and they were discussing sex in a totally different manner. He was appalled at the way people talked about modern trends. I am forty-five, and I am appalled at some of them. He similarly had been expressing his view on modern trends; they appalled him, and he said so.

–You boasted in this book of the success of the Jane cartoon? – A: I did not boast of anything. It is an objective book about the newspaper, on which I was then not working. I am able to recall that it was a success. I did not boast about it.

–I suggest that, having been largely responsible for it being a tabloid newspaper, you actually boasted of the newspaper? – A: Can you show me anywhere in this book where that suggestion is borne out?

–I suggest it is borne out throughout the book. The whole book is meant to praise the newspaper and its growth. – A: It is not meant to denigrate, but it does not boast about the fact that you mention.

–…'*Round-up*, the US paper in the Far East, described Jane' that is referring to the strip cartoon, is that right… 'a highly patriotic comely British lass whose one affliction at odds with her otherwise sterling character (if affliction it be) is that she has just one hell of a job keeping her clothes on'? – A: That is quite correct.

–'The Yanks, admitting that tweeds were seldom allowed to gum up the plot, waited a while to catch Jane *au naturel*. It happened, and *Round-up*, under the headline "Jane Gives All", commented: "Well, sirs, you can go home now. Right smack out of the blue and with no one even threatening her, Jane peeled a week ago. The British 36th Division immediately gained six miles and the British attacked in the Arakan. Maybe we Americans ought to have Jane, too."…'? – A: I think the whole point is in the last sentence. Maybe they should.

–The whole point of the Jane cartoon is when she is going to take her clothes off, is it not? – A: The whole point of the Jane cartoon at that time during the war, when a little fun was surely permissible, was because, when she 'peeled' as it is vulgarly said, she really peeled off. Life is more serious now. I thought the paragraph justified the policy, because the Americans wanted the same dame introduced there.

–The whole appeal of the Jane cartoon is an appeal to sex? –A: Sex of a rather genteel type.

–Genteel? – A: You cannot be frightfully sexy in a cartoon two inches deep. [Laughter.]

–Let us come to something which is more serious. You as the head of the Daily Mirror Newspapers…? – A: I am not the head. I am the editorial director.

–You, as the editorial director of the newspaper, are participating in the defence which has been set up in this case. You approve of it? – A: Of course.

–One is a complaint that my client made a disrespectful observation with regard to Princess Margaret. Do you remember that? I suggest that is utterly insincere and completely dishonest. You say it is not? – A: I do not think it is insincere; I do not think it is dishonest.

–Did your newspaper about that time conduct a poll in regard to Princess Margaret? – A: It did.

–A poll amongst its 4½million purchasers as to whether it was advisable that she should marry a certain person or not? – A: That is quite correct.

–Can you imagine anything more unpleasant for the lady in question? – A: I did not think that poll was unpleasant when it was published. I do not think so now.

–You seriously say that? – A: I do seriously say that.

–Neither to her nor to the royal family? – A: Definitely not.

–Do you think that, if the *Daily Express* were to conduct a poll amongst its millions of readers whether you should marry a certain lady or not, you would not find that unpleasant? – A: I do not think they would do so.

–Of course they would not. – A: It would not worry me. I am not a public figure. If I were a public figure I would not be frightfully surprised, in view of the previous problem arising over the Duke of Windsor.

–I did not ask you whether you would be surprised. Nothing by a *Mirror* journalist would surprise me. What I said was, would you find it unpleasant to have your personal marriage problem discussed among the 4½million readers of the *Daily Mirror*? – A: The *Daily Express*, you said.

–Right, the *Daily Express*. – A: if I were in Princess Margaret's position I would not be surprised. The poll was not conducted in an offensive manner; it was conducted in a kindly manner.

–You would not be surprised, but would you not find it most unpleasant and distasteful? – A: No, I would not.

–You do not think there was anything unpleasant about it? – A: I do not.

–You are also the editorial director of the *Sunday Pictorial*? – A: I am, but that newspaper is not a defendant to this action.

–I know, but you are a representative of both? – A: Correct.

–You were responsible for the...

GARDINER: I object on the ground of its inadmissibility to any issue in this action. If my friend says it is cross-examination as to credit, in order to seek to show that this witness is not telling the truth, he is quite entitled to do that, but of course neither of the defendants in this case is responsible in any way at all for the *Sunday Pictorial*.

MR JUSTICE SALMON: You must leave that to Mr Beyfus's discretion.

BEYFUS: Let me be quite frank. This is directed to the honesty of this witness, who is the principal representative of Daily Mirror Newspapers and who says that he remembers the defence which relies on an offensive observation alleged to have been made by my client about Princess Margaret. I suggest that no man could be honest in setting up that defence who published the *Sunday Pictorial* a fortnight ago. – A: To what question are you referring? Presumably you mean the question...

–I will find it for you. – A: I remember the issue, if it is that issue. There is no need to find it.

–It is clear, is it not, that that is a most unpleasant and insulting cartoon? – A: I agree the cartoon is unpleasant and insulting.

–And unpleasant and insulting in particular to Her Majesty the Queen? – A: I think it is unpleasant and insulting to anybody in this country.

–Primarily insulting to Her Majesty the Queen? – A: My own view is that it is insulting to anybody in this country. I agree primarily unpleasant as a cartoon.

–I did not ask you about that. I do not want to cross-examine about that; it would be a waste of time; but it is extremely insulting to Her Majesty the Queen? – A: The cartoon is insulting to Her Majesty the Queen, and insulting to all of us in this country.

–Do not bother about the insult to us. How is it headed? – A: The headline? 'A Stupid Insult', and above it are the words 'Thousands may laugh at this, but we call it A Stupid Insult'.

–That was published in the United States? – A: That is correct.

–You agree that, had your newspaper not re-published it in this country, it is unlikely that anybody in this country would have seen it? – A: Most certainly it would not have been seen, unless some other newspaper had published it.

–By your action, or the action of the company of which you are the editor in chief or editorial director, that was published to some 13 million readers? –A: That is correct.

–Who otherwise would not have seen it? A: Correct.

–You say that it was sent to you by a Canadian reader with a suggestion that you should… – A: When you say to me, I must please explain. This was sent to the editor of the *Sunday Pictorial,* who is Mr Lee Howard.

–Very well. You are not suggesting, or are you, I do not know, that that sort of publication would have taken place without your prior knowledge? – A: On this occasion the answer is 'Yes'.

–You did not see it? – A: I did not see it before it was published.

–Where were you? – A: I was on a boat in the river five miles away from here. I normally see the first edition. I did not do so that weekend.

–Had it not been discussed during the week? – A: It had not, because it had not arrived until late. If I may anticipate, I do approve of his publication.

–You do? – A: Yes.

–The excuse given for publishing it is that a Canadian writer who sent it had suggested you should publish the name of the magazine, so that in effect that magazine should be boycotted in this country. – A: I am sorry, I did not understand that.

–I have not got it in front of me, so I am speaking from recollection. The excuse given for publication, is it not, is that a Canadian writer sent it to you with the suggestion that it should be published, with the name of the American magazine, so that that magazine could be boycotted in this country? – A: I cannot see those words in this article. Indeed, they are not there.

–I was speaking from memory. Let us see how far I am right or wrong? – A: That is wrong.

–Let us see how far it is wrong. 'A Canadian reader was so disgusted he sent it to the *Pictorial* with this comment: "I feel that if you published this in your paper, enough people would complain to the magazine in question and discourage them from making further insults on the Royal Family".' – A: That is correct. You said 'boycott the magazine in this country', which is not mentioned there.

–Not boycott, but the whole point of publishing it, as suggested by the Canadian reader, was that you should give the name of the American magazine. – A: I beg your pardon. I am trying to see it. Would you mind repeating that?

–The reason suggested by the Canadian reader for your publishing it was that you should publish the name of the magazine in America, and so bring influence to bear on the owners of that magazine? – A: I cannot see the suggestion by the Canadian reader that we should publish the name in America.

–I did not say publish the name in America; I said, publish the name of the American magazine? – A: We did not publish it.

–Are you deliberately avoiding...? – A: I do not understand the question. I am extremely sorry.

MR JUSTICE SALMON: What was the point of publishing this extremely offensive cartoon, which could scarcely have been in worst taste? – A: The editor's explanation to me, which I accepted, was that if in a foreign country attacks are made upon the royal family, or upon politicians or upon any prominent person in this country, about which we know nothing in this country, we will be living in a vacuum if we do not publish them. This was a sincere attempt by saying 'This is what is being said abroad'. My mind goes back to the abdication period when American newspapers were publishing an amazing amount of material, which was suppressed in this country, and it came as a shock to the people here when it was suddenly released.

BEYFUS: I suggest it was not suppressed in this country; it was merely not published owing to the voluntary action of the newspapers. – A: It was in fact suppressed by agreement among a number of newspaper proprietors.

–That is the voluntary action of the newspapers. It is what the then editors of newspapers thought was the decent and proper thing to do. – A: That is not quite true. It was not the decision of the editors at all. It was a decision made by others.

–Suppression suggests the action of authority. Whatever there had been in not publishing then was a voluntary action by the proprietors of the newspapers concerned, a voluntary action? – A: It was a voluntary action until the voluntary action no longer applied, and then most newspapers,

283

and subsequently all newspapers, published the information about the Duke of Windsor.

–You used the word 'suppression'. When you referred to suppression, what you meant was that for a considerable period of time nothing was said about it because of the voluntary action of newspapers? – A: Quite. There have been misgivings since then about the wisdom of that action.

–You professed a moment ago not to understand my question? – A: I was not professing; I did not understand the question.

–Let me put the question again. You did not understand my question that the excuse you gave for publishing it was that a Canadian reader had suggested, if you published it, the people would complain to the magazine in question, which involved your giving the name of the magazine? – A: That is correct.

–But you did not give the name of the magazine? – A: No.

–The Canadian reader's idea that your readers should write to the magazine and complain could not be carried out? – A: No; that is correct, because the editor of the *Sunday Pictorial* thought that was an unwise suggestion, and he did not fulfil it.

–I suggest, therefore, there was no reason for publishing this, except the idea of boosting your circulation by a sensation? – A: I do not agree with that.

–That is for the members of the jury. Do you still say that you, approving of that type of insulting cartoon, insulting to Her Majesty, being published, rely upon the observation made by Mr Liberace in his reference to Princess Margaret? – A: I did not sign the affidavit of evidence, as you know perfectly well. I have heard you say that this statement was included in the defence, but…

–Do you approve of it and rely on it, as head of the *Daily Mirror*? – A: I approve of the way in which our case is being conducted.

–Do you approve everything which you have heard, of the way in which the case has been conducted? – A: Yes.

–That is true, is it? What you have just said is true, that you approve everything? – A: I approve of the manner in which our legal advisers are conducting our case.

–I did not say that. – A: I did.

–Is that the whole of the case? You approve of the way in which the whole of the case is being conducted? – A: I meant by our legal advisers. I approve everything else.

–Do you approve of everything which has been done by members of the staff of the *Daily Mirror* in the conduct of this defence? – A: I approve everything of which I am aware, and if there had been anything of which I disapproved I would have stopped it.

284

−Were you present when Mr Thompson was cross-examined? − A: No, I was not in court.

−Have you been told that he was approached by the dramatic critic of the *Daily Mirror* shortly after this action started, and was asked to supply the final copy of the song which he sang, because the dramatic critic wanted to tell it at a party, or wanted to have it told by a friend at a party, and the dramatic critic gave his word of honour that it would not be used for any other purpose? − A: I have heard that. I was not here.

−Do you approve of it? − A: I do not approve of it.

−It is somewhat shocking, is it not? − A: I did really mean I approve of the way in which our legal advisers are conducting the case. You have rather broadened the point. I must admit I do not approve of it.

−I have broadened it on purpose. − A: I realise that.

−What happened was that one of the staff of the *Daily Mirror* obtained a document by a false pretext, by a false promise. Does that rather horrify you? − A: I do not approve of it. I have said I do not approve of it.

−I am going a good deal further. Does it rather horrify you? − A: Yes, it horrifies me.

−Do you approve of the attack upon Mr Dimbleby by the second defendant? − A: By 'approve', do you mean approve before publication?

−No, I did not mean that. We will take it by stages. Did you approve it before publication? − A: I did not approve it before publication.

−You did not see it before publication? − A: I did not see it before publication, I am not the editor of the paper.

−What? − A: I am not the editor of the *Daily Mirror*.

−You are above the editor? − A: Correct, yes.

−You spoke of the position of Mr Connor: you said he has complete freedom to express his own views unless the editor objects? − A: That is correct.

−That means, of course, that the articles which he writes and are published are subject to editorial approval? − A: That means that the editor did not object.

−It must mean that everything of his that is published is subject in the end to editorial approval? − A: I explained, sir, that Connor has freedom to write what he wants to write, but that the editor, like all editors, has the right to exclude it. This was not excluded: therefore I assume that the editor approved of it.

−That is all I am putting. What is published in the *Daily Mirror*, whether written by Mr Connor or anybody else, is subject to editorial approval. − A: Of course.

−That is right? − A: That is what I mean, sir, yes.

−I was asking you with regard to the article on Mr Dimbleby and, of course, also on Mr Pickles, to save time. You did not see it before. Did you

285

approve it afterwards? – A: By 'approve' do you mean that I personally agree with Connor's views?

–Did you think it a right and proper thing to publish in the *Daily Mirror* about a popular figure? – A: Yes, I did.

–Obviously holding up to complete contempt and ridicule? – A: I do not think that at all, sir. I think it was an amusing article about Mr Dimbleby, who is a newspaper proprietor and he therefore presumably has a sense of humour. I have sat next to him at functions since, and I have not noticed any particular enmity from Mr Dimbleby.

–You do not think it held him up to contempt and ridicule? – A: I do not think so.

–I like to get your ideas on this matter. – A: Well, I do not think so.

–There is another thing I want to ask you. Are you a director of Associated Television Ltd? ... You have been a director for some time? ... How long? – A: March 29 1956.

–Were the television films of Mr Liberace which were produced in this country produced by that company? – A: They were not produced by that company: they were bought from America. They are American films.

–Bought from America by that company... And put on television by that company... In this country... For the purpose of making money, I presume? – A: Of course. It is commercial television.

–And was it that company that produced the television last night of my client at the Palladium... For the purpose of making money? – A: Of course, sir, yes.

–So you as a director of that company try to make money out of the performances of Mr Liberace; is that right? – A: I should point out, Mr Beyfus, that the Liberace films were all bought in the Autumn of 1955. I joined the company on March 29th, 1956. Secondly, that I have nothing to do with the buying of programmes in the company, which is done by Mr Val Parnell and the assistant director; and, thirdly, that I would in no way interfere with the appearance of an artist in this country because he had sued one of our newspapers for libel.

–I was not suggesting for that reason; but you did not resign? – A: I did not resign, because I do not entirely agree with Mr Connor's views of Mr Liberace; he has a right to express them.

–You did not resign from the company on the basis that Mr Liberace's performance was such as ought not to be seen by the British public? – A: I have not expressed that view myself, sir.

–It would be a ridiculous view? – A: I do not think it would be ridiculous, but that happens to be Cassandra's view. It is not my view, I differ on many points from Mr Cassandra.

–Since 1935, since the tabloid revolution, the *Daily Mirror* circulation has gone up and up and up, has it not? – A: Of course.

–And its capital has gone up and up and up, has it not? – A: Its capital, yes, it has.

–Indeed as recently as December last I think its capital went up by £4,000,000? – A: That is approximately correct, yes.

–It in fact rose roughly from £5,000,000 to £9,000,000? – A: Yes.

Re-examined by Gardiner:

–You were asked about the definition of sensationalism, and Mr Beyfus read this, where Mr Bolam expressed himself thus in a front-page manifesto:

> The *Mirror* is a sensational newspaper. We make no apology for that. We believe in the sensational presentation of news and views, especially important news and views, as a necessary and valuable public service in those days of mass readership and democratic responsibility.

…Now, if you look over the page, which Mr Beyfus did not read, you will see his explanation of that:

> We shall go on being sensational to the best of our ability. Sensationalism does not mean distorting the truth. It means the vivid and dramatic presentation of events so as to give them a forceful impact on the mind of the reader. It means big headlines, vigorous writing, simplification into familiar everyday language, and the wide use of illustration by cartoon and photograph.
>
> To give two examples. We used it during the war to launch a VD campaign which was vitally necessary for the welfare of the forces when a too-timid government department had the facts and dare not use them. We used it again when the national economic crisis demanded an explanation to the public which the government, not expert in these matters, was leaving bewildered and ill-informed.
>
> In both cases we were widely praised for our enterprise, and our methods were at once followed by the government. Today the needs for sensational journalism are even more apparent. Every great problem facing us – the world economic crisis, diminishing food supplies, the population puzzle, the Iron Curtain and a host of others – will only be understood by the ordinary man busy with his daily tasks if he is hit hard and hit often with the facts.
>
> Sensational treatment is the answer, whatever the sober and 'superior' readers of some other journals may prefer.
>
> As in larger, so in smaller and more personal affairs, the *Mirror* and its millions of readers prefer the vivid to the dull and the vigorous to the timid.
>
> No doubt we make mistakes, but we are at least alive.

…That is written by Mr Bolam. Do you agree with that or dispute it? – A: I agree with that. That is what I mean by sensationalism.

–Dealing with this case in which Mr Bolam was sent to prison, the facts of the case have not been before the jury. I do not want to read it all here. Was it an article published which it was found might be thought to refer to

287

John George Haig, the acid bath murderer, whose trial was pending? – A: That is correct, Sir, yes.

–And:

> The truth is that the *Mirror* had perpetrated a blunder. The law of England is that once a man is charged with a crime anything published in a newspaper which may tend to prejudice his fair trial constitutes a contempt of court; the veto holds good until the expiry of the period during which the accused may appeal against his sentence. That law is a good law. The editor took his punishment and did not complain.

...I think you told us he died after about three months of coming out of prison? – A: Yes, that is right.

–You were asked about a cartoon published during the war which the government did not like. In your view, was the government right or wrong to object to the cartoon? – A: I must explain, sir, that I was not in England at the time. I was away. I was in the Army away, and we therefore in this book re-examined the evidence, and, having been away at the time, perhaps I am not the best person to judge just what the effect of that cartoon was on the British public at that time, I can find it if you would like, but I do not think it would be hurtful; but that is not for me; but roughly it does say this...

–...Very well, I leave it. Now, it has been suggested that there is nothing in the *Daily Mirror* except sensationalism and sex. Do you not have regular correspondents upon foreign policy and other matters... economics? – A: We do, sir; the paper deals with affairs in a way which has been praised by many of the solemn serious newspapers on many occasions.

–Do you want to produce any cuttings about that? – A: Well, I have some in court, if I may do so. The *Economist* is reviewing the *Spotlight* pamphlet:

> The *Daily Mirror* 'Spotlight' series is a Fleet-Street phenomenon; for clarity, forcefulness and common sense, it is outstanding amid the present low ebb of analytical journalism on the left. Its *Spotlight on Trade Unions* published this week, shows those qualities again. Altogether this pamphlet says almost everything that needs to be said to and about trade unions, and it is particularly valuable that it should come from a source that cannot be written off as the voice of wicked capitalists.

BEYFUS: My lord, I do not quite know how far we go. I certainly was not going to object to any praise of the *Daily Mirror* which was found somewhere; but this is not the *Daily Mirror* but some pamphlet published by the same company, which is not the *Daily Mirror* itself. That in my submission is going far beyond anything which is permissible.

MR JUSTICE SALMON: It is quite irregular.

CUDLIPP: May I read some cuttings about the *Daily Mirror*?

BEYFUS: That, I have no objection to.

CUDLIPP: This is an editorial called 'Doctor's Orders':

> What is coming over our doctors? Here they are prescribing the *Mirror* as the paper no medico can afford to be without. This is indeed medical progress. First, a writer in the medical journal *The Lancet* suggests that the ideal 'composite newspaper' would include the *Mirror* strip cartoons on page one and Cassandra on page two.

...Then there is a quotation. I do not want to take up too much time. There is a quotation from the Manchester University *Medical School Gazette*, which also praises the paper. Mr, Drew Middleton, who is the London correspondent for the *New York Times*, a renowned journalist, writes about 600 words about the *Daily Mirror*, including the following reference to Cassandra:

> Cassandra (William Connor) is one of the hardest hitting and most provocative features in British journalism. The Communists hate him. He is a deflator of stuffed shirts, a pungent critic and a stout defender of the British worker.

...*The Observer* makes more amusing comment. This is Mr Hugh Massingham, their political writer, who wrote these words in *The Observer* about the *Mirror*'s exclusive account of the probe into the Labour Party's rusty organisation:

> The story really begins on the Monday when the *Daily Mirror*, in type slightly larger than life, gave a detailed list of the recommendations. 'When the truth is big news,' chuckled the innocent little darling, 'the *Mirror* can always find type big enough for it.' And that, as we have all learnt, is not an idle threat.

MR JUSTICE SALMON: Do you want anything else, Mr Gardiner?

GARDINER: No, my lord. I understood Mr Beyfus to say that the *Spotlight* publications were not *Daily Mirror* publications.

BEYFUS: I did not. I said they were not the *Daily Mirror*. I said I accepted that they were published by the proprietors of the *Daily Mirror*, but I said they were not the *Daily Mirror* itself.

GARDINER: Yes, I am much obliged. Now, you have been asked about a poll conducted by the *Daily Mirror*. Did you take the view that it was a good thing or a bad thing that what was being said abroad about the Duke of Windsor should be suppressed deliberately so that the British public did not know about it while everybody else did? – A: I thought that was wrong; and so did the chairman of our company at that time.

–So far as the poll is concerned, you say you did not see it until it was published? – A: The poll on Princess Margaret? I did see the poll on Princess Margaret before it was published, and I approved of it. I think the public should express their views as well as the dignitaries of the country.

–So far as Mr Thompson is concerned, he said in effect he was tricked into giving you the lyric of the song, but he said it was rather pointless because anybody could have gone to the theatre and taken a shorthand note of it. Do you know how that happened? – A: No, I do not; I do not know the details of that, but if the version given by Mr Beyfus is correct, I give my view that I do not approve of that way of getting evidence; but I do not know whether Mr Beyfus's version is correct.

–Is Mr Connor one of the part authors of some of the *Spotlight* pamphlets? – A: Yes, I think about three or four have been written, if not by him, certainly with his collaboration.

–Anglo-American partnership, and so on? – A: Yes, particularly that one.

–So far as Mr Connor is concerned, you have been read several things which you stated about him in your book. Is the paragraph this: 'The value of the man is that he writes superbly, is a born journalist, means what he writes, and writes without fear.' Is that your opinion of him? – A: Yes, that is the whole point of the man, and that is why he is renowned throughout the world; and the worrying thing about this case is that his virtues and his writings have not been fully dealt with, but merely those which concern the other side.

–Thank you, Mr Cudlipp.

That was the end of the case for the defence.

It was now late into the afternoon, in terms of court sitting times and the judge said he was loathe to allow Gardiner to start his closing speech and then have to finish it the following day. He suspected, however, that opposing counsel had differing opinions on what questions should properly be put to the jury, and these should be considered in the jury's absence.

In other words, having heard all the evidence from both sides, it had to be decided what it was all about. The jury was sent home early and most of the court reporters also left; after all, if the legal technicalities could not be heard by the jury, they could not be reported in the following day's newspapers.

GARDINER: Ordinarily in most cases the jury would be asked: Do you find for the plaintiff or for the defendant? I would have submitted that your Lordship might think it desirable here to ask the jury for a special finding as to whether they find that the words complained of, in their natural and ordinary meaning, bear the meaning which Mr Beyfus has suggested. My lord, I prefer not to put it into words, because there could be many alternatives. It has not been pleaded to bear the meaning which Mr Beyfus has expressed.

MR JUSTICE SALMON: The suggestion is that the words mean that the plaintiff is a homosexual. I am anxious to hear anything either of you have to say about it, but my present view is that that ought to be left to the jury separately.

GARDINER: My Lord, that is what I would respectfully submit.

MR JUSTICE SALMON: Do you agree with that, Mr Beyfus?

BEYFUS: My Lord, that they are incapable of that meaning? I agree.

MR JUSTICE SALMON: That is what we all have in mind, no doubt.

BEYFUS: My Lord, I think it is necessary to indicate what the meaning is. It cannot be left to the jury in the way I have suggested.

MR JUSTICE SALMON: The question I propose is: Do the words complained, of in the publication of September 25 1956, in their ordinary and natural meaning, mean that the plaintiff is a homosexual?

BEYFUS: Yes, my Lord. That would involve two verdicts as to damages.

MR JUSTICE SALMON: Well, I will just tell you what I have in mind. I think the second question should be: Without this meaning are the words complained of true in so far as they consist of statements of fact, and (b) fair comment in so far as they consist of expressions of opinion?

BEYFUS: That should be left, my Lord, yes, as a separate question. Normally one would just have a verdict for the plaintiff or defendant, but if separate questions are being left, that would be the right thing.

MR JUSTICE SALMON: Yes. Then: Damages (if any) in respect of the publication of September 26 1956. I would suggest that if the jury answer the first two questions in favour of the plaintiff, they should state how much of the damages are attributable to the imputation of homosexuality. That can only be done with your consent.

BEYFUS: Well, my lord, it can be done in two ways. The way which I was suggesting was that they should award damages on the view that it did not contain that meaning, and alternatively verdict and damages on the basis that it did.

MR JUSTICE SALMON: That would be another way of doing it, but I think it is important from both your points of view that the damages can, if necessary be separated hereafter.

BEYFUS: I agree, my lord.

MR JUSTICE SALMON: Do you agree, Mr Gardiner?

GARDINER: My lord, I respectfully disagree. In my submission it is not possible to do that. This is one publication. It has never, so far as I am aware, been done.

MR JUSTICE SALMON: No.

GARDINER: And I would respectfully not agree.

MR JUSTICE SALMON: Mr Gardiner, I think it cannot be done except by consent. The jury are not here, and I can tell you what I have in mind. Supposing a sum is awarded for damages and both the questions are answered in favour of the plaintiff; then you go to the Court of Appeal and say there is no evidence to support the first question. That would mean

291

there would have to be a new trial, because no one knows what they would have given if the words did not mean that. It is a matter of indifference to me which way this question is left, but I should have thought it can only save the parties costs in the long run. If you care to consider that, Mr Gardiner, it could be mentioned again in the morning. Mr Beyfus, there is no doubt that there is only one publication, and, unless Mr Gardiner consents – unless you both consent – the only question is damages.

BEYFUS: My Lord, with great respect, I do not agree with that at all. The ordinary case in which this arises is where there is an innuendo pleaded, and 20 years ago there would have been an innuendo pleaded in this case. But the alteration in the rules has changed the form of pleading. Now, my lord, at that time, if there had been an innuendo pleaded, one would ask whether the words bore the innuendo, and, my lord, one would have had to take a verdict of the members of the jury as to what the damages were without the innuendo and alternatively with the innuendo.

MR JUSTICE SALMON: I have never known that done, Mr Beyfus.

BEYFUS: I have not known it done, my lord, either, but this is a case in which my learned friend has made the specific submission that there is no case to go to the jury on the precise meaning which I am putting, simply and solely so that he can go to the Court of Appeal afterwards and upset the whole case and have a completely new trial because the words admitted to be defamatory...

MR JUSTICE SALMON: That is if you win.

BEYFUS: On the basis that I win on fair comment.

MR JUSTICE SALMON: It seems to me that would be a very sensible course, but, as there is only one publication, unless you are agreed, I do not think I will ask the jury to split the damages. I myself think it would be a very convenient and sensible course, but Mr Gardiner is entitled to take a different view and he does not agree.

BEYFUS: My lord, I entirely agree that your lordship cannot ask the members of the jury to split the damages; but what I am saying is that your lordship can invite them to give alternative verdicts, which is something quite different – alternative assessments of the damages – which is not splitting the damages at all. In my submission, there is nothing in the rules and nothing to be found anywhere in the books which would stop members of the jury saying: 'If the words mean so-and-so, we give them X damages, but if they go further than that and also mean so-and-so, then we give them Y damages', which is an alternative verdict to state the alternative conclusions to which they come on liability. They are alternative conclusions on liability, and in my submission you could have alternative verdicts on damages. I know nothing which requires any consent from counsel to enable alternative conclusions on liability to be followed by alternative conclusions on damages.

MR JUSTICE SALMON: They are not alternative conclusions. The jury will have to decide aye or no: do the words mean that he was homosexual? If they say they do not, no question arises, but supposing they say they do, then they are giving damages for one publication, and supposing they find that the words mean he is a homosexual, how can they be asked if the words mean that?

BEYFUS: My Lord, the words are admitted to be defamatory on any meaning.

MR JUSTICE SALMON: Yes.

BEYFUS: There is no doubt about that; it is common ground. So that if the defence fails, the members of the jury are bound to award me X damages; they are bound to on any view if it is not fair comment.

MR JUSTICE SALMON: Yes.

BEYFUS: I go on to say something further which is not common ground – that they mean something much worse than you admit, and in that case the damages must be increased. Therefore I ask your lordship to leave it to the members of the jury to say by how much would you increase the damages if you think they bear that meaning, which is alternative conclusions on one libel, followed, in my submission, by alternative corollary conclusions with regard to damages. My lord, I know nothing in any book which stops such a result being arrived at.

MR JUSTICE SALMON: Supposing the first question is answered in your favour, from your point of view is it necessary to have any further finding?

BEYFUS: Well, I would like it, in case my friend goes to the Court of Appeal. My friend is so persuasive, particularly in the Court of Appeal – in case they agree with it; but it is only because otherwise if the Court of Appeal agreed with it we should have to go through all this all over again and it would be for at least a six-day trial. My client is in the United States and lives normally in the United States and would have to come back for it. There is every reason for trying to avoid the necessity for a new trial; and, my Lord, the whole point of the taking of the point in the first place and then getting the two verdicts for damages is to necessitate a second trial. Unless my learned friend agrees to that, I object very strongly to any special question being put, because there is no point in it then. My learned friend can go ahead to the Court of Appeal if he likes, but in my submission there is no need for any special question to be put and I object to it unless the corollary is to follow, namely, alternative verdicts, and I should strongly object, having an admission that the words are defamatory, to there being any special question as to what particular meaning they may have unless it is followed by the two verdicts which would enable my learned friend to go to the Court of Appeal without the necessity for a second trial.

GARDINER: My lord, in my submission, the whole of the trouble here has been caused entirely by the plaintiff seeking to obtain all of the advantages of an innuendo without having pleaded it. It is a case, in my submission, in which he is really – whatever he may say – suggesting that the words have an innuendo, and indeed, so much so, that we have had dictionaries and we have had questions like, 'Do not you know that this particular word has some special meaning in some special part of the world.' That is still seeking, while not pleading an innuendo, to get all the advantages of it.

MR JUSTICE SALMON: Yes, I shall tell the jury they cannot take any notice of the supposed special meaning of the word.

GARDINER: My lord, might I consider the matter further?

MR JUSTICE SALMON: Yes. Of course, it may not arise at all, but in a certain event it could save a lot of time.

GARDINER: Yes, my lord.

MR JUSTICE SALMON: I think it would be unnecessary for the jury to hear about this discussion and I leave it to the good sense of the press to take notice of that.

[Adjourned to 10.30 am the following day.]

Having given the matter more thought overnight, the lawyers briefly resumed the discussion in the morning.

BEYFUS: With regard to the questions, I have been thinking it over very carefully, and in my submission, particularly having regard to the objection to the alternative verdict as to damages, I would prefer no special question about that at all. It can only concern the possibility of an appeal, and that chance I am willing to take. I prefer no special question as to that, and that the members of the jury be merely invited to find for the plaintiff or defendants on each of the two libels.

MR JUSTICE SALMON: Have you anything to say about that, Mr Gardiner?

GARDINER: I respectfully agree with the submission made by Mr Beyfus yesterday, that it is entirely for the court to decide what questions should be left to the jury. As your lordship knows, the House of Lords has remarked more than once that it is not the function of counsel; it is the responsibility of the court; counsel cannot confer a jurisdiction by consent which the court has not. In my submission it is entirely for your lordship to decide what questions should be left to the jury.

MR JUSTICE SALMON; I have reconsidered this matter, and I propose to leave five questions to the jury. The questions will be:

(1) Do the words complained of in the defendants' publication of September 26 1956 in their ordinary and natural meaning, mean that the plaintiff is a homosexual?

(2) Without this meaning, are the words complained of

(a) true in so far as they consist of statements of fact? and

294

(b) fair comment in so far as they consist of expressions of opinion?
(3) Damages (if any) for the publication of September 26 1956?
If the answers to Questions 1 and 2 are both in favour of the plaintiff: how much of such damages is attributable to the imputation of homosexuality?
(4) Are the words complained of in the defendants' publication of October 18 1956 fair comment?
(5) Damages (if any) for the publication of October 18 1956?
The trial was now in its sixth day, and Gardiner was about to address the jury.

Closing speech: Gerald Gardiner QC

Gerald Gardiner can have had no more cause for confidence in his case on the sixth day than he'd had at the end of the previous week when he had advised Cudlipp to end the trial and settle out of court.

The editorial director had tried hard to keep a straight bat in the witness box, but he had scored no runs. Like his old chum, Cudlipp had been hypnotised by the protracted and repetitious retreading and recycling of questions. Nothing had been gained by his appearance or by his evidence, but he had defended the *Mirror* and stood shoulder to shoulder with his old comrade in arms; without his contribution the defence case would have been worse than it was. The role of the other journalists had been merely to substantiate the cuttings they had written, and which supported part of the Cassandra column, while adding nothing to the defendants' case; but in so doing they had been exposed to the sometimes seemingly incomprehensible cross-examination of Gilbert Beyfus who, while not necessarily disproving anything, had possibly been able to cast doubt in the mind of jurors about the morals and the standards of accuracy in Fleet Street.

Gardiner still believed that the plaintiff's side had done nothing to substantiate the basis of its claim that Cassandra was suggesting Liberace was homosexual, while he thought he had proved that most of what had been said in the column was justifiable. The big problem was that the whole matter was an argument between one of the most popular entertainers in the world and a sensational tabloid newspaper. And it had to be decided by a jury... whose members he now had to address for the last time.

He started by praising the jury: nobody in the courtroom could have failed to have noticed their patience, he said, although it may be that 'there

295

are some other people not on the jury who would not have minded the burden of jury service, owing to the particular nature of the case!'

He told them they should be aware that some of the evidence had, in law, actually been inadmissible, but lawyers didn't like objecting to it in case the jury thought their side had something to hide. 'Very often it is better not to worry about it, and let the thing go.'

In most cases where a newspaper is sued for libel and pleads fair comment, he said, it does not call any evidence at all. They say it is for the complainant to prove that what was written was a view which an honest man could not have held. 'Whatever anybody may think about the *Daily Mirror*, at least it cannot be said that the *Daily Mirror* is a newspaper which runs away. I have not only called Mr Connor and a number of other witnesses, but I have also called Mr Cudlipp whom Mr Beyfus seemed at one point to be suggesting was being kept out of the witness box.'

And he reminded the jury that the plaintiff's side searched for, and brought up, 'any discreditable thing' that the *Daily Mirror* or the *Sunday Pictorial* had done in the last quarter of a century. He said he wasn't complaining, but the two newspapers were separate entities, and Mr Connor had no direct role in the management of either of them, and the old articles had no direct relationship to the case.

In the publications produced by or on behalf of Liberace, a great deal of material had turned out to be 'pure invention', even though the introductions expressly said everything in them was true. 'That is only relevant for enabling you to say how far you accept the evidence of the plaintiff.'

Similarly, with regard to Sheffield, a good deal had been said which in law, strictly speaking, was inadmissible and irrelevant. 'If someone had called out in the theatre in Sheffield, Go home, queer, that would only be the equivalent of the plaintiff giving evidence that someone else had told him that he thought that is what the article meant. It is one of those things which a witness cannot be prevented from saying, and therefore I thought it right to call before you a number of people who were in fact there.'

It was only at Sheffield that somebody was said to have shouted the word 'fairy', but witnesses had been produced who said that if Liberace had heard it on stage, they would have heard it too.

'But', said Gardiner, 'the whole incident, when you come to think of it, is substantially irrelevant. It depends entirely on what the plaintiff thought he heard; and I shall have to suggest to you later that the plaintiff appears to have something like a bee in his bonnet about people charging him with homosexuality.'

And so he would; in the course of his closing speech the QC made at least ten references to Liberace's apparent fixation with allegations that he was homosexual.

296

In any case, 'If anybody said it there is no evidence at all whether he said t because he formed that view himself; or formed that view from reading he article in the *Daily Mirror*; or because he had been to the Apollo Theatre, or saw the skit on television. At first blush one would say it would be more likely that he had read it in the *Daily Mirror*.'

However, he said, – 'As it happens, you have heard that the students came from two halls of residence, neither of which in fact takes in the *Daily Mirror*. A revue like *For Amusement Only* is just the sort of revue which tends, does it not, to attract the undergraduate of a university?

'When you find in addition to that the very curious circumstance that the people whom he now says made this allegation against him were not heard by others the position is this: First of all, the whole thing is strictly irrelevant because the question you have to decide is what *you* consider the ordinary reasonable reader would understand the words to mean. If it did depend, which it did not, on what someone had heard someone else say, there is no evidence at all why he said it and no evidence at all that he said it because it came from the *Daily Mirror*.'

The entertainer Jimmy Thompson had said that he had effectively been tricked into providing a copy of his script to the *Daily Mirror*, but there had been no evidence to support that, and anybody could have gone along to see the show, or watched it on television, and taken a shorthand note of the words.

But when Liberace arrived at the Savoy he found a 'dove of peace' from Mr Thompson, knowing it was because of the skit that he was doing.

'I understood him to say that when he received this dove of peace he made enquiries and was told that it was vulgar and embarrassing. He later had to agree that in the Café de Paris he put his arm round Mr Thompson and had them both photographed together. He said, 'Well, I did not know then that it was so vulgar and embarrassing.'

Then on the day before the skit was televised again, they were photographed together at the Savoy. When first asked about the Savoy he said he did not recall seeing Mr Thompson again, but when the photograph was produced he conceded it, saying: 'I do recall Mr Thompson telling me that he was going to appear on television.' What can he have thought Mr Thompson was going to do on television that would require them being photographed together if it were not his famous impersonation? It is an odd thing, is it not?'

All this time he had his own London theatrical venture. 'As you know from this action, since October 1956 he had his own London solicitors; his fans always rushed to his defence (there was that 'May you drop dead' letter to Cassandra). Is it really credible that in all that time, meeting all these different people in London, his own lawyers, theatrical agents, people in the world of the theatre, and all his fan letters, nobody told him
297

what was the nature of the impersonation in fact being done by Jimmy Thompson?'

No question apparently arose about suing the *Daily Mirror*, he told the jury, until Miss Ambler suggested it. And they could compare her evidence with that of both Mr and Mrs Connor

'What Mr Connor says is that the only reference which was made to the action was about the existence of it and the fact that he said he wondered who was going to look the bigger buffoon in the witness box, but the further conversation about which Miss Ambler spoke is completely untrue. Anybody can write anything down on a piece of paper behind anybody else's back at any time, and then go into the witness box and, as lawyers put it, refresh their recollection from a piece of paper, which undoubtedly adds an air of verisimilitude to an otherwise bald and unconvincing narrative.

According to Mrs Connor Miss Ambler said that she had met Liberace at a party, which obviously was not a very true statement, considering that she had accompanied him everywhere he went, and that he had mentioned Cassandra. Miss Ambler says that is quite untrue. You have seen Mrs Connor in the witness box; she was, in my submission, a simple, straightforward and obviously truthful witness. There was nothing to stop the plaintiff calling Mr McGhee in support of Miss Ambler's evidence. 'He has not done so, and you are entitled to draw your own conclusion from that.'

The same conflict existed between Miss Ambler and Mr Doncaster. 'You remember Mr Doncaster, a rather quiet and, in my submission, obviously truthful witness.' He had told how in Winifred Atwell's dressing room the plaintiff had said 'Let us have one for Cassandra'. He said that a short while afterwards Miss Ambler was talking rather loudly, and she said 'If Randolph Churchill can get £5,000 from *The People*, Liberace should get something from the *Daily Mirror*. I hope they have got a million.' He then asked Liberace: 'Are you really going to sue us?', and he said, no he was not. Miss Ambler again said that was untrue, and the jury had to judge between her evidence and that of Mr Doncaster, because of course the whole of this conversation, so far as Mr Connor is concerned, depended solely on the evidence of Miss Ambler.

The jury would remember the curious answer she gave on Day Two when she was asked about a book called *The Elusive Husband* which she had written. 'Do you think that, if you had written a particular book and a prosecution had taken place in which it had been declared to be obscene, that is a thing you would forget?' He had asked: (Q) You know that a bookseller in this country was fined for selling that as an obscene book? (A) No, I did not know that. 'I let her know that I had the press statement

298

which she made at the time and then she says, Oh, yes, she does remember.'

He said: 'It is a matter entirely for you whether you regard the lady as a witness of truth, when the whole of this evidence, so far as Mr Connor is concerned, depends entirely on her, when they do not choose to call Mr McGhee, when the witness is in direct conflict with both Mrs Connor and with what Mr Doncaster says, and generally when she is a lady who has sworn that she did not know that her book *The Elusive Husband* had been found to be obscene. Do you really think that, if that had happened to an authoress, a single lady, a book known to be obscene, she would have forgotten it?'

When he had finished his speech Mr Beyfus would address the jury, and then the judge would sum up, so he didn't reasonably expect them to remember much of what he was saying, but he wanted to deal with three main points. The first was that their verdict had to be unanimous: 'Just as people in this country are entitled to have strong views and to stick to them, so each one of you is entitled to find the facts in accordance with your own conscience and to stick to your own opinion.'

The second and third points were longer: namely, is the natural and ordinary meaning of the words in the box – 'you know what I mean by that' – what the plaintiff says it is; and, next, whether Mr Connor was saying what he honestly thought.

'On the first question it is of course clear that, whatever your verdict is, nobody in the country can interpret your verdict as meaning that the plaintiff is a homosexual, because, as has been made very clear from the outset, that is not what Mr Connor thought. It is not what occurred to him, and it is not what he intended to say. It is not what the defendants have ever suggested is true. The contest on that is whether this is the meaning of the words at all, if it is a contest.'

What they should not consider was what any of the words might mean in a different country. There was the expression 'fruit-flavoured'. While 'Old fruit', in this country was rather a favourable expression, they may remember that an American dictionary of slang was produced. What they had to consider was not what this meant in America but what the ordinary, reasonable reader of the *Daily Mirror* would understand it to mean.

'It is not suggested – this is one of the curious things in the case – that the meaning which the plaintiff puts on these words is a hidden meaning. It is not his case that some particular word has some particular hidden meaning. His case is that this is what the ordinary reasonable man, reading these words, would understand to be their natural and ordinary meaning. Of course, the great difficulty for the defendants is to know how on earth anybody can arrive at that conclusion.'

299

Until Mr Beyfus got up in court to open this case, and remembering all the correspondence which took place between the solicitors since the action started, this allegation had never been made, he said. 'Therefore, as you will imagine, having heard Mr Beyfus say that, I listened with interest to hear how on earth he got such a meaning out of the words. But he did not say anything about that in opening. He just said it obviously meant that he was a homosexual. When the plaintiff went into the witness box, partly I confess for curiosity how anybody could get that meaning out of these words and partly because it seemed right the plaintiff should have an opportunity of explaining it, I asked him; and of course Mr Beyfus put what he did to Mr Connor.'

In view of its importance he wanted to remind the jury exactly what Beyfus put to Mr Connor, and his replies:

(Q) Now let me put the way in which I suggest you intended these words to be understood by many millions of people. First of all, the words in the box start 'He is the summit of sex'. Is that right? (A) That is so.

(Q) Quite clearly, from, the words in the box, the subject which you are dealing with is sex? (A) Sex and sex appeal.

(Q) Sex. 'The pinnacle of Masculine, Feminine and Neuter. Everything that He, She and It can ever want' – sexually? (A) I object to the sentence being chopped up and divided. Sentences have a total meaning,

(Q) You may object to it, but I am afraid you are going to suffer it. 'He' in that context means another man or men, does it not? (A) Yes.

(Q) And you are saying that he is everything for something or other? (A) In the nature of his performance men are strongly attracted.

(Q) There is nothing in that paragraph about the nature of his performance, is there? (A) No, but there is in the rest of the article.

(Q) I know there is. He, Liberace, is everything that another man can ever want, sexually? (A) No, I do not agree 'sexually'.

(Q) That is what you are saying? (A) I did not say 'sexually'.

(Q) The word 'sex' at the top quite obviously governs what is in that box, does it not? (A) Would you just repeat that?

(Q) It is a simple question. The word 'sex' at the top quite obviously governs what follows in that box? (A) In that box?

(Q) Yes? (A) Yes.

(Q) That is what I am saying. Then we can take it that the next two phrases are used with a sexual connotation? (A) They are designed to draw attention to the fact that Mr Liberace is the most successful exponent of sex appeal in the theatre.

(Q) Everything that another man can want sexually, that is to say a body willing to participate in sexual practices with any man? (A) I entirely disagree.

(Q) I suggest that is the obvious meaning which you intended millions of people to understand? (A) I did not, and it did not occur to me.

300

(Q) Listen? (A) It did not occur to me. (Q) You agree with me that it is a most offensive piece of writing? (A) It is not as clear as it might have been.

Gardiner said: If one cannot understand how these words can possibly mean that someone is a homosexualist, of course one is in some difficulty explaining the thing at all. *Prima facie*, one would have supposed that, if there is a reference to He, She and It, to anybody suggesting that that referred to a homosexualist, the answer would be: Why the She?

'But, you see, the astonishing part about this case is that, when I asked the plaintiff, as it seemed only right and as I confess I wanted to know, how on earth he could get this allegation out of these words, we had long speeches saying, By God and my mother, that is what it means, but it was very difficult to get him to explain what it did mean, Mr Beyfus in opening the case not having explained at all how on earth this allegation could be got out of the words complained of. Eventually, after one of these references to God and his mother and so on, I said to him this:

> (Q) I am sorry to interrupt you, Mr Liberace, but I did not ask you to make a speech to the jury. I asked you to explain to them quite simply how the words 'Everything that He, She and It can ever want' can possibly be understood by anyone outside a lunatic asylum to mean that you are a homosexual. Would you explain to them? (A) I will try.
>
> (Q) Where do you find it in these words? (A) 'He, She and It'. 'It' refers to the sex, supposedly in between 'he' and 'she', right?
>
> (Q) That is what you are suggesting, is it? (A) That is what it means, yes.

'The plaintiff himself was relying entirely on the word *It*, and saying *It* refers to the sex supposedly in between He and She. There are, as we all know, men who are sexually attracted to men, and women, who are homosexuals, attracted to women, but it seems odd to refer to them, being still men and women, as the sex supposedly in between he and she. But that is his account of why he is asking you to say that the words Everything that He, She, and It can ever want, mean that he is a homosexual. He relies entirely on the word *It*.

'Mr Beyfus does not agree with that at all. Of course, strictly speaking, counsel cannot give evidence, but it is quite plain Mr Beyfus does not agree, from the question which he put to Mr Connor. He relies on *He* in that context meaning another man, and when it comes to *It* he sees no objection.'

Mr Beyfus had suggested that *It* was just thrown in for confusion. 'He is not relying on the word *It* at all; he is relying on the word *He*. His client apparently attaches no importance to the word *He*. The plaintiff himself says it is entirely in the word *It*, which for all we know may have some special connotation in America.

301

'In my respectful submission to you it is really quite fantastic to suppose that any ordinary, reasonable person, there being no question of some hidden meaning, reading his *Daily Mirror* on the way to work or wherever he reads it, would read this passage and then say: "I never knew Mr Liberace went to bed with men." It is fantastic. What Mr Connor was stressing was his sex appeal.'

It had never been suggested of the plaintiff by anybody – 'and goodness knows there have been enough criticisms' – that he is what is sometimes called a 'blue' artiste. Nobody has ever suggested that he told dirty jokes. There was nothing in this article suggesting it and nothing anybody ever said to suggest it. On the contrary, everybody knew that his great appeal is a family appeal, to the father, mother and child sitting round the television set. The only reason he was mentioning this was because Mr Milmo went on and on and on asking witnesses: 'Does he tell any dirty stories? Is there anything suggestive in what he does?' That had never been suggested, as he hoped he had made clear to the plaintiff. And he made it quite plain when he opened the defendants' case too.

'Those questions could only have been put in order to lead you to think that someone really was suggesting it, when they were not. That is one thing which nobody has ever suggested about him.'

There was nothing wrong, Gardiner said, in any artiste using sex appeal. 'All great artistes, singing love songs and so on, have always used all the sex appeal they have. Merely to say that an artiste has great sex appeal and has a very wide public, well, in my submission nobody who has not got homosexualism on the brain could possibly think that means the artiste is a homosexual.'

At an early stage he had put an extract from the *Daily Sketch* to the plaintiff: 'His playing sends women of all ages into ecstasies; they swoon and love it. Even bankers behave like bobby-soxers when they hear him.' And he had asked: 'You would not, I hope, suggest that the *Daily Sketch*, in saying that not only do women swoon but that bankers behave like bobby-soxers when they hear him, mean by that that you are homosexual?' And the plaintiff had agreed to that. 'What it obviously meant was that he had some sexual appeal to the bankers. His primary appeal is to women because, of course, he is a very good looking young man, but the bankers, when they behave like bobby-soxers, are not in any way sexually attracted to him; and nobody outside a lunatic asylum, reading that in the *Daily Sketch*, would have thought so.'

Liberace was extremely good looking, said Mr Gardiner – 'and when he sings a love song, obviously and perfectly properly, he uses that. Whether or not it is right to say, as was said on the cover of the book which he authorised, that he is the very heart throb of forty million women, the hottest personality ever to melt the TV airwaves, it is perfectly plain that

302

he has a great sex appeal for women. We must use a bit of common sense. He is a man who gets twelve proposals of marriage a month from women. How then can any ordinary, reasonable, sensible person, reading these words, think for one moment that they mean the plaintiff is a homosexual? You may think that to some extent he seems to have the subject on his brain. He seems to be always thinking someone is accusing him of something of this sort.'

The jury may remember the newspaper article, 'The truth about me, by Liberace', in which he had written:

I'd also like to smash the idea that my fans are all women. On the first chorus I invite the whole audience to yell. On the second I ask for women only. On the third, I say: 'Come on, boys!' You should hear *their* shouts. I've made a gag about it by saying, 'I told you, George! Men do come to my concerts.'

There was nothing wrong in that, but because the printers or the publishers had put the word *their* in italics he seemed to think even that suggests that he was a homosexualist.

What was wrong in that, and how could anybody possibly think that that meant there was some innuendo about it, simply because the newspaper had put the word *their* in italics?

But Liberace had said: 'This account of this particular number is distorted by the very fact the word 'their' is put in italics, adding some innuendo.' And Gardiner had asked:

(Q) What is the innuendo? (A) The way you read it, it sounded like an innuendo.

(Q) It certainly was not meant to be. (A) I took it that way.

(Q) Did you read everything as meaning you are a homosexual? I suggest there is nothing in it that refers to homosexualism.

'There is I suggest some evidence that the plaintiff rather has this particular subject on the brain and is apt to think that any perfectly ordinary words are an imputation on him of homosexualism by whomever it is that writes the words. Because the newspaper in the phrase – You should hear *their* shouts – puts the word *their* in italics, how could that conceivably lead anybody who had not got the subject on the brain to think that there was, there, some innuendo?'

He was sure the jury would remember that after the article was published he had accepted the hospitality of the *Daily Mirror* to go on a pub crawl. The original suggestion had come from him, but there was no reason whatever why he should go if he did not want to, 'if he really had thought that this article was an imputation of homosexualism, unless of course he took the view that whatever else happened any publicity was better than none'.

And in Manchester Mr Tossell and a colleague had introduced themselves as reporters from the *Daily Mirror* and had been received

'Quite cordially'. Had Liberace made any complaint against the *Daily Mirror*? – No.

'All the evidence tends to show that no suggestion of suing the *Daily Mirror* came until some time after Miss Ambler had first suggested it. How can it be contended that any ordinary person reading these words would understand that he was a homosexual, when all Cassandra is saying is that here is an artiste who has great sex appeal, which everybody knows, and who is remarkable for the universality of his appeal to people of every kind?

'Unless someone has got homosexualism on the brain, who in the world would have thought that being kissed by his mother and brother showed that he was a homosexualist? Someone in this case really has got homosexualism on the brain.'

The jury would not forget what Liberace had been quoted in the same issue that the article was published and was obviously very much in Mr Connor's mind: 'The secret of my success? It is a very simple thing – everyone in this world wants to be loved and I express that love to my viewers and listeners and they seem to respond to it.'

He had put that to the plaintiff this way:

(Q) You are always stressing the fact that you exude love, and you want the people to love you – there is nothing homosexual in that? (A) No.

(Q) Men, women and children? (A) That is right.

(Q) I suggest you really summed it up yourself in a sentence which you said at Southampton, and which was published in the same issue as the offending article, when you talk about expressing your love to your viewers. It is in the issue of September 26 1956, on the front page, in which you sum up for yourself what you describe as the secret of your success. 'The secret of my success? It is a very simple thing – everyone in this world wants to be loved and I express that love to my viewers and listeners and they seem to respond to it.' Your viewers and listeners include men, do they not? (A) Yes.

(Q) When you said they respond to it, you did not mean that in any improper sense? (A) No, I did not. I was speaking of love, humanity, brotherly love, the love between peoples. That I feel is sadly lacking in this world.

(Q) That I suggest is exactly what Cassandra was obviously referring to when he so described the universality of your appeal?

There had been a long pause, and then he said: 'Yes, I believe he was referring to that.'

'It is perfectly plain, in my submission, that is so, and that is how anybody would understand it, that is any ordinary person reading the *Daily Mirror*, whether he reads it in bed or whether he reads it in the train on the way to work. To no ordinary person reading this would it ever occur to him that this meant Mr Liberace was a homosexualist.

'Therefore, in my submission, when you come to consider the first question, Do the words complained of in the defendants' publication of September 26 1956 in their ordinary and natural meaning, mean that the plaintiff is a homosexual?, if you answer this question, as I am sure you will, accepting the law from my lord and in accordance with your own consciences, the answer to that question is plainly: No.'

The final question was: Was Mr Connor saying what he honestly thought? This referred to the article without that meaning. The jury was being asked in this form; 'Without this meaning, are the words complained of (a) true in so far as they consist of statements of fact? and (b) fair comment in so far as they consist of expressions of opinion?'

The facts were not really in dispute. The facts were known; they were not matters of opinion for this purpose. 'That is why the question contrasts what are facts with what are expressions of opinion. I only mention that because in this case if I say that he is a man forty-one years of age that cannot be said either he is or he is not; that is a question of fact. But the law regards as not being questions of fact those matters which in the sphere of public interest are expressions of opinion.'

The only facts in the article were, first of all, what happened in Berlin. Nobody suggested there was anything untrue in that, or that it was relevant at all. Secondly, what happened at Waterloo? He had asked the plaintiff: 'I gather from your learned counsel that you consider the account of this' – his arrival at Waterloo – 'given in the *Daily Mirror* is a fair account?' And he answered Yes.

> (Q) This article of which you complain says you had the biggest reception and impact on London since Charlie Chaplin arrived at Waterloo. I suppose you do not suggest that that is in any way defamatory of you... obviously not? (A) No.

The only other facts were the statements that the article says the plaintiff made to the press conference on the Queen Mary, which were reported at the time, about religion, mother love, world love and money. That was not a question of detail Gardiner said, but whether in substance he had said those things. 'It is not necessary for the defence to cross the t's and dot the i's, or, as the law puts it rather more formally, in an action for libel or slander in respect of words consisting partly of allegations of fact and partly of expressions of opinion the defence of fair comment shall not fail by reason only that the truth of every allegation of fact is not proved if the expression of opinion is fair comment having regard to such of the facts alleged or referred to in the words complained of as are proved.'

The jury had heard the evidence of reporters who took shorthand notes at the time and who sent back their articles to their papers. In addition to Mr Zec, who was himself from the *Daily Mirror*, he had called Mr Bonnett of

305

the *Daily Mail*, Mr Reid of the *News Chronicle*, Mr Lambert of the *Daily Express* and Mr Frost of the *Daily Telegraph*.

They did not necessarily all include the same statements made by Mr Liberace, but the *Daily Mail* reported: Liberace kissed her cheek, fondled her wavy brown hair, and talked of the trials of earning $1,000,000 a year. 'You see', he said, parting his lips around his milk-white-almost-too-perfect teeth 'I get only nine cents out of every dollar I make.' If I can deal with the money, that really was the only bit which Mr Liberace disputed. He says, 'I could not have said that because I did not know what the tax position was.' He then says this: 'I happen to be a religious man and I want my marriage to be blessed by my faith. Honestly', went on the bachelor, who loves to talk of marriage, 'I simply surround myself with married couples.' It is the first bit: 'I happen to be a religious man and I want my marriage to be blessed by my faith,' which was quoted verbatim in the article complained of.

Then, says the *Daily Express*: 'Do you really enjoy wearing such clothes?' I asked. 'Yes, I do', he said, 'I think people love lovely things – and they are deductible from income tax.' I asked him why he attracted middle aged women. He said, 'I think it is my mother love which so many of them do not get from their children.'

Then the *Daily Telegraph*: 'It cost me $400, to be able to pay that I have to earn $4,000. I earn about a million a year and could earn more if I tried harder; but I only manage to keep nine cents out of each dollar I earn.' Then he was asked, 'Do you like wearing these clothes?' Liberace replied: 'Of course I do, and also they are deductible.' Then there is this: 'I am a religious man, and a great believer in family life. That is my theme all the time. Mom is my inspiration. George, my brother, my colleague and my musical director, and we have a perfect telepathy. My love of family life I try to inculcate into my viewers and listeners, and especially the children. If I appeal to middle aged women it is because they want to mother me, and they see in my act my love for my mother.'

The *News Chronicle*, in substance, says the same thing about mother love, and 'Afterwards Liberace explained to us that his love for Mom helps strengthen Mom-love the world over.' Also this: 'Sounds a lot, I know, but how much do you think I keep from every dollar I earn? Not more than nine cents.'

It does not matter as to the details because in any case the plaintiff does not really dispute that he made statements substantially of this kind. The only one I have not troubled to read is the one about 'world love' and I did not because I took the view that it was not important, as it is admitted. The only one he really disputed was whether he said something about nine cents.

The only other possible implication of fact is the paragraph about Madison Square Garden. On the occasion in New York at a concert in Madison Square Garden when he had the greatest reception of his life and the critics slayed him mercilessly, Liberace said: 'The take was terrific but the critics killed me. My brother George cried all the way to the bank.' That he did say words to that effect he admitted.

The whole of the rest of the matters in the article were entirely expressions of opinion, Gardiner said.

The only point which he thought it was suggested might be open to argument was whether the adjective 'scent-impregnated' was fact or an expression of opinion. 'There is no reason why people should not use scent if they wish, but there is no real dispute you know about the facts, because nobody has suggested that that meant he used what might be called 100% perfume. The facts are not really in dispute. I asked him: (Q) Do you use scent or scented lotions? (A) I use after-shaving lotions and under-arm deodorants. (Q) Which are scented? (A) Yes. There is no dispute about that, but you have in fact heard the evidence of witnesses about it, and of course this was a thing which had been widely commented upon in the press as was nearly everything else which Cassandra said.

Indeed Mr Zec himself, in the article he wrote from the Queen Mary, said, 'With a song in his heart, a fixed dimpled smile and fragrantly perfumed with toilet water, Liberace, the Casanova of the keyboard, arrived here'. In the same way it had been noticed and commented upon by the *Daily Express*, which had referred to the scent in an article also written from the Queen Mary, and again in the *Evening Standard*.

'Of course this is a thing which had been so much commented upon, but if they like to use scent or scented toilet water or scented under-arm deodorant or scented after-shave lotion they are quite entitled to do it, but it had been so much commented upon that when his mother wrote an article for English readers she obviously thought it was a point with which she ought to deal, because in the article which begins, 'I know today I am the envy of every Mum in Britain', she prints this:

> Then there's other folk who criticise him because he likes flowers and colognes. Why shouldn't my boy like these things? I read him my history books. In them it said that some of the greatest men in history, especially in the days of your own Queen Elizabeth, liked flowers and scent.

She was commenting there on something which was well-known, the subject matter of comment by his critics.

The jury had heard from Mr Stephens that even in the antiseptic atmosphere of the first aid station at the airport the degree of the scent-impregnated toilet water or under-arm deodorant or whatever it was was so powerful that it overcame the smell of antiseptics.

All the rest of the adjectives were things Mr Connor had seen him doing himself, things which had for so long been commented upon by so many of his critics. Mr Connor was asked about the 'winking, sniggering, snuggling' and so on, but there had been a number of references in the articles which had been read, containing adjectives of that nature, and Mr Connor had observed him doing these things on television.

Now, said Gardiner, I come really to the heart of the matter. When you are considering whether what Mr Connor was saying was what he honestly thought, what in my submission you have primarily to bear in mind is both the size of the controversy and the sharpness of the controversy, because this is a thing which in my submission is without parallel in the history of the theatre.

Is it not only remarkable but, I suggest, quite unparalleled? You have here an artiste whose attraction to the public is such that in any country he can fill the largest hall, but you have a place like Madison Square Garden, which is really a sports arena, holding about 18,000 people, not one can imagine a very easy sort of place for an artiste to perform, but that does not matter; he fills it. And it is the same here. Never was an artiste so popular. He takes the Festival Hall and fills that. He takes the Albert Hall and fills that. He takes the Albert Hall again, and fills it again. Since this article was written it is exactly the same in *Sunday Night at the London Palladium*, and now he is off to a Royal Variety Performance to be performed before the Queen Mother. There never was an artiste who had such an enormous public following.

One of the astonishing features of the case of Mr Liberace is that, although you have this unparalleled position of the adoring and screaming public approving of him, there is this extraordinary unanimity, not very frequently marked among the critics, of the whole of the national press. I am not talking about the trade press or provincial newspapers where somewhat different considerations apply, but the virtual unanimity of the English about him and to a large extent that in America too. They come from the musical critics.

He says that the public have called him 'The Chopin of TV' but concedes himself that ever since he appeared on TV there has never been a favourable criticism from a music critic. The music critics, rightly or wrongly, are unanimous.

The more curious thing is that when Mr Mantovani was called as a witness on behalf of the plaintiff he said he thought he was a very good pianist. I asked Mr Mantovani this:

> (Q) ...Or take the Grieg piano concerto. Of this he throws away two movements, takes the stomach out of a third, re-orchestrates what's left and has the piano playing at one point when it should be resting'. Have you heard him do that? (A) Yes.

(Q) 'Beethoven's *Moonlight Sonata* is hacked to four minutes, lest American womanhood should yawn. Chopin, like Rachmaninov, becomes a stew of popular keyboard bits with orchestral effects impertinently added.' Would you agree with that or not? (A) Yes.

(Q) You would? (A) Yes.

Of course, although the musical critics have been unanimous, that is not the main ground on which the critics have felt so very strongly. The odd thing is that the things about which the critics have obviously felt so very strongly are the very things which his fans like most.

If he plays on the piano *Ave Maria* in a film, he then has this scene behind him – a stained glass window and a woman praying in agony to the Virgin Mary. It is quite obvious that some people regard that as somewhat profane. After all, this is commercial television. It is in between the advertisement for toilet paper or whatever it is. In the view of many people it just cannot be necessary, in order to hold the audience while he is playing the piano, to make use of a religious theme of that kind.

But when that view is put to him, while recognising that it is a matter of opinion, you may remember what he said: 'Oh, that is one of the most popular numbers' or 'one of the numbers which my public like best…'

But there is no doubt that some people do not like this. They are entitled not to like it. Some people obviously regard it as profane.

It is a matter of interest, is it not, that when the British press were writing about him, having seen week after week his films on television, something is said to the effect, 'You are all writing about him before he appears in the theatre'. But he made his name on television, and you could in fact see him better and closer on television than on the stage.

It is rather remarkable, is it not, that, having seen him in performances on the television, two national newspapers should pick out his feature showing people round his house and saying, 'This is where I live with my Mom and my poodle…' He then says, 'There is someone else who dwells with us, of whom I speak,' and he then sings the well-known semi-sacred song or hymn, *Bless this house, O Lord, we pray, Make it safe by night and day.*

Of course, there is no reason why he should not show people round his house and there is no reason why he should not sing that particular song, but, of course, the way of getting there from the black poodle is obviously a cue for the song, and it is quite plain from the fact that both the *Daily Herald* and the *News Chronicle* draw attention to this particular film that there are quite a lot of people who do not consider that that sort of thing is right and who regard it as profane.

There are a number of people who, rightly or wrongly – and they are as much entitled to their opinion as Mr Liberace's fans – do feel that all this 'Mom' business and all these references to God, or the president of the

United States, or Princess Margaret, or whatever it may be, that are brought in in order to support his performance are things which tend to make people, in effect, feel rather sick.

There is no dispute, of course, as to the sort of typical kind of performance in relation to his mother because I put it to Mr Liberace and he agreed:

> Has she appeared in your television performance? (A) Yes she has. (Q) Sitting on the stage? (A) Yes, she has. (Q) While you sing to her: 'I shall always call you sweetheart; that will always be your name'? (A) Yes. (Q) Then you kiss her? (A) Yes. (Q) The result of that is simply this, is it not, that with the majority it goes down splendidly but it makes a few people feel rather sick? (A) If that is the reaction, it is not my intention to derive that reaction. (Q) These things are very much a matter of opinion, are they not? (A) That is true. (Q) And, as with sugar, though it is very nice up to a point, there comes a point where too much sugar makes people feel sick? (A) That may be true, yes. (Q) And individuals differ as to what the point is? (A) That is right.

You will observe how many of the critics use the analogy of 'sugar', as one witness whom I called yesterday, in an article which I read, referred to him as 'candy floss'; and the critics – who are, in my submission, as much entitled to their opinion on what is obviously a question of opinion, as his fans – do feel that in a sickening way he plays on the emotions, and that the result is almost to create a sense of hysteria.

We know the income which the plaintiff earns and all the more credit to him; everybody in his field is trying to earn the largest possible income and all credit to the man who succeeds; but supposing you had been abroad and you had not read the papers, and you came back and you were told: 'There is a man this week in Queen's Bench Court IV and he is either American or English, I shall not tell you which, and he earns £375,000 a year gross, he can earn £20,000 a week; who do you think it is?'

And the answer, said Mr Gardiner, would not be a president or prime minister, or a captain of industry, not a life-saving surgeon, scientist or inventor, but... 'A pianist on the telly'!

You do not suppose, do you, that Mr Connor is the only person in this country who says there must be something wrong with our people when all the way from Southampton to Waterloo at intervals people are standing along the track in order that they might, perhaps, catch a glimpse of him as he goes by? That is the burden of Mr Connor's final paragraph: there must be something wrong with our people who attach such importance to this particular individual. Of course, anybody is equally entitled to say and to think the exact opposite, and that is why in fair comment the question is not whether you consider the comment fair in the ordinary sense; the question is: Was the defendant saying what he honestly thought? People are entitled to feel strongly, and there can be no doubt how very strongly, how quite exceptionally strongly, Mr Liberace's critics do feel, and they really are entitled to their view.

For that matter, anybody is entitled to their view of the *Daily Mirror*, because the *Daily Mirror*, being a national newspaper, is itself a matter of public interest.

If I may come back for a moment to the strength and violence of the national press, when at any time in your life do you remember any newspaper writing this about any artiste, British or foreign – and we have many fine foreign artistes here: 'Such dimpling and winking! Such tossing of curls and fluttering of eyelashes and flashing of teeth. Such nausea'...? Or in another national newspaper, the *Daily Herald*: 'This time for the man I vote the most unlikeable on our television screens. The man whose leers and dimples make me heave' – that means makes him feel sick. And again in the *News Chronicle* in the article which has been read, one of those which refers to the film about 'Someone who dwells with us', and so on: First of all as to his music: '... anything, in short, about dreams and amour, drip from his fingers like treacle, with lots of wistful lingerings and, to compensate for these, coy little scurries'. Then: 'Not that we need worry greatly. Music is not Liberace's true cause. Love is the thing. Mention of it brings that faraway, solemn look into his eyes: 'When I do a show', he explains, 'I exude Love', and so on... When did you ever hear ordinary English critics in the national press using language of that character about an artist?

Or the *Evening News*, which was the paper in which he wrote himself when he was here: 'Honesty compels me to reveal that upon me it has a slightly emetic effect.'

The reason I submit the controversy over Mr Liberace is really quite without parallel is, firstly, because of the immensity of his audience who adore him, scream for him and cheer him; secondly, because of the unanimity of the professional critic; and, thirdly, because they obviously feel so very strongly about his performance, which they absolutely cannot stand. If that is the position, they are entitled to say so, and entitled to say it strongly.

You have heard a good deal in this case about vitriolic language. Well – and you may find this interesting – you can compare that vitriolic language of Cassandra, of which you have heard several examples, with the language of Mr Beyfus in his final speech to you. I trust I shall offend no-one if I prophesy a dead-heat.

There are many occasions on which, especially when a matter of public interest is concerned, people are entitled to speak strongly. You see, Cassandra is in this very extraordinary position in Fleet Street, that whereas, of course, an editor always has the last word, in practice he is allowed to say what he thinks, and you have heard examples of articles he has written saying the exact opposite of what his own newspaper thinks.

Very often in a libel case, of course, there is some allegation of malice, but Mr Beyfus has expressly disclaimed any suggestion of personal malice on the part of Mr Connor because, of course, nobody suggests he had ever met Mr Liberace, or that they had had a row, or anything of that sort. So the only thing on which the plaintiff relies, or can rely, to suggest malice is that he was not saying what he honestly thought; he was writing something which he did not believe in order to increase the circulation of the paper. You have seen Mr Connor and you have seen something of the way in which the *Daily Mirror* is conducted, and that obviously is not so, is it? You may remember that Mr Connor said – and I have not got his exact words, but in substance he said – 'I don't give a damn what my readers think'. Having seen him in the witness box, that is obviously true, is it not?

You have seen Mr Connor being examined and cross-examined for some five hours. You may like him, you may dislike him. That he has strong views he would be the first to admit. One thing which, I suggest, is quite clear to anybody who has seen him is that he is telling the truth when he says that he felt strongly about this. There is not, in fact, anything in his article that has not already been said before by others. He puts it rather more shortly and, perhaps because he is a better writer, rather more bitingly; but when you come to address your minds to the question: Was this fair comment; was he honestly saying what he thought? – I do respectfully submit that each of you who heard Mr Connor giving evidence at length must know in your heart that Bill Connor was simply saying what he honestly thought on a subject about which he feels strongly, and that he would be saying it if nobody else in the country thought the same. It does happen to be the fact that nearly every critic in the country did feel the same, but that does not, strictly speaking, matter. Nobody who heard Mr Connor giving his evidence could doubt, if he was searching for the real truth, that Bill Connor was on this occasion, as always, saying what he thought honestly to be true.

So, when you come to consider these questions which my lord is submitting to you, it is, in my submission, fantastic, as I have submitted throughout, to suggest that, it not being alleged that these words have any hidden meaning, the ordinary reasonable reader would attach any meaning of homosexualism to these words as their ordinary and natural meaning. Secondly, when you come to consider the question whether, without this meaning, the words, insofar as they are fact and true, I suggest they are clearly true, although the facts are not really matters of much importance in this case. Then I suggest they are clearly fair comment insofar as they consist of expressions of opinion; he really was only saying what he believed to be true.

312

A good deal has been said about the book written about the *Daily Mirror* by Mr Cudlipp. In that book he said: 'It has never been a question of What Makes Connor Tick, but What Makes Connor Clang', and it may be that ought to be on his tombstone; but then he also added this – and he has known him for a long time: 'The value of the man is that he writes superbly, is a born journalist, means what he writes, and writes without fear', and it may be that that should be part of his epitaph too.

Thirdly, when you come to consider your verdict, if each of you considers his duty to each party, accepting the law as my lord directs you it is and finding the facts according to your own conscience, then I suggest that, for the reasons which I have endeavoured to put before you, your verdict in this case ought to be for the defendants.

Closing speech: Gilbert Beyfus QC

There was a formality with speeches in court, as at weddings where one party would thank the father of the bride, another would congratulate the bridesmaids on their beauty. In court the defence thanked the jury, whether they trusted them or not, on behalf of both sides; the plaintiff would congratulate the defence QC on his eloquence, whether he meant it or not; the judge would praise the barristers, whether they deserved it or not. So Mr Beyfus had to start with a tribute to his opponent:

Day by day, week by week and month by month my admiration for my learned friend and his conversational ability increases, and I have no doubt that you yourselves, having listened to the evidence for some five days, will have admired immensely the speech which he has just made. It is now up to me to say a few words on the other side.

Let me right at the beginning deal with what I venture to submit is the most important topic in this case. It is common ground – and my learned friend has just repeated it – that fair comment depends, in effect, on the answer to two questions: (1) Were the words such as any reasonable man could have written? and (2) Were they written honestly? And one of the first topics which you will have to consider is whether you can rely upon the honesty of Mr Connor; so I want you to consider his evidence on a number of topics.

One of the first questions I asked him was whether he was not aware – as Mr Cudlipp admitted – that the *Daily Mirror* was a sensational paper; that was on the Third Day. It may – in fact it probably will, certainly on the issue of damages – be a matter of importance, whether you consider that the *Daily Mirror* is or is not a sensational paper, a paper which, having been a decorous and gentlemanly paper up to 1935, has since then adopted a policy which ousted decorum and has since outraged decency. Mr Connor must have been extremely well acquainted with this book written by Mr Cudlipp, his boon companion, reviewed by him, and in answer to that question of mine: Are you not aware that Mr Cudlipp not only admits this newspaper, the *Daily Mirror*, is a sensational paper but boasts about it?, he said: 'I am not aware of that.' Then I had to put to him some passages in the book, in the first of which Mr Cudlipp himself said it was a sensational paper, and in the second of which Mr Bolam (the editor) and Mr Bartholomew (who was the head of both newspapers) boasted before the Royal Commission it was a sensational paper. That, I suggest, was a completely dishonest answer.

Then I asked him whether he did not agree that his strong point was vituperation, and he denied it; that is a point to which I will return. But you have heard what he said about doctors; you have heard what he wrote about Mr Dimbleby; you have heard what he wrote about Mr Wilfred Pickles; you have heard the way in which he expressed his dislike for poodles, and you have read this article. You have heard how he was described in a letter to the prime minister as a 'hard-hitting journalist with a vitriolic style'. You have heard how Mr Cudlipp described him as obviously having reached his home when he entered the profession of journalism, 'the only profession where', according to Mr Cudlipp, 'big-scale, incessant rudeness (skilfully written) is highly paid'. You remember the next passage, which he liked, the passage in which he thought Mr Cudlipp was making up for what he had written before, where, after describing how he read and masticated every paper, Mr Cudlipp wrote: 'He remembers every point of detail to the slightest disadvantage of the victim he picks up on the tip of his pen for public scrutiny in his column.' Can you have any doubt that when Mr Connor denied that his strong point was vituperation he was saying that which he knew to be untrue?

I cross-examined him with regard to this article on poodles which, of course, is remote from this case except insofar as it throws light on the honesty of Mr Connor. I asked him a very simple question on the Fourth Day, about an article he had written only a few weeks ago: 'Did you take an opportunity quite recently of expressing your detestation of poodles? (A) I did. (Q) Did you find it impossible to express your detestation of poodles without dragging in prostitutes? (A) I do not remember the phrase'. You will notice that I had not put any particular phrase to him, I merely said: 'Did you find it impossible to express your detestation of poodles without dragging in prostitutes?' and he, having written that article only a few weeks previously, gave that answer. What he had said was:

Of all the breeds to debase the coinage of animal and human self-respect, the poodle, now prancing round the West End in hordes, and significantly being found mincing and prancing in attendance on the fancier Tarts of the Town, is the worst...

'...prancing in attendance on the fancier Tarts of the Town'! I suggest that when in answer to my question he said, 'I do not remember the phrase', that was quite obviously a completely dishonest answer. It shows you the way in which, even in dealing with dogs, he cannot write honestly.

Having said: 'Of all the breeds to debase the coinage of animal and human self-respect, the poodle... is the worst', I asked him about it and he said: 'If I dislike a poodle it is because it is a dog which is often found in the company of people whom I dislike', and so forth. It is to be found, he said, 'in the company of prostitutes who use it as an advertisement'. So that when he answered 'I do not remember the phrase', the whole of his condemnation of poodles being due to the fact that some of them – fortunately not all of them – are owned by prostitutes, he must have been telling a lie.

Then when I suggested that the poll on the possibility of a marriage by Princess Margaret with a commoner sent to 4,500,000 readers must have been distasteful to her, do you think he was telling the truth when he told you he did not think that it would be distasteful to her? Could anything be more distasteful?

Perhaps you could not get a clearer example of his resolute determination to lie in the witness box if by lying he could defend the *Daily Mirror* than his declaration on oath that he did not consider that the publication of that cartoon a fortnight ago – which you have seen and which you will be able to look at when you retire – was a revolting attack on Her Majesty. I put to him: 'And this cartoon, if you look at it, is a most revolting attack upon Her Majesty both in regard to the caption and the drawing?' and he said: 'Mr Beyfus' and then, perhaps wrongly, I interrupted and said: 'Is that right?

> (A) I would not have published that if I had been editor of the paper, the *Sunday Pictorial*. (Q) That is not an answer to my question. This is a revolting attack upon Her Majesty both as regards the captions and the drawings? (A) I think it is a bit of folly. (Q) It is a revolting attack both as regards the caption and the drawing? (A) I think it is unwise. (Q) Do not bother about it being unwise. Is it a revolting attack on Her Majesty both as regards caption and drawing? (A) No, sir. (Q) Would you look at the last of those four pictures. Look at the second, the third and the fourth. Is that a picture of Her Majesty looking as sour as vinegar? (A) It is recognisable as being Her Majesty. (Q) Looking as sour as vinegar? (A) No. (Q) You do not think so? (A) No, looking unhappy.

You will have to consider the honesty of the witness in relation to those answers. Was it not endeavouring to defend the newspaper which has made him one of the highest paid columnists in Fleet Street by saying that which is quite obviously false? – Or do you think he was telling the truth? In my submission, there is only one answer.

Again, if you want to consider his truthfulness in the witness box, I cross-examined him as to the almost certain effect of this article which he wrote about Mr Liberace in which he called him this 'appalling, terrifying man', in which he called him 'vomit', and so forth. I will call your attention to the words of it again, although by now you must have heard them a great many times, I put to him, on Day Four:

> ... if a reader read that article and believed it to be true, do you not think Mr Liberace would become a hateful person in his eyes? (A) Not hateful, no. (Q) Do you think he would become a contemptible person in his eyes, the eyes of the reader who read it and believed it to be true? (A) Yes, his act would be so interpreted. (Q) You do not think Mr Liberace himself would appear to be a contemptible figure? (A) I do not know about that. Do you think that is true? (Q) Well, I want you to think. Do not you think that in the eyes of any reader who read it and believed it to be true he would become a contemptible figure? (A) I would think he would be an unworthy figure. (Q) What? (A) Unworthy. (Q) And ridiculous? (A) Unworthy. (Q) That is one word. I am asking about another. Do not you think it would be ridiculous? (A) No. (Q) You swear that? (A) I do. Then I said: I borrow a phrase from my learned friend. May the members of the jury judge the rest of your evidence, the truth of the rest of your evidence, on the basis of that answer? (A) Obviously they will. (Q) I hope so. Not ridiculous, and then I quoted the last sentence of the libel: 'There must be something wrong with us that our teenagers longing for sex and our middle-aged matrons fed up with sex, alike should fall for such a sugary mountain of jingling claptrap wrapped up in such a preposterous clown.' Do you not think that that would make him appear ridiculous? (A) I think it would reduce him to his correct proportions. (Q) And that his correct proportion would be that of a ridiculous person? (A) It would be those of a preposterous clown. (Q) Do you agree that a preposterous clown is a ridiculous person? (A) Yes.

Then I quoted again:

> 'Without doubt he is the biggest sentimental vomit of all time'. That is a pretty revolting phrase in itself, is it not? (A) It is a strong phrase, but it is a phrase which reflects and accurately reflects my reaction to Mr Liberace's public performances. (Q) Do you think it would make him appear contemptible and ridiculous? (A) I do not think it would increase his stature. (Q) Do you think it would make him appear both contemptible and ridiculous? (A) Ridiculous.

So it took me just on a page of cross-examination to get him to alter his sworn answer that he did not think these words would make Mr Liberace appear ridiculous to his eventual admission on the next page that they would, obviously, make him appear ridiculous.

316

Then I put: 'Not contemptible?' and he did not answer, and I put 'Not contemptible?' again and he did not answer.

Then you get the most astonishing answer of all. After I had put to him whether he had ever heard any other person in the world described as vomit and he said he could not recollect one, I asked: At any rate, the whole object of the article from beginning to end was to depreciate Mr Liberace in the public eye? (A) No, sir. (Q; It was not? (A) No. Now what can you think of a man who swears that that article, as violent and vicious an article as you have probably ever read, was not intended to depreciate Mr Liberace in the public eye? That was a lie told in the witness box, quite obviously, with the sole idea of reducing the amount of damages which you would probably give.

Then you will probably think he was obviously lying – at any rate I suggest to you he quite obviously was – when he said that he did not think that the expression admittedly used by my client when he had this enormous response in Madison Square Garden, 'The take was terrific but the critics killed me. My brother George cried all the way to the bank', was jocular. Would anybody reading that description by my client, with knowledge of the fact that his reception by the audience had been magnificent but the critics had been unfavourable, doubt that that was an obviously jocular remark? My client, referring to the unfavourable criticism of his musicianship by that very humorous remark: 'My brother George cried all the way to the bank', but he would not even agree that that was a humorous observation.

> Do you think it is the observation of a man making a joke against himself? (A) No. (Q) Do you think it is jocular? (A) No. (Q) I am not saying a good joke. (A) No. (Q) You obviously do not think that 'the take was terrific but the critics killed me. My brother George cried all the way to the bank' was jocular? (A) No.

Do you think he was really telling the truth when he expressed that opinion?

Then I go on with Aimee Semple McPherson. In his evidence-in-chief he had made it quite clear that he was not suggesting that she, a revivalist of some decades ago, was insincere, and yet he writes: 'Nobody since Aimee Semple McPherson has purveyed a bigger, richer and more varied slag-heap of lilac-coloured hokum.' I quoted that to him and I said: And that suggests falsity? (A) Humbug. Then I put to him:

> There is not much difference between falsity and humbug, is there, except one word is slang and the other is not? (A) That is right. (Q) Did you tell the members of the jury yesterday, when you were giving evidence, that when you wrote that you were not suggesting in the very slightest that this deceased lady was anything but completely sincere? (A) She may have been in what she thought, but what I thought of her performance was that it was humbug. (Q) Listen. She has been dead for

317

many, many, many years? (A) She has. (Q) Have you ever seen her? (A) No. (Q) I think she probably died before television came into existence? (A) I think she died about 1942. (Q) Certainly before television came into existence in the United States? (A) Yes.

Then, again, I asked him about the sentence: 'Nobody anywhere ever made so much money out of high speed piano-playing with the ghost of Chopin gibbering at every note.' This last bit was meant to add a little offensive note, 'the ghost of Chopin gibbering at every note'? (A) They are meant to reflect and to convey what I think of Mr Liberace's piano-playing. (Q) Do you think the ghost of Chopin does come down and gibber at every note? (A) I hope that he does come down and gibber at every note, and returns to the Shades from which he came. Then I asked him: Are you a musical critic? (A) I am not a musical critic. (Q) Have you ever heard Mr Liberace play Chopin? (A) I cannot positively identify that. (Q) At any rate, if you ever heard him, it did not make any impression on you that he played it badly? (A) No, I have seen other performances on the piano.

Then I dealt with the evidence of Mr Mantovani, and I went on: At any rate, you heard him express the opinion that he was a highly competent musician? (A) I did. (Q) You chose to write this about 'high speed piano playing with the ghost of Chopin gibbering at every note', without having heard him play Chopin? (A) To the best of my knowledge. (Q) Certainly without any knowledge that he played Chopin badly? (A) Yes, Chopin. That may, again, help you to wonder whether that sentence in the libel was honest.

Then you remember I read to you the article which he wrote about Mr Dimbleby. I do not want to read it again, but there are one or two phrases I want to repeat to you;

> 'The man shimmers in his own unction. He swells in a glycerine respect for his subject that makes the Royal Family look like an advertisement for an immensely costly hair tonic – for which Mr Dimbleby may sign up the advertising rights at any moment'... 'And still the result is the same – glossy pap soused with the mayonnaise of unlimited unction'... 'He stands to attention with cushioned respect'... 'To listen to Mr Dimbleby describing a Royal occasion is like tuning in to an oily burial service. But buried beneath the Dimbleby quilt they are reduced to scented flock.'

...that is the Queen and Prince Philip are reduced to scented flock. And the last one: 'He was quietly sizzling and gently bubbling like an over-rich Welsh rarebit.' You realise now why his chief wrote that he was a hard-hitting journalist with a vitriolic pen.

But I led up to asking about Mr Dimbleby by asking about my client: The whole of that article – that is the libel in this case – was bound, was it not, and I give you one last opportunity to deal with it, to cause Mr Liberace to be looked upon with great hostility by millions of readers? (A)

That was not the primary purpose. The primary purpose... and I said: I did not ask you that. (A) Then the answer is 'No'. I suggest that was not an honest answer, because the effect of the libellous article in this case was bound to cause Mr Liberace to be looked upon with hostility by millions of readers.

> My suggestion is that the primary purpose was to boost the circulation of this tabloid. (A) No. (Q) It was bound, was it not, to create grave hostility towards Mr Liberace and his performance? (A) That was not my purpose. (Q) I did not ask you that. Did you not think that it was bound so to do? (A) No. (Q) You say that on oath? (A) I do. (Q) You say the same thing in your article about Mr Dimbleby. That was bound, was it not, to hold him up to the most complete and utter ridicule? (A) No.

I have just read you some phrases from it. Do you believe that was an honest answer? Do you not think that that answer 'No' to my question 'That was bound, was it not, to hold him up to the most complete and utter ridicule?' was clearly and transparently dishonest?

When he said 'No', the learned judge intervened to say: If people accepted the opinions you expressed in this article, it would not be likely to endear Mr Liberace to them, would it? (A) I would agree with that. Those, again, are examples, I suggest, of the complete dishonesty of Mr Connor in the witness box.

The charge of profanity which he thinks it right to make is based, so far as Mr Connor's evidence is concerned, almost entirely on the fact that my client sang or played – I think played – *Ave Maria* with a background – which had obviously been arranged by those producing the film – of an actress dressed as a nun praying to the Virgin Mary. The whole of this charge of profanity is based upon his playing that music in that setting. A charge of profanity, mark you, not by an extremely religious man, a man of a deeply religious character, who might reasonably, or perhaps un-reasonably, take offence at anything which was even semi-sacred like the song *Ave Maria* when sung in a concert hall, but by an agnostic, a man who has no belief in religion whatsoever. Do you believe he was really making an honest comment when he accused my client of profanity because he has played that music in that setting on television? I suggest that all these facts which I have been mentioning make it quite clear the one thing on which you cannot rely is the honesty of Mr Connor; certainly not the honesty of Mr Connor as a witness.

Now let me come to the vitally important words in this libel, which we suggest were meant by Mr Connor to convey, and would convey, to the ordinary reader the idea that my client was a homosexual. The one thing you will probably be quite certain about, the one thing which is completely common ground in this case, is that Mr Connor is a most skilful writer. He is a master of the English language. Except in the disputed words, you will find in every single sentence he has written the utmost clarity, but with regard to these words he admitted to me they might certainly have been more clear.

One thing, of course, is certain, and that is that they were meant to mean something important; they were chosen by Mr Connor himself to be repeated in larger print in the box at the top of the article. He admitted – as quite obviously he would have to admit – that the words deliberately chosen for that privileged position were words that might be said either to constitute the highlight of the article, or to constitute the kernel of the article.

Another thing as to which there can be no dispute at all is that this article was a violent attack on my client and on his performance, and yet when the defendant (the author of these words) finds himself in a position where he has to explain what he intended to mean by them, he finds himself in the position that he has to tell you that those words were intended to convey the universality of my client's appeal, the fact that he appealed to people of both sexes and all ages, men women and children; and quite obviously, if that were so, they would be (as he had to admit) a very considerable compliment. I put that to him: 'Let us see what your explanation of them is. If your explanation of these words is true, they were a very considerable compliment to Mr Liberace, were they not? (A) They were'. Just try and consider where that leads us, or, above all, where that leads Mr Connor. In this wholly vituperative article – and one thing which cannot be denied, and indeed is not denied, by my learned friend is that this is an extremely vituperative article – he selects as the kernel of the article, as a highlight of the article, words which were intended to be, and on his view of what they meant were, a very considerable compliment to Mr Liberace. That is, is it not, the most utter and complete nonsense.

Those are the words of a man who, in the witness box on oath, is quite clearly intent on deceiving you as to what they meant. What I have suggested to you and what I submit to you – and what I hope you will accept as being the obvious truth in this case – is that this man, who can write as clearly as any man in Fleet Street, studiously and carefully sought out phrases which would convey to millions of the readers of the *Daily Mirror* the idea that my client was a homosexual, while at the same time enabling him to go into the witness box and swear to the contrary, to enable his counsel in, as I said before, an attitude of starry-eyed wonder to say to you: 'Where can you get that meaning?'

Well, you can get it in at least two ways. You can get it in the way which my client suggested, namely that my client thought that 'it' denoted a homosexual, as being something between male and female. Or you can get it in the way I suggest, particularly having regard to the admission of the defendant that the word 'sex' in the first sentence quite clearly governs the other words in the box. Then the last sentence must read in this way, must not: 'Everything that he, she and it can ever want sexually'. If it does not mean that, what on earth does it mean? It cannot, obviously, have the meaning which the defendants suggest of a compliment to my client inserted as the highlight and the kernel of this admittedly defamatory article. It cannot mean that, that is quite clear; and if it cannot have the meaning which the defendants suggest – the innocent, highly complimentary meaning which he suggests – then, quite obviously, it must, must it not, bear the meaning which we suggest. It was borne out – if you accept my client's evidence – by the shouts and jeers he heard at Sheffield, which caused him to telephone to his lawyer in California.

The remarkable thing about Sheffield was that the defendants called something like five witnesses. Two were right at the back of the stalls and quite obviously were not in a position to hear the shouts on the balcony. Then there was a student who was obviously head of a gang at one side of the balcony, who quite honestly told you that he could not say what shouts were coming from the rival gang on the other side. And the last man heard a lot of shouting but the only words which he could remember were: 'Hey, Mr Liberace, I am being thrown out.' He could not remember, or, indeed, hear clearly, anything else. From the mere fact that it was immediately after that, the very first opportunity after that, that my client rang up his lawyer, you can conclude that my client heard the words clearly used.

Let us look at one other aspect of whether the words mean what we suggest, which you may think is most important. The defendants have stressed – my learned friend stressed it in his opening speech and he stressed it in the speech he made this morning – that we did not in any letter before action, or indeed in any letter after action, and we did not in the Statement of Claim suggest in so many words that these words had the meaning that my client was a homosexual. How let me remind you of a most significant fact: Miss Ambler's evidence – and whatever view you may take as to who was telling the truth between Miss Ambler and Mr Connor, this part of her evidence would seem to be strongly confirmed – was to the effect that Mr Connor told her that the solicitors were searching out to see whether the same thing had not been said before by others, and one of the first things that happened, eighteen months or two years ago, before the defendants would have you believe they ever had any occasion to believe the words had this suggested meaning, they go round to Mr Jimmy Thompson, or they send round the dramatic critic, to get by trickery, by a false promise, out of him a song which he was singing – under instructions, as he says – which quite clearly – and you can have no doubt about it – imputed to my client that he was a homosexual. If they did not think that those words had that meaning, it never, according to them, having been suggested by us that they had that meaning, why on earth should they go round to Mr Jimmy Thompson and resort to the most

321

despicable trickery in order to obtain the words of a song which, quite obviously, suggested that my client was a homosexual?

We had no answer of any sort or kind to that question, and, in my submission, that is a second quite decisive reason why you should come to the conclusion that the words not only mean, but were quite clearly intended to mean, that which we say. Indeed, that confirms Miss Ambler and it does, indeed, confirm that part of Miss Ambler's evidence in which she said that Mr Connor, with his obvious ability, put his finger on the spot when, after saying 'he can take a lot of money off us', he said the gist of the libel was 'He, she or it'. Everything in this case goes to confirm her evidence to that effect: 'He, she or it'.

Mrs Connor was called for some reason or other, but the one thing she could not give any evidence about at all was as to what conversation took place between Miss Ambler and Mr Connor while she was absent upstairs in the bedroom trying to persuade the antagonistic cat to be less antagonistic to the photographer than it was, apparently, to Mr Connor, its master.

Two, at any rate, of the things she said are admitted: (1) That Mr Connor wondered whether he or Mr Liberace would appear to be the greater buffoon in the witness box, and (2) as to an article written by a Mr Beeby in New York as to which he telephoned his secretary. It is said: why should Mr Connor use words of this type to Miss Ambler? It is a legitimate question, but it would exclude, would it not, his saying anything like, 'Well, it will be interesting to see which of the two of us proves to be the greater buffoon in the witness box'. It tells just as much in respect of that part of the conversation as the other part, in my submission.

Looking at these points broadly, considering the impossibility of the defendant's explanation, the way in which they immediately rush round to get a copy of the song which obviously does make this imputation against my client, confirming, as it does, the very policy which Miss Ambler said they were following, can you have any doubt at all that I am right when I suggest that this master of language chose these particular phrases to convey to his readers that my client was a homosexual, while at the same time enabling him to deny it? It is the only way, of course, in which he could do it. He could not write in a newspaper, because no editor would have passed it: 'Every look, every gesture of his performance makes it clear that he is a homosexual.' It is quite obvious that he could not write it in plain and clear words like that, and so he had to use these very carefully chosen phrases to carry that meaning and, at the same time, to enable him to say in the witness box that he had no such intention.

I have dealt with the special meaning which we suggest these words bear, and now let me say a word or two about the rest of the article.

In the first place you remember that it is admitted beyond dispute that it is defamatory of my client, and all you have to consider is whether it is such that a reasonable man could have written it and whether in fact it was an honest article, or whether, as we suggest, it was written as part of the Cassandra daily task of writing some vitriolic article holding some victim – to quote the words used by Mr Cudlipp in his book – up to ridicule.

When Cortez invaded Mexico he found a wonderful civilisation, the Aztec civilisation, marred only by one thing, and that is that they had the habit of human sacrifice, by choosing the best looking boys and girls.

In our modern civilisation you may think that in the newspaper world we have the habit of butchering not people but reputations, butchering them not every day but possibly, in the case of the *Daily Mirror*, some five days a week, which was the number of days on which Cassandra wrote.

You have only got to look at the illustrations of the way in which he admittedly wrote to see, in my submission, that it was part of what Mr Cudlipp calls the tabloid revolution, the change from what had previously been a decorous newspaper into a sensational newspaper. You may have noticed yesterday that Mr Cudlipp agreed that it had ceased to be decorous but said it had not ceased to be gentlemanly. That is a distinction which you may find a little difficult to follow. There is no dispute at all that this tabloid revolution started in 1935 when Cassandra joined the paper and decorum was thrown overboard. You have only got to look at the type of articles which he wrote, in my humble submission, to be quite certain that he wrote those vitriolic articles for one purpose, and one purpose only – to create a daily sensation, to sell this sensational newspaper.

Let me just remind you. After all, we have got hold of a few illustrations. We get this from the book. I think someone said, 'Oh, that my enemy would publish a book.' Well, any prayer to that effect has been abundantly answered in this case. Let us see what Cassandra wrote about the medical profession:

> 'Of course I'm biased' he wrote. 'I'm agin doctors. I don't like 'em. For one thing their mumbo-jumbo, their smooth, lying inefficiency, and their blunt assumption that the disease-laden clients have the mentality of sick cattle. They are traders in the most valuable commodity we have – life itself. And they give poor value for money.'
>
> Cassandra opined that the General Medical Council was 'unparalleled in bigotry and autocracy' and described the ordinary doctor as a man with 'neither the wit nor the means to break into the big money'.

A shocking piece of writing you may think, but typical of the man.

You may too think it typical of the man the way he dealt with it in the witness box, when I cross-examined him about it on Day 3. I read it to him and I said this:

> (Q) Do you agree that is a piece of quite wicked, vitriolic writing? (A) I do not, but I think that I was entirely wrong, and I regret having written

323

it. (Q) It went on: Cassandra opined that the General Medical Council was 'unparalleled in bigotry and autocracy' and described the ordinary doctor as a man with 'neither the wit nor the means to break into the big money'? (A) I think I was wrong to write that, and I regret it.

(Q) Indeed, that is rather a shocking thing, is it not, to attack the ordinary GP, the General Practitioner, because he is content to earn a modest income doing his duty to his clients on the basis that he had neither wit nor means to break into big money? (A) Mr Beyfus, I have already said that I regret that. In the one million words which I have written and in the six thousand columns which I have written I do not pretend to be right, and I will admit when I was wrong, and when you read those words back to me they seemed foolish and stupid and wrong, and I am sorry I wrote them.

(Q) And shocking and vitriolic? (A) No, I will not agree that. I said I am sorry for them. I will not defend them anyway.

(Q) Do you agree that they are shocking? (A) I have said that I am sorry, and that I regret writing them.

(Q) I am not content with that. I am not the medical profession. You need not apologise to me. Do you agree that they are shocking? (A) I agree that they are wrong. (Q) I did not ask you that. Do you agree... (A) Yes, I agree that they are shocking (Q) Do you agree that they are vitriolic? (A) I did not think they were particularly vitriolic, but I will agree that they are vitriolic.

There is a passage in which it takes me nearly a page of cross-examination at last to extract from the defendant an admission of what should have been an obvious admission with regard to the words which he wrote.

Again dealing with the question whether these words are such as a reasonable man could have written and whether he wrote them honestly, just look at the way in which he dealt with this picture in the *Daily Mirror* on August 1 1949. What a light it throws, does it not, upon the way in which this paper is conducted? The days in August are usually known as the 'dog days', dull for newspapers, no daily sensations. So one of the employees of the *Daily Mirror*, a West Country photographer, stops a motor coach in which a number of men and women are travelling, gets the people out, asks them to pose looking over a wall, and takes a photograph and sends it up to London.

Then you got this utterly vitriolic attack upon those completely innocent people in which again Cassandra assumes the very worst against his fellow human beings, without any reason whatsoever. There are fifteen of them. 'The fifteen have every appearance of being on the gloat'. Then I see in big print the word 'Gloat' repeated. 'A horrible sounding word, well matched by its ugly meaning. But it fits this spectacle, they get a kick out of such things.' What conceivable reason was there for writing these words, even if the photographer had happened to see people looking over a

324

wall? They might have been looking over with sympathy; they might have been looking over with interest. They might have been interested in prison reform. It would be certainly a matter of interest to anybody to look at Dartmoor, to see how the men were allowed outside. They might have been considering the chances of prisoners escaping and wondering whether it was wise to take a house in that part of the country they were visiting. They might have been looking for every sort of reason, the ordinary, normal curiosity, but this is the man who always writes the worst of everybody – man, woman or dog. Remember the phrases: 'Gloating. They get a kick out of such things. It is all part of having a good time. A dirty part without pity and without decency. A filthy peepshow that degrades and reduces convict and freeman alike into creatures in a human zoo ... [reading to end of article].' He gets all that out of the back of fifteen people who are looking over a wall. Is that not typical of the man who has to serve up his daily sensation, and is quite determined to do so?

You can probably remember, as I have already cited phrases from it, the violent and vicious attack upon Mr Richard Dimbleby. But, says my learned friend, and he produces a copy of the *Daily Mirror* some weeks, months or years afterwards, I am not sure which, when reporting the Coronation he gives Mr Dimbleby a pat on the back. Of course Mr Dimbleby had served his turn. He had been the victim, a daily victim, and when Cassandra had finished with him he had served his purposes and there was no need in months afterwards to repeat it. He had held him up to the ridicule of all reasonable people.

That I venture to submit is the spirit and the manner in which you have to look at this article.

I am taking it now on the basis that it does not have the homosexual connotation which we suggest, but just look at it. First of all you have to consider whether this series of adjectives – deadly, winking, sniggering, snuggling, chromium-plated, scent-impregnated, luminous, quivering, giggling, fruit-flavoured, mincing, ice-covered heap of mother love – is a statement of fact or whether it is comment. If it is a statement of fact it is not suggested that it can be justified, except for the phrase 'scent-impregnated'. If you describe a man in those terms I suggest you are describing what you have seen, which is purely a question of fact. If you see a man laugh and you described the man as laughing, you are stating a matter of fact; it is not a question of comment. Here you have words like 'snuggling', and I do not pretend to know what 'snuggling' means, 'quivering', 'mincing', all unpleasant adjectives, deliberately chosen by this brilliant writer with his command of language to hold my client up to ridicule, and all purporting to describe his actual appearance.

Amongst them you have the word 'fruit-flavoured'. I say at once that, when I put this American slang dictionary definition to Mr Connor in the witness box, I was not putting it forward as evidence that the meaning in this country of 'fruit-flavoured' is that he is a homosexual, because I am not suggesting that it is generally known in this country that the word 'fruit' has that connotation. It is American slang, and not English slang. But I did put it to him that in his journeys to the United States he, this master of language, must have learnt it had this meaning, and for that reason, knowing that it would be repeated in America and in order that America should have no doubt at all what he meant, he used the phrase. It is a very, very odd phrase, 'fruit-flavoured', is it not? I think the defendant admitted that he had never used it before and had never seen it used. You may have to approach, as I suggest you should, the use of that word with the very greatest suspicion in considering the honesty or dishonesty of the defendant.

Then you get the description of my client as an 'appalling' man, not in the general sense in which one uses the word 'appalling' but in the literal sense of the word, 'terrifying'. Do you think that can have been an honest description of my client? You remember how he tried to get out of it. He said my client collected crowds and he disliked the herd instinct. It was that, and in that point of view, that my client was described as terrifying. Do you believe that for one moment? All important people collect crowds. There are the comparisons. Sir Winston Churchill collects crowds; royalty collects crowds; other entertainers collect crowds; an entertainer whose name I constantly forget, Bill Haley, whose visit to this country was sponsored by the *Daily Mirror*, collected crowds, and, indeed, apparently riotous crowds. It is the very nature of popular persons to collect crowds. Do you believe that he is telling the truth that, when he described my client as terrifying in the literal sense of the word, all he meant was that my client's popularity resulted in the fact that he collected crowds, as everybody does who has any popular appeal at all?

Then my client 'reeks with emetic language'. What possible justification can there be for that phrase? All sorts of things which my client said to various reporters at various press conferences in the course of years and years have been raked up against him. What possible justification is there for saying he reeks of language which makes you sick, which is what he means? That is a phrase of which he is so proud that within four or five lines he repeats it again – twice. There is that horrible phrase about grown up men longing for a quiet corner and an aspidistra, a handkerchief and the old heave-ho, and also, 'Without doubt he is the biggest sentimental vomit of all time'. I cross-examined him about that, and he had never heard of anybody being called a 'vomit', a most shocking, disgusting and beastly thing to say of any man.

326

He looked back with joy at the early 18th century when the vicious pamphleteers of that time wrote, but even amongst them apparently he did not find anybody who described anybody else as a vomit.

Then, still further, there was this:

'Slobbering over his mother, winking at his brother, and counting the cash at every second...' What possible justification is there for writing 'counting the cash at every second'? Nobody suggests my client is any more commercial minded than any other entertainer. My client, as any other entertainer, believes in getting as much by way of salary or at the box office as he could. There is nothing to be said against my client in that respect, and yet there he is counting the cash at every second. This man cannot avoid putting the most offensive phrases in every sentence of this article.

Then he goes on and sets out the various answers which my client had made at Cherbourg. One of them is, 'I earn about a million dollars a year and could earn more if I tried harder; but I only manage to keep nine cents out of each dollar I earn'. That was put to my client, and he said he had no recollection of having said it. I am prepared to concede to you the probability is that he did say something to that effect in answer to reporters, but in what particular context we do not know. You have seen a number of reporters, and you may have, I suggest, the very gravest doubt with regard to their accuracy. So far as that phrase is concerned one reporter, the *Daily Telegraph* reporter, said he said it in one particular context dealing with the prices of the suits he wore; another said that he used it in quite a different context. That was Mr Reid who wrote under the name of Francis Martin, and you may think he probably was as malicious a critic as one could find, a gentleman who objected strongly to my client playing extracts from any classical piece on the basis that, whatever might be true in other matters, in music half a loaf is not better than no bread, and that anybody who purported to play for four or five minutes an extract from a sonata was in fact a menace to the whole of the art world. That is that particular gentleman.

Indeed, if we are going into accuracy, there was Mr Lambert of the *Daily Express*, who told you in chief that my client said that he gave them – that is middle aged ladies – the love that they did not get from their husbands and sons. Some of you may have thought it was a rather offensive thing for my client to have said that he gave them the love that they did not get from their husbands and sons. In cross-examination it turned out that that was utterly and completely untrue. There was not one word of truth in the suggestion that my client had mentioned husbands at all. That is the sort of accuracy we get from these journalistic witnesses.

There is another man. You may have been shocked at the story of Mr Sayle who went on an aeroplane with another journalist whose passport had expired, and whose supposed article appeared under the name of Roger Lawrie. That perhaps does not matter a very great deal, but the importance is that there appeared, in this article, words which were relied upon by the defendants in their defence and as to which an interrogatory had actually been put to my client: Did you not say to Roger Lawrie... 'I appeal to women exactly as Marilyn Monroe appeals to men'? It was put to my client in cross-examination 'Did you not say that to Roger Lawrie?' There is not a word of truth in that at all. What Mr Roger Lawrie, or Mr Sayle to whom the name of Roger Lawrie was given by the editor of the *Sunday Graphic*, wrote started at the fourth paragraph. From beginning to end there is not one single syllable of truth in the suggestion that my client used those words put in the Interrogatory and in cross-examination. That is rather typical, is it not, of the type of witness we get from the newspapers?

There was Mr Donald Zec, a representative of the *Daily Mirror*. I wonder what you thought of him, going to visit my client in his home, being greeted most courteously and agreeing that my client was a friendly host, leaving him on the most friendly terms, and then writing that mocking article which has been read to you. That is the sort of performance we get from the *Daily Mirror* representative.

Then there was the other *Daily Mirror* representative who so utterly deceived Mr Jimmy Thompson and who gave his word of honour that he would not use a manuscript which was required simply and solely for the defence of this case.

Then, leaving the statements my client made, there is this: 'Nobody since Aimee Semple McPherson has purveyed a bigger, richer and more varied slag heap of lilac-coloured hokum', which can be translated into 'falsity'. That is my client. I dealt with that earlier; I will not repeat myself.

I have dealt with the next paragraph too, about Chopin.

Then the next phrase comes at the end, 'such a sugary mountain of jingling claptrap wrapped up in such a preposterous clown'.

Shortly afterwards 'grimacing Messiah' was the phrase used by the defendants with regard to my client. We are not claiming damages in respect of that. It is in a different publication. It may throw some light upon the honesty of this man, in which he accuses my client of profanity, based, as he says in his evidence, on the fact that my client played *Ave Maria* with the background which has been depicted to you.

It is for you to come to a conclusion. I suggest that to both the questions which you have to decide in your mind, without the meaning which we say applies to the words in the box, your answer should be 'No'. To the question whether any reasonable man could have written them I suggest the answer is 'No'; and to the question, 'Was he honest in writing them?' I suggest quite clearly, for the many reasons which I have been putting before you, the answer is 'No'.

From 1935 onwards, when the tabloid revolution began and was carried into effect, they lived, in the words of Mr Hugh Cudlipp, dangerously. What do you think was meant by that expression, 'lived dangerously'? Ousting decorum and decency? Do you not think that I am right when I suggest that they meant they were taking risks in their sensationalism, risks which I suggest came home to roost when they were fined over £10,000 and the editor was sent to prison, not merely because they had commented upon a pending criminal case but because the view of the court was that in so doing they had pandered to sensationalism? Do you not think they were living dangerously when, owing to the caption which Cassandra designed for that offensive cartoon, they were warned by the Home Secretary they were liable or likely to be suspended? Do you not think they were living dangerously when they printed articles such as this, exposing them to heavy damages at the hands of a jury?

Looking at it as a whole, are you not satisfied that the writing of these vitriolic articles was part of the policy of the *Daily Mirror*? The reason why Cassandra's or Connor's salary grew and grew, until he became one of the highest paid columnists in Fleet Street, was because he wrote in accordance with that sensational policy and served out a daily sensation to the readers of the *Daily Mirror*.

I think that is all I need say to you on the issue of liability, except one thing. I am going to take a leaf out of my learned friend's book and cite to you a passage from the leading case of *Merivale v. Carson*. He read to you a passage from the judgment of Lord Esher, but in the Court of Appeal there are three lords justices. I want to read to you from the judgment of Lord Justice Bowen. It is a passage which you may think, and I suggest you ought to think, is most apposite to this case. I do not know whether it was a play or a novel, and it does not matter, but it was a criticism of a literary production.

What Lord Justice Bowen said was this: 'In the case of literary criticism it is not easy to conceive what would be outside that region, unless the writer went out of his way to make a personal attack on the character of the author of the work which he was criticising. In such a case the writer would be going beyond the limits of criticism altogether, and therefore beyond the limits of fair criticism. *Campbell v. Spottiswoode* was a case of that kind, and there the jury were asked whether the criticism was fair, and they were told that, if it attacked the private character of the author, it would be going beyond the limits of fair criticism'. I suggest that is most apposite to this case.

Now let me go to the question of damages. There are one or two things I want to tell you about that, but they are always subject to the fact that my lord will direct you on the law. In the first place you have to give one verdict on damages against both defendants and not separate damages against each of them, but you have to give separate damages in respect of the separate libels – the first one, the long article published on September 26, and the second the short accusation of profanity in the issue of October 18.

Secondly, it is right that I should tell you that there are two bases on which you can give damages. The first is compulsory, and the second is at your choice. In the first place, if you find that the defence is not made out, you are bound to award to my client such damages as you may think will compensate him for the damage to his reputation and the distress which it has caused him. In considering that you are entitled to take into account the conduct of the defendants from the very moment that the defamatory article was published up to the very last word uttered by my learned friend in this case.

One of the things you will consider at once, in my submission, is their extraordinary conduct in running after Mr Jimmy Thompson some eighteen months or two years ago, when he was known to be singing a song which imputed homosexuality to my client, got hold by trickery of the full and complete version of the song, and eventually call him as a witness here. Why should he be called? I can tell you in a sentence. The excuse for calling him is that my client had given evidence that at Sheffield he was called 'Queer' and 'Fairy'. The suggestion was that some of those who were in the gallery at Sheffield, and called 'Queer' and 'Fairy' from the gallery, might have come to London, visited the Apollo Theatre and heard that song. That is the excuse for calling him, but long before he was called I put to Mr Connor, 'Which do you think is more likely, that these people in the gallery at Sheffield were some of your thirteen million readers who had read this article or who had come up to London and been to the Apollo Theatre?', and he gave the only possible answer. 'It is much more likely that they were readers of the *Daily Mirror.*' Then why call Mr Thompson to say that he was singing a song imputing to my client that he was a homosexual?

Why the long and prolonged cross-examination of my client, whether he did not know the nature of the skit being performed at the Apollo Theatre? My client said he was told that it was vulgar and embarrassing. If you were a friend of Mr Liberace and had seen that skit, do you think you would go further than that? Would you not seek to dissuade him from going to the Apollo Theatre? In order to dissuade him from going, do you not think you would have said something to the effect that it was vulgar and embarrassing?

But why drag in Jimmy Thompson and his song? To try to create the atmosphere that he really was one? In spite of their denial here, to try to create an atmosphere that, really being one, he had not got the courage to bring an action against the management of the Apollo Theatre and the

330

producer? Is that the argument? What else is the idea of dragging in Jimmy Thompson and his offensive song than the suggestion that my client is a homosexual? I suggest you take that into very serious consideration when you are considering the conduct of the newspaper in dealing with this action.

Take another matter of their conduct. They rely on and put in the forefront of their defence, so much in the forefront of it that in relation to this matter it is repeated twice in their Particulars, the fact that my client made a jocular observation with regard to Princess Margaret, saying he would like to see her, that she is pretty and she is single. You may think that is a harmless jocular observation, but it was one about which, when he was tackled on it, he immediately apologised, saying that he certainly did not mean it to be in any way offensive.

What do you think of the honesty of that defence, members of the jury, when you see how they treated Princess Margaret and Her Majesty The Queen? A different newspaper it is true, but the same management – Mr Hugh Cudlipp. What do you think of the honesty of that? Do you think it would be possible to imagine a more dishonest defence set up by the *Daily Mirror* than to repeat it twice in their Particulars that he made this offensive observation with regard to Princess Margaret when they treat Princess Margaret and Her Majesty The Queen in the way that you know, and then to go in the witness box and say they would not be offensive or distasteful to Princess Margaret and this was not of interest to Her Majesty The Queen but only to us, the people of England? Those are matters which you have to consider when you consider the conduct of the defendants in relation to this action.

But apart from such compensatory damages you are also entitled to award punitive or exemplary damages if you think, and only if you think, that the defendants' conduct is such that it deserves to be punished, or if you think it is such that an example ought to be made of it so that other newspapers will not be tempted into pursuing the same path.

In this respect you may perhaps wonder why I do not suggest to you the sort of sum which I would like you to award. I can assure you, members of the jury, I would very much like to do so, but unfortunately I am prevented by a rule of practice which so far as I know has no legal justification whatever. It is this rule of practice which prevents me from so doing, and inasmuch as it does exist I am not going to be a pioneer in destroying it or seeking to destroy it. Indeed I do not suppose my lord would allow me to do so, even if I wanted to do so. But I hope I can give you ideas on the subject.

The fact that the plaintiff is presumably well off, from the gross income which he earns, after his expenses have been taken away and the tax collector has done his worst, is a matter which you are bound to disregard

331

in assessing damages. It can be used either in favour of the defendants or against them. It could be used against them by saying, 'Well, to compensate a man who has so much money you must give him an enormous sum'. That would be wrong. It could be used in their favour by saying, 'Well, money is not much use to him. You must not give him much'. That would be equally wrong. I think I am right in saying that in assessing damages the wealth of the plaintiff is something which you should disregard entirely, either in favour of or against the defence.

But, of course, in considering what would punish the defendants and in considering what it might be hoped would deter them from the course which they have pursued in butchering reputations you cannot disregard their financial position. Nor I suggest can you disregard the sort of sums which they have incurred in their 'dangerous living' and which are treated by their headman, Mr Cudlipp, as really of no account at all. Mr Cudlipp dealt in his book with the £10,000 fine for pandering to sensationalism and the three months' imprisonment. In effect he says it was well deserved.

Also it is worth considering that their circulation is 4½million. At 2d a copy, which was the price in 1956, they would get every day something in the nature of £37,000 gross. I do not suppose they would get the whole of that because they have to pay the costs of distribution, but if the costs of distribution were one third they would get about £25,000 for one issue, apart from the advertising revenue; and for the two issues which contained the two libels of which we complain they would have received something like £50,000. That again is the sort of matter which you may think it right to take into consideration.

You may also consider that converting it from a decorous paper into what it is has apparently so paid off that last December they increased their capital from £5 million to £9 million.

The wicked flourish mightily you may think, and if you are going to give to my client the sort of sum which will deter these people, or which it may be hoped will deter these people, from carrying on this sensational policy you may think it will have to be a very, very heavy one.

Mr Cudlipp wrote of Mr Connor that he did not grasp the danger of words. You may think it really is time that he was taught, and taught by a jury, to grasp the danger of words, and to be stopped from this incessant rudeness which apparently pays off, according to Mr Cudlipp, so well in the journalistic profession.

I put to him a phrase which he did not know. It was from the preface to *Adonais*, Shelley's preface to Adonais, which was written on the death of Keats, which was alleged in part to be due to the effect on him of an article of criticism in the *Quarterly Review*. It finished by saying; 'Nor shall it be your excuse that, murderer as you are, you have spoken daggers but used none'. Words can be daggers, and the defendant Connor knows how to use them as such.

I was invited by my learned friend to try to match the language of Cassandra in my final speech to you. I do not think I can do it. He has put me on my mettle, but I am afraid I cannot match him. But if this in any way resembles the language of Cassandra, might I suggest that this newspaper is vicious and violent, venomous and vindictive, salacious and sensational, and ruthless and remorseless? I do not think that is quite up to Cassandra's standard, but it is the best I can do.

[Laughter.]

I did not want to end on a note of laughter, but I suggest to you the words which I have used are really a proper description of this newspaper and its daily policy, and the only way in which it can be stopped is such an assessment of damages as will really make its directors think, when they come to deal with the balance sheet at the end of the year and what libel has cost them, and when they read what this libel has cost them, 'Well, we must trim our sails a bit. We have gone a bit too far. In future, if we cannot be decorous and gentlemanly as the paper was in 1935, at any rate we can speak a little more decorously and a little more gentlemanly than we have in the last few years.' If you members of the jury can bring about that second revolution in the policy of the *Daily Mirror*, a counter revolution perhaps it could be called, then in my submission you will have rendered a service to this country.

Summing up: Mr Justice Salmon

It is now our duty, yours and mine, to consider this case quietly, calmly and reasonably. During the course of what I am going to say to you I will explain the law as clearly and as briefly as I can. The law is entirely my responsibility. You must accept from me what I tell you about the law. The facts are entirely your responsibility.

Now it may be that during the course of the summing up I shall express some view about a fact, or you may think from what I say or the way I say it that I have formed some view about a fact. If your view happens to be the same as mine you will give effect to it, but if having listened to what I say your view about a fact is different from what you may think mine is, it would be quite wrong for you, and quite contrary to the traditions of an independent British jury to say, and I am sure you would not, 'The judge thinks so and so. He obviously must be right', because if your view about any fact is different from what you may think my view is then it is not only your right but it is your duty to give effect to your own view and not to what you may think mine is.

The second general observation I want to make to you, and this is most important, is that you must put out of your mind any prejudice which you may feel for or against any of the parties in this case. Feelings have run high, as you can see from the evidence you have heard and from what you have heard read to you about Mr Liberace, or at any rate they did in 1956. Feelings have admittedly run high about the Daily Mirror since 1935. You may be amongst Mr Liberace's greatest admirers, or you may not. You may applaud or deplore the manifestations of hysterical enthusiasm which his public appearances have engendered. You may greatly admire or detest the *Daily Mirror* and Cassandra. But any feelings which you may have either for or against any of the protagonists here must be put and I am sure you will put them, behind you; and you will decide this case on the evidence, without fear or favour, affection or ill-will.

Now, the first question you have to decide is a question of very great importance to the parties. It is this: Do the words complained of in the defendants' publication of September 26 1956 in their ordinary and natural meaning, mean that the plaintiff is a homosexual? According to the plaintiff he says that the words obviously mean just that, and if they did not he would not have been bringing this action. According to the defendants, they say the words obviously do not mean anything of the kind; and if they did they would not be defending the action because there would be no defence to it.

The test is not what the plaintiff thinks the words mean; nor what the defendants think the words mean; nor what anybody thinks the words mean, except you.

You have heard evidence from the plaintiff that when he went to Sheffield a few days after this article was published he was greeted with cries of 'Go home, queer', or words to that effect. You may accept or reject that evidence. He is the only person, I think, who has been called to say that they were spoken. You have heard a number of witnesses called, some of them quite disinterested, who did not hear those words, although they heard other interjections. But, of course, the words could have been spoken without any of the witnesses called by the defence hearing them. I gather there was a good deal of noise at the time, but what people thought in Sheffield, what anyone thought, is of no importance. The question for you on this part of the case, and the only question, is: what do these words in their ordinary and natural meaning mean to the ordinary man and woman? That is you.

The plaintiff has to satisfy you, if you are to answer this question in his favour, that the words mean that he is a homosexual, that is to say that he is a sexual pervert who indulges in homosexual practices with other men.

Now the test is not what some very suspicious or dirty minded man or woman might wring out of those words. Nor is the test what some

334

exceptionally innocent or unworldly person might think they mean. The test is what would you, reading them in the circumstances of this case, in their context, conclude they meant. What is their ordinary and natural meaning to you?

I do not think that I can really help you very much further on that particular question. I do not want to read these words to you all over again. You have heard them read in this case *ad nauseam*. The words occur in the article in this way. I think I had perhaps better read some of them. After Cassandra reports his experiences in Germany on the eve of the war and speaks about the drinks that he had, which apparently were called '*Windstarke Funf*', he says: 'I have to report that Mr Liberace, like *Windstarke Funf*, is about the most that man can take. But he is not a drink. He is Yearning-Windstrength Five. He is the summit of sex – the pinnacle of Masculine, Feminine and Neuter. Everything that He, She and It can ever want.' That is in the contents of the article. You will remember that in the box, which is the bit at the head of the article, the words are lifted: Cassandra says: 'He is the summit of sex - the pinnacle of Masculine, Feminine and Neuter. Everything that He, She and It can ever want.'

As I indicated you have to be satisfied that means that he is a homosexual pervert, that he indulges in homosexual practices. If all that it means is that he seems to have a tremendous attraction not only for women but also for men and possibly also for some homosexuals, that does not mean, does it, that he is a homosexual himself?

What is the fair meaning to attribute to those words? It is argued on behalf of the plaintiff that there can be no object in using the words 'Sex - masculine - feminine - neuter - he- she - it' unless they have the sinister meaning the plaintiff attributes to them. On the other hand, it is said on behalf of the defendants, 'Well, all that Cassandra was doing was to remark on the really phenomenal appeal this man seems to have for everyone.'

It is said: Well, sex is mentioned, too, in the publicity which at this time was being put out about Mr Liberace with his authority. His sexual appeal was very strongly underlined; he had, I think, twelve proposals of marriage every month. That is one of the things put out about him. Women and girls, apparently, fainted and screamed at his every public performance and they fought to touch the hem of his garment.

Again, it is said in the publicity which has been read to you he did not only make an appeal to women, but men were his fans also, and it is suggested to you, on behalf of the defendants, that read fairly this is, really, an observation on that remarkable fact. It was put to Cassandra – and I remind you that it does not really matter what Cassandra thought about it on this point, but it is very important later – Well, was it intended

335

as a compliment, would not this be a compliment? But, you see, if you read those words, the very way they are put together is obviously ironic and derisive. The point you have to consider is whether the real meaning was that the man was a homosexual, or whether the real meaning was that he had this astonishing universal appeal in which sex played a very considerable part.

One matter I ought to mention to you is this: I have told you already that in considering this question you have got to consider it in its context, that is to say, with the whole of the rest of the article, and you have heard a good deal about the word 'fruit' and 'fruit-flavoured'. Now, in considering what this article means you must put the word 'fruit' and 'fruit-flavoured' out of your mind in considering whether it means homosexual or not. We have in this country a rule that if a man brings a libel action, or brings any action, he has to put his claim down in writing in what is called a Statement of Claim. If he says the words, in their ordinary, natural sense mean so-and-so, so be it, he does not have to mention that because it is obvious from the words what they mean; but if he is alleging that the words have some special meaning, that there is some phrase that would be understood by people not in its ordinary natural sense but in some special context, then he has to say so. Now in this case Mr Liberace had the advantage of having his pleadings, his Statement of Claim, drawn up by one of the most able and experienced advocates at the Bar, and if when this Statement of Claim was drawn up it had been thought that there was any chance of persuading a British jury that the word 'fruit' was understood in this country as slang for a homosexual, you may conclude that it would have been in that Statement of Claim; but it is not there, and you have got to put that entirely out of your mind.

But you are, members of the jury, entitled to take all the other words in the article into account and look at the words in the box in that context, and it is for you to say, having done that, whether, in your opinion, read fairly in their ordinary, natural meaning, it means a homosexual. It has been said – and you may give this argument such weight as you think it is worth – that in this connection it is obvious that Mr Connor and the defendants, although they now say the words had no such meaning, must have thought that they had such a meaning because eighteen months or two years ago Mr Jimmy Thompson was canvassed and that extremely, you may think, salacious lyric was extracted from him. Mr Beyfus says: 'Well, if the defendants did not think it meant that why were they going after the lyric?', but I think I ought to remind you that the plaintiff has said that, although the allegation that the words mean that the man is a homosexual were never made formally, were never said formally, during the course of Interlocutory proceedings – and there are all sorts of proceedings before the case comes into court before what we call a Master

336

where Counsel appear – counsel for the plaintiff, at one of these Interlocutory proceedings, had said their case was that the words meant that the man was a homosexual, and the first Summons before the Master was on January 18 1957, which is a good deal longer than two years ago. So you may think the point is a formidable one about finding the lyric from Jimmy Thompson; on the other hand, you may think that the defendants may have been appraised by one of these remarks before the Master, sometime before two years ago and before they went for the lyric, what the plaintiff was going to say about it.

Anyway, as I told you, it does not really matter much what the plaintiff thinks of it or what the defendants think of it, it is what you think, as ordinary men and women, those words fairly mean. This is a very important point, and it is one which you must very carefully consider.

The next question, members of the jury, is this: without any homosexual meaning, are the words complained of true insofar as they consist of statements of fact, and fair comment insofar as they consist of expressions of opinion?

Looking at the first part of that question, it will be for you to say whether they are true insofar as they consist of statements of fact, and it will also be for you to say what is fact and what is comment. But may I, first of all, deal with what is admittedly fact. If you have the libel before you, there is a heading: 'Religion, Love, Money', and then the plaintiff's alleged sayings on religion, on Mother love, on world love and on money are set out in full. There is no real dispute by the plaintiff that he did say those things. There was some dispute at one time as to whether he had said that he kept only nine cents out of each dollar, but now Mr Beyfus has very rightly said he no longer contests that point; it would, indeed, be very remarkable – unless the tax laws of the United States are far more beneficent than ours – that out of an income of some £376,000 he should keep more than the not inconsiderable sum of £36,000 or £37,000. So there is no dispute about those facts.

The next fact stated is that: 'On the occasion in New York at a concert in Madison Square Garden when he had the greatest reception of his life and the critics slayed him mercilessly, Liberace said: 'The take was terrific but the critics killed me. My brother George cried all the way to the bank.' There is no dispute about that either. The only dispute, members of the jury, is on this paragraph immediately under the words, 'Not Since 1921', and those words, as you remember, say this: 'They all say that this deadly, winking, sniggering, snuggling, chromium-plated, scent-impregnated, luminous, quivering, giggling, fruit-flavoured, mincing, ice-covered heap of mother-love has had the biggest reception and impact on London since Charlie Chaplin arrived at the same station, Waterloo, on September 12 1921.'

Now the plaintiff says that is a statement of fact; the defendants say that is merely an expression of opinion, and it is for you to say what you think about that. Is it really a statement of fact, or is it merely giving rise – and whether it is a good opinion or not I will deal with in a moment – to an opinion and impression about the plaintiff? If it is the latter, then it is not a statement of fact. If 'scent-impregnated' is a fact, the defendant said he did use scented lotion and there is no argument about that; it may be a rude way of putting it, but as a fact it is true.

The first part of that question, therefore – 'without the meaning of homosexuality are the words complained of true insofar as they consist of statements of fact' – may not give you very much trouble.

But the second part of the question is: 'and are they fair comment insofar as they consist of expressions of opinion?' Now this question, members of the jury, raises a matter which is of very great importance, not only to the parties but everyone. It concerns what is somewhat misleadingly described as the defence of fair comment, and it is very important that you should understand, and I should clearly explain to you, the law on this topic, because our law on this topic is the very foundation of freedom of speech in this country. This is a vital freedom, for without it all freedom withers and dies. Freedom of speech is the freedom of everyone to state his honest opinion about any matter of general importance. This is not a right that is peculiar to newspapers and journalists; it is a right which is common to us all; we are all free to state fearlessly to anyone our real opinion, honestly held, upon any matter of public interest. We are free to state such opinions in any way we like, diffidently, decorously, politely and discreetly, or pungently, provocatively, rudely and even brutally. We may not, of course, tell a defamatory lie about anyone; that is to say, we must not make any untrue statement of fact about anyone which tends to lower his reputation in the mind of right-thinking people. But where we are stating an opinion it matters not that it is defamatory if it is our real opinion, honestly held, and is such that any fair-minded man might honestly hold.

Let me give you an example: Whether a man is a sexual pervert is a question of fact. If you state untruthfully that a man is a homosexual, it is no defence to say that you honestly believed what you stated. If, on the other hand, you said that a man's behaviour is nauseating, that is a matter of opinion. If you honestly believe what you state about a matter of public interest, however wrong your view may seem to the court, your statement is not actionable providing that your opinion is such that a fair-minded man could honestly hold it.

Here it is common ground the plaintiff's behaviour in public is a matter of general interest, and the primary question for you to determine on this part of the case is whether Mr Connor honestly held the opinions stated in the article complained of. The question is not whether you agree with the

338

comment, whether you think it is fair. Were this so, the limits of freedom of speech would be greatly curtailed. The enthusiast, the crank, the man with deep feelings, with strong and even prejudiced and obstinate views is just as much entitled to express his honest opinion as the meek and mild, the sweetly-reasonable man. It has truly been said that it would be a sad day for freedom of speech in this country if juries were to apply the test whether they agreed with a comment instead of the true test: Was this the defendant's honest opinion; would any fair-minded man, however prejudiced he might be, however exaggerated and obstinate his views, honestly have written this criticism of the plaintiff? The right which the law gives to anyone to state his honest opinion about matters of public interest, and the way that right has been upheld by British juries, is the foundation of freedom of speech in this country.

If you are satisfied that Mr Connor honestly believed what he wrote and that a fair-minded man could honestly have written what he wrote, your verdict should be for the defendants on this question, even if you thoroughly disagree with Mr Connor's views. In such circumstances you can say with Voltaire, 'I do not agree with a word you say, but I will defend to the death your right to say it'. If, on the other hand, you come to the conclusion that Mr Connor did not honestly believe what he wrote, that a fair-minded man could not honestly have written this article, then you will answer this question in favour of the plaintiff.

There has been a good deal of argument on one side and the other on this very important point. I have dealt with the law on the subject and you will take that from me; it is very important that you understand it, it is equally important that you apply it.

Now you have seen the defendant Cassandra in the box and you have read the article. The article is admittedly couched in very strong language, as you may think in violent language. It is said that no fair-minded man could honestly have expressed that criticism and that, certainly, Mr Connor did not hold that view, and that is the point you have to decide. The violence of the language and the circumstances in which it is written are matters from which you could say: 'Well, that points to someone not holding that view honestly; no-one could honestly think that'; but violence of language does not necessarily mean that the views expressed are not honest views, or views that could be held by fair-minded men.

I will deal, first of all, with the way the case is put for the plaintiff. Mr Beyfus says this newspaper is a sensational newspaper. It is concerned to increase its circulation. The defendant Cassandra wrote this article, not because he believed any of this about Mr Liberace, but merely because he was trying to write something sensational that would help to sell the paper. If that is right, the defence of fair comment cannot succeed, because it would follow, would it not, that he did not honestly believe what he said,

339

and if he did not honestly believe what he said, that is the end of fair comment. You have got to be satisfied of two things: that he honestly believed what he said, and that any fair-minded man could honestly have written this criticism.

The case for the plaintiff is that, having seen Mr Connor in the box, you ought to disbelieve him because on a large number of matters, specified by Mr Liberace's counsel, he was, it is suggested to you, lying – at any rate, was not being frank with the court. I think I ought to refer to those matters.

It was said, first of all, that he refused to admit that the *Daily Mirror* was a sensational newspaper and that the public and everybody else connected with it had agreed that it was a sensational newspaper – as they all have. You remember Mr Connor's evidence on this and you will give all the weight to that criticism of it which you think it can truly bear. His explanation – which you may or may not accept –was that he quarrelled with the word 'sensational'. He looks upon a sensational paper as one that publishes a sensation merely because it is a sensation in order to sell the paper. Mr Cudlipp, on the other hand, and, I think, Mr Bolam, regarded a sensational paper as a paper which did not publish something sensational because it was sensational, but which published important news in a sensational way to make an impression on the public. Well, it may be you may think Mr Connor was not being frank with the court; you may think that was an argument about the meaning of words, because he agrees that it did present important news in a sensational way, in a pungent and provocative fashion.

Then the next point taken is that he refused to admit that he was a vituperative writer, and he did, when he is. Whether you think the fact he would not admit it helps you in judging the value of his evidence is a matter entirely for you.

The next point taken was in relation to the article on poodles. I am sure we are all delighted to learn (as we did during the course of the evidence) that no writ for libel has yet been issued on behalf of any poodle! It is said that he was dishonest because when he was first asked about this article, although it had only been written a short time ago, he said he could not remember the phrase about poodles. Well, there are many things which could be said in defence of what seem to some people to be a very brave and rather sporting race of dog – and we are not all affected in the way that Mr Connor seems to suggest. But I do not know; does that lead you to believe from his answers to those questions that his evidence is not worthy of testimony? – Because that is the point that is for you.

Then there was the question – which I do not want to explore, but you will remember it – about the poll as to whether a certain Royal person should or should not marry, and he would not have it that that poll was distasteful.

Then a cartoon was put to him in the *Sunday Pictorial* which I suspect every one of you strongly deplored, and he would not admit that it was revolting. He said he would not have published it, but he would not admit that it was revolting, and it is said: 'Well, it is so obviously revolting that anyone who refuses to admit that in defence of a paper which is associated with the paper employing him obviously ought not to be believed. He would not have it that it was hateful and contemptible, and for the same reason it is suggested you must consider that he is not a frank witness.

Then he would not have it that the object of the article that he wrote about Mr Liberace was to depreciate Mr Liberace in the eyes of the public. If you remember – and this is, you may think, an important point – it was also put to him that the article obviously held Mr Liberace up to ridicule and contempt, and he would not have that at first, and it took Mr Beyfus, I think, a page to get him to admit that it was holding the plaintiff up to ridicule. He said that the object of the article was not to depreciate Mr Liberace in the eyes of the public but to express his dislike of the man, as he did not care fourpence what the public thought, in fact. You may think it would have been much better if Mr Connor had said, 'Quite obviously the article holds the man up to ridicule and contempt', but he did not and Mr Beyfus, very properly, takes that point against him.

Then he was asked whether he did not think the observation, 'My brother George cried all the way to the bank', was a jocular one, and he would not have that. What he said, you remember – and I am not quoting his exact words, but this is the effect of what he said – was I thought this was typical of the man: he did not mind all the criticisms about the error of taste, he did not mind the behaviour that was being criticised, so long as it could bring in money for him. That was his answer to that: 'I did not think it was jocular, I thought it was a revealing remark.' Well, you may think it may or may not have been a revealing remark, but you may have little doubt that it was a jocular one. But, of course, it may or may not have been revealing according to the view you take.

The next point was relating to the passage in the article complained of about Mr Liberace playing with the ghost of Chopin gibbering at every note, and Mr Connor admitted that he had never heard Mr Liberace play Chopin, or he could not remember it and it is suggested that, therefore, this criticism of his playing Chopin could not have been genuine, could not have been anything he believed. He says – and it is for you to consider it – that he had read everything he could lay his hands on that had been written about Liberace before he wrote the article, and it is conceded that the critics, at any rate the musical critics since 1952, had all, rightly or wrongly, been extremely condemnatory of Mr Liberace as a musician.

The next point that is taken is the article about Mr Dimbleby, and that was read to you to your considerable amusement. The first thing that is

341

said about that article is: Well, he could not really have believed that of Mr Dimbleby, nobody could. You can form your own opinion about that. But what was said also – and this may be an important point, it is for you to say – is that he would not admit that the article held Mr Dimbleby up to ridicule. You may think it obviously did, and you may think it would have been very much better for Mr Connor if he had not made any bones about it.

Then it is said that when he accuses – as he is said to have done – Mr Liberace of profanity, he is an agnostic and, insofar as he is an agnostic his accusation of profanity cannot be genuine. Well, members of the jury, that is a matter entirely for you. You may think it was not genuine, or you may think that even an agnostic might form the view that someone is a humbug and should not bring religious subjects on to television for a commercial television broadcasting programme.

Then you will have heard his writing about doctors. It was said: Well, that is a deplorable piece of writing. It shows he could not have believed it; it shows the sort of thing this man does in order to gain publicity for his paper. Well, you have got to apply your common sense and knowledge of the world to that problem. Mr Connor says: Well, I am very sorry I wrote it. It was stupid and wrong and I ought not to have written it. The plaintiff says: Well, you did write it, and that shows that, insofar as you could write an article of that sort, you are not to be believed on your oath; you could not genuinely have held the views that you now profess, or did profess, about Mr Liberace.

Then the next point was the picture, you will remember, and the article about those persons who were peering over the wall of Dartmoor at the prisoners – or were supposed to have been. When Mr Connor was first cross-examined about this, the information that had reached the plaintiffs, apparently, was that in the article Mr Connor had said that he was there himself and had seen it, and, of course, that would have been a grossly dishonest thing for him to say because he was not there. But, when the article was produced, as it was, the day afterwards, it was discovered that he never said anything of the sort, and that what happened was that he had been supplied, or the paper had been supplied, with a copy of a picture from one of their photographers in, I think, Plymouth and they had been informed that here were the people looking over the wall at the prisoners, and Mr Connor says: I believed that, and I think it is disgusting of people to intrude upon, and gloat upon, the misery of their fellow human beings. I do not know whether you think that is a possible view or whether you do not. Of course, they might have been interested in prison reform and the conditions of the prisoners. But supposing you were told that a lot of holiday-makers had got on to the wall overlooking the prison and were looking at the convicts, some of them with cameras, some with binoculars,

342

how would you have felt about it? Do you think that a man might feel considerable indignation about a matter of that sort? Mr Connor wrote an extremely indignant article about it, and you may or may not be surprised. We learn now that he was completely deceived by the photographer who sent in the picture because, far from these unfortunate people prying into the prison, they were invited by the photographer to get up to look over the wall while that photograph was taken. The photographer behaved quite disgracefully, but what is in question in this case is not the behaviour of that photographer, but the veracity of Mr Connor.

This is a matter entirely for you. You saw him in the box. It is for you to judge from your knowledge of human beings and to use your common sense, and to make up your mind whether you think he is speaking the truth. Bear in mind all these criticisms that have been made about his evidence; remember, if you think it is right, that he was in some passages very slow to admit that his articles held people up to ridicule or contempt and you may think that they obviously did. He denied it at first, and that may shake your whole confidence in his evidence, or it may not; it is for you to say.

What is suggested on behalf of the defendants, by Mr Gardiner, is that he may be a very difficult and vitriolic gentleman, but there is no sum of money that could persuade him to write what he does not believe and it would take an almost super-human to restrain him from writing about something in which he did believe. That is what the defendants suggest. You saw him and it is for you to say what you think about him, because this question of fair comment really depends almost exclusively on what you think of Mr Connor's honesty. Supposing you were not persuaded that Mr Connor honestly believed what he wrote about Mr Liberace – that is an end of the defence of fair comment; but if you think that Mr Connor did honestly believe it, you have still got to consider the other aspect of it: could a fair-minded man, however prejudiced or obstinate he might be, have honestly written this article about Mr Liberace?

It is a little important to remember that the article was being written, not about Mr Liberace's performances since 1956 let alone about his performances on television recently, and certainly not about his performances in this country. If the aspect of Mr Liberace which was being criticised was the aspect which you saw in this court, you may well think that no honest man could have written that article, no honest fair-minded man could have written that article. If an article of that kind had been written about, say, Mr Moiseiwitz the well-known pianist, you would obviously think it impossible that anyone could honestly believe that about him, it is impossible that an honest, fair-minded man could have written that about him. But this article was written about Mr Liberace's performances on television and about his public appearances prior to

September 26 1956, and what the defendants said – and it is for you to consider what strength you give to it – was that the aspect which he then presented to the public something wholly different from the aspect he presented to the jury in this court. If it had not been, can you imagine hysterical women fighting to touch the hem of his garment, or rushing up on to the stage to feel his knee and swooning and the like? The defendant says that he read everything there was to be read about Mr Liberace before he wrote the article, and in particular he read accounts of his reception at Waterloo, and he had seen photographs. Now, members of the jury, one of the photographs is that one which you have, no doubt, seen. Well, you may think it is a very pretty scene of a young man, a single man, very naturally responding to the advances of a young lady, or it may make you sick. But the question is: Do you think, because it makes you sick, it is possible it might have made any fair-minded man sick, and, more particularly, did it make Mr Connor sick?

You have seen the other pictures which were before Mr Connor of the crowds, and the woman fainting and being carried away, and the girl with 'Liberace' written on her sweater. Again the question is: Do you think that might make any ordinary man rather sick?

You have read the accounts – and this is not denied – of girls sobbing, screaming and fainting at Mr Liberace's appearances. I think they sobbed, and screamed and fainted at Waterloo or Southampton; standing all the way along the track to get a glimpse of him.

Then he read the stories in the press – which are not denied – about Mr Liberace – who has, no-one doubts, a deep and sincere love for his mother – having his mother brought up on to the stage and singing a song to her to the effect, 'I will always call you sweetheart' with the spotlight on her, and then he kisses her and his brother George kisses her. It is quite possible to take the view that that is a delightful domestic scene and that it is really doing good in this world. You have to consider whether a fair-minded man could honestly take the view that it was commercialising mother-love. That is what the defendant, Mr Connor, says he thought about it. He says there is obviously nothing wrong in mother-love, it is something sacred; but it is not something out of which you ought to try to make money, it is not something that ought to be exploited. Whether he is right or wrong in that, or whether he honestly took that view, is entirely a matter for you to say.

Then he referred also, I think, to a press conference of Mr Liberace's where he said – or Mr Connor wrote that he had said, and I do not think it is disputed that he did say it – that a girl, at his bidding, had left an iron lung, and that two cripples who had never walked before had walked because he asked them to, or told them to. Well, that is a very remarkable power to possess. Mr Liberace says he possessed it and that happened and

344

there is no reason at all to doubt him, but the question is whether an honest, fair-minded man might take the view that to try to get publicity out of that is revolting. Mr Connor says that is what he thought. The suggestion on the part of the plaintiff is that is absolute moonshine; there is no reason in the world why he should not have said what he had done, and no honest man could think there was.

Then Mr Connor said he read the article about what he regarded as the astonishing home of Mr Liberace, where everything, so it is said – certainly everything except the main structure and certain of the fittings – is shaped like a piano. He read how Mr Liberace had a piano on his ring, a piano motif on his tie, and all over the house, and so on. There is no reason at all why he should not, but Mr Connor says, in effect, that that sort of what he calls 'publicity mongering' is horrible. You may agree with him, or you may not; but is it a point of view which a reasonable man could take; does he honestly believe it. If he does, if he keeps within anything like the bounds, he is entitled to say so.

Then he talked about the rather exotic or glamorous clothes that Mr Liberace wears, not only on the stage and at television performances, but on occasions when he meets the public and the press. You will remember he arrived here, as he was perfectly entitled to do, in a silk tweed with a gold thread, and Mr Connor did not like it – so he says, of course, he may have admired it greatly. Then there are all the other clothes that he wears.

Then he refers also – you may think entirely wrongly and you may think without any foundation at all – to what he says is Mr Liberace's parade of religion. Mr Connor says he is an agnostic; he wishes he was not. He says that it makes him sick when he sees people parading and exploiting their religion in order to make money out of the ensuing publicity. You may think there is no sort of reason for any honest minded man to form that view, or you may not.

He had seen about four television performances and he had seen the report of the music critic in the *News Chronicle* on a performance which took place in his home at California when, apparently, Mr Liberace says, during the course of the performance, 'Mother and I are vurry, vurry happy there' and, according to the reporter, he said, after a smug twinkle: 'So is my little French poodle who lives with us. (Eyes slide sideways, face goes solemn). And there is Someone Else who dwells with us and to Whom I speak. (Lights dim. Liberace sings) *Bless this house.....*'

He said he had read the article, and he said he did not like it and he does not think it ought to be done. The question really is: Was that his honest view; would an honest man take that view?

I see it is now 4 o'clock and I cannot hope to finish this summing-up for, I think, half an hour or probably an hour because there are several matters with which I have to deal. If you were then to retire this evening you would all be tired and you could not, really, give your best attention to these questions I ventured to state, because it might take you a very long time to arrive at your decision. Therefore, I think it would be better if I break off now and we resume tomorrow morning when we are all feeling fresher.

When the court rose yesterday I was dealing with the matters which according to the defendants so aroused Mr Connor's indignation and disgust that he wrote the article complained of. There are very few matters with which I have not dealt already; I think there are only two.

You will remember that Mr Connor said that one of the things to which he strongly objected was that when Mr Liberace was playing the *Ave Maria* on commercial television, in what Mr Liberace describes as his glamorous clothes, there was a figure of a nun kneeling in what is said to have been the emotional agony of prayer, and also a statue of the Virgin Mary. Mr Connor says that, although he is an agnostic, he thought that was highly objectionable inasmuch as, according to him, it was another instance of the plaintiff exploiting what many people hold sacred, and for commercial purposes.

On the other hand Mr Liberace says that is sheer humbug because this man is an agnostic, and whoever else that might offend it could not offend an agnostic.

Well, that is a matter for you to decide. Mr Connor says it does not matter if you are a devout Protestant, Catholic or not; it does not matter if you have no belief at all. It is a matter which would offend anyone in all the circumstances, even an agnostic. The plaintiff says nonsense. That is a matter for you to decide.

The other matter concerned the broadcast by Mr Liberace at his home to Mr Edward Murrow, which was to be relayed all over America. In the course of that broadcast Mr Liberace did refer to a certain royal personage in the sense that might be understood, you may think, that he regarded her as a likely prospect for marriage. The case for the defendants is that that remark was in the worst possible taste, and aroused Mr Connor's indignation and disgust.

The way it is put is thus: anyone may inadvertently make an indiscreet and silly remark in private. I daresay we have all done it. But what is said is that Mr Liberace was well versed in the art of publicity, and there was no question of this having been said unguardedly in private. The way it is put by the defendants – it is for you to consider whether you think it is right or not – is this: They say, 'Well, Mr Liberace's home is furnished and decorated for publicity. Mr Murrow, who is one of the foremost commentators in the world, had come to his home to put the interview on the whole of the American network, or at any rate many of the stations'.

346

What the defendants say is that this reference was dragged in not by mistake but because it was recognised by Mr Liberace that the name of that person had a good deal of publicity value. It is another example, so the defendants say, of any means to get publicity, and through publicity to get money. As I say, you have got to consider not whether that view is right but whether Mr Connor genuinely believed it and whether any fair minded man could have taken that view.

The case for the plaintiff on that is that it is absolute nonsense. It was an innocent, jocular remark for which there was an apology. The defendants say the apology was also publicised. The plaintiff says it is quite insincere for the defendants to put this point forward because he says, 'Look at what they do themselves'. You remember they referred to the poll in respect of the desirability of this person's marriage. He says: 'Look at the *Sunday Pictorial* cartoon which is about as offensive and in about as bad taste as anyone could imagine. There could not have been the slightest excuse for publishing that. How could anyone really have taken offence and been disgusted at Mr Liberace's broadcast to Mr Murrow? How could Mr Connor have been disgusted by the broadcast if the *Daily Mirror* and the *Sunday Pictorial* have that sort of picture?' That is a powerful argument you may think, but it is for you to consider it.

Of course it is only fair to Mr Connor to say that what you are considering here is his honesty. You are not, in deciding this question, registering your disgust at some of the things the *Sunday Pictorial* may have done. He is not responsible for that. Nor is he responsible for the editorial policy of the *Daily Mirror*. If you accept the evidence it is quite plain that he is often in violent conflict with it. You have got to consider whether the article relied upon on behalf of the plaintiff really does reflect Mr Connor's state of mind at the material time, because on this part of the case that is what is of crucial importance.

When I was dealing with the plaintiff's case, the reasons which counsel advanced, the evidence which they relied on in their submission that Mr Connor did not honestly believe what he wrote, I think I omitted to deal with the evidence of Miss Ambler, upon which the plaintiff relies very strongly. I want to deal with it briefly now. Miss Ambler is a lady who was commissioned by a newspaper called *The People* to write about Mr Liberace's visit to this country in 1956. We have heard that she was with him for the greater part of every day. She went with him everywhere, even apparently to the theatre when he took an evening or a few hours off. That lady, after the writ had been issued, a few days after the writ had been issued and Mr Liberace had gone to Rome, went down to visit to Mr Connor in his home. She is a freelance journalist, and she was commissioned to write an article about Mr Connor and his cat. Whether the suggestion that the article be written came from her or came from the

Picture Post we do not know. The fact is that she went down a few days after the writ was issued and interviewed Mr Connor, and according to her evidence, by pure coincidence, Mr Connor raised the question of this action which Mr Liberace was bringing against him and the *Daily Mirror.* The lady spent most of every day for about a fortnight with Mr Liberace. The writ had been issued, and down she goes to see Mr Connor, and by pure coincidence the Liberace case is mentioned. Well, you have seen the lady. You may believe that, or you may think it puts a strain on your credulity which it is wholly unable to bear.

The defendants say that the lady went down as a spy, to see if she could be of some use to Mr Liberace in the case which he was bringing against the defendants. I do not know what view you will take about that, but I want to warn you of this. Even if you came to the conclusion that she was a spy, and it perhaps is not a particularly attractive role, it may not lend any great credibility to her evidence, but it would by no means necessarily follow that because she was a spy she was not speaking the truth. Sometimes spies bring back false or embroidered stories to suit their masters, but sometimes spies bring back the truth. It does not follow by any means that merely because she was a spy, if you think she was, she must have been wrong.

There was a very great conflict of evidence between her and Mr Connor as to what was said when she went there. You will remember she said in effect that the defendants appreciated that it was a libel when they wrote it, that they thought it would be worth it for a week's publicity, that they knew there was no defence to the case, and that the real trouble was the words 'He, She or It'. If you believe that what she told you is true and accurate about that conversation it is a very strong point, you may think, in favour of the plaintiff, because you heard the evidence not only of Mr Connor but of Mrs Connor.

Probably, and it is entirely a matter for you, you took the view that Mrs Connor was a transparently honest woman, but of course she does not carry the case much further, because it is not suggested that this conversation took place in her presence. By a happy or unhappy coincidence it is said to have occurred when no one was there except Mr Connor and the lady herself. The defendants say it is a palpably unlikely story. Mr Connor admits having said in a jocular way, 'It will be interesting to see who is the bigger buffoon in the box', but no one has suggested that Mr Connor is other than an extremely intelligent man, and it is highly unlikely that within a few days of the writ being issued he would be saying to a perfect stranger, 'There is no defence to this. We know it was a libel. He will take a great deal of money from us.' Both the plaintiff and Mr Connor are very intelligent men. The defence is that it is very unlikely he would have said it, and he denies it, except as to the jocular remark which according to the defence anyone might have made.

There is one other matter. This lady was asked about a book she had written, called *The Elusive Husband*, and at first she could not remember anything about having written a book of that kind. Then she was told, 'Well, was not the publisher of the book prosecuted and fined for publishing that as an obscene book?' She said, in effect, 'I do not know anything about that'. Then Mr Gardiner made it known to her that he had a statement which she had made to the press about this, and as soon as that became apparent to the lady she said, 'Oh, yes, I remember now'. You saw her. The fact, of course, that she wrote an obscene book is of no importance as far as this case is concerned, but what may be important, if you think that she did, is that she told a lie about it when she said she could not remember, until she was reminded of the statement.

I want to warn you about this, because it is only fair. Even if you thought that she lied about that matter, again it might not commend her to you as a witness but it would not necessarily follow that because she was lying about that she was lying to you about the other matters about which she told you. You have got to weigh up her evidence. You saw her in the box, and you saw Mr Connor. You have got to decide who is the more credible witness. We know that she made a note of the conversation, I think within an hour or two of it having taken place. On the matter whether she went and spied, perhaps that may be – I do not know what you think about it – of some value. If she did go as a spy you might expect her to make an immediate note. Whether you think the note helps you in deciding whether she or Mr Connor is telling you the truth about that interview I do not know.

Of course, if what she says is accurate and truthful, it is a very big point in the plaintiff's favour. Of course, if you do not give any credence to her evidence or if you think she would not have been above giving it a certain twist in favour of the plaintiff, and what she told you is not very reliable, you may regard it differently.

So, you have to consider this second question, this very important second question of fair comment. The language of the article you may think is violent, indeed very violent, but in matters where feelings run high the violence of the language does not necessarily exceed fair comment. Indeed, where feelings run high, it has been said that matters of fair comment should be liberally construed by a jury.

Therefore, in deciding this question, there are two factors about which you have got to think. Let me remind you of them. Did Mr Connor honestly hold the view that he expressed in the article? His case is that he did. The plaintiff's case is that he felt nothing of the kind, that the article

349

was written merely as a sensational article to boost sales. You have got to decide, having heard the evidence, what you believe.

The second factor in deciding this question of fair comment is this. Could a fair minded man have had his indignation and disgust so roused by the public appearances and performances of Mr Liberace before September 25 1956 that he could have written such an article as Mr Connor wrote?

If you come to a conclusion against Mr Connor on either of those questions, the defence of fair comment fails and you would answer the second question 'No'. If you came to a conclusion on both those matters, and it must be both of them, in favour of Mr Connor, you would answer the second question 'Yes'.

Before I leave the issue of liability there is only one other thing I want to say to you, and it is this. You remember the first question which you are going to answer, whether the words in their ordinary and natural meaning mean that the plaintiff is a homosexual. When you come to consider that you must consider the first question entirely independently of the second. Let me tell you what I mean. Even if you thought Mr Connor believed every word that he wrote and that any ordinary fair minded man might in the circumstances of this case well have taken the same view and written the same article, even if you felt that strongly, nevertheless if in your opinion the words mean that Mr Liberace is a homosexual, then it would be your duty to say so because whatever views you may take on the second question they have got absolutely nothing to do with the first question. It turns merely upon what is the meaning that the ordinary man and woman, reading those words, would attach to them. Would they say, 'Well, this means that Mr Liberace indulges in homosexual practices'?

But when you are considering the second question of fair comment, if you were to answer the first question against the defendants, that is to say, if you thought that the words meant that Mr Liberace was a homosexual, and Mr Connor believed it and knew it when he wrote it, that would have, or might have, a very powerful effect upon the view you take about the matters concerned in the second question.

I want to come to damages in respect of the article of September 26 1956, but it is only if you come to a conclusion in favour of the plaintiff on one or other or both of the first two questions that any matter for damages arises in respect of this article. If you were against Mr Liberace on both the first two questions, then you would not in any way be concerned with the third question.

I want to say a word about damages, which arise only if you are in Mr Liberace's favour on one or other or both the first two questions. Mr Beyfus has told you that he cannot mention any sum for damages to you. Well, members of the jury nor can I. And I am not going to try. I am sure

350

that, if I did, I could not make such a successful attempt as Mr Beyfus did! First of all this question, and you appreciate the basis on which I am addressing you now is that you answer one or both the first two questions in favour of Mr Liberace, would depend, would it not, on whether you thought the words meant that he was a homosexual because, if you answer that question in his favour, I imagine that the damages which you award him would be much greater under that head than the damages in respect of the rest of the article. All I can tell you about damages is this. If a man is libelled he is entitled to some fair compensation from the jury for the libel. You have got to give him a sum which will show to the world that there is absolutely nothing in it. The defendants have said that of course, as far as the alleged imputation of homosexuality is concerned, it is rubbish; they did not intend it, never have, and do not for one moment suggest that it is true.

If you come to consider damages you must not be niggardly – on the other hand you must not be extravagant. You have got to give this man, if you find in his favour, a sum which in your good judgment is fair and reasonable.

The plaintiff says that this article caused him the greatest pain and shock, and that, more especially, it upset him because it made his mother so ill that she nearly died, and, indeed, ever since the article has been published and as a result of its publication the lady has been ill.

You cannot give Mr Liberace any money because his mother is not well. The position in this respect you may think is somewhat curious. This gentleman, as I say, tells you that what really is affecting him almost more than anything about the article is the great injury to his mother's health, the fact that it nearly killed her. Apparently the article was shown to the lady on September 26, the day on which it was published, and she was immediately struck down by illness as a result, and a physician was called. That is what you are told, and it is fair to say that there is not any evidence the other way.

But on October 1st, about a week later, one of the *Daily Mirror* reporters, who has been called before you, Mr Doncaster, wrote a letter to Mr Liberace's manager, upon which Mr Liberace was consulted, in those terms:

> You may recall that I spoke to you last week and again today on the telephone about fixing a picture feature on Mr Liberace visiting a London pub. I also wrote a letter to Mr Liberace some weeks ago suggesting this feature for the Mirror after talking with him about a London pub when I was in Hollywood. Some other newspapers, I fear, have a similar idea and I am therefore anxious to try to keep this exclusively to the Mirror - with your kind co-operation - because we have been planning this with some eagerness...

And Mr Liberace went with the *Mirror*. This is the paper which according to him he believed had accused him of being a homosexual and had struck his mother almost a death blow only a week before. I do not know what you think about it.

He gives two excuses. He says, 'Well, I promised to do this visit to the London public houses when I was in Hollywood, and I also find that people, although they may not like me at first, get to like me when they know me better.' Ask yourself the question, if anyone had written something which you believed meant that you were a homosexual, and it had so upset your mother that she nearly died, would you within a week accept an invitation of this sort? Would you say, 'I said I would, in Hollywood', or would you say to them... well, perhaps it is not for me to forecast what you might have said to them in those circumstances.

The defendants say the excuse is nonsense. This is important on a question of damages, if the question ever arises, because the real reason for his going is to be found, so they say, in another paragraph in this letter, which reads thus:

> I can assure you that, if it is exclusive to us, it will be given the utmost prominence and display in the *Daily Mirror* – the paper with the greatest daily sale on earth.

They say, and it is for you to consider it, that such is Mr Liberace's thirst for publicity that that is the thing which did the trick, and that he went because he wanted the publicity. Whatever his thirst for publicity is, say the defendants for your consideration, he cannot have been so terribly upset by that article as he would now have you believe, because, if he was, how on earth could he have gone? Well, there it is. It is a matter for you to consider.

When and if it comes to a question of damages, you give him what in all the circumstances of the case you think would be fair to compensate him for this libel, if you think it is a libel, if you answer one or other of the first two questions in his favour.

But Mr Beyfus has said that one of the elements that you are entitled to consider in assessing these damages is the conduct of the defendants towards the plaintiff from the moment they published the libel right up to the moment that you give your verdict and he is absolutely right. If you think that this is a case for damages, if you answer either of the first two questions in favour of the plaintiff, you would be entitled, if you thought right, in your award for damages to include the element of what is called 'punitive damages', if you thought their conduct towards this man merited such an award.

I think I ought to warn you about what you are not entitled to take into account. A good deal has been said about that revolting cartoon in the *Sunday Pictorial,* which you may think reflects very little credit, or indeed, great discredit, on those who published it. A great deal has been said about the other troubles into which the *Daily Mirror* has apparently fallen, wholly unconnected with Mr Liberace. What you are not entitled to do in considering damages is to say, 'We want to teach these people that they must not publish the sort of thing that is in the *Sunday Pictorial*, and we want to express our disapproval of what they have done on other occasions. We are going to soak them for that reason'. That would be wholly wrong. It has got nothing to do with this case; and it would be most improper if you were to take any matter of that sort into account. For one thing the *Sunday Pictorial* is different from the *Daily Mirror*, although of course there is a close financial connection and there is one man responsible I think for the editorial policy of both papers, but that has got nothing to do with it. Even if that cartoon had been published in the *Daily Mirror*, which I hope it never would have been, it cannot have anything to do with the question of damages in this case.

All you have got to consider is how they behaved towards Mr Liberace.

One of the matters you are entitled to take into account, as has been referred to by Mr Beyfus, is this.

You take it into account if you consider damages, and if it commends itself to you. That relates to what we have heard in this case about the lyric sung in a revue by a certain Mr James Thompson. That lyric made the clearest imputation of homosexuality against Mr Liberace. There cannot be any doubt, can there, about that? I am not going to read that to you again, but you will probably say to yourselves, 'Well, no ordinary man or woman could read that without saying at once that of course this says what the plaintiff says it says'; and, indeed, it is not denied by the defendants. Indeed, it is put forward by the defendants as a lyric which does make that imputation. The only way in which it could conceivably be relevant to the case for the defendants is on damages. If you think that the words complained of in the article mean that Mr Liberace is a homosexual, then the defendants could rely on that lyric, for what it is worth, and say you ought not to give him so much damages as you would otherwise have done because literally thousands and thousands of people have heard the same thing in the theatre and on television.

What relevance you think that has and what weight you think that has, if you came to consider damages, is a matter for you, but Mr Beyfus says, and it is for you to consider it, that is not the real reason why it was produced at all. He says in effect that this is trying to justify by the back door; they have not the courage to say that this man is a homosexual; but this is dragged in for the purpose of conveying that impression to the jury. The defendants say that is absolute nonsense, and, 'We merely use it in mitigation of damages should that issue arise'. It is for you to consider which of those two views you accept. If you thought Mr Beyfus's contention was correct on that point then that would be a matter which, if you thought right, you might consider merited punitive damages. That is the only way in which I suggest to you on this question of damages the lyric should be considered. It either mitigates damages, if it is used genuinely for that purpose, and if so, well, you will give it such weight as you think right, or it aggravates damages because it was not used genuinely for that purpose.

Therefore in considering this question of damages, if you do come to consider it, you will, as I say, give something which on your view of the case in all the circumstances is fair and reasonable; and it would be of great help, if you answered both the first questions in favour of the plaintiff, if you say how much of the damages you award are attributable to the imputation of homosexuality. That only arises if you answer both the first two questions in favour of the plaintiff.

All I can say on this is what I said at the beginning. This is a case in which feelings may well run high one way or the other. In considering the questions before you, you have got to free your minds of prejudice one way or the other. It may not be easy but I am sure you will do it, as juries always do.

Before I pass to the second libel or the second defamatory publication I only want to say this. You have heard Mr Beyfus pay a very just tribute to the extremely able way in which Mr Gardiner has conducted this case on behalf of the defence. I would like to say to you, members of the jury, that you and I have been privileged to hear an outstanding, forceful and brilliant example of advocacy from Mr Beyfus who is a master of the art and, indeed, one of the outstanding advocates of our time. If it is not impertinent for me to say so, his performance is characterised by his usual extreme fairness.

Now let us look together at this second article about which we have heard hardly anything at all. You may think that is not surprising because it is comparatively of very little importance, but you have got to decide it, and I have got to say something to you, and I ought to say something to you, very briefly about it.

In their issue of October 18 1956, in Cassandra's column, these words appear under the heading of 'What's On':

> 'In their daily programme of events called 'Today's Arrangements' *The Times* was yesterday at its impassive, unsmiling best. It said: 'St Vedast's, Poster Lane, Canon C B Mortlock, 12.30. St Paul's, Covent Garden, The Rev Vincent Howson, 1.15. St. Botolph's, Bishopsgate, Preb H H Treacher, 1.15. All Souls', Langham Place, Mr H M Colling, 12.30. Albert Hall, Liberace, 7.30.' Rarely has the sacred been so well marshalled alongside the profane.'

Well, I do not know what you think about that, members of the jury, it is certainly you may think somewhat incongruous – and I daresay Mr

Liberace would be the first to admit it, because he does not pretend to be sacred – to see an announcement of one of your concerts in that company, just as it would be somewhat incongruous to see the announcement of a religious performance in a theatre guide. The comment on that is, 'Rarely has the sacred been so well marshalled alongside the profane'. You will not have to worry whether that is defamatory, because it is admitted to be so.

Of course, when you talk about sacred and profane music, that is not a reflection on the profane music; and, as far as I know, when you talk about sacred and profane love, that is not a reflection on profane love.

The question here is, again, is this an opinion which Mr Connor honestly held when he wrote it; and is this the sort of thing that a fair minded man might honestly have written about an announcement of this kind?

I do not really think this merits me saying anything more to you about it than I just have. I have put to you the question about it, which is Question 4. If you thought it was not fair comment, then you would say just how much damages you think it merits.

You have listened extremely patiently to this case over many days; and it is now your task to arrive at your decision. Will you kindly consider your verdict?

The jury filed out at 11.25am and people in the well of the court took the opportunity to stretch their legs or, in some cases, to find a friendly nearby drinking-place. The *Mirror* team was fairly buoyant. Beyfus had been quite brilliant, as the judge had suggested, in his summing up, but they still didn't think he had proved his case. The 'He, She and It' words in the box did not say that Liberace was a fairy, and everything else in the Cassandra column had been substantiated or, to anybody who had seen his act, was surely fair comment.

And Beyfus, for all his expertise, had been so preoccupied with that single quote that he'd missed a big one. Cassandra had written:

> I spoke to sad but kindly men on this newspaper who have met every celebrity arriving from the United States for the past thirty years.
>
> They all say that this deadly, winking, sniggering, snuggling, chromium plated, scent-impregnated, luminous, quivering, giggling, fruit-flavoured, mincing, ice-covered heap of mother-love…

Beyfus had even made a sarcastic aside, *sotto voce*, possibly not even intended to be heard by the jury, doubting whether the *Mirror* actually employed any 'kindly' men. So, if he was so god-damned brilliant, why hadn't he asked Cassandra who these people were, and which of them had offered him each particular adjective? The columnist wouldn't have had a leg to stand on.

No: the Old Fox was losing his cunning. He was past his sell-by date. What was that nonsense with Pat Doncaster about, 'What is your real name?... I thought you were called Johnson...'

If there was any justice... But the long established retort of experienced silks was that justice was not necessarily the same as verdicts.

The judge also thought that the *Mirror* team would most probably emerge as victors in the jury room. That was part of the reason he had been so enthusiastic in his praise for Beyfus; as a young barrister he had been his junior. Now Mr Justice Salmon suspected this would be the Old Fox's last case and thought he should pay him an appropriate final tribute. If he was going to lose, the judge didn't want him to think it was on account of his age or his ill health, or that he had been anything less than his usual magnificent self in pleading his client's case.

But Beyfus was feeling supremely confident. He had again noticed the sympathetic woman juror. It was the seventh day and she had appeared again in a change of clothes. He believed that no English jury would side with a team that attacked the Queen and her sister, the church, the government, family doctors and popular icons like Richard Dimbleby and Wilfred Pickles. And Liberace fans. And dogs; even if there were cat lovers among the jury, Connor himself had made it clear that his own cat didn't think much of him. Beyfus needed one sympathetic juror on his side and he was fairly certain he had that.

A court reporter approached him in the corridor by the door of the court and congratulated him on the judge's remarks. Beyfus enjoyed a good working relationship with the regular members of the press bench who referred to him as 'Gillie', just as they knew his junior Helenus Milmo as 'Buster', said to date back to his success as an MI5 interrogator during the war. Beyfus often made their job easier by delivering them the telling phrase that would make headlines the following day, and he would peer over his glasses at them to ensure they'd got it. When he was incarcerated in a TB sanatorium the first person who telephoned to enquire after his health – by which time he'd been in five weeks – had been a court reporter.

'Was that your valediction, Gil?' the reporter asked, referring to the judge's personal praise. 'Are you going to quit, now?'

'Only if I'm knocked over by a bus as I leave the court,' said a beaming Beyfus.

The jury were out for three hours and twenty-five minutes. They were all in their seats before the judge was back on the bench and the lawyers at the front of the court looked to see whether they could deduce the verdict from the expressions on the jurors' faces. It wasn't necessary. The woman juror who had been transfixed by the plaintiff throughout the trial now looked at him, nodded, winked broadly, and silently mouthed the words, 'It's all right'. The message quickly went round the court – 'He's won.' Liberace, in grey suit and grey silk tie, mopped his brow with a monogrammed handkerchief and smiled his famous smile (with the dimple).

Nevertheless, the questions had to be put.

They had answered all the questions and were agreed on their answers, said the foreman.

Question 1: Do the words complained of in the defendants' publication of September 26 1956 in their ordinary and natural meaning, mean that the plaintiff is a homosexual? Answer – Yes.

Question 2: Without this meaning, are the words complained of (a) true in so far as they consist of statements of fact? – No.

And (b) fair comment in so far as they consist of expressions of opinion? –No.

Question 3: Damages (if any) for the publication of September 26 1956? – £8,000.

The jury had assessed the damages as £2,000 for saying Liberace was homosexual and £6,000 for publishing comment they did not think was fair. They found the plaintiff's case against the publication of October 18 – *'Rarely has the sacred been so well marshalled alongside the profane'* – to be 'not proved'; in other words they considered it was fair comment and awarded no damages.

To the lawyers in the case and to the headline writers, £8,000 represented the highest award for libel ever made in an English court.

In his attempt to explain the wealth of the *Daily Mirror* to the jury, and thereby to give a broad hint as to what sort of amount might be sufficient to make them think twice about uttering any future libel, Beyfus had been somewhat wayward in his calculation. The economics of the newspaper in the 1950s were basically that they received one-third (not, as he suggested, two-thirds) of the cover price after the wholesalers and retailers had subtracted their share; in other words, at 2d a copy (at the time the offending article was published) on 4.5million sales their net income was in the region of £12,500 a day from circulation; advertising would lift that figure by approximately 50 per cent (in most other newspapers, with far lower sales, the circulation-advertising ratio would have been roughly reversed). By the date of the trial the cover price had increased to 2½d – a 25 per cent hike in the days before 'inflation' was part of the vocabulary of everyday life, but a halfpenny was the smallest coin in circulation. A huge proportion of all newspapers was home-delivered in the 1950s, therefore £8,000 was an amount that would be covered by the defendants before breakfast the following day.

It may also have been peanuts to the entertainer, who could earn more than twice that amount in one night's sell-out performance, and whose earnings that year, one commentator calculated, would have paid for the entire judicial bench of England. But in 1959 the maximum win on the Premium Bonds (introduced in 1957) was £1,000 – in 2009 it was £1,000,000; a top Fleet Street journalist could have been earning £1,000 a year in 1959 (although, fairly obviously, Cassandra would have been earning considerably more than that). Gilbert Beyfus picked up £2,415 in total of fee and daily 'refreshers' for handling the trial; it was the highest pay-rate of his life and fifty years later it would have cost 40 or 50 times more to hire a QC of his calibre. The average price for a house in the UK was about £2,000.

Beyfus formally asked for judgment for £8,000 with costs, but Gardiner said he had a submission he wished to make first, and as it was a question of law the jury need not be detained.

The judge said that, before he heard anything more he had something he wanted to say: 'I think counsel ought to know that during the course of this case I received a number of anonymous letters. All except one appear to have been written by lunatics, and they have gone straight into the wastepaper basket. The letter I referred to arrived this morning. It is a sinister and wicked attempt to pervert the course of justice. I need hardly say that it has had absolutely no effect on me, except to fill me with disgust at the conduct of the writer. I intend to send this letter to the Director of Public Prosecutions, for his consideration.' He did not explain what he was talking about.

He told the jury there were more arguments he needed to hear; they could leave if they wished to. But having endured, or enjoyed, the case this far, they wanted to stay to the bitter end.

GARDINER: At the conclusion of the plaintiff's case I submitted to your lordship that the words in the box were not capable in their natural and ordinary sense of the meaning which the plaintiff placed upon them. I agreed that it would be convenient, as the jury were here, that their verdict should be taken, but the question whether words are capable of a particular meaning is a question of law.

It would appear that there are four conceivable meanings of these words, and when I say 'conceivable', I mean in its literal sense, which people have conceived.

There is, firstly, the meaning ascribed to them by the plaintiff, that the words mean that he is a homosexual pervert.

358

There is, secondly, the meaning ascribed to them by the defendants, namely, that he is an artiste who uses to a considerable degree sex appeal, and that his appeal, as is well known, is of a universal character, he having achieved his fame on television which is a medium where success depends on his appeal to the whole family, father, mother and child sitting at home around the television set.

A third possible view is one which I have adumbrated to the jury, and that is that it is one of those sentences which sound very well but really, when you come to analyse it, means very little.

A fourth might be that he is a man who attracts all kinds of people to him, to his performances, but that does not mean that he is himself a homosexual pervert. A good example perhaps is what Mr Cudlipp wrote in that book about Mr Connor when he said this:

> According to subject and the state of his liver, he can make his column purr or bark, nuzzle or bite, canter or gallop, soothe or repel. And, a rare gift, his words appeal alike to men and women, young and old, intellectuals and ignoramuses, priests and atheists, judges and old lags, heterosexuals, homosexuals and hermaphrodites

…a statement which plainly no one could read as meaning that Mr Connor was a homosexual.

Your lordship will not want authority for the proposition first stated in *Capital and Counties Bank v. Henty,* and ever since repeated, that if there are several meanings no one is entitled to pick out the worst one.

Your lordship will bear in mind that in most cases the argument is whether the words are capable of bearing an innuendo. Of course, it has been my submission throughout this case that what the plaintiff has really sought to do is to have all the advantages of innuendo without the disadvantages. Ever since *Watson v. Hall* a claim in libel for innuendo has to be regarded on two counts – firstly, the words in their natural and ordinary meaning, and, secondly, with the innuendo; and therefore, not infrequently, the court has had to consider, in considering whether the words complained of are capable of bearing the innuendo alleged, whether or not they were capable of being defamatory in their natural and ordinary meaning.

The authorities are summarised in this case in *Gatley* at page 126.

> In determining whether the words are capable of a defamatory meaning the judge will construe the words according to the fair and natural meaning which would be given them by reasonable persons of ordinary intelligence, and will not consider what persons setting themselves to work to deduce some unusual meaning might succeed in extracting from them. That clearly is not the test.
>
> 'The test according to the authorities,' said Lord Selborne (and this is in the *Capital and Counties Bank v. Henty*) 'is whether, under the circumstances in which the writing was published, reasonable men to

whom the publication was made would be likely to understand it in a libellous sense.' The law is perfectly well settled. Before a question of slander or libel is submitted to a jury, the court must be satisfied that the words complained of are capable of the defamatory meaning ascribed to them. That is a matter of law for the court. If they are so, and also of a harmless meaning, it is a question of fact for a jury what meaning they did convey in the particular case.

In applying this test 'the judge ought not to take into account any mere conjectures which a person reading the document might possibly (though unreasonably) form. He should 'consider what might be conveyed by the letter to a reasonable fair-minded man, and not what might be inferred from it by a man with a morbid or suspicious mind.

'The question is, has the plaintiff satisfied the onus of proof, as well as of allegation, that the words used would convey to reasonable minds of fair men who read them the meaning he seeks to have put upon them?

'The proposition has been established now upon authority which it is difficult to question... that it is not enough to say that by some person or another the 'words *might* be understood in a defamatory sense'. It is unreasonable that, where there are a number of good interpretations, the only bad one should be seized upon to give a defamatory sense to the document'. If, then, a defamatory inference *might* be drawn from the words complained of, but there are other inferences of an innocent character which naturally suggest themselves to the mind of any reader of average intelligence who is not induced to put a malignant construction on the words, the judge ought to withdraw the case from the jury unless the plaintiff has proved that there are extrinsic circumstances which would reasonably lead those to whom the words were published to draw the defamatory inference.'

The words here complained of are ordinary English words. There is nothing whatever to convey or to suggest homosexuality at all; and it is of course of the essence of the plaintiff's case not that there was here some hidden meaning, not that there was here some phrase which night be read by some people in a peculiar sense, but that this was the ordinary and natural meaning of the words. I find myself in some difficulty through an inability really to understand out of what words this meaning can come. Your lordship will remember that the plaintiff himself relied on one word, and by his counsel he relied on another.

There have been many cases in which, and I am not saying this with reference to anything in this case, on a submission to the court that the words complained of in an action as defamatory are not reasonably capable of bearing the meaning ascribed to them by the plaintiff, the court has intimated that it is in sympathy with that view, but as the jury is here it might be wise to take their opinion. Once a jury has expressed the view that the words do bear that meaning the court has in effect said that, whatever indication it may previously have given, it might be wise to leave it to the Court of Appeal. The answer to that is that it adds considerably to the costs of both parties and achieves no result useful to the plaintiff.

In my submission these words never were, and are not, in their natural and ordinary meaning, capable of the meaning ascribed to them by the plaintiff.

MR BEYFUS: In my submission they quite clearly were capable of such meaning.

My learned friend read from the speech of Lord Selborne in the House of Lords, and the important words seen to be these: 'The test, according to the authorities, is whether, under the circumstances in which the writing was published, *reasonable* men to whom the publication was made would be likely to understand it in a libellous sense.' The very important words seem to be 'under the circumstances in which the writing was published'.

My lord, with regard to the alternative possible meanings to which my learned friend has referred, *Gatley* at the bottom of page 127 gives a citation from the judgment of Lord Justice Scrutton in a case which may well be remembered by the defendants because it is *Cassidy v. Daily Mirror.*

It is this: 'I do not agree with some dicta to the effect that if words are capable of several meanings, some defamatory and some innocent, they should not be left to the jury.'

In this particular case the question has been left to the jury as twelve reasonable men and women, and they have decided that, particularly I imagine having regard to the circumstances in which the words were published, they do bear this meaning.

Your lordship will remember the whole of my case on this point was to the effect that the defendant Connor had deliberately used phraseology which would convey to the ordinary, reasonable, man this imputation but which would at the same time leave him free to deny it in the witness box, and to raise this point in court. In my submission the test whether reasonable readers would read it in this sense has in fact been determined by the members of the jury.

MR JUSTICE SALMON: Of course, I have got to exercise my judgment without having regard to that finding.

BEYFUS: My lord, if the defendants' counsel chooses to leave the argument until after the jury have given their verdict, in my submission that is not a matter which should be wholly excluded from your lordship's mind. I do not know that I have ever seen that point raised or determined.

MR JUSTICE SALMON: It is quite usual to leave this point of law to be discussed after the verdict, is it not, because, after all, the verdict of the jury might be that the words do not bear the defamatory meaning they have been asked. If they had not been asked, to go all the way to the Court of Appeal and back again...

BEYFUS: That is so, but your lordship asked whether your lordship should wholly disregard it. My answer to that is, in my submission, no. What weight your lordship should attach to it is quite a different matter, but wholly to disregard it seems in my submission wrong. Of course my case has always been that, inasmuch as it was quite impossible for Mr Connor to write this indicates a homosexual, or something which quite frankly and openly makes that suggestion, he was obliged to use phraseology which would lead to that imputation but leave it possible for him to deny it. On that basis, having regard to the place in which these words were published, namely, the box and in larger print, it would call particular attention to them in an article which was devised from beginning to end to vilify my client. Inasmuch as in effect the members of the jury had a choice between accepting the meaning put forward by Mr Connor in the witness box and the meaning put forward by Mr Liberace and by me on his behalf – the other two meanings were not I think put forward on behalf of the defendants to the members of the jury – if the meaning which Mr Connor ascribed to the words which he himself wrote is quite clearly an impossible one and an absurd one, a meaning which means that he was paying a high compliment to my client, 'a considerable compliment' were the words which he ascribed...

MR JUSTICE SALMON: I am not sure that he did. It was put to him, 'If it means that he makes a universal appeal, that would be a compliment', and he said, 'Yes', but I gather that the way it is written shows, and I think he made no bones about it, that he was not trying to pay any compliment.

MR BEYFUS: He cannot have it both ways. If he says this was a reference to his universal appeal, the fact that he appeals to men, women and children, people of both sexes and of all ages, if that is so it would be a considerable compliment, and he says, 'Yes'. In my submission he cannot get away with it by reason of the fact that he has used that particular type of language.

MR JUSTICE SALMON: If you say a man makes a universal appeal to anyone, but it is said in such a way that it means Heaven knows why, that is hardly a compliment.

MR BEYFUS: I do not know. At any rate, he had not got the courage in the witness box on oath to develop that line at all. When I asked him, 'Is that not a considerable compliment?' he answered 'Yes'.

My learned friend in his argument started by saying: Well, there are four possible meanings – my client's meaning, Mr Connor's meaning; the third one that the words were meaningless, as I understood it; and the fourth one that my client attracts homosexuals. If those are the four possible meanings, my lord, the members of the jury have accepted the first. In my submission your lordship ought not to rule the words are incapable of that meaning, but ought to leave the defendants to go to the Court of Appeal, if they desire to take the point there.

MR JUSTICE SALMON: Mr Gardiner, do you desire to reply?

MR GARDINER: Dealing first of all with what Mr Connor said, Mr Beyfus only read one question and answer to the jury, and that was in fact qualified by what followed. (Q) Let us see what your explanation of them is. If your explanation of those words is true, they were a very considerable compliment to Mr Liberace, were they not? (A) They were (Q) And you are inviting members of the jury to believe that, having written this highly deprecatory article about Mr Liberace and his performances, you chose to highlight, to print in the box in larger print, words which were highly complimentary to him? (A) No, I am not saying that at all. May I say what I am saying? What I was emphasising was the totalitarian nature of his performance, which has been one of the most astonishing phenomena of our time, to say for instance that he gets 16,000 people in Madison Square Garden. Then my learned friend asked for the previous question to be read, and your lordship said: The question was, 'If those words mean that he has a universality of appeal, that would be a great compliment to him?', and he agreed that. Then he was asked whether he meant them to be complimentary. Then Mr Beyfus said, (Q) In other words, what you are saying is that these words were intended to describe and convey to the public the universality of his appeal? (A) It was. (Q) That would be a compliment, surely? (A) Not necessarily. In the context of the article they could be read annexed to the caption; they could be read annexed to the views which I expressed.

On the question whether your lordship should take into account the view of the jury, what I am submitting to your lordship is a question of law. The jury are not lawyers, and in my submission your lordship would not be entitled to take that into account.

With regard to what Lord Justice Scrutton said in *Cassidy v. Daily Mirror* that was an observation by one of the Lords Justice, and since then *Sim v. Stretch* has been decided in the House of Lords, and in that case their lordships expressly restated with approval what had been said in *Capital & Counties Bank v. Henty,* namely, that it seems unreasonable, where there are a number of good interpretations, the only bad one should be seized upon to give a defamatory sense to the document.

MR JUSTICE SALMON: The question I have to decide is a question of law, whether these words are in law capable of meaning that the plaintiff is a homosexual. Would reasonable men and women be likely to understand them as meaning the plaintiff is a homosexual? Are they capable of that meaning? The question, as I understand it, whether I think they mean that he is a homosexual is entirely beside the point, just as I think it is beside the point that the jury have found that that is their meaning.

I come to the conclusion that on the whole the words are capable of this meaning. I look at the words; I look at them in their context; and further down in the article I see these words applied to the plaintiff – sniggering, snuggling, scent-impregnated, giggling and mincing. I am quite unable to say in these circumstances that the words are not capable of the meaning which the jury have attributed to them.

A possible view, of course, is that they really do not mean anything of the sort, and that there is no connection between the words in the box really in this sense and what comes after, but it seems to me that, although I am by no means saying I should have come to the same conclusion of fact, in law these words in their context are just capable of the meaning which has been attributed to them; and that is my finding.

Mr Justice Salmon made judgment for £8,000 and costs, and Mr Gardiner immediately accepted that the plaintiff was entitled to it. But he claimed that the defendants were entitled to judgment and costs in respect of the second article that had been complained about.

The case, he said, was 'one in which the plaintiff has succeeded on one issue and failed on the other. It is a quite separate publication. I submit that the defendants are plainly entitled to their costs on the second publication, that there should be a set-off as to costs, and the money in court as security for costs should remain in court until the costs have been taxed'.

He asked for a stay of execution – his clients, 'as your lordship knows, have always strongly contended that the words were certainly not intended to have any such meaning. Also we desire to take the opinion of the Court of Appeal upon that point. Also the point arises upon the first article whether there is evidence on which the jury could properly have found the facts were not true.'

MR JUSTICE SALMON: That is immaterial, if they found against you on the second limb.

GARDINER: Not necessarily, because the comment is comment on facts. If they ought to have found the facts were true, facts which they considered on the evidence were not true, that would not necessarily follow. I am prepared to bring the money into court, but I ask for it to stay there. I put that on the fact that the plaintiff is resident abroad, and of course, if he takes the money out, it would be useless to prosecute the appeal. I am only asking for a stay on the usual terms.

MR JUSTICE SALMON: Mr Beyfus, what do you say about the second publication, to start with? I suppose it is right, is it not, that the defendants are entitled to judgment in respect of the second publication?

BEYFUS: That seems to be right.

MR JUSTICE SALMON: Some of the costs must be attributable to that?

BEYFUS: I should have submitted that, having regard to the way this case was conducted, there would be no extra costs in respect of that publication, because it consisted of one word, and no special effort so far as I knew was applied to that. If your lordship says judgment for the defendants with such costs, if any, as may be attributable to that second cause of action, I cannot really oppose that.

MR JUSTICE SALMON: No.

BEYFUS: With regard to the stay, it would be wrong for me to oppose a stay of execution. With regard to the £2,000 on which there is the point of law I do not want the money paid into court. It is a great mistake to have money brought into court by the defendants because I do not get interest on it, whereas it is 4% if it is not paid in. I do not ask for the money to be brought into court.

In my submission there is no ground at all for a stay with regard to the other £6,000 in so far as the members of the jury have found that the facts are not true. In so far as they consisted of statements of fact, I contended at any rate that all the adjectives were statements of fact.

MR JUSTICE SALMON: Mr Beyfus, the defendants may be wanting to go to the Court of Appeal on a misdirection.

BEYFUS: I cannot conceive that!

[Laughter.]

MR JUSTICE SALMON: I cannot think that it will impose any hardship on Mr Liberace.

BEYFUS: The defendants have not intimated that they want to go to the Court of Appeal on a misdirection. If they did so intimate, I could not resist it. Unless they intend to go to the Court of Appeal on a misdirection, in my submission there should be no stay in regard to the £6,000.

MR JUSTICE SALMON: I give judgment for the plaintiff in respect of the first publication for £8,000 and costs; and judgment for the defendants in respect of the second publication, with costs. I think there ought to be a stay of execution on the usual terms, and I think that the money paid into court as security should be paid out to the plaintiff's solicitors without further authority.

GARDINER: And a set-off on the costs?

MR JUSTICE SALMON: There will be a set-off on the costs.

Afterword

But the Liberace and Cassandra extravaganza did not end when the curtain figuratively came down at the end of the show.

There was 'The Case of the Winking Juror.'

When Liberace and his team of lawyers and assistants arrived back at the Savoy Hotel they were confronted by the woman juror who had been facially expressing her sympathy with the plaintiff throughout his trial. Now, smiling broadly, she advanced on the entertainer with a piece of paper for his autograph.

Spotting her, solicitor David Jacobs grabbed Liberace's arm and told him: 'Quick, run for it! If she speaks to us it could mean a new trial.' They fled along one of the hotel corridors and locked the door behind them.

The juror, Mrs Jean Friend, a grey-haired 49-year-old widow, didn't get to speak to her idol but she spoke to reporters.

'He's a real smasher,' she said. 'I was tremendously thrilled with our verdict. I was bubbling over with it.'

About revealing the verdict before it was announced, she said: 'I wanted to end his suspense, to let him know everything was all right. Any woman of feelings would have done the same. I felt for him all the time. I never wavered for a minute from the second I sat down.'

Within seconds news of this statement had reached Geraldine House and the *Mirror* lodged notice of appeal, although it did not pursue it.

Newspapers did not normally identify jurors, nor interview them. But most Fleet Street lawyers decided that this was a statement made in public, that anybody could have heard, and carried the story on the following day's front pages. The headline in the *Daily Herald* was: 'Woman in Liberace jury sensation.'

Mrs Friend was encouraged to telephone Liberace's suite at the Savoy. But he had already left to play before a packed house at the Chiswick Empire. Mr and Mrs Beyfus were in the audience in a box as special guests. Liberace accepted a three minute ovation and spoke from the stage, glancing up at a jubilant Beyfus: 'It has been said many times, ladies and gentlemen, that English justice is the finest in the world. I am absolutely convinced of it now.'

When a woman in the stalls shouted: 'Let's have one for Mr Connor!' Liberace turned to the keyboard, with the smile (and the dimple) and banged out *Jealousy*...

The next day's *Daily Mirror* had a stark front page: Liberace – £8,000, and announced that an appeal was being considered. It did not mention

Mrs Friend. For the time being, at least, the newspaper was not living dangerously.

Gilbert Beyfus, again opposed by Gardiner, represented the social secretary of Margaret, Duchess of Argyll, in a libel case against her former employer winning £7,000 in damages. At the end of the trial, which he suspected would be his last, he commented: 'Not bad for a dying man, eh?' He died in October 1960... with another high profile libel suit awaiting his attention on his desk.

Mark Carlisle, the young lawyer who had first queried the Cassandra copy, became a Conservative MP in 1964 and was education minister in 1979. He was created a life peer in 1987 and died in 2005.

William Connor, bloodied but unbowed by the trial result, continued writing his often splenetic column until 1967 when he died, aged 57. In the meantime this scourge of the church, the government, of doctors, broadcasters and poodles, was knighted in 1965 for services to journalism.

Hugh Cudlipp succeeded Cecil King as chairman of the Mirror group of newspapers (later IPC, the biggest publishing company in the world). He was knighted in 1973 and a year later created Baron Cudlipp of Aldingbourne. For a number of years he hosted a Liberace Reunion Dinner, attended by the judge (by now Lord Salmon) and his wife and counsel and their wives. He died in 1998.

The circulation of the *Daily Mirror* continued to rise after the trial, and peaked in 1967 with an average daily sale of 5.28million.

Patrick Doncaster went from the first rock and roll days with Bill Haley to in-depth coverage of the next musical phenomena, The Beatles and the Rolling Stones. He later became features editor of the *Daily Mirror* and wrote biographies of Cliff Richard and Beatle Pete Best. He retired in 1973.

Neville Faulks was appointed a QC in 1959 and became a high court judge in 1963.

Gerald Gardiner successfully defended Penguin Books on a charge of obscenity for publishing *Lady Chatterley's Lover* in November 1960 and in 1964 was appointed Lord Chancellor in Harold Wilson's government.

Liberace's solicitor David Jacobs became known as the 'solicitor to the stars', requiring a team of six secretaries to service more than 5,000 show business clients including Lord Olivier, Judy Garland, Marlene Dietrich, Zsa Zsa Gabor, Brian Epstein and The Beatles. He hanged himself in the garage of his home in Hove in 1969, while being investigated by police in connection with an incident on Hampstead Heath. He was 56.

Liberace made the *Guinness Book of Records* as the world's highest paid entertainer of the 1960s and 1970s – when Elvis Presley and The Beatles were at their peak. He died of AIDS in 1987, aged 67.

Tony Miles, who had accompanied Pat Doncaster on the Liberace pub crawl, became editor of the *Daily Mirror*, then succeeded Cudlipp as editorial director and later as chairman of Mirror Group Newspapers. He resigned when Robert Maxwell bought the company in 1984.

Helenus Milmo, who had been a member of the prosecution team in the Nuremberg war trials, became a QC in 1961 and was knighted and became a high court judge in 1964. He died, aged 80, in 1988.

Editor Jack Nener, who had succeeded jailed editor Sylvester Bolam in 1953, retired in 1961 and died in 1982.

Sir Cyril Salmon became Lord Salmon of Sandwich in 1964. In 1976, he led a Royal Commission on Standards of Conduct in Public Life, following the Poulson corruption scandals; Hugh (by now Lord) Cudlipp was a member of it. Salmon died in 1991.

Murray Sayle wrote a novel based on his experiences and became a trailblazer in investigative journalism for the *Sunday Times*, for whom he also covered wars from Vietnam to Northern Ireland. Later he was Asian editor of *Newsweek*. He retired to Sydney in 2004 where he received an honorary degree from the university and also the Order of Australia.

Peter Stephens remained bureau chief in Paris for both the *Daily Mirror* and the *Sunday Pictorial* (later the *Sunday Mirror*) and retired in 1984.

Donald Zec became the doyen of Fleet Street show-business writers, and his columns were syndicated worldwide. He retired in 1977 and wrote biographies of Sophia Loren, Lee Marvin, Barbra Streisand, Cubby Broccoli and the Queen Mother. He won a national press award in 1967 and was made an OBE for services to journalism.

Further Reading

The Old Fox, A Life of Gilbert Beyfus QC by Iain Adamson (Muller) 1963. Out of print.

Liberace: An American Boy, by Darden Asbury Pyron (University of Chicago Press) 2001.

Cassandra At His Finest And Funniest, edited by Paul Boyle, foreword by Hugh Cudlipp (Revel Barker Publishing) 2008.

Read All About It! 100 sensational years of the Daily Mirror, by Bill Hagerty (First Stone) 2003.

A Crooked Sixpence, by Murray Sayle (Revel Barker Publishing) 2008.

Laughter in Court, by Hugh Cudlipp: *British Journalism Review*, Vol. 3, No. 2, 20-31 (1992)

Publish And Be Damned, The Astonishing Story of the *Daily Mirror*, by Hugh Cudlipp (The Bodley Head) 1953. Out of print.

Other books from Revel Barker Publishing

Slip-Up: How Fleet Street found Ronnie Biggs and Scotland Yard lost him; the story behind the scoop by Anthony Delano.

Forgive Us Our Press Passes by Ian Skidmore.

The Best Of Vincent Mulchrone selected articles by the Daily Mail's finest writer.

Ladies of The Street by Liz Hodgkinson.

More information from

www.booksaboutjournalism.com

CASSANDRA

At His Finest And Funniest

For thirty-two years – with time off to go to war – William Neil Connor wrote his famous column in the London *Daily Mirror* using the nom-de-plume of Cassandra.

Its crisp and trenchant sentences set a new standard for columnists, copied everywhere but never bettered. Cassandra's rivals envied him many things but, most of all, the cut and thrust of his style, so devastating in chopping opponents down to size.

Three decades was a long time to occupy a pulpit in public print.

Cassandra did it brilliantly, with never a yawn from his daily congregation of fifteen million. But he observed in his first column after four years away on active service: "As I was saying when I was interrupted, it is a powerful hard thing to please all of the people all of the time..."

To satisfy Cassandra's fans – and the more literate of his enemies – in one book is a powerful problem indeed. These pages can only skim the cream of his genius. Included is some of his finest and best remembered writing side by side with certain jocular items (much relished by *Mirror* readers) such as the saga of the Goose-Egg Man, the Fourteen Day Soup, and Cassandra's private collection of Square-Wheel English.

This is a book for all occasions and all moods, a delight for those who love to see their own language used stylishly, a primer for young writers who are willing to learn from a master of words.

Published by Revel Barker Publishing

ISBN: 978-0-9558238-2-4

A CROOKED SIXPENCE

By Murray Sayle

It has taken 47 years for Murray Sayle's classic book about popular newspapers to become readily available.

A CROOKED SIXPENCE tells the tale of a young Australian reporter, fresh off the boat, brimming with excitement, enthusiasm and ambition, securing casual shifts on a mass-circulation Fleet Street Sunday scandal-sheet… and the disillusion that set in very shortly afterwards.

It has been described as:

'A classic' – Peter Stothard, editor, *Times Literary Supplement*…

'The best novel about journalism – ever' – Phillip Knightley…

'Effectively a documentary, lightly disguised as a novel' – Neville Stack…

'Wonderful – the best book about British popular journalism. Every journalist should read it' – Roy Greenslade…

And 'the best novel never published' – Anthony Delano.

In fact the book was published, by MacGibbon and Kee in London and by Doubleday in New York, in 1961. A CROOKED SIXPENCE became an instant hit, and sold to Hollywood for a movie, but it lasted in print only for a number of days.

This was because a near-penniless London aristocrat believed that he was identifiable in the story and wanted to sue.

Incredibly, the would-be litigant was actually a friend of Sayle's; he had no real beef but thought that, since he'd heard that all publishers had libel insurance, he could collect a load of cash without anybody being seriously harmed.

But his get-rich-quick plan backfired because instead of paying up, or bothering their insurers, the publishers simply recalled the book and pulped it. And the Hollywood project was abandoned.

The book had lain dormant, then, until being revived in this edition.

Published by Revel Barker Publishing

ISBN: 978-0-9558238-4-8

Printed in the United States
153165LV00006B/61/P